Archive and Artifact

ARCHIVE AND ARTIFACT:
SUSAN HOWE'S FACTUAL TELEPATHY

W. SCOTT HOWARD

Talisman House, Publishers
Northfield, Massachusetts • 2019

Copyright © 2019 W. Scott Howard

All rights reserved

No part of this book may be reproduced in any form or by any means, electronic or mechanical, including printing, photocopying, recording, or by any information storage or retrieval system, without permission in writing from the editor and Talisman House, Publishers, LLC

Published in the United States of America by
Talisman House, Publishers
PO Box 102
Northfield, MA 01360

11 12 13 7 6 5 4 3 2 1

ISBN: 978-1-58498-141-1

ACKNOWLEDGMENTS

Grateful acknowledgement is made to the following artists and authors, libraries and publishers for permission to include passages from their works, as noted here:

Susan Howe and the Beinecke Rare Book and Manuscript Library, Yale University, Susan Howe Papers, YCAL MSS 338, Series II, Writings, [1994]-2007, Box 9, "Work for Ether/Either, Fall, 1996"; –, YCAL MSS 338, Series II, Writings, [1994]-2007, Box 5, "Work on Preterient"; –, YCAL MSS 338, Series III, Notebooks and Diaries [1984-2007], Box 11, "Sketch Book Journal, 1995, 1 of 13"; –, YCAL MSS 338, Series III, Notebooks and Diaries, 1984-2007, Box 12, Folder 24, Notebook: Dickinson Material (Spring 2001).

Susan Howe and Special Collections & Archives, UC San Diego, Susan Howe Papers, 1942-2002, MSS 0201, Box 3, Folder 5.

Susan Howe and Brita Bergland, *Articulation of Sound Forms in Time*, Windsor, VT: Awede Press, 1987.

Susan Howe and Leslie Miller, *Frolic Architecture,* New York: The Grenfell Press, 2010.

Continued on the following three pages,
which constitute an extension of the copyright page

Susan Howe and The Museum of Modern Art, *TOM TIT TOT,* New York: MoMA, 2014.

Excerpts of "Articulation of Sound Forms in Time" from *Singularities* © 1990 by Susan Howe. Published by Wesleyan University Press and reprinted by permission.

By Susan Howe, from *EUROPE OF TRUSTS*, copyright ©1990 by Susan Howe. Reprinted by permission of New Directions Publishing Corp. By Susan Howe, from *PIERCE-ARROW*, copyright ©1999 by Susan Howe. Reprinted by permission of New Directions Publishing Corp. By Susan Howe, from *THAT THIS*, copyright ©2010 by Susan Howe. Reprinted by permission of New Directions Publishing Corp. *THE SPONTANEOUS PARTICULARS: THE TELEPATHY OF ARCHIVES*, copyright ©2014 by Susan Howe. Reprinted by permission of New Directions Publishing Corp. By Susan Howe, from *DEBTHS*, copyright © 2018, 2014, 2015, 2016, 2017 by Susan Howe. Reprinted by permission of New Directions Publishing Corp.

PATERSON, copyright ©1946 by William Carlos Williams. Reprinted by permission of New Directions Publishing Corp.

"As You Came from the Holy Land," copyright © 1973 by John Ashbery. Originally appeared in "Poetry"; from *SELF-PORTRAIT IN A CONVEX MIRROR* by John Ashbery. Used by permission of Viking Books, an imprint of Penguin Publishing Group, a division of Penguin Random House LLC. All rights reserved.

"The Idea of Order at Key West," "The Plain Sense of Things," "Vacancy in the Park," "The Creations of Sound," and "The Owl in the Sarcophagus" from *THE COLLECTED POEMS OF WALLACE STEVENS* by Wallace Stevens, copyright © 1954 by Wallace Stevens and copyright renewed 1982 by Holly Stevens. Used by permission of Alfred A. Knopf, an imprint of the Knopf Doubleday Publishing Group, a division of Penguin Random House LLC. All rights reserved.

THE POEMS OF EMILY DICKINSON: READING EDITION, edited by Ralph W. Franklin, Cambridge, Mass.: The Belknap Press of Harvard University Press, Copyright © 1998, 1999 by the President and Fellows of Harvard College. Copyright © 1951, 1955 by the President and Fellows of Harvard College. Copyright © renewed 1979, 1983 by the President and Fellows of Harvard College. Copyright © 1914, 1918, 1919, 1924, 1929, 1930, 1932, 1935, 1937, 1942 by Martha Dickinson Bianchi. Copyright © 1952, 1957, 1958, 1963, 1965 by Mary L. Hampson.

Charles S. Peirce Papers, MS AM 1632 (277). Houghton Library, Harvard University.

Thanks also to my former University of Denver students from English 2716: *Anglo-American Metaphysical Poetics* for permission to include passages from their essays: Laura Davis, Jillian Knapp, Caroline Leong, Karen Mah, Meg Satrom, Jonathan Soweidy, and Matthew Williams.

Grateful acknowledgement is also made to the editors of the journals in which some of the essays collected in this book first appeared in shorter forms: "Teaching, How/e?: *not per se*," *Denver Quarterly* 35.2 (2000): 81-93; "Anglo-American Metaphysical Poetics: Reflections on the Analytic Lyric from John Donne to Susan Howe," *The McNeese Review* 46 (2008): 36-52; "Literal / Littoral Crossings: Re-Articulating Hope Atherton's Story After Susan Howe's *Articulation of Sound Forms in Time*," *Water: Resources and Discourses*, ed. Justin Scott Coe and W. Scott Howard, *Reconstruction: Studies in Contemporary Culture* 6.3 (2006): https://web.archive.org/web/20080828020123/http://reconstruction.eserver.org/063/howard.shtml [;] "Archives, Artifacts, Apostrophes: Susan Howe's *Spontaneous Particulars*," *Denver Quarterly* 50.3 (2016): 99-107; "Art in Art / Stone on Stone: Susan Howe's Quarrying," *Talisman: A Journal of Contemporary Poetry & Poetics* 44 (2016):
http://talismanarchive3a.weebly.com/howard-howe.html [.]

Special thanks to Susan Howe for permission to include the complete text of our conversation, "Accidental Purpose: Chance and Discipline from *My Emily Dickinson* to *Debths*," which appears here for the first time; and for permission to include my photographs from her 2013 exhibition of *TOM TIT TOT* at the Yale Union gallery in Portland, Oregon. Thanks also to Steve Van Eck and Scott Ponik for permission to include those photographs. Grateful acknowledgment is also made to xtaxtl for editing and collaging those images for this book's front and back covers, respectively titled "bird-like things" and "~~Knowing that~~"[.]

This book's engagement with the field of archival research has been shaped by the sage guidance of Moira Ann Fitzgerald and Nancy Kuhl (at Yale); Robert Melton and Heather Smedberg (at UCSD); Kate Crowe, Peggy Keeran, and Rebecca Macey (at the University of Denver). Thanks to you all.

Grateful acknowledgment is made to the University of Denver for research grants and sabbaticals that supported my work on this book; and also to Yale University for the 2015 Donald C. Gallup Fellowship in American Literature at the Beinecke Library, which was essential for my research in the Susan Howe Papers Collection.

Special thanks to Edward Foster, Zoe Kharpertian, and Christopher Sawyer-Lauçanno for reading the typescript and offering expert advice for the work's path forward. Thanks also to my Indexers, Cameron Duder and Judy Gordon.

The essays collected in this volume have traveled many roads. I am ever grateful for the nonconformist wisdom of my colleagues, students, and teachers. This book is for you.

For their love and understanding beyond measure, my deepest thanks goes to my family (Jenny, Kat, and Gwendolyn) for always being with me at the centers and circumferences of each day.

Image Credits:

Front Cover: "bird-like things" by W. Scott Howard and xtaxtl. Collaged from the author's photographs of Susan Howe's 2013 gallery exhibition of *TOM TIT TOT* at Yale Union in Portland, Oregon. Reproduced with permission from Susan Howe and Yale Union.

p. 61: Facing pages from the 1987 Awede Press edition of *Articulation of Sound Forms in Time*. Reproduced with permission from Susan Howe and Brita Bergland.

p 244: "Hannah bird" by Susan Howe, *Spontaneous Particulars* (NDP, 2014) page 62. Reproduced with permission from Susan Howe and New Directions Publishing.

Back Cover: "~~Knowing that~~" by W. Scott Howard and xtaxtl. From the author's photographs of Susan Howe's 2013 gallery exhibition of *TOM TIT TOT* at Yale Union in Portland, Oregon. Reproduced with permission from Susan Howe and Yale Union.

Contents

"signal escapes": the fabric of poetry • *1*

"colliding phenomena": *factual telepathy* as Editorial Poetics & Praxis • *8*

Art in Art & Stone on Stone: *The Quarry* • *17*

Metaphysical Poetics: Reflections upon the Analytic Lyric
from John Donne to Susan Howe • *31*

"scape esaid": Radical Contingency and Historical Figuration
from *Articulation of Sound Forms in Time* to *The Quarry* • *54*

Accidental Purpose: Chance and Discipline
from *My Emily Dickinson* to *Debths* • *189*

Archives, Artifacts, Apostrophes: *Spontaneous Particulars* • *236*

Bibliography of Works Cited • *247*

Archive and Artifact

"signal escapes":
the fabric of poetry

"books are not seldom talismans and spells"[1]

"The uniqueness of a work of art is inseparable from its being imbedded in the fabric of tradition. This tradition itself is thoroughly alive and extremely changeable."[2]

"Poetry brings similitude and representation to configurations waiting from forever to be spoken"[3]

Susan Howe is a poet of *signal escapes*,[4] and this is a collection of essays from someone who fell under an enchantment with her work in the midst of a bookstore near the Willamette River on a rainy day.

From January 1991 to August 1993 (with the Portland, Oregon-based documentary film artist, Vanessa Renwick),[5] I co-managed the *Small Press/Journals* section and the *dew.claw* reading series at Powell's Books (the Burnside Store). Collection development, ordering and pricing, sorting and shelving were orchestrated autonomously (often with endearing idiosyncrasies) by the section managers during those years before computerized inventory. Our haptic and happenstance practices

---

[1] William Cowper, *The Task*, vi, cited in Holbrook Jackson, *The Anatomy of Bibliomania* (New York: Charles Scribner's Sons, 1932), 24.

[2] Walter Benjamin, "The Work of Art in the Age of Mechanical Reproduction," *Illuminations*, ed. Hannah Arendt, trans. Harry Zohn (New York: Schocken, 1968), 223.

[3] Susan Howe, *The Europe of Trusts* (Los Angeles: Sun & Moon, 1990), 14; and (New York: New Directions, 2002), 14.

[4] George Sheldon, *A History of Deerfield, Massachusetts: the times when the people by whom it was settled, unsettled and resettled: with a special study of the Indian wars in the Connecticut valley, With genealogies*, 2 Vols. (Deerfield, MA: E. A. Hall & Co., 1895-1896), [Greenfield, MA: Press of E. A. Hall & Co.], 1:166; and Susan Howe, *Articulation of Sound Forms in Time* (Windsor, VT: Awede Press, 1987), unpaginated (np).

[5] Oregon Department of Kick Ass: http://www.odoka.org/about/[.]

were immersed in tactile and *tychic*[6] forces that we acknowledged and respected. There was an undeniable animist-materialist-vitalist agency dwelling among and between, within and through the books themselves—something kindred to what Howe, looking back on her writing of *Articulation of Sound Forms in Time*, would describe as "the telepathic solicitation of innumerable phantoms."[7] This was the context in which Susan Howe's poetry and prose found me. These are some of the facts.

I arrived at Powell in August of 1990, thinking that I knew something about poetry (having recently completed an M.A. in English). A few weeks of working in the Poetry section (and in the warehoused acres of packed shelves and unopened boxes)[8] easily disabused me of that notion. Powell's was then, and still is today, the "largest independent used and new bookstore in the world."[9] In the midst of the daily and weekly ebb and flow of helping customers and working with colleagues, there were countless moments for reading. We all anticipated these moments, knowing they were unpredictable and transitory—shaped by the interruptions and whims of the retail floor. Sitting on ladder tops. Leaning against bookcases. Sorting, alphabetizing, shelving. Wherever and whenever we could find available time, we would be reading at intervals

---

[6] "Peirce called his doctrine that chance has an objective status in the universe *tychism*, a word taken from the Greek word for 'chance' or 'luck' or 'what the gods happen to choose to lay on one'. Tychism is a fundamental doctrinal part of Peirce's mature view, and reference to his tychism provides an added reason for Peirce's insisting on the irreducible fallibilism of inquiry. For nature is not a static world of unswerving law but rather a dynamic and dicey world of evolved and continually evolving habits that directly exhibit considerable spontaneity." Robert Burch, "Charles Sanders Peirce," *Stanford Encyclopedia of Philosophy*, ed. Edward N. Zalta (Winter, 2014): http://plato.stanford.edu/entries/peirce/#anti.[.]

[7] *Souls of the Labadie Tract* (New York: New Directions, 2007), 14.

[8] The vastness of the Powell's enterprise was overwhelming. I remember hearing Michael Powell, one afternoon, as he walked through the Green Room, talking with Susan Wells and Bob Duran. Michael had just purchased the contents of several freight train cars. "Pennies on the dollar. Pennies on the dollar." Michael's refrain echoed with the distant thundering of rail wheels crossing the Midwest.

[9] Powell's City *of* Books: http://www.powells.com/[.]

between tasks. And when we weren't reading, we were talking about books with customers and with one another. The everyday atmosphere was all-consuming, invigorating, and exhausting. I worked four ten-hour days, often until closing at 10 p.m. In my dreams, this literal/littoral stream of activities was (and still is) endless, uncanny.

Mark Johnson[10] should be recognized for his advocacy for small press publications at Powell's prior to 1990. Working with others, including Wayne Pernu,[11] Mark had been (over many months, if not years) surreptitiously ordering and shelving (in the Poetry and Literature sections) his favorite works of experimental poetry, poetics, and contemporary fiction. Mark was especially interested in the Objectivists, the L=A=N=G=U=A=G=E writers, and the OULIPO writers. Although these fugitive texts were shelved *under-the-radar*—that is, unbeknownst to the Poetry and Literature section managers—David Emmons and Robert Gerke in the Order Office were allies. Mark was a trickster. Sometime in early 1991, he moved from the Burnside Store to a new Powell's location on SE Hawthorne St. I can't say for sure whether it was Mark or Wayne (or David or Robert) who first introduced me to Howe's poetry and prose.

Vanessa and I were fortunate to be in the right place at the right time. We somehow convinced our supervisors and the store's general manager that Powell's should represent a greater variety of small press publications, especially because there was a thriving local and regional community of readers, writers, book arts specialists, typographers and printers, magazines and publishers. Since the humble origins of Powell's in 1971, the store had, of course, made countless efforts to promote local and regional artists, writers, and organizations. This was the early 1990s, I might add, and another factor undoubtedly contributed to our successful

---

[10] Mark Johnson, *The Poetry Project* (October 27, 2014):
https://soundcloud.com/poetry-project-audio/mark-johnson-claire-wilcox-oct-27th-2014[.]

[11] Christina Cooke, "An Old-School Book Scout," *The New Yorker* (March 9, 2012):
http://www.newyorker.com/books/page-turner/an-old-school-book-scout[.]

bid for the creation of a *Small Press/Journals* section: the growth of Borders and of Barnes & Noble, both of which were already moving into the greater metro area. Portland had then (and still has today) more bookstores per capita than any other city in the U.S. Like all of the independents during those years (such as Laughing Horse Books), Powell's had to compete with the national chains, which would be neither the most likely nor the most hospitable environments for retail sections devoted to the small presses. And so, Vanessa and I began to build *SP/J*. We designed the floor and wall spaces; ordered like crazy from SPD, Bernard de Boer, Small Press Traffic, Book People, Paul Green's Spectacular Diseases, and Bookslinger (among other distributors & wholesalers, many of which are now defunct); and happily watched the section grow.

SP/J was located in the northeast sector of the Blue Room, along the edges of the high-brow Literature section. We asked for a large rectangular slot-wall section in the middle of the north wall so that Vanessa and I could display books face-out via a variety of moveable, clear plastic boxes and inclined shelves. This open, central area was framed on both sides by unusually tall, slender rectangular bookcases that reached upward into the exposed rafters and ducts. The western edge of *SP/J* was distinguished by a custom-built island that combined regular shelving with inclined wood surfaces. Portland artist Tom Cramer painted a mural (commissioned by the store managers) that we hung above the central slot-wall area. *SP/J* became a semi-autonomous zone. We were activists and our authors and their publications were agents for artistic and social change. We launched the *dew.claw* small press reading series (which continued into 1993 and beyond) that featured West Coast poets from the U.S. and Canada.

I remember the omnipresent dampness in Portland during the winter months. The woolen clouds. Flannel shirts and mugs of coffee. Days like weeks of rain and mist interspersed with what Portlanders were (and still are) fond of calling 'sun breaks'. Thrift shop boots and coats. Sidewalk moss. More coffee. Commuting by bicycle across the Hawthorne Bridge. The Willamette's ebb and flow.

On such a day in 1993, Mark brought a curious book to me. He had been working in one of the warehouses, moving and unpacking boxes that were at risk of water damage (due to a leaky roof). In one of the boxes, a slim volume instantly caught his attention because the spine was blank: *Hope Atherton and His Times* by Arthur Holmes Tucker (Deerfield, MA: Pocumtuck Valley Memorial Association, 1926). Mark knew that I was obsessed with the Awede and Wesleyan editions of *Articulation of Sound Forms in Time*, and that I was preparing for a presentation at the *Practicing Postmodernisms* conference in May at the University of Oregon. None of the book buyers at Powell's could remember ever having encountered this title; there was no purchase record.

Tucker's was the first of several books that set me on a spiral path into the *debths* of Howe's reading/writing against the grain of history, as I relate in this collection's most contextually embedded essay.

Some volumes are magic books. Where and how does such entangled precariousness live? What are the circumstances that influence its appearance and/or disappearance through and within, between and among contingent and contiguous manifestations (each singular) of the work that continues to change through a process of intermittent adaptation and reconfiguration? The Awede edition of *Articulation of Sound Forms in Time* (1987) and the paradigm press edition of *a bibliography of the king's book; or, eikon basilike* (1989) are, for me, such talismans—always already imbedded "in the fabric of tradition," paradoxically weaving together what Walter Benjamin calls *cult value* and *exhibition value*. The greater the degree of embeddedness, the more enchanting the book.

Noah Webster's 1828 *American Dictionary of the English Language* defines "fabric" as: "*noun* [Latin, a frame, a workman.] 1. The structure of any thing; the manner in which the parts of a thing are unitied by art and labor; workmanship; texture […] 2. The frame or structure of a building; construction. More generally, the building itself; an edifice; a house; a temple; a church; a bridge, etc. […] 3. Any system composed of connected parts; as the *fabric* of the universe. 4. Cloth manufactured

[…]."[12] As a *verb intransitive*, fabric means "to build; to construct." Noah also reminds us that fabrics are texts, from the Latin *textus*, meaning "woven."

In *Frame Structures*, Howe speaks of *telepsychology*, how we "have always been in contact with one another, keeping on never letting go, no distance as to time".[13] In *Spontaneous Particulars*, she gives thanks for the "inward ardor" she feels "while working in research libraries" which she says is intuitive—"a sense of self-identification and trust, or the granting of grace in an ordinary room, in a secular time."[14]

Bookstore fabric of *configurations waiting from forever to be spoken*. Language fabric of the poem's sacred & secular bridge, weaving/texting to the universe and back again.

One of the enduring characteristics of Howe's works, I would say, concerns their contextual and tropological synergy—that is, the dynamic *fabric* (shaped by chance encounters) of poetic language dwelling within everyday acts and materials of attention, intuition, motion, sound, texture, and vision. Or, in other words, *betweenness*—always already in the midst of things.

The texts in this collection modulate between intensities and tones from conversational discussions to theoretical discourses, becoming increasingly embedded in generative, unpredictable intersections among archives, artifacts, and factual telepathy.

These essays are cross-genre hybrids of creative and critical engagement with the works of Susan Howe (through print and electronic, video and vinyl, manuscript and typescript, gallery installation and special collection forms) over many years between my communities from New

---

[12] Noah Webster, *American Dictionary of the English Language*, 1828 edition online: http://webstersdictionary1828.com/[.]

[13] *Frame Structures: Early Poems, 1974-1979* (New York: New Directions, 1996), 25. Here and in other discrete instances throughout this book, I choose to deviate from stylistic conventions (concerning the placement of punctuation marks inside of quotation marks) in order to represent Susan Howe's language exactly as it appears in her works.

[14] *Spontaneous Particulars: The Telepathy of Archives* (New York: Christine Burgin / New Directions, 2014), 63.

England to the Pacific Northwest to the Intermountain West and the Colorado Front Range. Between Powell's and Portland State University; the University of Washington and the University of Denver; the University of Louisville; the University of California, San Diego; and Yale.

These materials have traveled many roads between coasts, continents, and coffee shops via scraps of paper and keyboards; through pixels to flash drives and across mountains via servers and satellites. The works herein have circulated between home and office; garden and classroom. Among family and friends, colleagues and students. With birds and cats and dogs and bugs in the dirt and flowers and grasses and weeds and trees and small fish in Blue Lake and Little Dry Creek. With dragonflies in sunshine. With owls and toads in moonlight. While riding my bicycle and humming and thinking and looking and listening. Between logistical evasions; sleeping and waking, shopping and cooking and cleaning, remembering and forgetting, laughing and crying, saying unsaying.

These essays move within and against fields of study (mainly history, literature, and philosophy plus a few others here and there); across and through time periods (from the early modern to now). They follow a nonconformist's helical quest '*after*' the poet's signal escapes.

"colliding phenomena":[15]
factual telepathy as Editorial Poetics & Praxis

[B]ewilderment is like a dream: one continually returning pause on a gyre [...,] the shape of the spiral that imprints itself in my interior before anything emerges [...] For to the spiral-walker there is no plain path, no up and down, no inside or outside. But there are strange recognitions and never a conclusion.[18]

I have vivid memories of my first moments with the Awede edition (1987) of *Articulation of Sound Forms in Time* and the paradigm press edition (1989) of *a bibliography of the king's book; or, eikon basilike*. These volumes were (and for me still are) *bewildering*. I had no idea then of what sorts of difficulty and pleasure these books were bound to bring my way; how deeply they would sink into my life and change my world. Their audacious, fierce, playful, and hauntingly elegiac quests immersed my senses of perception (and visceral proprioception) in charged, helical, unbound intersections of archives and artifacts. Looking back these

---

[15] This essay first appeared as a conference presentation, "'colliding phenomena': Susan Howe's *factual telepathy* as Editorial Poetics & Praxis," *National Poetry Foundation*: June 29, 2017, Department of English, University of Maine, Orono, ME.

[16] *Articulation of Sound Forms in Time* (Windsor, VT: Awede Press, 1987), unpaginated (np).

[17] *a bibliography of the king's book; or, eikon basilike* (providence: paradigm press, 1989), unpaginated (np).

[18] Fanny Howe, "Bewilderment," *The Wedding Dress: Meditations on Word and Life* (Berkeley and Los Angeles: University of California Press, 2003), 9.

many years later (by way of Fanny Howe's meditations), I recognize that path as a spiral-walker's endless journey of uncanny wonderment.

These two small press volumes—*Articulation* and *Eikon*—were subsequently republished, respectively, in *Singularities* (1990) and *The Nonconformist's Memorial* (1993). And through those reconfigurations, the poems (and my relationships with them) were transfigured anew, following a radical *"movement of the Same towards the Other which never returns to the Same."*[19] With some hindsight, I can see now that these openwork texts are concrete, lyrical/social, polyvocal strophic assemblages of *factual telepathy* embodying major turning points in Susan Howe's materials and methods that would shape her poetics and praxis in other works going forward, including essays such as "Encloser" (1990), "Sorting Facts" (1996), and "Ether Either" (1998), and especially the books, *Pierce-Arrow* (1999), *Souls of the Labadie Tract* (2007), *Frolic Architecture* (2010), *THAT THIS* (2010), *Spontaneous Particulars* (2014), *TOM TIT TOT* (2014), and *Debths* (2017). In all of these dynamic works, we simultaneously experience language through both sides of the page and across facing pages; these cross-genre, sequential collages invite our dialogue with inter- and intra-texts—recalling the Latin, *textus*—experienced as woven compositions of *radical contingencies*.

By 'radical', I mean a fundamental concern for and critique of the linguistic roots of reality; and by 'contingency', I mean chance affinities among and within, against and through materials/methods that are neither designed nor foreseen, yet possible due to accidents, conditions, or forces whether immanent or imminent. Howe's factual telepathy—engaged as an editorial gesture (~~sieve catacomb~~)[20] and constitutive trope (a / pi / v / o / t)—occupies physical and phenomenal territories, playing at

---

[19] Emmanuel Levinas, *Collected Philosophical Papers*, trans. Alphonso Lingis (Boston: Martinus Nijhoff, 1987), 91.

[20] This early instance (among the first) of Howe's typographic gestures *sous rapture* occurs on [page 13] of the unpaginated Awede text of *Articulation*, and echoes with a recent companion instance of emphasizing what is said unsaid: "TANGIBLE THINGS // Out of a stark oblivion ~~disenter~~". *Debths* (New York: New Directions, 2017), 49.

the edges of font and figure, sound and sense. Across and through, within and between the pages in *Articulation* and *Eikon* (as well as in the other essays, poems, and volumes invoked above), numerous instances (too many to address in this short essay) may be encountered of Howe's collagist-typographic field of action.

If you're familiar with Susan Howe's books from the 1970s collected in *Frame Structures* (1996) and/or with her volumes from the 1980s collected in *The Europe of Trusts* (1990, 2002), you might be saying to yourself at this point, "Well, sure, Susan has always worked in these ways." And you would be correct! Howe's poetry and prose from *Hinge Picture* (1974) to *The Quarry* (2015) and beyond lovingly and persistently recovers and releases "language Lost // in language / Wind sweeps over the wheat // mist-mask on woods"[21] threshing the linguistic and material ruins of history for voices and visions, ghosts and gifts on the brink of oblivion that could repair personal and collective traumas. YES and yes AND YET [...] what I'm also noticing is that distinctive collagist-typographic, polyvocal gestures of "invisible colliding phenomena"[22]—which I'm tracking here vis-à-vis the kindred notion of "*factual telepathy*"[23]—first emerge in *Articulation* and *Eikon* and the other works collected in *Singularities* and *The Nonconformist's Memorial*—editorial/tropological artifacts that are not quite yet present in Howe's typescripts and published works from the earlier 1980s and 1970s, including her early word squares and watercolor broadsides (c. 1958-1973).[24] To my eyes and ears, *Articulation* stages the first perfor-

---

[21] "Speeches at the Barriers," *The Europe of Trusts* (Los Angeles: Sun & Moon, 1990), 99; and (New York: New Directions, 2002), 99.

[22] Susan Howe, "Sorting Facts; or, Nineteen Ways of Looking at Marker," *Beyond Document: Essays on Nonfiction Film* (Hanover: Wesleyan University Press, 1996), 341.

[23] "Sorting Facts; or, Nineteen Ways of Looking at Marker," New Directions Poetry Pamphlet #1 (New York: New Directions, 2013), 7.

[24] Susan Howe Papers, YCAL MSS 338, Series VI, Art Work, 1958-1973, Box 21, Artist's Book, "Untitled, handmade artist's/poet's book including original drawing, painting, collage, and text;" and Boxes 22-30, Drawings, "Includes drawings/manuscripts done in series by Susan Howe, representing transitional

mance of Howe's telepathic radical contingency. These distinctive features—similar to instances of *dynamic cutting*[25] in film editing, or of *splicing*[26] in audio editing—emerge within context, beginning c. 1987 and becoming more prevalent throughout the 1990s.

During those years, Howe navigated at least three significant transitions in her prolific career: teaching full time at the University at Buffalo; shifting from analogue to electronic compositional practices; and migrating from small press publishing (with presses such as Kulchur, North Atlantic, Awede, paradigm, Sun and Moon) to new relationships with Wesleyan and New Directions. These changes in practice and production, techniques and technologies amplified and complicated Howe's agency as a documentary and visionary poet. The transition to electronic word processing was especially challenging. In the interview included in this collection, she reflects: "It was a big thing for me to shift, in my poetry, from typewriter to computer [...] With the poetry it was just somehow the tactile *thing*, which brings it all around to touch, to acoustics—because it's a ritual."[27] Howe rediscovered her work in new ways in the midst of these multi-modal and trans-discursive shifts. Her emerging collagist-typographic polyvocal gestures shaping factual telepathy

---

works; drawings by Susan Howe, 'Birds 71 72 Gardens 72 73?'; drawing by Susan Howe of the Amethyst Hotel (Achill Island, Ireland); and two drawings by Jonathan Shahn, one of Henry Geldzahler when he was at Harvard and one of Susan Howe when she was at the Museum School." Beinecke Library, Yale University: http://drs.library.yale.edu/fedoragsearch/rest/[.]

[25] "Sorting Facts; or, Nineteen Ways of Looking at Marker," *The Quarry* (New York: New Directions, 2015), 127.

[26] "For quite a few years, I produced poetry programs on the radio (at WBAI in the 70s) and I edited tape and I loved doing it—the materiality, the *slash*, the cutting with the razor—and I became so sensitive because every single poet has a verbal tic. And what do you do—how far do you go in editing?" Susan Howe, interview typescripts and e-mails to the author (April, 2016; May, 2016; June, 2016).

[27] Interview typescripts and e-mails to the author (April, 2016; May, 2016; June, 2016).

underscore the persistence and precarity of handmade (often highly re-mediated) artifacts that signify an *unspeakable thisness*[28] recovered from the archival wilderness of radically contingent, contiguous inter-/intra-texts where words "will always escape into their own mystery."[29]

During the 1990s, Susan Howe's works of poetry and prose were numerous and yet characteristically radically singular. There were at least twelve books from *Singularities* (1990) to *Pierce-Arrow* (1999); at least four essays plus numerous poems appearing in journals such as *Avec, Dark Ages Clasp the Daisy Root, Hambone, How(ever),* and *Temblor* (just to name a few).[30] In all of these published volumes, instances of Howe's factual telepathy may be found. Each of these books gathered smaller books, discrete sequences, individual texts, and ephemera from earlier years of work.[31] And all of those reconfigurations shaped a poetics and praxis of radical contingency specific to each volume. Each of

---

[28] W. Scott Howard, "*Apophatic Haecceity*: William Bronk & the Analytic Lyric," *William Bronk in the Twenty-First Century*, ed. Edward Foster and Burt Kimmelman (Greenfield, MA: Talisman House, 2013), 91.

[29] "Encloser," *The Politics of Poetic Form: Poetry and Public Policy*, ed. Charles Bernstein (New York: ROOF Books, 1990), 195.

[30] Some of these other journals include: *a.blek, American Poetry Review, Conjunctions, The Difficulties,* and *Verse*.

[31] *Singularities* (Wesleyan, 1990) includes: *Articulation of Sound Forms in Time* (Awede, 1987); *Thorrow*; and *Scattering As Behavior Toward Risk*. The *Europe of Trusts* (Sun & Moon, 1990; New Directions, 2002) includes: "There are Not Leaves Enough to Crown to Cover to Crown to Cover;" *Pythagorean Silence* (Montemora, 1982); *Defenestration of Prague* (Kulchur, 1983); and *The Liberties* (Loon, 1980). *The Nonconformist's Memorial* (New Directions, 1993) includes: *The Nonconformist's Memorial* (The Grenfell Press, 1992); *Silence Wager Stories*; *a bibliography of the king's book; or, eikon basilike* (paradigm, 1989); and *Melville's Marginalia*. *Frame Structures* (New Directions, 1996) includes: "Frame Structures;" *Hinge Picture* (Telephone, 1974); *Chanting at the Crystal Sea* (Fire Exit, 1975); *Secret History of the Dividing Line* (Telephone, 1978); and *Cabbage Gardens* (Fathom, 1979). *Pierce-Arrow* (New Directions, 1999) includes: *Arisbe*; *The Leisure of the Theory Class*; and *Rückenfigur*. Other works by Howe published between 1990 and 2000 include: *Heliopathy, Temblor* 4 (1990); "Encloser," 175-196; "Sorting Facts" (1996): 295-343; *Marginalia de Melville*, trans. Bernard Rival (Courbevoie: Théâtre Typographique, 1997); "Ether Either," *Close Listening: Poetry and the Performed Word*, ed. Charles Bernstein (New York and Oxford: Oxford University Press, 1998), 111-127;

12

Howe's texts is simultaneously centric and eccentric; all of her works share affinities and echoes beyond anticipation or plan; and yet each singular work also destabilizes that field of editorial and tropological synergy. In other words: language escapes the works and vice versa on centripetal and centrifugal dimensions. These many swerving adaptations of individual volumes and collected books could be usefully studied via mereology[32] except that Howe's colliding phenomena subvert transitive predications. Howe's poetics and praxis affirms Julia Kristeva's argument that "there is within poetic language [...] a *heterogeneousness* to meaning and signification."[33] The dynamics of factual telepathy in Howe's work is animist, contextual, materialist, phenomenological, and vitalist.[34]

Howe's first published articulation of the phrase "factual telepathy" occurs within the context of "Sorting Facts; or, Nineteen Ways of Looking at Marker," which first appeared in *Beyond Document: Essays on*

Deux et (Courbevoie: Théâtre Typographique, 1998); and "Heterologies: Community of Form in Practice and Imagination," *The Recovery of the Public World: Essays on Poetics in Honour of Robin Blaser*, ed. Charles Watts and Edward Byrne (Burnaby, Canada: Talon Books, 1999), 217-220.

[32] Mereology is the study of parts and the wholes they form, emphasizing the logic of partial ordering as "a reflexive, transitive, antisymmetric relation" informed by three core (albeit contradictory) principles: everything is part of itself; any part of any part of a thing is itself part of that thing; two distinct things cannot be part of each other." See Achille Varzi, "Mereology," *The Stanford Encyclopedia of Philosophy*, ed. Edward N. Zalta (Winter 2016): https://plato.stanford.edu/archives/win2016/entries/mereology/ [.]

[33] Julia Kristeva, *Desire in Language: A Semiotic Approach to Literature and Art*, ed. Leon S. Roudiez, trans. Thomas Gora, Alice Jardine, and Leon S. Roudiez (New York: Columbia University Press, 1980), 133.

[34] In this regard, Howe's *factual telepathy* does not invoke transcendental signification, but rather dwells among internal realisms kindred with the works of C. S. Peirce. "All scientific concepts must somehow be traceable back to phenomenological roots. Thus, even when Peirce calls himself a 'realist' or is called by others a 'realist,' it must be kept in mind that Peirce was always a realist of the Kantian 'empirical' sort and not a Kantian 'transcendental realist'. His realism is similar to what Hilary Putnam has called 'internal realism.' (As was said, Peirce was also a realist in quite another sense of the word: he was a realist or an anti-nominalist in the medieval sense.)" Robert Burch, "Charles Sanders Peirce," *The Stanford Encyclopedia of Philosophy*, ed. Edward N. Zalta (Winter, 2014): https://plato.stanford.edu/archives/win2014/entries/peirce/ [.]

Nonfiction Film (1996).[35] The essay was subsequently translated by Bénédicte Vilgrain and Bernard Rival and published in 1998 as "Triage Des Faits; ou, Dix-neuf façon de regarder Marker."[36] "Sorting Facts" has more recently appeared in *Framework* Vol. 53, No. 2 (Fall 2012); subsequently as New Directions Poetry Pamphlet #1 (2013) and also as one of the essays collected in *The Quarry* (2015), making it one of Howe's most frequently remediated works. Arguably one of Howe's most rigorous and rewarding essays, "Sorting Facts" celebrates Chris Marker's films, *La Jetée* and *Sans Soleil*, which she describes as "haunted by indwelling flames of spirit" (1996:297). "*La Jetée* et *Sans Soleil* sont hantés d'intimes flammes d'esprit" (*Deux et*, 55).

Howe places Marker's life and work within comparative contexts of Russian formalist cinema (via Dziga Vertov and Andrei Arsenyevich Tarkovsky), Russian futurist poetics (via Vladimir Mayakovsky), and an eclectic range of topics and figures from anagrams, existentialism, historical materialism, pragmatism, and semiotics to, respectively, Anne Bradstreet, Hamlet, Walter Benjamin, William James, and Roland Barthes (among many others). "Sorting Facts" is also a bracing and beautiful work of remembrance and "Refused mourning" (1996:342) for Howe's second husband, David von Schlegell.[37] The essay's first section begins with memories of David's life and their twenty-seven years together. In the concluding lines of that section, Howe invokes Jean-Luc Godard's interview with Philippe Sollers, in which Godard cites a passage from Antonin Artaud: "'I want soul to be body; so they won't be able to say that body is soul, because it will be the soul which is body'" (1996:297). And then she writes: "Surely nonfiction filmmakers sometimes work intuitively by factual telepathy. I call poetry *factual telepathy*." "J'appelle la poésie *télépathie factuelle*" (*Deux et*, 55). A few pages later, Howe elaborates:

---

[35] Ed. Charles Warren (Hanover: Wesleyan University Press, 1996), 295-343.

[36] *Deux et* (Courbevoie: Théâtre Typographique, 1998), 51-109.

[37] David von Schlegell (1920-1992) abstract artist, sculptor, and head of the Yale School of Art, Sculpture Department, from 1971-1990.

Editorial use of split sequences, "disruptive-associative montage," emphasis on the mysterious patternment and subliminal structures of images (icons), sensitivity to the sound shape (even in a silent film) of each pictured event, awareness of the time-mystery of simultaneous phenomena (co-occurrence and deployment)—I am an American poet writing in the English language. I have loved watching films all my life. I work in the poetic documentary form, but didn't realize it until I tried to find a way to write an essay about two films by Chris Marker. (1996:300)

Within and against these contingent, contiguous contexts of formalist cinema, futurist poetics, and anagramatological revelations of hidden purposes, dynamic cutting is, for Howe, "a highly stylized form of editing" that attempts "to recapture someone something somewhere looking back" (1996:332). Akin to the "use of split sequences" in film, Howe's collagist-typographic polyvocal gestures in the works collected in *Singularities* and *The Nonconformist's Memorial* also engage factual telepathy as an artifactual poetics and praxis for recovering marginalized voices and visions by amplifying contradictions among and between, within and against archival sources. Howe reflects upon these priorities in her essay, "Encloser" (1990), where she argues that what "gradually gets edited out in a narrative is singularity". As a counter-method against such linguistic (and historiographic) erasures, Howe's dynamic cutting "involves a fracturing of discourse" used as a regenerative inter-/intra-textual force in order to rescue "an echo of an undervoice that was speaking from the beginning"—that is, a singular and "peculiarly American" *other voice* that keeps on "speaking *against* the grain."[38] Howe's inter- and intra-textual *phénomènes invisibles collisions* (*Deux et*, 107) signify her desire to "find some truth that had been edited out of our history" (1996:195)—a quest *to hear and speak* echoes of undervoices that goes back, for Howe, to the many years of her dedicated close listening to

---

[38] "Encloser," 191-192.

Emily Dickinson's manuscripts (c. 1980 and ever since), to Mary Rowlandson's and Anne Hutchinson's narratives (c. 1982-1993), and to her transformative encounter with Hope Atherton's nonconformist experience. Recalling her bewilderment with Hope's undervoice in George Sheldon's *A History of Deerfield, Massachusetts* (1895-1896), which by hap found the poet at work (c. 1982) in the "sleeping wilderness" of Yale's Sterling Library, Howe would, decades later, describe her propitious correspondence with "Font-voices [that] summon a reader into visible earshot."[39]

Howe's editorial and tropological/typographical factual telepathy in the works collected in *Singularities* and *The Nonconformist's Memorial* shaped her work in ways that anticipated her attunement to the "visual and acoustic shock"[40] she would encounter (c. 2005) in the *Diary* of Hannah Edwards Wetmore (as transcribed by her daughter, Lucy Wetmore Whittelsey) in the "vast collection of Edwards family papers" at the Beinecke Library.[41] *Articulation* and *Eikon; Thorow, Scattering As Behavior Toward Risk, The Nonconformist's Memorial, Silence Wager Stories, Melville's Marginalia,* and *Frolic Architecture* are kindred breakthrough works for Howe: collagist-typographic, polyvocal, strophic assemblages of embedded inter-/intra-texts, guiding the poet's understanding that "language attaches to and envelops its referent without destroying or changing it".[42]

Howe's *invisible colliding phenomena* of folding *floreate flare* imbricate/intercalate the artifactual and the archival in gestures of recovery, reconfiguration, and regenerative release.[43]

---

[39] *Souls of the Labadie Tract*, 14, 15.
[40] *Spontaneous Particulars*, 52.
[41] *The Quarry*, 36.
[42] *Souls of the Labadie Tract*, 14; *The Quarry*, 31.
[43] "In the light-bound space of the mind, the floreate flare ... // It is a child that sings itself to sleep, / The mind, among the creatures that it makes, / The people, those by which it lives and dies." Wallace Stevens, "The Owl in the Sarcophagus," *The Collected Poems* (New York: Vintage Books, 1982), 436.

Art in Art & Stone on Stone:[44]
The Quarry

I am a North American author. I was born in 1937. Into World War II and the rotten sin of man-made mass murder [...] Where did the poison of racial hatred in American begin? Will it ever end? Why are we such a violent nation? Why do we have such contempt for powerlessness?[45]

For me there was no silence before armies [...] I wish I could tenderly lift from the dark side of history, voices that are anonymous, slighted—inarticulate.[46]

Poetry is *factual telepathy* for Susan Howe (*The Quarry*, 91, 111). By this phrase, Howe means that her writing occupies charged contradictory zones among phanopoetic, physical, and phenomenal territories. Readers will find the essays collected in *The Quarry* challenging and rewarding, transgressive and transporting—not only for their relevance within the scope of Howe's work since 1974, but especially for their celebrations of rigorous creativity (in cinema, literature, philosophy, and visual art) that regenerate legacies of violence into works of hope. Howe's writing searches through the linguistic and material ruins of history for voices and artifacts, ghosts and gifts that could repair personal and collective traumas. Her essays forge elegiac passages of resistance and rescue across the "River of battlefield ghosts" in collaborative quests for the "River of peace and quietness" (23). Howe's abiding care with

---

[44] A shorter version of this essay first appeared as "Art in Art / Stone on Stone: Susan Howe's Quarrying" in *Talisman: A Journal of Contemporary Poetry & Poetics* 44 (2016): http://talismanarchive3a.weebly.com/howard-howe.html[.]

[45] Susan Howe, *The Birth-mark: unsettling the wilderness in American literary history* (Hanover and London: Wesleyan University Press, 1993), 38, 164.

[46] *The Quarry*, 177, 181.

(and concern for) our cultural and intellectual inheritance is revolutionary and redemptive. Her work is a force for social change. We need Susan Howe's learned and generous nonconformity today perhaps more than ever.

This essay primarily concerns *The Quarry*, but I'll occasionally also refer to Howe's companion collection, *The Birth-mark*—first published in 1993 by Wesleyan University Press—which New Directions republished and released on the same day as this new volume: Pearl Harbor Day. Legacies of disaster—of cultural, racial, and spiritual violence—of traumas collective and personal—invest Howe's writing with a dynamic and austere force for recovery. As the entwined epigraphs for this essay illustrate, *The Birth-mark* and *The Quarry* are contingent & contiguous elegiac twins—fierce, merciful, and visionary volumes of poetic prose juxtaposed within "the double and paradoxical nature" (*The Quarry*, 103) of Howe's kaleidoscopic array of interdisciplinary and multimedia performances and publications. This timely release of both books (in 2015) celebrates Howe's scrupulous-aleatory research, avant-gardist criticism, and visionary poetics since 1974, underscoring her preeminence as one of the most innovative and influential American writers of her generation and our time.

In her conversation with Maureen McLane published online in *Paris Review* (2012), Howe affirms that she believes "in the sacramental nature of poetry."[47] And in *Spontaneous Particulars* (2014), Howe refers to her artistic practice as an intuitive "sense of self-identification and trust, or the granting of grace in an ordinary room, in a secular time".[48] How does she accomplish such paradoxical fusions between fact and fiction, personal and political, sacred and secular realms? Howe's volumes of poetry combine a documentarian's scrupulous attention to detail, a visionary's defiance of authority, and a minimalist's care for dynamic relationships between form and content, figure and ground in all media. This is also

---

[47] Susan Howe, "The Art of Poetry: Interview by Maureen N. McLane," *The Paris Review* (Winter 2012):
http://www.theparisreview.org/interviews/6189/the-art-of-poetry-no-97-susan-howe[.]

[48] *Spontaneous Particulars*, 63.

true of her essays, which are cross-genre works of ecstatic prose that subvert generic categories, disciplinary boundaries, and historical chronologies. The word *ecstatic* is key, for Howe's writing often conveys imagistic magnetism kindred with heterodox mysticism. Her work pursues "philosophical questions about reality" through "unfathomable source[s]" until "knowledge derived from sense perception fails, and the unreality of what seems most real floods over us" (*The Quarry*, 3). At the same time, however, her writing subverts transcendental priorities and dialectical equations that would privilege spirit over matter. Howe's uncanny *unreality of what seems most real* is always already deeply embedded within the linguistic and material strata of our shared (if shattered) experience. "But if you write poems that are structured the way a piece of glass is when dropped from a great height, you probably mean something different by the word 'poem' from what most people mean. Whatever poetry may prove to be, Howe's is a material construction."[49]

Howe's cubist-like collages of poetic prose in *The Quarry* are keenly attuned to the political requirements of living in a nation shaped by legacies of violence. In company with the parabolic transgressiveness of Maggie Nelson's *The Argonauts* (2015) and the disabusing polemics of Claudia Rankine's *Citizen* (2014), for example, Howe's self-effacing and sagacious critiques are deeply contextual because, as she tells us: "This is my historical consciousness. I have no choice in it. In my poetry time and again, question[s] of assigning *the cause* of history dictate the sound of what is thought" (180). Howe's factual telepathy is experimental and ethical; her intuitive intensity transmits messages from a more hopeful future dwelling within the archive of our nation's dire past. Special collections and public libraries, for Howe, protect and provide those collective foundations for and passages to freedom.

In Howe's poetic prose, dates are like facts are like shattered windows moving down a city sidewalk; her writing emerges within and against ground-zero zones between ruins. While there's nothing particu-

---

[49] Anon., "Susan Howe: TOM TIT TOT," *Exhibition Pamphlet* (Portland, OR: Yale Union, 2013): http://yaleunion.org/susan-howe/[.]

larly unusual about slight adjustments to publication schedules, the revised release date (November 17 to December 7, 2015) for *The Quarry* resonates significantly for this North American author. In fact, five texts in the volume draw upon Howe's memories of that particular day when she was four years old, living in Buffalo, NY, with her mother (Mary Manning), father (Mark DeWolfe Howe), and sister (Fanny Howe). She visited the zoo in Delaware Park with her father, as she intimates (on page 178) in "There Are Not Leaves Enough to Crown to Cover to Crown to Cover": "B u f f a l o / 12.7.41 // (Late afternoon light.) / (Going to meet him in snow.)" Readers familiar with Howe's work will hear echoes of these lines in the "Pearl Harbor" section in *The Europe of Trusts* (1990, 2002). For Howe, this "treasured memory of togetherness before he enlisted in the army and went away to Europe" (*The Quarry*, 143) marks a turning point after which, as she notes, "I became part of the ruin. In the blank skies over Europe I was Strife represented" (179).

My own selective sequencing of events here—forwards, backwards, forwards—connects fragments from different textual layers in *The Quarry*, which, as readers, we are impelled to do while self-consciously risking the dynamics of their embedded contexts. This is where Howe's writing (compared with Nelson's and Rankine's) escapes capture and conversion (in every sense of the word) and resists (while requiring) interpretation. The uncanny contextual fusions among photographs and narratives, histories and hallucinations in W. G. Sebald's *Rings of Saturn* (1995) seem more apt companions here. Howe's texts are so deeply immersed in their historical moments and materials that they pull us into the ruin's lingering tempest, which may cause some readers to recoil (at first). The fierce and playful collaged erudition of Howe's essays can be daunting and destabilizing. Her agency is like that of a witness who "walks quickly down a city sidewalk carrying a long pane of broken glass," which is "a window not a mirror" (117). Howe's ecstatic prose dares us to walk briskly alongside, looking upon as well as through both sides of the relational medium—"a language of remains" (105)—that does not represent reality (as if in a mirror) but which continuously frames and reframes the shifting ground for the scattering & scattered figures of our individual and collective experiences. Howe's essays require our leap of faith *into the quarry*. Her writing transforms her materials; when we emerge from the whirlwind, we realize that our active, embodied interpretation has fundamentally changed the way we read the past and ourselves.

Theorists such as Cathy Caruth, Shoshana Felman, and Dori Laub have studied psychic trauma as a force that requires innovative ways of listening to and searching for truth so that the irreducible specificity of intense suffering might be channeled into creative paths without being reduced to common explanations.[50] This is true for Howe's elegiac works except that her fusions of fact and fiction escape conventional notions about how language and memory constitute and alter reality. Against problematic distinctions between true and false recovered memories, for example, Howe's writing subverts questions of origins and endings through asynchronous hybrid forms that combine autobiographical vignettes with philosophical investigations, historical details with artifacts and anecdotes from visual and material culture. Her "inexplicable intricacies of form and measure" (3) amplify the "discontinuity between nature as original creation, and the inward perception or sensation through words clear as crystal formed in rock" (14). What exactly may this mean? This is neither object-oriented fictive realism nor psychoanalytic meta-history. This is factual telepathy, and if Howe invokes *inward perception* as a metaphor for her own methods, then she also calls upon our collaborative, imaginative, and physical struggle to search the ruins for our own clarity of conviction, which is a call for regenerative action.

This means that our ways of reading and writing are also forms of making and acts of rescue. Howe's poetics is deeply praxical. Interpretation, like quarrying, requires precise cutting, recovery, and reconfiguring. One of the most remarkable achievements in Howe's essays is their

---

[50] See, respectively, *Trauma: Explorations in Memory*, ed. Cathy Caruth (Baltimore: The Johns Hopkins University Press, 1995), 3-12; 13-60; and 61-75. See also Shoshana Felman and Dori Laub, *Testimony: Crises of Witnessing in Literature, Psychoanalysis, and History* (New York: Routledge, 1992).

uncanny ability to regenerate their sources, returning to the archival groundwork "the silent voice of stone on stone" (218). That immersive, artifactual and contextual *thisness* is Susan Howe's ending-beginning "Art in art" (214). Her linguistic collages, which alternate between philosophic rigor and poetic rapture, invite our intuitive co-creative agency, as in this deftly complex passage from "Sorting Facts":

He loses her to look for her. Escape into air from living underwater, she could be his mother glimmering into sight

                      if a bird beats the air must it oh

oh must it not resound

        across the moving surface of time, a dark wing the hauntedness all that is in the other stream of consciousness. (*The Quarry*, 98)[51]

In these lines, Howe imbricates/intercalates her readings of Chris Marker's film, *La Jetée* (1962), Laurence Olivier's cinematic production of *Hamlet* (1948), and her memories of watching "newsreels, cartoons, previews of coming attractions" (103) during the 1940s at the University Movie Theater in Cambridge, Massachusetts—among numerous other contextual motifs and materials engaged in this particular essay—in her search "across the moving surface of time" for "a dark wing the hauntedness all that is in the other stream of consciousness." Everything has co-creative agency when placed within and against Howe's animist-materialist-vitalist canvasses, which juxtapose fragments into dialogues between "materialism and spiritualism" (157)—always critically attentive to the roles of language and silence, time and space as mediators of human experience. Howe's poetic prose reconfigures personal and public forms of grief expression, relentlessly and lovingly folding texts and contexts over and over, entangling her archival source materials within and

---

[51] These lines have been reformatted for presentation here.

against, between and through one another into cubist-like, artifactual paragraphs and facing page columns. Her essays stage fields of constructivist-intuitive action until the chance magic of remediation sparks regenerative "infinite and finite local evocations and wonder [for] how things are, in relation to how they appear" (45). In the spirit of Benjamin's historical materialist, Howe "regards it as [her] task to brush history against the grain."[52]

Such a poetics and praxis places Howe's work in line with Marita Sturken's concept of "cultural memory" which she figures as "a means through which definitions of the nation and 'Americanness' are simultaneously established, questioned, and refigured [...] without letting the tension of the past in the present fade away."[53] And yet and yet. Howe's quantum entanglements escape theorizing. "Time (take Zeno's flying arrow) sets out in a past we place ourselves in. If the present is connected to the past by a series of infinitesimal steps (The Law of Mind) a past cannot be wholly past" (72). Her spellbinding prose poems in *The Quarry* lead us to a new "awareness of the time-mystery of simultaneous phenomena" (94). Passages such as these may alternately fascinate and frustrate readers looking for more explicit historical and political critiques. Howe anticipates and counters such expectations at every turn. "Specialists want to nail things down. Poets know to leave Reason alone" (199). Her work variously combines the Greek notion of *poiesis* (substantial making); the Latin *praxis* (action, direct experience) and *vates* (prophet); the Old Irish *fáith* (Bard), and the Welsh *gwawd* (to scorn); the Russian formalist principle of *ostranenie* (defamiliarization), a postmodern antinomian's resolute (even recalcitrant) intuition, and a late-modernist's affinity for image/text sonic remixing. In other words, Howe's prose is packed full of kinetic materials and potential wonders,

---

[52] Walter Benjamin, "Theses on the Philosophy of History," trans. Harry Zohn, ed. Hannah Arendt, *Illuminations* (New York: Schocken Books, 1968), 257.
[53] Marita Sturken, *Tangled Memories: The Vietnam War, the AIDS Epidemic, and the Politics of Remembering* (Berkeley and London: University of California Press, 1997), 13.

and invokes our attentive and rigorous *quarrying* (in every sense of the word).

And yet, if generic categories, disciplinary boundaries, and any lingering concerns for origins and endings, identity and discourse formations are seriously challenged here, as Howe's whirlwind poetics & praxis suggest, then each and every discrete reconfiguration of texts and contexts in each essay would constitute an irremediable "catastrophe of bifurcation" (*Birth-mark,* 1993:77). By this phrase (from the 1990 *Talisman* conversation in *The Birth-mark*) Howe compares her methods to René Thom's algebraic formula of the *singularity*, "the point chaos enters cosmos, the instant articulation" (173). Howe's freethinking nonconformity, however, does not liberate either her writing or our interpretive work from history, her favorite subject since childhood. As she says in that conversation with Edward Foster: "I am trying to understand what went wrong when the first Europeans stepped on shore here […] There are things that must never be forgotten" (*Birth-mark,* 1993:164).

Readers familiar with Howe's poetry and prose will readily grasp the significance of December 7, 1941 and WWII among other legacies of violence from Metacom's War (1675-1678) to the post-9/11 global war on terror that charge her work's persistent ethical concern and redemptive force. Across the ten essays gathered in *The Quarry*, Pearl Harbor Day formatively shapes "Sorting Facts," "Frame Structures," and "There are Not Leaves Enough to Crown to Cover To Crown to Cover" and more indirectly informs "Vagrancy in the Park" and "The Disappearance Approach." Each of these prose poems integrates personal experience with artistic, literary, historical, and philosophical texts and contexts that converge upon and diverge from this pivotal moment in Howe's life. Social and political conditions during and after the war years in Europe, Ireland, and the US weave through the linguistic collages of two other sections in *The Quarry*, "Where Should the Commander Be?" and "The End of Art." Bombs and destruction, wounds and ghosts abound in these seven essays where "Pain is nailed to the landscape in time" and "Language surrounds Chaos" (180). Like Olson following Melville following Ahab into oblivion, Howe plumbs the *debths* in order to rescue "the shadow-aspect" (196) of herself and our collective North American inheritance, hoping to repair and restore "psychic reality and its relation to external reality" (130). She seeks "the unpresentable violence of a negative double" because "Something has to remain to rest a soul against stone" (31). Two other essays in *The Quarry*—"Personal Narrative" and "Arisbe"—respectively return to far earlier (though no less persistent) legacies of violence—the Turners Falls Massacre (1676) and the Trojan War—as framing contexts for Howe's archival search through "Lethean tributaries of lost sentiments and found philosophies" for "life-giving effect[s] on the *process* of [her] writing" (51 52). Special collections and public libraries, for Howe, are quarries "of freedom and wildness" where, "surrounded by raw material paper afterlife, [her] spirits [are] shaken by the great ingathering of titles and languages" (54).

In these heroic quests *across the moving surface of time* for *all that is in the other stream of consciousness,* Howe is viscerally aware of the risks and responsibilities involved in her relationships with the dead. She acknowledges that she "take[s] [her] life as a poet from their lips, their vocalisms, their breath" (54). Her quarrying through catastrophe in search of "TANGIBLE THINGS / Out of a stark oblivion"[54] pits destruction against deliverance, chaos against cosmos, as she expressed in the following reflections upon (and for) an exhibition of *TOM TIT TOT* at the University of Denver (2015):

> *TOM TIT TOT* broke my poetry, opened a new path to follow that began with the poems in *Frolic Architecture* and has been encouraged in acoustic directions while working on collaborations with the musician and composer, David Grubbs. I still felt somehow that *Frolic* was anchored-down to some material, a document or fact—to Hannah Edwards' original text—whereas

---

[54] Susan Howe and R. H. Quaytman, *TOM TIT TOT* (New York: The Museum of Modern Art, 2014), unpaginated.

25

> *TOM TIT TOT* tosses chance and discipline together in a more kaleidoscopic way [...].[55]

Each essay in *The Quarry* is a collage of vocalisms and swerving sources, of "configurations waiting from forever to be spoken" (181). Howe's erudite and ecstatic fusions of archives and artifacts engender reading (and performative) experiences similar to moiré effects that resist synthetic interpretation. Nine of these ten geometric prose-poems have been hewn from previous publications—monographs, edited collections, and journals—where they each arguably play more dynamic roles as hybrid works set within whole compositions. Given the radical linguistic and material synergies at work in Howe's immersive contexts, the selection process must have been agonizing. This is the risk taken in the production of *The Quarry*, and some readers may lament the absence of Howe's facing page sequences and paratextual materials (including book cover images, drawings, letters, transcriptions, and other remediated artifacts) from those earlier volumes. Some fans may even protest against such inter-/intra-textual violence, especially given Howe's celebrated defense of "poetry as a physical act," of "the print on the page," and of "the shapes of words, at the surface—the space of the paper itself" together with her outspoken frustration with "publishers and editors [who] let the machine rule the text" (*Birth-mark,* 1993:157, 175).

In fact, the one essay in *The Quarry* that I haven't yet addressed, "Errand," suffers most from these cross-volume transpositions. This one-page reflection upon Jonathan Edwards's practice of "pinning a small piece of paper on his clothing" as an idea would occur to him while traveling "alone on horseback from parish to parish" (47) sets magic in motion in Howe's book, *Souls of the Labadie Tract* (2007). There, the less-well-known Edwards anecdote echoes a companion moment in another one-page essay (also called *Errand*) many pages later in the book, where

---

[55] W. Scott Howard, "TANGIBLE THINGS / Out of a stark oblivion": Spellbinding *TOM TIT TOT*," (University of Denver, 2015): https://dulibraries.wordpress.com/2015/08/05/tangible-things-out-of-a-stark-oblivion-spellbinding-tom-tit-tot/[.]

Howe offers a kindred reflection upon Wallace Stevens's more widely known practice of "jott[ing] down ideas and singular perceptions, often on the backs of envelopes and old laundry bills cut into two-by-four-inch scraps he carried in his pocket"[56] during his daily two-mile walk from home to office. Although *The Quarry* begins with Howe's homage to Stevens, "Vagrancy in the Park" (which first appeared online),[57] the metaphoric and material reverberations among these previously embedded artifacts and errands in *Souls of the Labadie Tract* have been lost (as others may be found anew, here).

However, quarrying involves cutting and re-arranging, and Howe's work celebrates morphological and metamorphic transformations. And although this occasion of *The Quarry's* release date suggests a theme of ruin and repair, the multidisciplinary cross-genre texts gathered here illuminate myriad facets in Susan Howe's life and writing from her early interests in visual minimalism and concrete poetry through various forms of constructivism and modernism, historicism and romanticism, pragmatism and symbolism (among so many other influences and practices). Reading Howe's ecstatic prose requires our leap into "the immediate chaos of violent motion" in order to "recuperate the hiddenness and mystery of this 'visible' world" (93). If the essays in *The Quarry* seek regeneration through violence dwelling among linguistic and material details where history "intersects with unanswered questions [...] heavy as marble against the liberty of life" (35), then these dialogues with the dead somewhere between materialism and spiritualism ultimately lead us to a "sixth sense of another reality even in simplest objects [which] is what poets set out to show but cannot once and for all" (45).

Is this all we really need to know—that *Beauty is truth, truth beauty*? Howe follows Dickinson following Keats following Shakespeare & etc. As she notes in *My Emily Dickinson* (1985), "The lyric poet reads a past that is a huge imagination of one form."[58] Skeptics of such methods

---

[56] *Souls of the Labadie Tract*, 73.
[57] "Vagrancy in the Park," *The Nation* (October 15, 2015): http://www.thenation.com/article/vagrancy-in-the-park/[.]
[58] *My Emily Dickinson* (Berkeley: North Atlantic, 1985), 106.

should read the earliest and most recent essays—respectively "The End of Art" (1974) and "Vagrancy in the Park" (2015)—which, taken together, illuminate the arc of Howe's persistent "search for infinity inside simplicity […] to find simplicity alive with messages" (221). After crossing many rivers of battlefield ghosts, Howe's essays lead us to peace and quietness, where there is much hope for the future. "Vagrancy in the Park" offers a most remarkable constellation of discoveries that follow from this vital affirmation: "The poetry of Wallace Stevens makes me happy. This is the simple truth" (3). In *The Quarry*, we find Howe's endings always already beginning again with *art in art* and *stone on stone*.

Howe's ecstatic prose immerses us in highly charged tensions between centripetal and centrifugal forces, propelling our attention simultaneously toward discrete details recovered & reconfigured within precisely located moments (events, lives, materials, words) through portals in space-time (contradictions, erasures and gaps, paradoxes, secrets and silences, undocumented materials) across centuries and oceans, invoking our co-creative, interpretive, and regenerative work among micro-, macro-, and meta-archives, collections, and libraries. In each essay's dense and disjunctive quarry of texts and contexts, Howe deftly and intermittently articulates a poetics & praxis of inter-/intra-textual synergies and intuitive actions. "Vagrancy in the Park," for example, offers this sequence (among others) of lines and passages:

> Secret perceptions in readers draw near to the secret perceptions in authors (11) […] Poetry is an incessant amorous search under the sign of love for a remembered time at the pitch-dark fringes of evening when we gathered together to bless and believe […] Sound is sight sung inwardly. I am folding tangled threads of royal purple for a robe wrapped tightly round to keep the breath of the night wind warm (12) […] Illumination means simple understanding (13) […] According to William James: 'Both the sensational and the relational parts of reality are dumb. They say absolutely nothing about themselves. We it is who have to speak for them'. This is what Wallace Stevens does—he sounds

the myriad ever shifting sensations—fragmentary, unpredictable, unspoken, invisible—of seemingly simple objects or events [...] This interaction between reality and imagination is the benevolent, relentless vitality of nature and of poetry" (20).

Reading and writing, like quarrying, require precise cutting, recovery, and reconfiguring; each ellipsis in this block of prose marks a fracturing of the linguistic strata—a form and function of an argument in-progress here, which respects and yet also risks the precariously contingent & contiguous integrity of Howe's contextual striations.

For Susan Howe, archives and libraries, artifacts and histories, languages lost in language found, and compelling works of art are "inexhaustible quarr[ies]" (200). As she notes in *The Birth-mark*, her concern for "North American voices and visions that remain antinomian and separatist" has often "returned by strange paths to a particular place at a particular time, a threshold at the austere reach of the book" (1993:2). One of the key resources for Howe's research and writing over the years has been Webster's *An American Dictionary of the English Language* (1828 and 1854), which would remind us of the many possible meanings for *quarry* and for *quarrying*, including respectively: "a square; as a quarry of glass; an arrow with a square head; in falconry, the game which a hawk is pursuing or has killed; among hunters, a part of the entrails of the beast taken, given to the hounds; a place, cavern or pit where stones are dug from the earth, or separated from a large mass of rocks; a vast cavern under [a city], several miles in extent;" and "to prey upon [as an eagle]; to dig or take from a quarry; as, to quarry marble."[59] Attentive readers of *The Quarry* will encounter these denotative and connotative resonances (among others) in the morphological and metamorphic forms and forces dwelling among & within these challenging prose poems as herein reconfigured and "Revolving beyond forgetfulness" (25).

The Quarry sequences Howe's essays in reverse chronology (2015-1974) which complements and counters the generally forward-looking

---

[59] *American Dictionary of the English Language*, 1828 edition online: http://webstersdictionary1828.com/[.]

arrangement of essays (1984-1993) in *The Birth-mark*. Together these volumes offer a retrospective of Howe's writing. Comparisons between the two collections will inevitably follow in tandem with reassessments of Howe's incisive critiques of literary- and cultural-historical frameworks, artistic and philosophical movements, colonialism and late capitalism; as well as of her exhilarating (often paradigm-shifting) encounters with antinomians, constructivists, eccentrics, minimalists, and nonconformists—including respectively (among so many others): Anne Hutchinson and Nathaniel Hawthorne; Gertrude Stein and Chris Marker; Emily Dickinson and C. S. Peirce; Hilma af Klint and Ad Reinhardt; Anne Bradstreet and Herman Melville. Most readers will recognize Howe as a poet. She is also a cultural and literary critic, a scholar and historian, a visual and electronic media artist. *The Quarry* emerges from a prolific and multifaceted career.

From her minimalist paintings (c. 1965-1972), word drawings (first exhibited in 1971 at the Kornblee Gallery), earliest poetry collections (e.g. *One of Them*, c. 1969; *Circumnavigator*, c. 1970), and radio programs for WBAI-Pacifica (c. 1977-1981) to her numerous books of poetry and prose since *Hinge Picture* (Telephone Books, 1974), her nineteen years (1988-2007) of teaching at the State University New York at Buffalo (where she held the Samuel P. Capen Chair in Poetry and the Humanities), and her multifarious studio recordings and sonic performances (since 2003) with the composer, David Grubbs; from her recent residencies (e.g. Gardner Museum, 2012) and exhibitions (e.g. Yale Union 2013, Whitney Biennial 2014, Morgan Library 2017) to her latest artist books (*Concordance*, 2019), and vinyl/digital sonicimagetexts (*Stray*, 2019), Susan Howe's generous and collaborative spirit transfigures her materials and audiences. These are some of the facts from Howe's dynamic cutting through quarries old and new.

Metaphysical Poetics:[60]
Reflections upon the Analytic Lyric
from John Donne to Susan Howe

The earliest occupation of man is poetizing,

~~The infa~~ is Feeling and delighting in feeling.[61]

I will print you a syllabus

Continuity probability even

the predictability of drift [62]

Innovation & Tradition

What exactly are the implications of teaching the work of an innovative, twenty-first-century American poet within and against the context of a poetic tradition that emerges (primarily in England) in the seventeenth century? To suggest, in the first place, that there could be 'implications' for adopting such a pedagogy underscores what perhaps may be a strong resistance, in some scholarly and writerly communities, to

---

[60] Shorter versions of this essay first appeared as: "Teaching, How/e?: *not per se*," *Denver Quarterly* 35.2 (2000): 81-93; and "Anglo-American Metaphysical Poetics: Reflections on the Analytic Lyric from John Donne to Susan Howe," *The McNeese Review* 46 (2008): 36-52.

[61] Charles S. Peirce, MS 277, "The First Chapter of Logic," Charles S. Peirce Papers 1859-1913, Houghton Library, Harvard University, Cambridge, Mass. Reproduced in Susan Howe, *Pierce-Arrow* (New York: New Directions, 1999), 4. These lines continue, thus: *"That is what the infant in his cradle seems ~~to be doing~~ mainly to be about."* Given Peirce's double cross-outs and the difficulty of deciphering some letters and words, I have taken the liberty of interpolating onto this typographic transcription of the manuscript page my reading of ~~The infa~~ vis-à-vis this subsequent sentence, above.

[62] *Pierce-Arrow*, 22.

the assertion that experimental poetry shines most brilliantly when read, discussed, and studied in relation to established artistic traditions.[63] This essay investigates that premise through a series of reflections upon my recent experience of teaching an undergraduate course in which students examined literature, criticism, theory, and philosophy from the sixteenth through the twentieth centuries.[64]

---

[63] Only one monograph to date embraces the capaciousness of this vibrant, heterogeneous legacy from early modern English and European to modern and postmodern American poetry & poetics. See Arthur Clements, *Poetry of Contemplation* (Albany: State U of New York P, 1990). Clements's concern with postmodern poetry, though, figures minimally in that volume. (The field of criticism/scholarship suffers due to various points of resistance between creative writers and academics as well as between studies in either English or American literature and culture.) Clements differentiates his approach from that of Louis Martz, who builds a paradigm (English and European) of 'meditative' poetry and poetics that harkens back to seventeenth-century Jesuit devotional practices. See respectively Louis Martz, *The Poetry of Meditation* (New Haven: Yale UP, 1954); and Edward Dawson, *The Practical Methode of Meditation* (London, 1614). For two related and equally influential perspectives, see Helen Gardner, *The Metaphysical Poets* (Oxford: Oxford UP, 1961); and Barbara Lewalski, *Protestant Poetics and the Seventeenth-Century Religious Lyric* (Princeton: Princeton UP, 1979). A new direction here would be to reconfigure the field via a robust investigation of the analytic lyric that originates in the late sixteenth century as lyric poetry becomes estranged from both manuscript culture and musical accompaniment, turning increasingly inward upon the emerging, secular dimensions of autonomous subjectivity, individuality, literary production and reception. On that topic, see W. Scott Howard, "'That Noble Flame': Literary History & Regenerative Time in Katherine Philips's Elegies and Society of Friendship," *Dialogism & Lyric Self-Fashioning: Bakhtin and the Voices of a Genre*, ed. Jacob Blevins (Cranbury, NJ: Susquehanna University Press, 2008), 136-162.

[64] The syllabus for English 2716: *Anglo-American Metaphysical Poetics* included the following course description: "William Bronk, winner of the 1982 American Book Award for poetry, was recently described (in *Hungry Mind Review*) as 'arguably the most metaphysical poet of his generation.' What does it mean to call a contemporary American poet 'metaphysical'? Is there a tradition of American metaphysical poetry? This course traces the trajectory of *metaphysical poetics*, beginning with selections from the works of Renaissance and early modern English poets (such as William Shakespeare, John Donne, George Herbert, Aemilia Lanyer and Thomas Traherne), then engaging in close studies of poems by Anne Bradstreet, Edward Taylor, Emily Dickinson, Walt Whitman, Wallace Stevens, T. S. Eliot, Marianne Moore, Elizabeth Bishop, Jack Spicer, Robert Duncan, William Bronk, Gustaf Sobin, Rosmarie Waldrop, Michael

32

The challenge of teaching Susan Howe's poetry and prose, for example, with regard to the trans-Atlantic and trans-historical current of metaphysical writing—from Donne to Dickinson, Browne to Bishop and Bronk—yields rewards which, I believe, augment the value of literary influence and innovation, tradition and transgression that may only be gained through honest engagements with a cluster of difficult questions, including:

- What kinds of critical commentary should one offer in response to experimental texts that posit, as a central tenet and/or theme, radical breaks away from literary and scholarly conventions?
- How might a reader celebrate a writer's singularity and the innovative work's autonomy without betraying those motives and characteristics by subordinating them to so-called conventions?
- What kinds of agency are constituted and/or subverted (for writers and readers alike) by texts that propose a new 'making-of-an-unmaking'?
- How might a reader enjoy, defend and/or question the experimental work's difference from tradition without transforming the text's otherness and 'recklessness' into sameness and predictability?

Questions such as those go straight to a paradox at the heart of the innovative writer's struggle: *experimental texts need experienced readers*. A similar challenge was also true for John Donne, who sought to break free from the influence of Petrarch—"For Godsake hold your tongue, and let me love"—and yet, in order to strike the fresh "patterne" of new poetry, needed readers well-versed in the standard conceits of neo-Platonic love lyrics.[65] But at what point does a reader's experience with experiment engender a normative point of view? In the classroom—either under-

---

Palmer, and Susan Howe. This comparative approach will also involve examinations of cultural and poetic theories pertinent to the life and work of each poet."

[65] John Donne, "The Canonization," *English Seventeenth-Century Verse*, vol. 1, ed. Louis Martz (New York: Norton, 1969), 48-50.

graduate or graduate—a consequent question might be: how do we assess the sufficiency of that readerly expertise in order to achieve a successful study of innovative literatures?

In 1995, while a graduate student, I was fortunate to attend a conference and poetry festival—*The Recovery of the Public World*—in honor of Robin Blaser, his poetry and poetics.[66] The event was a dazzling gala: four days of readings, panel presentations, musical performances, banquets, parties, and other festivities. By the fourth day the conference had truly acquired a character of its own; there was a distinctive tenor to the readings, papers, and discussions, all of which had been offered in the spirit of celebrating innovative writing and art from Canada and the US. There was also, by that time, what I recall as a notable silence in that chorus of song, an absence concerning the question of 'tradition'—to be exact: any literary tradition prior to Charles Olson and the Black Mountain School that might be deemed worthy of recognition for contributing a defining influence upon experimental writing in the late twentieth century.[67] And then there was Charles Altieri's presentation, which signaled (for me anyway) a pivotal moment on that fourth day. Altieri began with an apology: instead of reading the paper he had prepared for the festival (on continuities and discontinuities between language writing and literary aesthetics from the Renaissance through the modern eras) he would offer an extemporaneous talk about the importance of allowing innovative texts to stand on their own merits and to be judged in terms of the

---

[66] This conference was held at the Emily Carr Institute of Art and Design, Vancouver, British Columbia, June 1-4, 1995. Many of the papers presented at that festival (including Susan Howe's presentation) were subsequently published in *The Recovery of the Public World: Essays on Poetics in Honour of Robin Blaser*, ed. Charles Watts and Edward Byrne (Burnaby, BC: Talonbooks, 1999).

[67] I should emphasize the idiosyncrasy of these reflections, which are contingent (for their relevance) upon my memory and my notes. However, I suspect that I am not alone in having a strong impression, though years have gone by, that the discussions at the conference would have been enlivened by more direct engagement with the challenges of placing experimental writing within and against various traditions, such as (and only for example): artistic (e.g. baroque and/or futurism); literary (e.g. dialogue and/or lyric); and philosophical (e.g. formalism and/or phenomenology).

breaks from tradition they devise and defend.[68] The talk was both engaged and engaging, but it seemed as though an important opportunity to 'grasp the nettle' had just been missed—that is, to provoke and investigate the most central, exacting, and invigorating question of all. How and why do we recognize, understand, value, discuss, write about, and teach relationships among the old, the new, and the really new literary work?

Experimental writing absolutely must be valued apart from any strict reliance upon artistic conventions. However, two key words here are: *strict* and *reliance*. I would also underscore two related points: 1) no poet, "no artist of any art, has [their] complete meaning alone;"[69] and 2) literary tradition, much like personality, should neither be exploited nor evaded—as Bin Ramke asserts in his deft commentary on Eliot's oft-quoted essay, "Tradition and the Individual Talent."[70] How, then, do we assess the ways in which innovative poets (such as Donne, Dickinson, and Howe) transfigure literary influences, thereby writing within and against poetic conventions?[71] Each influenced each, poet to poet, across the centuries, while also contributing their individual accomplishments

---

[68] In reply to my recollection and use, in this essay, of his presentation, Altieri comments: "I guess my talk was mostly extempore but that seems hard to imagine now. On my content I think you get it right, but a little partial. My point was that I felt my own paper was too mired in expectations shaped by tradition and so was not sufficiently responsive to the differences the poets were trying to establish. I was not arguing a theoretical point, but narrating a practical discovery for me. I do agree that eventually one would have to come back to 'tradition', but sometimes one has to suspend it if [tradition] leads too easily to negative terms and insufficient openness to what might be new." Charles Altieri, e-mail to the author (June 8, 2005). In *The Recovery of the Public World*, see Altieri's essay, "Some Problems About Agency in the Theories of Radical Poetics," 411-427.

[69] T. S. Eliot, "Tradition and the Individual Talent," *Selected Prose of T. S. Eliot*, ed. Frank Kermode (New York: Farrar, Straus and Giroux, 1975), 38.

[70] Bin Ramke, "Elegy as Origin," *Denver Quarterly* 23.3-4 (1989): 37.

[71] This essay contributes to a larger project that studies the analytic lyric from Shakespeare to Bronk, and Donne to Howe. See W. Scott Howard, "'roses no such roses': Jen Bervin's *Nets* and the Sonnet Tradition from Shakespeare to the Postmoderns," *Double Room* 5 (2005): http://webdelsol.com/Double_Room/issue_five/Jen_Bervin.html[.]

to the ongoing, international, and trans-historical reconfiguration of the devotional, metaphysical, meditative, contemplative, and analytic lyric traditions.[72]

Their texts share, I wish to argue, an unmistakable attentiveness to: the elaboration upon (rather than the explanation of) a poetic conceit; rapid developments of comparisons between dissimilar ideas; sudden contrasts (without explicit transitions) between ideas and images; simple language and difficult syntax; and intellectual passion shaped into a manifold of sensibility—all characteristics that have been ascribed to works in the trans-Atlantic, trans-historical legacy of metaphysical poetry and prose.[73] But does the presence of those common characteristics—if even variously articulated—necessarily mean that Donne, Dickinson, and Howe, for example, work *together* within an identifiable literary mode or artistic tradition? What best defines a 'legacy' or a 'tradition'—*writerly* or *readerly* practices; or both, or neither?

One of the greatest pleasures and values of teaching Susan Howe's writing with regard to a metaphysical line of poetry and poetics, I believe, is the discovery that for her, as for Donne and Dickinson, innovation and tradition depend equally upon *both* "a trust in radical form, however [scrupulously] achieved"[74] *and* a working context of artistic change rather than some abstract, preconceived belief in an unchanging, transcendent literary pattern against which all poems must be measured.

---

[72] The important nuances—similarities, differences, tensions—among these various strands in the legacy of metaphysical poetry and poetics are considerable. An account of those perspectives is beyond the scope of this essay. In addition to the critical studies already noted above, see Alex Preminger et al., eds., *The New Princeton Encyclopedia of Poetry and Poetics* (Princeton: Princeton University Press, 1993).

[73] T. S. Eliot, "The Metaphysical Poets," *Selected Prose of T. S. Eliot*, ed. Frank Kermode (New York: Farrar, Straus and Giroux, 1975), 60-64. See also Marjorie Nicolson, *The Breaking of the Circle*, rev. ed. (New York: Columbia UP, 1960); and A. J. Smith, *Metaphysical Wit* (Cambridge: Cambridge UP, 1991).

[74] Edward Foster, "Preface," *Postmodern Poetry: The Talisman Interviews* (Hoboken: Talisman House Publishers, 1994), vii-viii.

How/e, 'Metaphysical'?: *not per se*

In the undergraduate special topic course, my students read "Arisbe," the first section of *Pierce-Arrow*. Howe published an abbreviated edition of that poetic sequence in *Profession 1998*, the MLA's annual showcase for essays that concern pressing academic and pedagogical matters. Presented within that forum, Howe's "Renunciation is a P[ei]rcing Virtue"—a title inspired by Dickinson's verse—gains the dubious responsibility of professing to professional academics the "secret affinity between symbolic logic and poetry".[75] My encounter with that early version of "Arisbe" (and that text's allusion to Dickinson) shaped my decision to introduce my students to Howe's *Pierce-Arrow*. One or two of my colleagues (and a few friends as well) not unreasonably voiced strong doubts about teaching Susan Howe and C. S. Peirce to undergraduates: "you're teaching Howe and Peirce, *how*?!" I knew this would be a great challenge—a certain risk—but I also (not unreasonably) expected my students to rise to the occasion and hoped that, given a productive teaching context, they would be prepared to argue for and/or against her work's contribution to the poetic tradition we were investigating.[76]

When I was studying literary theory early in my graduate school years, class discussions often turned to the topic of canon formation and the status of experimental texts. Our professor, Greg Goekjian, was fond of saying, "as critics, we have one of two choices to make: we can write about non-canonical texts in a non-canonical fashion and risk alienating our audience, or we can celebrate innovative writing in a canonical manner, making familiar the strange, and perhaps gain new readers for experimental literatures."[77] Susan Howe has clearly chosen both of those

---

[75] "Renunciation Is a P[ei]rcing Virtue," *Profession 1998*, ed. Phyllis Franklin (New York: MLA, 1998), 51.

[76] We did not, however, examine Peirce's affiliation with the so-called Metaphysical Club that included William James, Oliver Wendell Holmes, Jr., Nicholas St. John Green, Joseph Bangs Warner, John Fiske, Francis Ellingwood Abbot, and Chauncey Wright. See Louis Menand, *The Metaphysical Club* (New York: Farrar, Straus and Giroux, 2001), 201-232.

options in the writing of *Pierce-Arrow*, nearly all of which investigates and re-imagines the life, work, and legacy of Charles Sanders Peirce, enigmatic progenitor of American pragmatism, or pragmat<u>ic</u>ism as Peirce further refined his nomenclature in order, Howe reminds us, "'to keep it safe from kidnappers'" (19). My evaluation here, though, is not entirely just; for, in *Pierce-Arrow*, Susan Howe writes neither purely as a creative artist nor simply as a critic, but works simultaneously in both capacities and/or *otherhow*. If unsympathetic readers should object to Howe's criticism and scholarship concerning Peirce, I'll wager they will just as strongly find themselves moved by her exuberant (often visionary) discoveries.

And what exactly are those discoveries in *Pierce-Arrow*? Does Howe elucidate Peirce's relationships with his first wife, Harriet Melusina (Zina) Fay Peirce, and with his friend and lover, Juliette de Portales? Does she present a compelling new reading of Peirce's philosophy together with a critique of the academic discourses and institutional power structures that ostracized Peirce during his lifetime and that continue to portray him as an intellectual maverick and social outcast? My answer to those questions is unequivocally yes and/or *not per se*. Much like *My Emily Dickinson*, her earlier signature text of creative and scholarly collage, *Pierce-Arrow* reveals as much—perhaps more—about Susan Howe's poetics & praxis as about the life and work of the book's quasi-biographical subject.

We have come to expect nothing less from Susan Howe than vitalist/materialist, creative/critical brilliance and passion: a singular writing style that explores "the implications of breaking the law just short of breaking off communication with a reader"[78] applied to literary subjects, characters, and historical contexts both uncanny (such as the *Eikon*

---

[77] This essay is dedicated to Greg for his outstanding teaching at Portland State University, where I first studied critical theory and poetics.

[78] *My Emily Dickinson*, 11.

Basilike) and popular (such as King Lear's youngest daughter, Cordelia).[79] If Howe has chosen to engage (in some passages) with the texts of Peirce in a non-canonical fashion, has she risked alienating her audience? Howe's devoted readers have been pleased (though not unproblematically so) with *Pierce-Arrow*.[80] The book shines as strongly, but not as warmly, as her unforgettable *My Emily Dickinson* (a second edition of which was published by New Directions in 2007). Whereas *My Emily Dickinson* has (since the 1990s) become recognized as a foundational text (for readers of Dickinson and of Howe), *Pierce-Arrow* has not yet received an equally significant amount of attention as a key work—either in the development of Howe's poetics & praxis; or, for incisive ways of reading Peirce (although such emphasis should be equally given). This difference in Howe's literary reception perhaps arises partly from the obscurity of Peirce's philosophy and partly from Howe's disjunctive methods. Whereas *My Emily Dickinson* dwells in the possibility of bringing the reader closer to Dickinson's life and work, *Pierce-Arrow* amplifies Peirce's distance from us: "The original remains perfect by being perfectly what it is because you can't touch it" (6). Yet, if Howe estranges an already alienated iconoclast in *Pierce-Arrow*, she also celebrates what remains inscrutable about Charles [Santiago] [Saunders] [Sanders] S. Peirce (7).

There were twelve students in my course—mostly sophomores and juniors—only two of whom were English majors. Our classroom conversations concerning three topics were essential to the establishment of our working context: the tradition of metaphysical poetry as articulated by T. S. Eliot; Susan Howe's inter-/intra-textual poetics & praxis; and a brief introduction to Peirce's philosophy. During the quarter, we had

---

[79] See respectively the following texts: *a bibliography of the king's book; or, eikon basilike* (providence: paradigm press, 1989); and "The Liberties," *The Europe of Trusts*, 147-218.

[80] See, for example, Stephen Collis, *Through Words of Others: Susan Howe and Anarcho-Scholasticism* (Victoria: University of Victoria, 2006); Will Montgomery, *The Poetry of Susan Howe: History, Theology, Authority* (New York: Palgrave, 2010); and, especially, Kristen Case, *American Pragmatism and Poetic Practice Crosscurrents from Emerson to Susan Howe* (Rochester: Camden House, 2011).

been tracing the trajectory of metaphysical poetics and poetry from John Donne to Emily Dickinson to Robert Duncan, focusing particularly upon the analytic lyric. Other writers under consideration also included, in chronological order: Shakespeare, George Herbert, Aemilia Lanyer, Anne Bradstreet, Thomas Traherne, Sir Thomas Browne, Edward Taylor, Walt Whitman, Wallace Stevens, T. S. Eliot, Jack Spicer, Marianne Moore, Elizabeth Bishop, William Bronk, Gustaf Sobin, Rosmarie Waldrop, and Michael Palmer. Eliot's essay on the metaphysical poets was especially useful for our preliminary discussions about whether or not metaphysical poetry is a coherent literary genre, or mode, or movement, or sensibility, or style. After opening with the precaution that not "only is it extremely difficult to define metaphysical poetry, but difficult to decide what poets practise it and in which of their verses" (59), Eliot carefully offers a cluster of defining characteristics, as noted above: the elaboration upon (rather than the explanation of) a poetic conceit; rapid developments of comparisons between dissimilar ideas; sudden contrasts (without explicit transitions) between ideas and images; simple language and difficult syntax; and intellectual passion shaped into a manifold of sensibility (60-64).

I argued in class that only the last of these points would need modification if we were to weigh and consider Eliot's views with regard to Howe's *Pierce-Arrow*. Whereas the 'manifold sensibility' of Donne, following Eliot, involves the experience of a centered subject that lights upon and delights in the linguistic de-centering of subjectivity, the 'inter-/intra-textual sensibility' of Howe concerns the predicament of de-centered subjects covered by and recovered within and against language. For Donne, as Eliot sees it, the locus of poetry resides with the reader's realization of the writer's manifold experience of artistic creation:

> A thought to Donne was an experience; it modified his sensibility. When a poet's mind is perfectly equipped for its work, it is constantly amalgamating disparate experience; the ordinary man's experience is chaotic, irregular, fragmentary. The latter falls in love, or reads Spinoza, and these two experiences have

nothing to do with each other, or with the noise of the typewriter or the smell of cooking; in the mind of the poet these experiences are always forming new wholes. (64)

Take, for example, just this one moment from "A Valediction: of weeping,"[81] where Donne amplifies the poem's central conceit:

>   On a round ball
> A workeman that hath copies by, can lay
> An Europe, Afrique, and an Asia,
> And quickly make that, which was nothing, *All*,
>   So doth each teare,
>   Which thee doth weare,
> A globe, yea world by that impression grow,
> Till thy teares mixt with mine doe overflow
> This world, by waters sent from thee, my heaven dis-
>   (solved so,
>   O

---

[81] John Donne, "A Valediction: of weeping," *P O E M S, By J. D. WITH E L E G I E S ON THE AUTHORS D E A T H*. (London: Printed by *M.F.* for John Marriot, 1633), 228-229; quoted from page 228. In this transcription, I have tried to reproduce the poem's concrete embodiment of manifold synergy: the polysemous and polyvocal registers (in the final line(s) of this stanza) of heaven being simultaneously "dissolved so" and "dis- solved so" are amplified by the poem's materiality at this liminal metaphysical space between stanzas and between pages. The aleatory catchword, O, embodies the complexity of that typographic immanence/imminence and of Donne's central conceit—the ingenious generative trope that engenders the poem's formal and thematic coherence. In Donne's 1633 text, the poem's next stanza continues at the top of page 229: "O more then Moone, / Draw not up seas to drowne me in thy spheare, / [...]." Modern editions typically do not represent the dynamic presence of catchwords, as if their tychic agency were silent and transparent. See, for example, this poem's appearance in *English Seventeenth-Century Verse*, vol. 1, ed. Louis Martz (New York: Norton, 1969), 58-59. On *catchwords* and other key principles of letterpress printing and book publishing, see John Carter, *A B C for Book Collectors* (New York: Alfred A. Knopf, 1990).

For Howe, as I see it, the place of poetry turns upon the reader's transformation of the work's vitalist/materialist, creative/critical synergies. Consider the following lines from two different sources: "In poetry all things seem to touch so they are" (*Pierce-Arrow*, 13), and "Approaching poetry all things seem to touch so they are".[82] Howe's remixing, I argued in class, is inter-/intra-textual; in *Pierce-Arrow* we see, as in *My Emily Dickinson*, the poet crafting a field of archival/artifactual relationships among and between texts.[83]

Whereas Eliot notes a characteristic telescoping of images in metaphysical poetry (60), Howe imbricates/intercalates discourse onto a map. Her poetics & praxis in *Pierce-Arrow* is metaphysical, I believe, because her text elaborates upon the conceit that heterogeneous discourses interanimate one another through the poet's and the reader's active interpretation, as the following section from "Arisbe" illustrates:

> NAME IN FULL: Charles S. Peirce (I am variously listed in print as Charles Santiago Peirce, Charles Saunders Peirce, and Charles Sanders Peirce. Under the circumstances a noncommital S. suits me best) [MS 1611]. PIERCE *v*; to run into or through as an instrument or pointed weapon does. PURSE *n*; a small bag closed with a drawstring and used to carry money. Even if he trained himself to be ambidextrous and could amaze his undergraduate classmates at Harvard by writing a question on the blackboard with one hand while simultaneously answering it with the other, Peer/se pronounced Purr/se blamed most of his problems on his own left-handedness (7).

---

[82] "Ether Either," 112.

[83] On the significance of borders, gaps, and margins in Howe's works, see: W. Scott Howard, "'writing ghost writing': A Discursive Poetics of History; or, Howe's 'hau' in Susan Howe's *a bibliography of the king's book; or, eikon basilike*," *Talisman: A Journal of Contemporary Poetry & Poetics* 14 (1996): 108-130; and, especially, Elisabeth W. Joyce, *"The Small Space of a Pause": Susan Howe's Poetry and the Spaces Between* (Lewisburg: Bucknell University Press, 2010).

Howe interpolates her own writing here within and against a passage from one of Peirce's manuscripts and two dictionary definitions, each discourse touching upon the other—contiguous and contingent—but *not yet quite* divulging an explicit account of the subject matter that these inter-/intra-texts reconfigure.

This radically contingent, analytic poetics & praxis also informs the remediation of Howe's language from one publication to another. Lines from "Arisbe" are adapted from earlier sources in which they serve different contexts and purposes. For example, the following section from "Arisbe"—

> It is strange how the dead appear in dreams where another space provides our living space as well. Another language another way of speaking so quietly always there in the shape of memories, thoughts, feelings, which are extra-marginal outside of primary consciousness, yet must be classed as some sort of unawakened finite infinite articulation. Documents resemble people talking in sleep. To exist is one thing, to be perceived another. I can spread historical information, words and words we can never touch hovering around subconscious life where enunciation is born, in distinction from what it enunciates when nothing rests in air when what is knowledge? (6)

—appears also in "Ether Either" (111), but in a completely different context. In "Arisbe" this passage immediately follows a prose account of Howe's encounter with the copy machines at Yale University Libraries and precedes a verse meditation upon the implausibility of both ontology and epistemology. In "Ether Either" this same section directly follows two portions of text: 1) a quotation from *Shelley Memorials* concerning Shelley's affection for his first child and his dislike of both the child's wet nurse and his own sister-in-law; and 2) four sentences reflecting upon the subjects of rumor, iteration, and reiteration (111). This juxtaposed passage in "Ether Either" also precedes a reproduction of a photograph (figure 5.1, page 112) that shows a young Susan Howe in the arms of her mother, Mary Manning Howe, upon their return to Boston from Ireland (October 10, 1938). Four more sentences and one fragment then follow this passage in "Ether Either," the first and last of which also appear in "Arisbe":

> Demosthenes with his mouthful of pebbles had to talk without choking himself or allowing the pebbles to drop from his mouth who ever saw him who ever saw him bite? Never the nurse of the child, the wife of the wild, the soon to be abandoned rumor. What is your fortune, my pretty maid? My face is my fortune, sir, she said. Approaching poetry all things seem to touch so they are (111-112).

My students considered these apposite structures after having read both the first section of *My Emily Dickinson* and selections from C. S. Peirce's *Letters to Lady Welby*. Many were truly fascinated with Howe's study of Dickinson's life and work, and found in that text numerous passages that indirectly offered commentaries upon Howe's own poetics & praxis, especially the following section:

> HER INTELLECTUAL CONSCIENCE
> Must never be underestimated. A tear is an intellectual thing. Dickinson ignored the worst advice from friends who misunderstood the intensity of her drive to simplicity, and heeded the best, culled from her own reading. Her talent was synthetic; she used other writers, grasped straws from the bewildering raveling of Being wherever and whenever she could use them. Crucial was her ability to spin straw into gold. Her natural capacity for assimilation was fertilized by solitude. The omnivorous gatherer was equally able to reject. To find affirmation in renunciation and to be (herself) without. Outside authority, eccentric and unique (28).

Here my students recognized not only Howe's reflection upon her own inter-/intra-textual methods, but also her keen affection for intellectual iconoclasts, a theme that constitutes perhaps the strongest link between *My Emily Dickinson* and *Pierce-Arrow*. In fact, Howe invokes Dickinson in the concluding passages of "Arisbe" for that very reason:

> On the fifteenth of April 1862, Emily Dickinson sent a first letter to her future editor, probably in response to his "Advice." She enclosed four poems, including "We play at Paste—," and a separate card bearing her name.

> Lewis Mumford noted in *The Brown Decades: A Study of the Arts in America 1865-1895* (1931) that the publication of Peirce's manuscripts had lagged for lack of a few thousand dollars to guarantee the initial expenses of his "Collected Works" and compared the situation to the concealment of Emily Dickinson's manuscripts by overzealous guardians (21-22).

Howe grounds her devotion to the life and work of both figures in the vitalist materiality of their manuscripts, arguing that Dickinson's and Peirce's original works confront us with artistic and scholarly difficulties that provoke the most imaginative and rigorous of responses. In particular, Howe praises the extent to which Dickinson's and Peirce's manuscripts embody the action of thought and the modalities of vision, feeling, and being.

The pursuit of such phenomena was perhaps the most provocative aspect of Howe's poetics & praxis for my students—something tangible they could situate in relation to Peirce's semiological analysis of the processes by which objects accrue symbolic values. In selections from Peirce's *Letters to Lady Welby* they read his accounts of Firstness, Secondness, and Thirdness:

The typical ideas of Firstness are qualities of feeling, or mere appearances […] The type of an idea of Secondness is the experience of effort, prescinded from the idea of a purpose […] In its genuine form, Thirdness is the triadic relation existing between a sign, its object, and the interpreting thought, itself a sign, considered as constituting the mode of being of a sign.[84]

These formulations became vivid when my students considered *Pierce-Arrow's* generous gathering of photographic reproductions of Peirce's manuscript pages (which animate those tri-partite dynamics through cross-outs and doodles, some of which are quite enigmatic and entertaining). Howe presents these exhibits as poetic documents in their own right: "Putting thought in motion to define art in a way that includes science, these graphs, charts, prayers, and tables are free to be drawings, even poems" (ix). One manuscript page in particular, as it is reproduced within *Pierce-Arrow* (4), offers vital reflections upon the concepts of Firstness, Secondness, and Thirdness that my students found to be very helpful for our work. My transcription here approximates Peirce's cross-outs:

1907 Oct 6
The First Chapter of Logic,

O Creator out of blank nothing of this Universe whose ~~ime~~ immense reality, sublimity, and ~~beauty~~ so little thrills me as it should, inspire me with the earnest desire to make this chapter useful to my brethren!

The earliest occupation of man is poetizing, ~~The infa~~ is Feeling and delighting in feeling. That is what the infant in his cradle seems ~~to be doing~~ mainly to be about.

---

[84] "Letters to Lady Welby," *Critical Theory Since 1965*, ed. Hazard Adams and Leroy Searle (Tallahassee: UP of Florida, 1986), 639-642.

But feeling – ~~pre gives birth to~~ generates dreams; dreams, desires; desires, impulses to do things. So the main business of a normal man's ~~life becomes~~ comes to ~~be action~~ ~~consist~~ in Action.

But ~~action soon makes~~ any man that has any ~~ripening power potentiality of possibility~~ ability to ripen is soon made by ~~a life of action~~ active life to realize that his different acts must not stand each for itself, unrelated to the others, that mere action is fatuous unless it accomplishes some thing [85]

In 1993, when I first included Susan Howe's writing in a different undergraduate course, *Avant-Garde North American Poetics and Poetry*, my primary objective was to get my students talking about their resistance to her texts: where and why their attention broke and whether or not those interruptions offered insights into Howe's materials and methods. That teaching strategy turned upon placing Howe's poetry & prose within/against an artistic and philosophical tradition that involved a combination of legacies and methodologies: Russian formalism, abstract expressionism, deconstruction, and L=A=N=G=U=A=G=E writing. In the more recent course, I was also interested in hearing about the moments in Howe's texts when my students were having trouble reading. Near the end of the quarter, I asked them to write one of their weekly, informal, two-page essays in response to *My Emily Dickinson*, "Arisbe," and the open question of Howe's placement within and/or against a tradition of metaphysical poetry and prose. The following seven passages are selected from those papers.[86]

---

[85] Charles S. Peirce, MS 277, "The First Chapter of Logic," Charles S. Peirce Papers 1859-1913, Houghton Library, Harvard University, Cambridge, Mass. Reproduced in Susan Howe, *Pierce-Arrow* (New York: New Directions, 1999), 4.

[86] Thanks to the following former students for permission to reprint these passages from their essays, respectively following the sequence of paragraphs, below: Laura Davis, Jillian Knapp, Caroline Leong, Karen Mah, Meg Satrom, Jonathan Soweidy, and Matthew Williams.

Beyond Thirdness: An Elegant Collage?

Reading Susan Howe is very similar to reading a Samuel Beckett play [...] all the guidelines that we base meaning upon when reading something are taken away from us. Her ideas are purposefully fragmented, but they always find a way of gluing themselves together by the end of the poem. I enjoy reading Howe because you are never quite sure whether she means what she is saying directly or if she means the exact opposite of what she is saying. She admits in *My Emily Dickinson* that a poet is a mirror. A mirror shows exactly what is happening, but in the eye of the human, the mirror is showing everything backwards.

*   *   *

Similarly to [George] Eliot—Dickinson's "lane to the Indies"—Dickinson herself is for Howe an "emblematical Concord River"—and for similar iconoclasm. Since Howe, like the other post-modernist poets in the metaphysical tradition, is no longer concerned with God, the "gift of belief," which she suggests that Dickinson's "greatness denied her," is not a belief in God, but a belief in something like the existence of appreciation of her work.

*   *   *

The subjectivity of the poet will always exist. Susan Howe is admittedly the lens through which we meet *her* Emily Dickinson. Recognizing the poet brings greater objectivity through the ability to understand, analyze and if necessary abstract the poet's viewpoint. "Yet I see a great many thinkers who are trying to construct a system without putting any Thirdness into it," writes Peirce. Susan Howe could represent qualities beyond

Thirdness; to understand Howe to understand Dickinson to understand the world Dickinson saw seems extraneous, except that each level of understanding contains beauty. "Forcing, abbreviating, pushing, padding, subtracting, riddling, interrogating, re-writing, she pulled text from text."

*   *   *

"Arisbe," similarly to *My Emily Dickinson*, explores the importance of a literary influence on Peirce and translates this influence into an influence on Howe's own writing. As with Dickinson, Howe rejects a previous critical view, offering her alternative to Max Fisch's explanation of the name "Arisbe." Howe's poetry incorporates references to both Homer […] and to Peirce's own writing: "[…] Hector was the third slayer / Actuality is something brute / Unspelled Firstness is first […]." In *My Emily Dickinson* and "Arisbe," Howe's discussion of the influences on Dickinson and Peirce becomes a way for her to analyze her own writing through both explicit and implied comparisons.

*   *   *

No matter who you are, how much education you have, or your level of interest in poetry, you will find Susan Howe […] challenging to understand. Howe's collective book of poetry, *Pierce-Arrow*, is difficult and hard to follow. The poetry intertwined into the commentary makes trying to dissect her point challenging, confusing, and just plain frustrating. However, in her book, *My Emily Dickinson*, Howe is clear and fairly concise on her argument of the writing and life-style of Dickinson. What I found interesting and inspiring in both books was the discussion of women and their roles in society as women, but more specifically as women artists/writers in society.

*   *   *

I believe Howe does an excellent job of digging into Dickinson's life and bringing up facts that can give us a better understanding of the poet. I find the title of the book fitting [...] because all of Howe's work is a construction of Dickinson from fragments she left behind: with no real model to look at, Dickinson becomes an interpretive concept. It reminds me of Bronk's and Spicer's work and how everything is made up of fragments, and words only have meanings due to their context and those are not absolute [...]. I still have yet to grasp *Pierce-Arrow*. I can only assume it is similar to *My Emily Dickinson*, for they are both reconstructions of identities through fragments and the mind. Is the ingenious conceit of this metaphysical poet the way the fragments are pieced together, giving a semblance of an identity?

*   *   *

Having critiqued Howe's style of "elegant collage," I stand at a crossroads. I'm not sure my hours in the library number enough for me to begin my collage. I'm not reading Howe on microform. I never had a great appreciation for squinting at the dim screens of language magnified from reduction. I understand just enough to know that the microfilm could be important. "The original remains perfect by being perfectly what it is because you can't touch it," Howe suggests. Yet Howe does touch the perfection of the words by writing about them. Culture alters. Computers outdate microfilm. Whole sections of my life occur through digitized print, the bite of HELLO. The relationship [among] Howe, Dickinson, and Peirce defies simplification. Howe quotes Peirce as saying of Lady Welby, "She thinks that modern conceptions call for a modern imagery of speech. But we fear that she does not realize how deep the knife would have to go into the body of speech to make it really scientific." Howe is difficult because so much has gone before.

Tradition & Innovation

Our context (for discussions and written work) underscored Howe's pursuit, through both Dickinson and Peirce, of "the vital distinction between concealment and revelation" (*My Emily*, 27) and of "the elements of appearance" (*Pierce-Arrow*, 14)—that is: the mysterious processes by which poetic language forms and informs the inchoate world. In response, my students often asked: why must the writing be so difficult?[87] They considered Eliot's reply to that very reasonable question:

> It is not a permanent necessity that poets should be interested in philosophy, or in any other subject. We can only say that it appears likely that poets in our civilization, as it exists at present, must be *difficult* […]. The poet must become more and more comprehensive, more allusive, more indirect, in order to force, to dislocate if necessary, language into his meaning ("Metaphysical Poets," 65).

---

[87] Stephen Burt and Robert Pinsky and have engaged with this very question. Burt's critical survey goes as far back as Eliot, and is particularly rich and attentive vis-à-vis language writing and an array of more current poetic practices in the US. Pinsky's *chrestomathy* briskly covers a lot of ground, including George Herbert's "Jordan" poems. See, respectively, Burt, "Close Calls With Nonsense: How to Read, and Perhaps Enjoy, Very New Poetry," *The Believer* 2.5 (2004):
http://www.believermag.com/issues/200405/?read=article_burt[;] and Pinsky, "In Praise of Difficult Poetry," *Slate* (Monday, April 23, 2007):
 http://www.slate.com/id/2164823/pagenum/all/#page_start[.] The open access poetics journal, *Reconfigurations*, devoted an entire issue to the topic of 'difficulty', including "Difficult Praise," a collaboratively-authored response (facilitated via a Wiki) to Burt's and Pinsky's essays. See *Reconfigurations: A Journal for Poetics & Poetry / Literature & Culture* (November, 2007):
http://reconfigurations.blogspot.com/2007/11/difficult-praise.html[.]

51

A pervasive obsession with *difficulty* in modern poetry, argues Eliot, sometimes engenders conceits and techniques very similar to those employed by the metaphysical poets. But how and why does the analytic, lyrical difficulty of modern and/or postmodern poetry, poetics & praxis move readers differently in comparison to the 'difficulty' of the early modern metaphysical writers? Most of my students in this particular course would have agreed, at the beginning of our investigation, that poetry in general is something of an acquired taste! By late November, I believe several would have reaffirmed that same perspective, especially considering the more obscure works of Lanyer, Traherne, Browne, Taylor, Eliot, Spicer, Duncan, Sobin, R. Waldrop, Palmer, and Howe. Nearly all of my students, however, expressed much enthusiasm for the poetry of Shakespeare, Donne, Herbert, Bradstreet, Dickinson, Whitman, Stevens, Moore, Bishop, and Bronk. (Remember that ten out of my twelve students were non-English majors.)

In that secondary gathering, Donne, Dickinson, Stevens, Bishop, and Bronk emerged as the five most central figures (according to my students' experiences and perspectives) in the trans-Atlantic, trans-historical legacy of metaphysical poetry & poetics. At once lyrical and philosophical, worldly and mystical, their poetries, I believe, moved my students to ask profound questions about themselves and their education that required critically reflective effort, the kind of which should be central not only to the liberal arts. For my students in this particular course, Howe's *My Emily Dickinson* also sparked that kind of generative engagement, while *Pierce-Arrow* engendered more resistance to their reading/writing (as well as for our discussions in productive ways). At the very least, however, the course's literary and cultural contexts articulated a bridge between "Arisbe" and a proven poetic tradition that inspires readers to delight in the play of language and thereby see anew the world (and themselves).

The greatest challenges and rewards, I believe, in teaching experimental writing result from honest attempts (and failures) to identify and investigate continuities and discontinuities among older, newer, and really new works, especially when those interrelationships include the possibility of a text's precarious departure (scape esaid) from artistic, cultural, and philosophical conventions. Such are the inter-/intra-textual difficulties for Howe; such were the readerly & writerly necessities for Donne and Dickinson.

"scape esaid":
Radical Contingency and Historical Figuration
from *Articulation of Sound Forms in Time*
to *The Quarry*

    from seaweed said nor repossess rest
    scape esaid [88]

These talismanic lines float in the middle of the first page of Susan Howe's *Articulation of Sound Forms in Time*—letterpress printed during March 1987 by Brita Bergland of Awede Press (Windsor, VT) in an edition of 1000 copies. They form a literal/littoral epigraph signifying destination and theme through numerous sources and voices, reverberating and rippling among kindred passages within and across centuries and contexts. Their source of utterance (*from seaweed said*) resists regained recovery (*nor repossess rest*) escaping speech (*scape esaid*) said of scapes.[89] Or, perhaps there is no escape (to be said) of the rest nor to

---

[88] *Articulation of Sound Forms in Time* (Windsor, VT: Awede Press, 1987), unpaginated (np). Unless otherwise noted, all quotations from and references to *Articulation* will follow this edition and will not be cited beyond this first mention. Sometimes these passages will be randomly selected, thereby invoking the play of chance in the spirit of Howe's poetics and praxis.

[89] The manifold meanings of *scape* (as noun, verb, interjection, and in compounds of combining forms) amplify these resonances: an act of escaping; a transgression against codes of conduct; an inadvertent mistake or clerical error; unharvested grapes; surplus steam or wind released; the shaft of a column; the tongue of a balance; a long stem or stalk rising from the root or rhizome; the main stem of a feather; the word "scape" itself—that is, the stem of the combining forms of –scape; the first joint of an antenna; an expanse of land; after Gerard Manley Hopkins, a reflection or impression of the individual quality of a thing or action; an escapement or one of its parts; an imitation of the cry of the snipe when flushed; a literal or figurative view or picture. *Oxford English Dictionary*: http://www.oed.com/[.] Unless otherwise noted, all electronic resources cited in this essay were accessed during March, 2018.

repossess from what was or is or may be from seaweed said.[90] This openwork essay places these generative, haunting eight words within the context of the poem's archival and historical sources, thereby diving into the *debths* of Howe's poetics and praxis, following *some trace of love's infolding* (*Birth-mark*, 1993:4). By 'poetics', I mean substantial making; by 'praxis', forms of action—two fundamentally interwoven aspects of socially engaged artistic production. Howe's deft, deviant reading/writing against the grain of the poem's colonial and early modern historiographies recovers, remediates, and releases Hope Atherton's story—his *undervoice*—through the artifactual wilderness, speaking truth to power. "A sonic grid of homely minutiae fallen away into posterity carries trace filaments. Tumbled syllables are bolts and bullets from the blue."[91]

Since the appearance of this first edition of *Articulation*—arguably one of Howe's most elegantly designed early letterpress books[92]—many

---

[90] "Is a story said from seaweed what is also repossessed? Or is a story said because the rest, what lies beyond its ends, can't be repossessed? Will a view (landscape or seascape), or escape (from the Middle English *scapen*, short for *escapen*) emerge from scape, or will a story said from seaweed grow into a scape (flower stem or column bottom) supporting more sayings?" (76). John Palattella, "An End of Abstraction: An Essay on Susan Howe's Historicism," *Denver Quarterly* 29.3 (1995): 74-97. I am grateful for Carolina Ebeid's unsettling of the archival wilderness at *Denver Quarterly*.

[91] "Personal Narrative," *Souls of the Labadie Tract*, 13; "Writing *Articulation of Sound Forms in Time*," *The Sound of Poetry/The Poetry of Sound*, ed. Marjorie Perloff and Craig Dworkin (Chicago: University of Chicago Press, 2009), 199; and "Personal Narrative," *The Quarry*, 51.

[92] Howe's first edition of *Secret History of the Dividing Line* (Cambridge and Somerville, Massachusetts: New England Free Press and Telephone Books, 1978) is a kindred letterpress volume that combines book design, typography and printing, inks, papers, and images with Howe's writing to achieve a whole composition of nuanced complexity. Few books achieve such balanced synergy, and few critics attend to the whole work as integral to the poem's multi-modal composition. In an essay first published on her website in 1997, Marjorie Perloff considers *Articulation* within the context of artist books, letter press publications, and hybrid works of "intermedia art" that amplify synergies between textual and visual components. Perloff reflects briefly upon some of the differences between the Awede and Wesleyan editions of *Articulation*, noting generally that the poem "as represented in *Singularities* is simply not the same poem." Perloff, "Textuality and the Visual: A Response," (1997):

readers have attempted to decipher these eight words for their literary allusions and mystic resonances, investigating the dynamically destabilizing intertextuality here, and throughout the poem, in terms of "collisions (and sometimes, it may be, collusions) of three codes—the historical, the mythic, the linguistic—all three, it should be added, as informed by an urgent, if highly individual, feminist perspective."[93] Neil Schmitz

---

https://web.archive.org/web/20160409172458/http://marjorieperloff.com/essays/ [.] See also Jerome McGann's discussion of Howe's *Pythagorean Silence* (New York: Montemora Foundation, 1982) in his influential volume, *Black Riders: The Visible Language of Modernism* (Princeton: Princeton University Press, 1993), 98-106.

McGann positions Howe's work within and against L=A=N=G=U=A=G=E poetics, aiming to celebrate *Pythagorean Silence* as the poet's "trope for what literary historians call American transcendentalism" (100). This move emphasizes antinomian linguistic iconoclasm in contrast to Pythagorean vitalist materialism—a contradiction that McGann playfully acknowledges (101)—thereby engendering a conflicted attunement to Howe's "almost mystical involvement with the materialities of writing," "jammed entanglement[s]," and "magical or primitive turn[s]" (104) within the context of individual pages, but neither across nor between facing pages (which are among the poet's signature gestures). McGann's investment in the visible surface of "each individual page" (101) underscores his main argument (via Blake, Yeats, and Stein) that "the composition of the page *is* its explanation" (102) yet hinders his ability to follow synergies and tropes throughout the book, such as his attention to "sonic mirrorings" (104) in the first two lines of Howe's epigraph to the volume without any concern for other key instances of such heightened linguistic imbrication, including "ceremony / ceremony" and "humanchild / humanchild" (Howe, *Pythagorean Silence*, np).

[93] Marjorie Perloff, *Poetic License: Essays on Modernist and Postmodernist Lyric* (Evanston: Northwestern University Press, 1990), 299. Joel Lewis (1988) reads such code switching in *Articulation* as "the fulfillment of Olson's dream of the historical process" (9). Stephen Ratcliffe (1989) engages the cross-disciplinary intertextuality of *Articulation* through his essay's collage of italicized quotations from the poem, thereby illustrating Howe's "*sideup upside* turning attention" (43). Janet Rodney (1989) sees the poem's "language respond[ing] to deeper levels of meaning, Reality in its broadest sense, human and psychological" (48), mirroring the "backward-forward movement of a sequence" (49). Paul Metcalf (1989, 2010) places *Articulation* within the context of the Objectivist legacy, reading the intertextual, internalized "ramblings of Hope Atherton" as a documentarian, historicist, and psycho-geographic composition inflected by Howe's "absence of technique" and "mistrust of metaphor" (55). Maureen Owen (1989) counters Lewis, asserting that the poem is not "a concrete tongue but a mystery [...,] a dismantling of discovery of the undefinable, not an archeological

find to be dusted off and catalogued" (58). Bruce Andrews (1989) celebrates Howe's intertextuality through paragraphs that collage quotations from *Articulation*, thereby animating Howe's poetics of *the reverse shot*—"a mirror, identified with the audience, whose members identify (as individuals) with the producer (the writer, the camera)"—which sutures the gaps and wounds so that the "ghosted spectator can see—'the absent-one'—through a shot/reverse shot sequence & continuity editing" (68). Peter Quartermain (1989, 1992) studies the poem's intertextuality for "turning points, limits, shifts, the nameless edge of mystery where transformations occur and where edge becomes centre." Charles Bernstein (1989) finds in *Articulation* "a concrete method" for examining "our captivity in [our] history" (86) of colonization and conquest in North America. Rachel Blau DuPlessis (1990) sees *Articulation* as an allegorical "vision of the center as marginal, marginalized, prone to a hopeless—yet potentially saving—breakup of its most cherished paradigms" (138). Linda Reinfeld (1992) examines *Articulation* as a "journey of literary scholarship" (122) informed partly by Howe's research "into the myth of her own very specific locality as it appears in the printed histories of Hadley and Hatfield, Massachusetts" and also by "a matrix of theory from which Howe's signature is never quite detached" (126). Ming-Qian Ma (1994) invokes Howe's "Collision or collusion with history" to link *Articulation* to the poet's interest in mathematical singularities, chaos theory, and the "coils and complications of Saying's assertions" (735). Susan M. Schultz (1994: np) reads the poem as an "American epic of reduction and reconstruction" that performs a "linguistic sex-change operation," transforming Hope Atherton's quest into "a feminine aspiration" of Hope for the woman poet in America. Marjorie Perloff (1997: np) sees the "EXTRACT from a LETTER" as a "frame structure for the lyric text" of *Articulation*. Lynn Keller (1997) places the poem's counter-discourse within the context of Howe's abiding concern with "historical figures" who have suffered from "near absence" or "misrepresentation in historical record[s]" (193). Nicky Marsh (1997) argues that "the contradictions and ambiguities implicit in [Howe's] construction of an authorial self" undermine her "challenges to the marginalization of historical narrative" in *Articulation*, which consequently "valorize[s] the indeterminacy inherent in the written word," thereby reaffirming elitist power dynamics (124-137). Paul Naylor (1999) reads *Singularities* as a collection of "lengthy serial poems that engage, on a very material level, various mythical and historical texts" as well as "hidden or repressed texts" (52). David Baker (2000) characterizes *Singularities* as a book of "three long poems" that "describe a fairly conventional view of American history" (120). In *Articulation*, Howe "seeks to tell the history of the individual by tracing the history of language, reiterated, renewed, and revised in its reuse," thereby crafting the poem as a palimpsest "overwritten by subsequent texts" (121). Baker sees Atherton as "Howe's personification of American experience, where a journey into the wilderness is more likely to result in tribulation and default than in spiritual vision or material creation" (121). Megan Simpson (2000) investigates a fundamental contradiction "at the heart of Howe's feminist project of historical recovery": on the one hand, her "poetics implies a positivist belief that historical 'voices' are somehow really there to be recovered;" and yet her work also deconstructs the notion that "historical documents can be read unproblematically as transparent representations of a 'real' past" (164). *Articulation* thus *performs* such antinomian tensions between extra-textual spirituality and intertextual materiality—dramatized most powerfully through Howe's polyvocal word squares—as a mode for "encountering history on the level of the linguistic monad" (186) that paradoxically might "allow even the most uncontainable elements in history to persist and survive" (185), thereby encountering "the past more directly" (186). Susan Vanderborg (2001) places *Singularities* within the context of what she calls *poetic palimpsests*. In such works, Howe reconfigures "a canonical work or a historical archive that presents subjects alienated from their community in conflicts over private and public identity" (65), often amplifying the role of gender politics. Ming-Qian Ma (2002) finds in *Articulation* a deft countermethod that critiques Cartesian "language trap[s]" which threaten to silence "the undervoice" and kill "the knowledge of the Other" (336). Stephen Collis (2006) studies the poem's "anarcho-scholastic" (9) intertextuality via the tropes of *emblem* and *enclosure*, following "fluid creative force[s]" (36), "emblazoned threads" (39), and "hinging juxtaposition[s]" (52). G. Matthew Jenkins (2008) tracks linguistic self-reflexivity in *Articulation* to the trace of the author that links "the poem to the most primordial element of language, the saying, or the call of the Other" (167). Miriam Nichols (2010) investigates the poem's "margin-center paradigm" that "contaminates everyone," engendering the poet's incessant wandering after "shadowy, half-articulated figures[,] tramp[ing] through the rising and falling of empires" (253). Uta Grosmann (2012) interprets the poems in *Singularities* vis-à-vis Howe's invocation of Gilles Deleuze's and Félix Guattari's notion of *multiplicity*: "when the individual opens up to the multiplicities pervading him or her, at the outcome of the most severe operation of depersonalization, [...] he or she acquires his or her true proper name" (91).

For the works cited above, see respectively: Joel Lewis, "Dreamers That Remain," *American Book Review* 10.1 (1988): 9; Stephen Ratcliffe, "Idea's Mirror," *The Difficulties: Susan Howe Issue*, ed. Tom Beckett (Kent, Ohio: Viscerally Press, 1989), 43-45; Janet Rodney, "Language and Susan," *The Difficulties* (1989), 46-51; Paul Metcalf, "The Real Susan Howe," *The Difficulties* (1989), 52-56; and "Hope Atherton's Wanderings" (2010): http://www.english.illinois.edu/maps/poets/g_l/howe/hope.htm[;]
Maureen Owen, "Susan Howe's Poetry," *The Difficulties* (1989), 57-58; Bruce Andrews, "Suture—& Absence of the Social," *The Difficulties* (1989), 67-70; Peter Quartermain, "And the Without: An interpretive essay on Susan Howe," *The Difficulties* (1989), 71-81; and *Disjunctive Poetics: From Gertrude Stein and Louis Zukofsky to Susan Howe* (Cambridge: Cambridge University Press, 1992), 182-194; Charles Bernstein, "'Passed by Examination': Paragraphs for Susan Howe," *The Difficulties* (1989), 84-88; Rachel Blau DuPlessis, *The Pink Guitar: Writing as Feminist Practice* (New York: Routledge, 1990); Linda Reinfeld, *Language Poetry: Writing as Rescue* (Baton Rouge: Louisiana State Uni-

recalls his first encounter (summer, 1989) with Howe's *Articulation*: "It was indeed the coincidence of these different literary operations […], their collision and commingling, that so mesmerized me, each page high postmodernist poetry, constructed, positioned, text, yet also powerfully Biblical, the planctus of Rachel, the voice of God, absolute authority, Poetic Truth speaking."[94] The co-presence of Brita Bergland's letterpress artistry also collides, colludes, and comingles with the book's opening incantation, I would say unsay from *seawede* said.

Here and throughout *Articulation*, Howe's language plays at the edges of sound and sense, "gesturing beyond itself in a speech that is none, open[ing] itself to the nonlanguage that precedes it and that follows

---

versity Press, 1992); Ming-Qian Ma, "Poetry as History Revised," *American Literary History* 6.4 (1994): 716-737; Susan M. Schultz, "Exaggerated History," *Postmodern Culture* 4.2 (1994): https://muse.jhu.edu/article/27452 [;] Marjorie Perloff, "Textuality and the Visual: A Response," (1997): https://web.archive.org/web/20160409172458/http://marjorieperloff.com/essays/ [;] Lynn Keller, *Forms of Expansion: Recent Long Poems by Women* (Chicago: The University of Chicago Press, 1997); Nicky Marsh, "'Out of My Texts I Am Not What I Play': Politics and Self in the Poetry of Susan Howe," *College Literature* 24.3 (1997): 124-137; Paul Naylor, *Poetic Investigations: Singing the Holes in History* (Evanston: Northwestern University Press, 1999); David Baker, *Heresy and the Ideal: On Contemporary Poetry* (Fayetteville: University of Arkansas Press, 2000); Megan Simpson, *Poetic Epistemologies: Gender and Knowing in Women's Language-Oriented Writing* (Albany: State University of New York Press, 2000); Susan Vanderborg, *Paratextual Communities: American Avant-Garde Poetry Since 1950* (Carbondale and Edwardsville: Southern Illinois University Press, 2001); Ming-Qian Ma, "Articulating the Inarticulate: *Singularities* and the Countermethod in Susan Howe," *American Women Poets in the 21st Century*, ed. Claudia Rankine and Juliana Spahr (Middletown: Wesleyan University Press, 2002), 329-352; Stephen Collis, *Through Words of Others: Susan Howe and Anarcho-Scholasticism* (Victoria: University of Victoria, 2006); G. Matthew Jenkins, *Poetic Obligation: Ethics in Experimental American Poetry After 1945* (Iowa City: University of Iowa Press, 2008); Miriam Nichols, *Radical Affections: Essays on the Poetics of Outside* (Tuscaloosa: The University of Alabama Press, 2010); Uta Grosmann, *Poetic Memory: The Forgotten Self in Plath, Howe, Hinsey, and Glück* (Madison: Farleigh Dickinson University Press 2012).

[94] "Introduction: The Planctus of Rachel," *I Have Imagined A Center // Wilder Than This Region: A Tribute to Susan Howe* (Cuneiform Press, 2007), 15.

it."[95] The other sides of language are / era egaugnal fo sedis rehto ehT.[96] Such a playful gesture here emulates Howe's polyvocal re(verse)alisms: perhaps most vividly dramatized (near the end of the poem's first section, "*Hope Atherton's Wanderings*") by the double-helical facing pages[97] beginning with "Posit gaze level diminish lamp and asleep(selv)cannot see // *is* notion most open apparition past Halo view border redden / possess remote so abstract life are lost spatio-temporal hum". Across and between, within and through these playfully inscrutable, entangled, and precarious facing pages, Howe shows us that language seen one way (upside / sideup) swiftly shifts (sideup / upside) suddenly swerving—

ReddenBorderViewHaloPastApparitionOpenMostNotion *is*

—quickened by the phenomenon of perspective: "*is* notion most open apparition". Seeing is simultaneously hearing and touching; perception and proprioception, sensation and supra-sensation inter-animate our shared, contingent experiences.[98] Howe's poetics and praxis engender

---

[95] Daniel Heller-Roazen, *Echolalias: On the Forgetting of Language* (New York: Zone Books, 2008), 18.

[96] "Howe is uniformly contradictory, 'teilweise strukturalistische, teilweise sprachmystische' [Möckel-Rieke, 281]. That is, if she is part speech-mystic, she also provides a structural anatomy of mysticism. One can witness this dynamic at work in her word squares, which do serve a definite analytical purpose." Brian Reed, "'Eden or Ebb of the Sea': Susan Howe's Word Squares and Postlinear Poetics," *Postmodern Culture* 14.2 (2004): http://pmc.iath.virginia.edu/issue.104/14.2reed.html [;] and (quoted by Reed) Hannelore Möckel-Rieke, *Fiktionen von Natur und Weiblichkeit: zur Begründung femininer und engagierter Schreibweisen bei Adrienne Rich, Denise Levertov, Susan Griffin, Kathleen Fraser und Susan Howe* (Trier, Germany: WVT Wissenschaftlicher Verlag Trier, 1991), 281.

[97] In the Wesleyan edition of *Articulation*, these are pages 14 and 15. *Singularities* (Middletown, CT: Wesleyan University Press, 1990), 1-38.

[98] Along with the epigraph to the Awede edition of *Articulation*, these particular facing pages have received ample commentary since 1987: all of the poem's readers agree that these entwined passages resist interpretation, and yet each reader turns these enigmatic pages to the advantage of their respective ar-

the reader's lyrical and social, embodied precarity through and within the work's constitutive tropological field of action.[99]

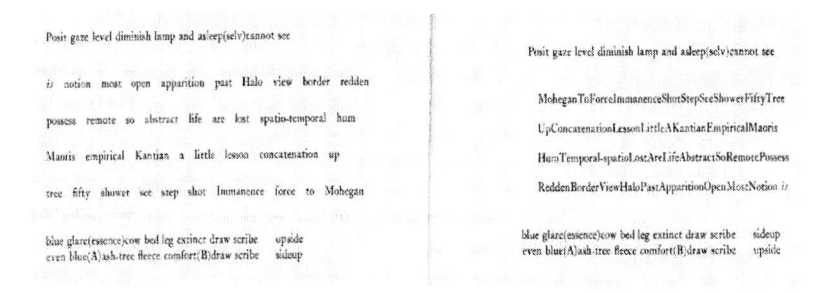

Howe's dynamic intertextuality amplifies the contingency and synergistic reversibility of the senses just as painterly mirrors magically convert "things into spectacle, spectacle into things, [oneself] into another, and another into [oneself]."[100] Merleau-Ponty's materialist-vitalist phenomenology resonates deeply here. Indeed, Howe's "Correct Final

---

gument. In each instance, those divergent readings reveal methodological principles at work; the history of that ongoing conversation illustrates the shifting course of argument in this field.

[99] (These facing pages escape the camera!) In other words, Howe's writing amplifies the powers of figurative language to construct a work that does not merely represent reality, but which embodies the reader's and the writer's lyrical and social engagement through the world of the poem's making. By *poetics*, I mean substantial making; by *praxis*, forms of action. See Hazard Adams, *Antithetical Essays in Literary Criticism and Liberal Education* (Tallahassee: Florida State University Press, 1990), 10. "To claim that language is *fundamentally* tropological is to say that metaphor, synecdoche, metonymy, and irony are the warp and woof of language," and that "in its tropes" language "is always trying to tell us something about our relations to the other and the relations of one other to another" through our shared precarity.

[100] Maurice Merleau-Ponty, "Eye and Mind," *The Merleau-Ponty Aesthetics Reader: Philosophy and Painting*, ed. Galen A. Johnson, trans. Michael B. Smith (Evanston: Northwestern University Press, 1993), 130. See also Howe's *Frolic Architecture*: "That this book is a history of / a shadow that is a shadow of // me mystically one in another / Another another to subserve". Susan Howe

Version" of her annotated typescript for *Articulation* includes an epigraph from his 1945 essay, "Cézanne's Doubt": "The truth is—this work called for this life".[101] Throughout the poem, Howe's sonic, tactile, and visual playfulness reminds us that language is a charged medium—that words are *articulations of sound forms in time*—palimpsestic, polysemous, and polyvocal.[102] Her precise attunement to these multimedia and multisensory dimensions generates imbricated passages of inter- and intra-textual artifacts escaping capture; each line requires and resists interpretation, especially when placed within the larger field of spatio-temporal action across and between facing pages:

HumTemporal-spatioLostAreLifeAbstractSoRemotePossess

Another typescript for the poem presents a title in two lines fused together (one on top of the other) so that the character terminals create an openwork stitched horizon (reminiscent of Howe's *dividing line*): "ARTICULATION OF SIGNS IN TIME / ARTICULATION OF SOUND

---

and James Welling, *Frolic Architecture* (New York: The Grenfell Press, 2010), np; and Susan Howe, *THAT THIS* (New York: New Directions, 2010), 39.

[101] Susan Howe Papers, 1942-2002, MSS 0201, Box 3, Folder 5, Geisel Library, Special Collections and Archives, UC San Diego: http://libraries.ucsd.edu/speccoll/findingaids/mss0201.html[.]
See also Merleau-Ponty, "Cézanne's Doubt," *Sense and Non-Sense*, trans. Hubert L. Dreyfus and Patricia Allen Dreyfus (Evanston: Northwestern University Press, 1964), 20. "The truth is that *this work to be done called for this life*."

[102] In her 1990 interview with Edward Foster, Howe reflects upon possible sources for the book's title: "I think it's a definition Schoenberg gives of music [...] But then I ran across the idea in a couple of other places. I can't remember where. I think there is a definition of language in the wonderful 1848 Webster's that is almost that. But I only found that last year. Poetry is a sort of music." Edward Foster, "An Interview With Susan Howe," *Talisman: A Journal of Contemporary Poetry and Poetics* 4 (1990): 30. "**LAN'GUAGE**, *noun* [Latin lingua, the tongue, and speech.] **1.** Human speech; the expression of ideas by words or significant articulate sounds." Noah Webster, *American Dictionary of the English Language*, 1828 edition online: http://webstersdictionary1828.com/ [.]

FORMS IN TIME".[103] That typescript also includes a subtitle, "Patriarchal prophesy at heels of hope / Futurity" (words which also appear within the poem's second section, "Taking The Forest"). The least sign/sound counts.[104]

Howe's collected papers reveal the *radical contingency*[105] of her co-creative relationship with an archive of source materials and the chance artifacts of her collagist compositional process working throughout the folders for *Articulation* at UC San Diego.[106] Her poetics and praxis engage language as a charged, embodied, indeterminate, and phenomenological medium even (or especially) through absence and silence. She composed *Articulation* through the archive of her sources, her manuscripts and typescripts, and the multifarious artifacts that emerged by chance from her reconfiguration of those materials, which includes a range of haptic and happenstance gestures inflected by the technology of

---

[103] Susan Howe Papers, 1942-2002, MSS 0201, Box 3, Folder 4, Geisel Library, Special Collections and Archives, UC San Diego: http://libraries.ucsd.edu/speccoll/findingaids/mss0201.html[.]
See also *Secret History of the Dividing Line*, 7, 30.

[104] "'Before and after reading each poem, Stevens spoke of the nature of poetry [...] the least sound counts, he said, the least sound and the least syllable'." Susan Howe, "Vagrancy in the Park / The essence of Wallace Stevens: Roses, roses. Fable and dream. The pilgrim sun," *The Nation* (October 15, 2015): http://www.thenation.com/article/vagrancy-in-the-park/[.]

[105] By *radical*, I mean a fundamental concern for and critique of the linguistic roots of reality; by *contingency*, chance affinities among materials that are neither designed nor foreseen, yet possible due to either present or absent accidents, conditions, or forces. In this regard, Howe's poetics and praxis echoes Rorty's resilient belief in poetry: "To see one's language, one's conscience, one's morality, and one's highest hopes as contingent products, as literalizations of what once were accidentally produced metaphors, is to adopt a self-identity which suits one for citizenship in such an ideally liberal state." Richard Rorty, *Contingency, irony, and solidarity* (Cambridge: Cambridge University Press, 1989), 61.

[106] Susan Howe Papers, 1942-2002, MSS 0201, Box 2, Folder 17; Box 3, Folders 1-5; and Box 42, Folders 7-9; Geisel Library, Special Collections and Archives, UC San Diego: http://libraries.ucsd.edu/speccoll/findingaids/mss0201.html[.] Box 42, Folders 12-15 chart the transition from *Articulation* to the emergence of Howe's *a bibliography of the king's book; or, eikon basilike* (providence: paradigm press, 1989).

the times (c.1982-1987), such as: scribbling annotations, comments, questions and references (in pencil and pen) on typescript pages; cutting and pasting (with tape and/or glue) sections of text; erasing or blotting or crossing-out words or lines or passages; folding, inverting, reversing or shuffling passages; and removing numerous pages from what ultimately became the working typescript for the Awede edition.

Such an aleatory, craftivist, generative process—*"whirlwind handwritten"*—continued through the production of the Wesleyan edition (1990) as well as throughout the openwork sequence of Howe's elaborations upon these materials and methods from *Articulation* to *The Quarry* (2015) and beyond.[107] That centripetal/centrifugal collage becomes all the more complex in light of the co-presence, within the fabric of *Articulation*, of imbricated/intercalated passages from other works, such as the poem that appears on page 34 in the Wesleyan text, which may also be found in one of Howe's most frequently adapted and republished works (between 1985 and 2015) that goes by multiple names, most recently appearing in *The Quarry* as "There Are Not Leaves Enough to

---

[107] *Articulation of Sound Forms in Time* was republished in *Singularities* (Wesleyan, 1990), 1-38. Howe's commentaries on the poem have appeared as "Personal Narrative," in *Souls of the Labadie Tract*, 11-19; as "Writing *Articulation of Sound Forms in Time*," in *The Sound of Poetry / The Poetry of Sound*, ed. Marjorie Perloff and Craig Dworkin (Chicago: University of Chicago Press, 2009), 199-204; and as "Personal Narrative," in *The Quarry*, 49-56. In each of these instances, Howe varies the context and presentation of para-textual materials that illustrate her research and writing process. She also discusses her work on *Articulation* in published conversations, including: Edward Foster, "An Interview With Susan Howe," *Talisman* 4 (1990): 14-38; Edward Foster, "Susan Howe," *Postmodern Poetry: The Talisman Interviews* (Hoboken: Talisman House, 1994), 48-68; Susan Howe, "*Talisman* Interview," *The Birth-mark* (1993): 155-181; Lynn Keller, "An Interview with Susan Howe," *Contemporary Literature* 36.1 (1995): 1-34; Jon Thompson, "Interview with Susan Howe," *Free Verse* (2005): https://english.chass.ncsu.edu/freeverse/Archives/Winter_2005/interviews/S_Howe.html [;] and Susan Howe, "*Talisman* Interview, with Edward Foster," *The Birth-mark* (2015): 155-181. This openwork sequence of adaptations and remediations of *Articulation* continues, most recently in the collaborative sound sculptures from Susan Howe, Nathaniel Mackey, and Shannon Ebner collected in *STRAY: A Graphic Tone* (Amsterdam, Netherlands: Roma Publications, 2019): https://www.printedmatter.org/catalog/52888/[.]

Crown to Cover to Crown to Cover."[108] Innumerable instances of such inter-/intra-textual transformation in the poem's disjunctive sequence across decades—including the absent presence of unpaginated [page 26] in the Awede text which does not appear in the Wesleyan text—shape and also subvert origins and endings for *Articulation*. Although some of the poem's reconfigurations are more robust than others, such continued (if intermittent) engagement underscores the radical contingency of Howe's *historical figuration*.[109] Just as "fiction seeps quietly and continuously into reality, creating that remarkable confidence of community in

---

[108] "There Are Not Leaves [...]" did not appear as such within *Pythagorean Silence* (1982), but was first published as "Statement for the New Poetics Colloquium" in *Jimmy and Lucy's house of 'K'* 5 (November, 1985), 13-17; thereafter reappearing as "THERE ARE NOT LEAVES ENOUGH TO CROWN TO COVER TO CROWN TO COVER" as a preface to a reconfigured sequential work, *PYTHAGOREAN SILENCE*, in *The Europe of Trusts* (Los Angeles: Sun & Moon, 1990), 9-14; and also in *The Europe of Trusts* (New York: New Directions, 2002), 9-14; subsequently appearing as "*There Are Not Leaves Enough to Crown to Cover to Crown to Cover*" in *American Women Poets in the 21st Century*, 325-328; and then again as "There Are Not Leaves Enough to Crown to Cover to Crown to Cover" in *The Quarry*, 177-181.

[109] By *historical figuration*, I mean a dynamic fusion of historical discourse and poetic figuration that amplifies the constitutive tropological agency of metaphoric transference. This formulation amplifies the synergy that Hayden White articulates among myth, fiction, and historiography. See *The Content of the Form: Narrative Discourse and Historical Representation* (Baltimore: The Johns Hopkins University Press, 1987). "In other words, just as the contents of myth are tested by fiction, so, too, the forms of fiction are tested by (narrative) historiography" (45). My formulation also complements Michel de Certeau's compelling insight that all discourse "is incessantly articulated over the death that it presupposes, but that the very practice of history constantly contradicts;" *historical figuration* (I would add to de Certeau's text) specifies the immanent/imminent wilderness where "language is confronted with its origins" (47). See *The Writing of History*, trans. Tom Conley (New York: Columbia University Press, 1988). On *contingency*, *historical figuration*, and *the historical imagination* as resources for social change, see W. Scott Howard, "Landscapes of Memorialisation," *Studying Cultural Landscapes*, ed. Iain Robertson and Penny Richards (London: Arnold, Inc., and New York: Oxford University Press, 2003), 47-70; and "'Fire harvest: harvest fire': Resistance, Sacrifice & Historicity in the Elegies of Robert Hayden," *Reading the Middle Generation Anew: Culture, Community, and Form in Twentieth-Century American Poetry*, ed. Eric Haralson (Iowa City: University of Iowa Press, 2006), 133-152.

anonymity,"[110] Howe's poetics—that is, her reading/writing against the grain of history—ultimately celebrates a long-standing notion of praxis, one that underscores the artist's social responsibility as activist and maker, reformer and visionary dwelling in the midst of contradicting forces, "splitting nature's shadow / splitting the world".

Since the Awede text of 1987, Howe has revised and republished *Articulation*; she has also produced para-textual materials and other creative/critical texts in dialogue with this body of work—each of which offers reflections upon her life and writing. Why has this poet returned in those various ways to these passages and their haunting legacies—these "Portents of lonely destructivism"? How have those changing texts and contexts for Howe's reading, writing, editing, and publishing—each unique in their own ways—informed her art?

That inter- and intra-textual staccato score—"emblazoned in tent-stitch"—tracks the slanted emergence and development (c. 1982-2017) of Howe's *factual telepathy*, which recovers voices on the brink of ruin—"TANGIBLE THINGS // Out of a stark oblivion ~~disenter~~"[111]—by amplifying and remediating contradictions among and between contexts, documents, and technologies. Howe's reflections upon Dickinson's "synthetic" talent offer kindred observations: "abbreviating, pushing, padding, subtracting, riddling, interrogating, re-writing, she pulled text from text."[112] Like Dickinson, Howe composes not just "'through

---

[110] Benedict Anderson, *Imagined Communities: Reflections on the Origin and Spread of Nationalism* (London: Verso, 1983), 40.

[111] Susan Howe and R. H. Quaytman, *TOM TIT TOT*, np; and Susan Howe, *Debths*, 49.

[112] *My Emily Dickinson*, 28, 29.

words of others',"[113] but through the "gallymafry of diverse articles"[114] and materials that shape the warp and weft of our reading and writing

---

[113] Stephen Collis's *Through Words of Others: Susan Howe and Anarcho-Scholasticism* (Victoria: University of Victoria, 2006) offers one of the most insightfully rigorous studies of dynamic inter-/intra-textuality in Howe's writings. Collis posits a sequence of events in a sentence that implies the embedded, proleptic germ for his book's title: "After more than a decade on Dickinson (1974-1985), the passage 'through words of others' ('Marginalia' 92) became a 'Lane to the Indies' (Dickinson, Letter 456)—so she was able to move on swiftly through Mary Rowlandson[,] Anne Hutchinson[,] Hope Atherton—Thoreau[,] Melville[,] and Peirce" (Collis, 6). Howe's work on "Melville's Marginalia" did not immediately follow *My Emily Dickinson* (1985), as Collis suggests, and (according to the UCSD Howe Papers) was not emergent until 1989 at the earliest. Between 1985 and 1989, Howe published (among other works): "The Captivity and Restoration of Mrs. Mary Rowlandson," *TEMBLOR: Contemporary Poets 2* (1985): 113-121; *Articulation* (1987); "Thorow," *Temblor* 6 (1987): 3-21; and *a bibliography of the king's book; or, eikon basilike* (providence: paradigm press, 1989)—all of which prepared the ground for her work on "Scattering As Behavior Toward Risk" (1990) and "Melville's Marginalia" (1993) among other projects going forward. Howe's papers at UCSD for *Singularities* and "Melville's Marginalia" span the years from 1990-1995; the earliest point of contact there with Melville are her notes for a talk on "Billy Budd" (1989) which would inform "Scattering As Behavior Toward Risk;" the latest, seminar notes on "Bartleby" (1997). Susan Howe Papers, 1942-2002, MSS 0201, Box 56, Folder 7; Box 63, Folders 5-8; Box 64, Folder 1; Box 67, Folders 1-2; and Box 68, Folders 4-8; Geisel Library, Special Collections and Archives, UC San Diego: http://libraries.ucsd.edu/speccoll/findingaids/mss0201.html [.] Melville's influence on Howe's reading and writing, however, certainly goes back farther and further. Her 1989 conversation with Tom Beckett underscores Melville's presence within the context of Howe's *Pythagorean Silence*: "In a certain sense, for me, Melville is Pythagoras." Beckett, "The Difficulties Interview," 18. "Scattering As Behavior Toward Risk" first appeared in *Singularities*, 61-70. "Melville's Marginalia" was first published in *The Nonconformist's Memorial* (New York: New Directions, 1993), 91-159; and later appeared as *Marginalia de Melville*, trans. Susan Howe, Bénédicte Vilgrain, Richard Sieburth, and Bernard Rival (Paris: Théâtre Typographique, 1997), which was the first publication of *Melville's Marginalia* as a single volume book. "Melville's Marginalia" was also adapted, appearing as the second track in the first studio CD by Howe and David Grubbs, *THIEFTH* (Chicago: Blue Chopsticks, 2005), which was later reissued on vinyl, *THIEFTH* (New York: ISSUE Project Room, 2015). As Howe might agree, and as she has often said in interviews, all of this ultimately goes back to her work on Dickinson. "It would be hard not to discover Dickinson. She is part of the New England landscape." Janet Ruth Falon, "Speaking With Susan Howe," 33.

practices: bookmarks, conversations, drawings and dreams; envelopes, fabrics and furniture; ghosts and gifts; houses, letters, memories, photographs and places; relationships, visions, etc. In *Articulation*, we witness Susan Howe composing between and across facing pages, as her reconfigurations of archives and artifacts engender trajectories for her pivotal trope of factual telepathy through and within infinitely finite sound forms in time.

>from seaweed said nor repossess rest
>scape esaid

On the other side of the poem's opening lines, the ghostly typographic presence of a passage from "*EXTRACT from a LETTER*" haunts the figure-ground field of intuition and touch, sound and vision in the Awede text in a powerful instance of Peircean *dialetheism*.[115] We experience the language through both pages (and through their many sources) simultaneously; these multi-sensory letterpress gestures invite our dialogue with inter- and intra-texts—recalling the Latin, *textus*—encountered as a woven composition among kindred works.[116] Some of these

---

[114] Edward Clodd, *Tom Tit Tot: an essay on savage philosophy in folk-tale* (London: Duckworth & Co., 1898), epigraph from Montaigne's essay, "Of Names." See also Michel de Montaigne, *The Essayes of Michael Lord of Montaigne*, trans. John Florio (London: George Routledge and Sons, Ltd., 1894), 136.

[115] "*Dialetheism* is the view that there are dialetheias. One can define a contradiction as a couple of sentences, one of which is the negation of the other, or as a conjunction of such sentences. Therefore, dialetheism amounts to the claim that there are true contradictions. As such, dialetheism opposes the so-called *Law of Non-Contradiction* (LNC) (sometimes also called the Law of Contradiction)." Graham Priest and Francesco Berto, "Dialetheism," *The Stanford Encyclopedia of Philosophy*, ed. Edward N. Zalta (Spring 2017): https://plato.stanford.edu/archives/spr2017/entries/dialetheism/[.]
See also Laurence Goldstein, "A Problem for the Dialetheist," *Bulletin of the Section of Logic* 15.1 (1986): 10-13.

[116] Text, *n.1*: "<French *texte*, also Old Northern French *tixte*, *tiste* (12th cent. in Godefroy), the Scriptures, etc., <medieval Latin *textus* the Gospel, written character (Du Cange), Latin *textus* (*u*-stem) style, tissue of a literary work (Quintilian), lit. that which is woven, web, texture, <*text*-, participial stem of *texĕre* to weave." *Oxford English Dictionary*: http://www.oed.com/[.]

vital gestures particular to the Awede edition disappear from subsequent remediations of *Articulation* and among the poet's disjunctive elaborations upon her "Personal Narrative" therein while other artifacts and details emerge in each instance of the work's asymmetrical singularities across decades from *Articulation* to *The Quarry*.

Within this context of shifting methods and materials, where does the poem live? When we invoke Susan Howe's *Articulation of Sound Forms in Time*, to which body of work do we refer? Does each instantiation of the work offer a part of the whole, or a whole of parts? Or, both/and as if through either/or between & among all and yet *as such* as such?

Howe is a poet of reconfiguration; each of her volumes incorporates varying degrees of material from earlier projects adapted anew, discretely revised. Some of her most frequently remediated works include "THERE ARE NOT LEAVES ENOUGH TO CROWN TO COVER TO CROWN TO COVER" (noted above), "Thorow," "Melville's Marginalia" (above noted), "Sorting Facts; or, Nineteen Ways of Looking at Marker," *Frolic Architecture*, and *TOM TIT TOT*.[117] Such a recur-

---

[117] "Thorow" first appeared in *Temblor* 6 (1987): 3-21; was republished in *Singularities* (Wesleyan, 1990), 39-59; then translated, appearing as "Passe-Thoreau" and "Thorow" in *Thorow*, trans. Bernard Rival (Paris: Théâtre Typographique, 2002), 7-32, 49-76; and then adapted, appearing as the first track in the first studio CD by Howe and David Grubbs, *THIEFTH* (Chicago: Blue Chopsticks, 2005), which was later reissued on vinyl, *THIEFTH* (New York: ISSUE Project Room, 2015). "Sorting Facts; or, Nineteen Ways of Looking at Marker" appeared first in *Beyond Document: Essays on Nonfiction Film*, ed. Charles Warren (Hanover and London: Wesleyan University Press, 1996), 295-343, and was later republished under the same title as the first in a series, New Directions Poetry Pamphlet #1 (New York: New Directions, 2013); thereafter reappearing in *The Quarry*, 88-139. "Sorting Facts […]" was also translated, appearing as "TRIAGE DES FAITS; ou, Dix-neuf façons de regarder Marker," in *Deux et*, trans. Bénédicte Vilgrain and Bernard Rival (Paris: Théâtre Typographique, 1998). *Frolic Architecture* was published as a fine press limited edition by Howe with photograms by James Welling (New York: The Grenfell Press, 2010); also appearing as "Frolic Architecture" in Howe's *THAT THIS*, 37-95; and was later released as the studio CD by Howe and David Grubbs, *Frolic Architecture* (Chicago: Blue Chopsticks, 2011). *TOM TIT TOT* premiered as a

sive, recombinant poetics and praxis engenders deft articulations and reticulations that suggest and subvert origins and endings; each work embarks on a trajectory of converging and diverging hybrid forms reminiscent of Eco's notion of *open works in movement* that "display an intrinsic mobility, a kaleidoscopic capacity to suggest themselves in constantly renewed aspects."[118] Such asymmetrical and self-reflexive, contiguous vitalist-materialist contingencies shaping the field of the work's precarious emergence could be usefully studied via mereology[119] except that Howe's factual telepathy evades transitive predications. Through this kinetic context of Howe's infinitely immanent/imminent sequential works, *Articulation of Sound Forms in Time* invokes a centripetal and centrifugal disjunctive collage of "signal escapes wonderful in themselves".

This essay celebrates that sequence of disruptively generative materials and methods through kindred appositional engagements with Howe's radical contingency, historical figuration, and factual telepathy,

---

gallery installation in Portland, OR, "Susan Howe, TOM TIT TOT" (Portland, OR: Yale Union, October 5–December 1, 2013):
http://yaleunion.org/susan-howe/ [;] then traveled to NYC, "Susan Howe," *Whitney Biennial* (New York: Whitney Museum of American Art, 2014): http://whitney.org/Exhibitions/2014Biennial/SusanHowe [;] then was published in a fine press limited edition, Susan Howe and R. H. Quaytman, *TOM TIT TOT* (New York: The Museum of Modern Art, 2014); later adapted, appearing in Howe's fourth studio CD with David Grubbs, *WOODSLIPPERCOUNTERCLATTER* (Chicago: Blue Chopsticks, 2015); and was subsequently published as a section in Howe's *Debths*, 43-100. During 2018, selected "word collages from [*TOM TIT TOT*] were exhibited in Brussels and in Vienna […], also Japan." Susan Howe, "'colliding phenomena' in Kraków," e-mail to the author (November 7, 2018).

[118] Umberto Eco, *The Role of the Reader: Explorations in the Semiotics of Texts* (Bloomington: Indiana University Press, 1979), 56. See also Joseph M. Conte, *Unending Design: The Forms of Postmodern Poetry* (Ithaca: Cornell University Press, 1991), 47-104. Conte's notion of *infinite serial form* also resonates with Howe's poetics: "having no beginning and no end; a limitless interrelation of parts; the absence of an externally imposed schema; mobility; and an intentionally incomplete condition of form" (49).

[119] For a comparative consideration of how Howe's immanent/imminent openwork sequences might be said to function at the atomic, quantum level of constitutive figuration, see Hilary Putnam's discussion of the Copenhagen Interpretation and the Many Worlds Interpretation in *Realism With a Human Face*, ed. James Conant (Cambridge: Harvard University Press, 1990), 3-18.

which are central to her works of mourning that resist transcendent forms of consolation and closure in order to shape conditions for positive social change.[120] Contradictions and echoes, erasures and paradoxes will guide my concern for this poet's "Cries open to the words inside them / Cries hurled through the Woods". This essay investigates *Articulation* through Howe's critique of the poem's source documents; through her studies of the captivity narrative which informed that critique; through new historical evidence concerning the so-called excursion of Rev. Hope Atherton,[121] which Howe "assume[s] [...] for an emblem foreshadowing a

---

[120] Howe's texts and sonic performances combine ecstatic and elegiac modes of narrative discourse and poetic figuration. On the theme of elegiac resistance to consolation as a modality for cultural critique, see Melissa F. Zeiger, *Beyond Consolation: death, sexuality, and the changing shapes of elegy* (Ithaca: Cornell University Press, 1997); Marita Sturken, *Tangled Memories: The Vietnam War, The AIDS Epidemic, and the Politics of Remembering* (Berkeley: University of California Press, 1997); W. Scott Howard, "'The Brevities': Formal Mourning, Transgression & Postmodern American Elegies," *The World in Time and Space: Towards a History of Innovative American Poetry in Our Time*, ed. Edward Foster and Joseph Donahue, *Talisman: A Journal of Contemporary Poetry and Poetics* 23-26 (2002): 122-146; and Judith Butler, *Precarious Life: The Powers of Mourning and Violence* (London and New York: Verso, 2004), 19-49.

[121] Hope Atherton (baptized August 30, 1646; died June 8, 1677) was the tenth child of Humphrey Atherton and Mary Wales. Hope graduated from Harvard College in 1665 "at the age of nineteen, and later became the only teacher in the only school in his native town" of Dorchester in 1668. Arthur Holmes Tucker, *Hope Atherton and His Times* (Deerfield, MA: Pocumtuck Valley Memorial Association, 1926), 4-7. Hope Atherton was ordained as First Minister of Hatfield, MA on May 10, 1670. Rev. Atherton accompanied a garrison of soldiers in Hatfield (commanded by Captain William Turner) who attacked a peaceful gathering of Native Tribes at Peskeompscut (Great Fall) at daybreak of May 19, 1676. Atherton witnessed the massacre, fled during the military rout, then wandered in the woods for three days before returning to Hadley, MA, which is on the other side of the Quinetucket (long tidal) River. Daniel White Wells and Reuben Field Wells, *A History of Hatfield, Massachusetts, in Three Parts* (Springfield, MA: F. C. H. Gibbons, 1910), 60-84. Hope's improbable survival, crossing of the river, return to Hadley on Monday, May 22, and narrative account of his sufferings—delivered as a sermon to his congregation in Hatfield on Sunday, May 28—were, each and all, widely denounced on the grounds that he was beside himself. Sylvester Judd, *History of Hadley, Including the Early History of Hatfield, South Hadley, Amherst and Granby Massachusetts* (Springfield,

Poet's abolished limitations in our demythologized fantasy of Manifest Destiny";[122] and through the arc of the poem's disjunctive elaborations (from the Awede text to *The Quarry's* "Personal Narrative") which further Howe's reading/writing against the grain of the historiography of Atherton's experience and legacy. On all of those levels, this essay offers new arguments and details, consequences and facts to the field.

My recursive wanderings follow the curving scarlet arrows in the Awede text—"Invisible festival / halves drawn into a circie"—which engender a ritual of rescue, remediation, and regenerative release through a precarious landscape of embedded swerving stories, an "axe-edge wording of each ramping lion".

This compelling, haunting "poem including history"[123] (which has been characterized as an "epic in reverse")[124] amplifies these many contested, nested narratives within and against, across and through centuries and contexts, unsettling origins and endings at each articulation of the work's radical contingency and historical figuration; and, of the reader's collaborative attunement to Howe's factual telepathy. In that dynamic spirit, this essay's openwork sequence will be cross-stitched by three asterisks, which invoke "a world of possibilities … [that] approaches the impossible … [and yet] remains nevertheless hypothetical."[125] These star

---

MA: H. R. Hunting & Co., 1905), 173; Wells & Wells, 84-85; and Tucker, 65-70.

[122] "The Falls Fight," *Singularities*, 4.

[123] "An epic is a poem including history. I don't see that anyone save a saphead can now think he knows any history until he understands economics." Ezra Pound, "Date Line," *Literary Essays of Ezra Pound*, ed. T. S. Eliot (New York: New Directions, 1954), 86. See also Robert Duncan, *A Poet's Mind: Collected Interviews with Robert Duncan, 1960-1985*, ed. Christopher Wagstaff (Berkeley: North Atlantic Books, 2012), 443.

[124] Schultz (2001): http://www.scc.rutgers.edu/however/v1_6_2001/current/readings/encounters/schultz.html[.] See also Schultz (2005), 152-153.

[125] Heller-Roazen, 110-111.

signs also emulate Howe's prosaic collages that shaped the groundwork for *My Emily Dickinson*, *The Birth-mark*, and *The Quarry*.[126]

*   *   *

The opening eight words in the Awede text of *Articulation* cast a powerful spell through their woven soundscape of slant rhymes *(sea / weed, said / repossess / rest)* and internal rhymes *(said / esaid)*; alliteration of *s*'s, assonance of *e*'s and of *o*'s; consonance *(weed / said / esaid)* and occlusion *(from / nor)*; fricatives *(f, s, s, s, s, s, s, s, s)* and plosives *(d, d, p, t, p, d)*; alveolar trills *(r, r, r, r)*, diphthongs *(ea, ee, ai, ai)*, and schwas/vowels *(o, e, a, e, e, a, i, o, e, o, e, e, a, e, e, a, i)*; solitary labiovelar glide *(seaweed)* and singular voiceless velar stop *(scape)*. Such incantatory music invokes a shared mnemonic culture of literal and littoral crossings,[127] rearticulating Hope Atherton's story before and after Howe's *Articulation*. In these mesmerizing lines, echoes from Eliot's *The Waste Land*, Hopkins's "Spelt from Sibyl's Leaves," Melville's "Billy in the Darbies," and Rowlandson's *Narrative of the Captivity and*

---

[126] See respectively "Part Two: Childe Emily to the Dark Tower Came," *Code of Signals: Recent Writings in Poetics*, Io #30, ed. Michael Palmer (Berkeley: North Atlantic Books, 1983), 196-218; "The Captivity and Restoration of Mrs. Mary Rowlandson" (1985); and "The End of Art," *Archives of American Art Journal* 14.4 (1974): 2-7.

[127] This essay emerges and diverges from earlier presentations and publications: W. Scott Howard, "Anecdote as Reflexive Field in the Poetry of Susan Howe," *Practicing Postmodernisms*: University of Oregon, Eugene, May 7, 1993; "'signal escapes wonderful in themselves': Hope Atherton's Wanderings in Susan Howe's *Articulation of Sound Forms in Time*," *Redisciplining America*: University of Washington, Seattle, April 20, 1995; "Literal/Littoral Crossings: Re-Articulating Hope Atherton's Story After Susan Howe's *Articulation of Sound Forms in Time*," *Reconstruction: Studies in Contemporary Culture* 6.3 (2006): https://web.archive.org/web/20110726035138/http://reconstruction.eserver.org/063/howard.shtml[;] and "'signal escapes': Susan Howe's *factual telepathy* from *Articulation* to *Debths*," *The Louisville Conference on Literature and Culture Since 1900*: University of Louisville, Louisville, February 24, 2018.

Restoration (among many other texts, including Job 1:15)[128] have been discerned and discussed by Howe's readers.[129]

---

[128] "And the Sabeans fell *upon them*, and took them away; yea, they have slain the servants with the edge of the sword; and I only am escaped alone to tell thee." The Holy Bible: King James Version (New York: Meridian, 1974), 442.

[129] Among those works of Howe criticism addressed above, consider especially Perloff, *Poetic License* (297-310, 343), and Reinfeld, *Language Poetry* (122-130, 134-147), in addition to the following publications, which collectively represent the most detailed and thorough engagements with *Articulation* thus far in the field: George F. Butterick, "The Mysterious Vision of Susan Howe," *North Dakota Quarterly* 55.4 (1987): 312-321; Bruce Campbell, "'Ring of Bodies / Sphere of Sound': An Essay on Susan Howe's *Articulation of Sound Forms in Time*," *The Difficulties: Susan Howe Issue* (Kent, Ohio: Viscerally Press, 1989), 89-96; Marjorie Perloff, *Radical Artifice: Writing Poetry in the Age of Media* (Chicago: University of Chicago Press, 1991), 50-53, 129; Peter Middleton, "On Ice: Julia Kristeva, Susan Howe and avant-garde poetics," *Contemporary Poetry Meets Modern Theory*, ed. Antony Easthope and John O. Thompson (Toronto: University of Toronto Press, 1991), 81-95; John Palattella, "An End of Abstraction: An Essay on Susan Howe's Historicism," *Denver Quarterly* 29.3 (1995): 74-97; Hank Lazer, "'Singing into the draft': Susan Howe's Textual Frontiers," *Opposing Poetries*, vol. 2 (Evanston: Northwestern University Press, 1996), 60-69; Peter Nicholls, "Unsettling the Wilderness: Susan Howe and American History," *Contemporary Literature* 37.4 (1996): 586-601; James McCorkle, "Prophecy and the Figure of the Reader in Susan Howe's *Articulation of Sound Forms in Time*," *Postmodern Culture* 9.3 (1999): https://muse.jhu.edu/article/27712 [;] Kathleen Crown, "Documentary Memory and Textual Agency: H.D. and Susan Howe," *How2* vol.1, no.3 (2000): http://www.scc.rutgers.edu/however/v1_3_2000/current/readings/crown.html[;] David Clippinger, "Between the Gaps, the Silence and the Rubble: Susan Howe, Rosmarie Waldrop, and (Another) Pound Era," *Denver Quarterly* 36 1-2 (2001): 189-205; Susan M. Schultz, "The Stutter in the Text: Editing and Historical Authority in the Work of Susan Howe," *How2* vol. 1, no.6 (2001): http://www.scc.rutgers.edu/however/v1_6_2001/current/readings/encounters/schultz.html[;] Rachel Tzvia Back, *Led By Language: The Poetry and Poetics of Susan Howe* (Tuscaloosa and London: The University of Alabama Press, 2002), 17-18, 37-50, 51, 53; Elisabeth A. Frost, *The Feminist Avant-Garde in American Poetry* (Iowa City: University of Iowa Press, 2003), 108-135, 195-196, 198; Brian Reed, "'Eden or Ebb of the Sea: Susan Howe's Word Squares and Postlinear Poetics," *Postmodern Culture* 14.2 (2004): http://pmc.iath.virginia.edu/issue.104/14.2reed.html[;] Susan M. Schultz, *A Poetics of Impasse in Modern and Contemporary American Poetry* (Tuscaloosa: The University of Alabama Press, 2005), 141-158; Peter Middleton, "Open Oppen: Linguistic Fragmentation and the Poetic Proposition," *Textual Practice* 24.4

Such ineluctable, innumerable resonances among kindred works are simultaneously definite and indefinite, autological and heterological, both/and as if neither/nor while yet & also whenas anon. This is the Howe paradox—*scape esaid*—which plays somewhere between the Grelling–Nelson paradox and Russell's paradox. Anagrams invoke aptagrams, antigrams, lipograms, palindromes, portmanteaus, and semordnilaps. So deeply informed by synergies among elisions and erasures, morphemes and phonemes—Howe's wordscapes occupy charged figure-ground relationships where language self-reflexively folds through and across, against and within itself in recombinant, vitalist-materialist articulations of sound forms in time.

We thus arrive at a wildly generative aporia: the poem engenders and evades interpretation, propelling us centripetally and centrifugally across centuries and through countless possible texts and contexts. The delightfully serious, sonorous play in these eight words—their polyvocal and polysemous resonances—intensifies the dynamics among denotative and connotative, literal and figurative, cultural, literary, historical, and metrical registers. These two opening lines in the Awede text[130] of *Articulation* serve and swerve simultaneously as cryptograph and epigraph; as apostrophe, epitaph, and invocation. We are called upon, as if from a mythic realm—"Impulsion of a myth of beginning"—to search through

---

(2010): 623-648; Will Montgomery, *The Poetry of Susan Howe: History, Theology, Authority* (New York: Palgrave, 2010), 4, 34, 44, 70, 78, 80, 85-98, 100, 103, 122, 189; Elisabeth W. Joyce, *"The Small Space of a Pause": Susan Howe's Poetry and the Spaces Between* (Lewisburg: Bucknell University Press, 2010), 16, 24, 52, 146, 152, 157, 166-196, 218-219, 225, 230-231; and Nancy Gaffield, "Susan Howe's Landscapes of Language: *Articulation of Sound Forms in Time* and 'The Liberties'," *Women: A Cultural Review* 26:3 (2015): http://dx.doi.org/10.1080/09574042.2015.1069141 [.] After Perloff's (1990) and Reinfeld's (1992) foundational readings, these critical texts offer the most robust studies of *Articulation* to date (to the best of my knowledge) and will be addressed in more detail, below.

[130] In the Wesleyan edition, these lines appear italicized and centered below an untitled woodcut image by an unknown artist from Kachergis Book Design of Pittsboro, NC. Anne Kachergis noted that they "often have several designers on staff" and expressed regret that they "didn't credit the art anywhere." E-mail to the author, "Re: Susan Howe's *Singularities*," (June 10, 2016).

the linguistic and material ruins of history for voices and artifacts, ghosts and gifts on the brink of oblivion that could repair personal and collective traumas: "Rugged solacing on surge sheltering". Beyond the solitary *"EXTRACT from a LETTER"* (which haunts these opening eight words from the other side of the page) the Awede text of *Articulation* provides no other citations from noted historical documents.[131]

May these enigmatic lines mean anything we would wish for them, or do they signify more precisely? How far across centuries and through cultures of literary and historical discourse might these words resonate? Whose stories and which sources are most relevant?

For example, if we should turn to *The Waste Land* (as other readers, noted above, have done) we would hear striking, cadenced echoes from *What the Thunder Said*:

DA *Datta* DA *Dayadhvam* DA

---

[131] The Wesleyan text of *Articulation* in *Singularities* adds several new, disruptive elements to the poem: a prose preface, "The Falls Fight," with an epigraph from Increase Mather (without source citation); several paragraphs of historical context with details and unacknowledged direct quotations; one vague allusion to "the historian" (3); and one quotation from John Cotton (also without source citation). The poem's placement as first in a sequence of other poems (*Thorow*, and *Scattering As Behavior Toward Risk*) in the Wesleyan volume introduced significant complications for formatting and page layout. Perhaps the most vexing problem in that regard concerns the integrity of Howe's facing pages in the Awede text, which were reconfigured in the Wesleyan text into stacked passages (on pages 6, 7, 8, 10, 11, 22, 25, and 35) interrupted by horizontal lines. In her personal copy of *Singularities*, Howe has tried to remove these lines with whiteout. Another problematic consequence of the poem's reformatting is that one whole page of poetry from the Awede text (page 26) has disappeared. The Wesleyan edition's inclusion of anonymous, untitled woodcut images; epigraphs from D. H. Lawrence and H. D.; and back-cover blurbs from Robert Creeley, Marjorie Perloff, and Charles Bernstein further destabilize *Articulation* while also enriching the poem's disjunctive, openwork reading/writing against the grain. Such details will be addressed, below. In her 1995 conversation with Lynn Keller, Howe discusses some of the challenges she faced in adapting *Articulation* from the Awede text to the Wesleyan volume of *Singularities*. See Lynn Keller, "An Interview with Susan Howe," *Contemporary Literature* 36.1 (1995): 1–34; and "Susan Howe/TOM TIT TOT," Yale Union: http://yaleunion.org/susan-howe/[.]

Damyata [132]

But would we also be right to listen more closely for traces of Eliot's deletions from the poem's field of composition on those manuscript pages (in dialogue with at least three co-poets/co-editors)?

~~friend my friend have for responsive shore~~
~~empty hands~~ [133]

Or, might we also discern the lingering presence (which haunts *The Waste Land*) of the first line of *The Iliad*—"μῆνιν ἄειδε, θεά, Πηληϊάδεω Ἀχιλῆος" ("Anger be now your song, immortal one, Akhilleus's anger, doomed and ruinous")[134]—within Howe's more compressed and variable metrics, her "Hook intelligence quick dactyl"? If we divide Homer's line of sixteen beats into units—dactyl (μῆνιν ἄ), dactyl (ειδε, θε), spondee (ά, Πη), dactyl (ληϊά), dactyl (δεω Ἀχι), spondee (λῆος)—we may compare with one possible scansion of Howe's two lines of twelve beats total: dactyl (from seaweed), sponde (said nor), dactyl (repossess), anceps (rcst) / dactyl (scape esaid), [sixth foot missing]. In Homer's line, the hephthemimeral caesura occurs after the third foot's first syllable—(ά,)—that is, between the seventh and

---

[132] This is not a direct quotation. My selective transcriptions from these discontinuous passages in Eliot's poem echo the cadence and the lineation from Howe's text. T. S. Eliot, *The Waste Land: A Facsimile and Transcript of the Original Drafts Including the Annotations of Ezra Pound*, ed. Valerie Eliot (New York: Harcourt Brace Jovanovich, Inc., 1971), 76-79. This edition documents the influence of Vivien Eliot, Ezra Pound, and John Quinn on Eliot's composition of the poem.

[133] Eliot, *The Waste Land*, 76-79, as noted above. In both of these instances, my selective quotations exaggerate the proposition that echoes from Howe's opening two lines in the Awede text of *Articulation* may be found embedded precisely and also randomly throughout the fabric of poetic exemplars.

[134] For the Homeric text, see *Iliad*, Perseus Digital Library, ed. Gregory R.Crane:
http://www.perseus.tufts.edu/hopper/text?doc=Perseus:text:1999.01.0133[.] Accessed May 8, 2017. For the translation, see *The Iliad of Homer*, trans. Robert Fitzgerald (Garden City, NY: Anchor Books, 1974), 11.

eighth accents, which Howe's music emulates through the shift in stress between re / po // ssess.[135] The variable metrics in Howe's two lines, including the absent sixth Homeric foot—spondee (λῆος)—shows the co-presence of "indeterminate unit[s] of versification" informed by the ubiquity of modernist free verse and perhaps more specifically by Hopkins's sprung rhythm that "involves 'feet from one to four syllables, regularly, and for particular effects any number of slack or weak syllables'."[136]

And yet, in Howe's music we might also detect Melville's speech from the depths: "I am sleepy and the oozy weeds about me twist."[137] Or, Rowlandson's invocation of Job 1:15, "*And I only am escaped alone to tell the News*"[138] (which Howe includes among the epigraphs to her 1985 essay, "The Captivity and Restoration").[139] And yet again, if we should recall Howe's abiding admiration for *Paterson*, would we be right to hear the co-presence of Williams's variable foot—"We know nothing and can know nothing / but the dance [...]"[140]—inflecting the score of these

---

[135] On my comparative scansions, see "Hexameter," *The New Princeton Encyclopedia of Poetry and Poetics*, ed. Alex Preminger and T. V. G. Brogan (Princeton: Princeton University Press, 1993), 525-527. There are other possible scansions for Howe's lines, including: spondee (from sea), spondee (weed said), dactyl (nor repo), spondee (ssess rest), dactyl (scape esaid), [sixth foot missing]. In this reading, the caesura would again fall between (repo) and (ssess). I am grateful to my colleague, Victor Castellani, for his sage guidance in these matters.

[136] See respectively Timothy Steele, *Missing Measures: Modern Poetry and the Revolt Against Meter* (Fayetteville and London: University of Arkansas Press, 1990), 99-100; and Gerard Manley Hopkins, *The Poems of Gerard Manley Hopkins*, ed. W. H. Gardner and N. H. MacKenzie (New York: Oxford University Press, 1967), 47.

[137] Herman Melville, "Billy Budd, Sailor," *Great Short Works of Herman Melville*, ed. Warner Berthoff (New York: Harper & Row, 1969), 505.

[138] *Narrative of the Captivity and Restoration of Mrs. Mary Rowlandson*, Project Gutenberg (2009): https://www.gutenberg.org/files/851/851-h/851-htm[.] Accessed June 2, 2017.

[139] *TEMBLOR* (1985): 113; and *The Birth-mark* (1993): 89.

[140] William Carlos Williams, *Paterson*, ed. Christopher MacGowan (New York: New Directions, 1995), 236. In a note added to the end of Book 1, which may be seen in the Kent State University page proofs for *Paterson*, Williams alluded to the emergence of his notion of the *variable foot*, which increasingly

opening twelve beats in the eight words of these two mere lines in a volume that also alludes to Schoenberg's notion of musical phrases as *articulations of sound forms in time*?[141]

Such allusive/elusive/illusive readings—relevant as they may be for their reaffirmation of artistic and literary traditions—arguably take us farther and further away from Hope Atherton and his times. The inter-/intra-textual reverberations here are endless and, as Howe has often said, *it's all about the echoes*. If *Articulation* invites a hermeneutics of bibliomancy, then how and where shall we turn from figure to ground? Which sources and whose stories are most resonant and relevant? Which writers and works have most often been invoked, and why? Which have been forgotten, and why and how so?

On the other side of the poem's first page, the Awede edition provides a solitary historical source text: "*EXTRACT from a LETTER (dated June 8th, 1781,) of Stephen Williams to President Styles*". Perhaps that single document is, as Blake might affirm, "Enough! Or Too much."[142]

*   *   *

The poem's opening two lines initiate a sequence of entangled, precarious facing pages, which have been described as "ecstatic or mystic speech" (Crown, np) that abandons "normative language functions"

---

shaped his poetry from 1953 onwards. See, for example, "The Problem" (c. 1953) or "The Descent" and other poems collected in *The Desert Music* (1954). On the Kent State University page proofs, see *Paterson*, ed. MacGowan, 267. For Williams's elaborations upon the variable foot, see "A New Measure," *Twentieth-Century American Poetics: Poets on the Art of Poetry*, ed. Dana Gioia, David Mason, and Meg Schoerke (Boston: McGraw Hill, 2004), 49-50, the text of which has been transcribed from Williams's letter to Richard Eberhart (May 23, 1954), *The Selected Letters of William Carlos Williams*, ed. John C. Thirlwall (New York: New Directions, 1957), 325-327.

[141] Foster, "An Interview With Susan Howe" (1990): 30; and Howe, *The Birth-mark* (1993): 172. See also Arnold Schoenberg, *Style and Idea: Selected Writings of Arnold Schoenberg*, ed. Leonard Stein, trans. Leo Black (New York: St. Martin's Press, 1975).

[142] William Blake, *The Marriage of Heaven and Hell*, ed. Morris Eaves, Robert N. Essick, and Joseph Viscomi (London: Tate Gallery, 1993), 158.

(Back, 40). Some readers have celebrated (and emulated) the poem's radical inter-/intra-textuality as "Language Engendering" (Rodney, 50), while others have called for restraint: "Obviously there are many ways of interpreting the eight words in these two lines, which is not to say that they can mean anything we want them to mean" (Perloff, 1990: 299). This complex, haunting poem has generated considerable debate in the field since 1987, most of which has emphasized artistic/literary and philosophical/theoretical perspectives, which (with a few notable exceptions) have surprisingly overlooked the importance of the poet's source materials for the work's historiographic engagement—even among those critics who have celebrated Howe's "historical poetics" (Montgomery, 85) and "the intersection of the personal and historical" (Gaffield, 271) in *Articulation*. A wide range of kindred artists and writers have been invoked from Dickinson to Duncan, and from Shakespeare to Scalapino.[143] And a dizzying variety of methodological approaches have shaped converging and diverging paths of argument and inquiry. In my first genealogy of criticism—from Joel Lewis (1988) to Uta Grosmann (2012)—three primary paths emerge concerning Howe's radical contingency in *Articulation*: trans-discursive contextualizing; center/margin, self/Other critiques; and Objectivist/Language poetics—each inflected by varying theoretical emphases (deconstructionist, feminist, historicist, linguistic, materialist, psychoanalytic, semiotic, etc.) and all three increasingly overlapping as the field develops. In my second genealogy of criticism—from George F. Butterick (1987) to Nancy Gaffield (2015)—

---

[143] In addition to those figures already discussed or mentioned in this essay, others include: Samuel Beckett, Charles Bernstein, John Cage, Paul Celan, Stephen Crane, Johanna Drucker, Robert Duncan, Kathleen Fraser, Ian Hamilton Finlay, Madeleine Gagnon, H. D., Lyn Hejinian, James Joyce, Nathaniel Mackey, Jackson Mac Low, Agnes Martin, Steve McCaffery, Charles Olson, Ezra Pound, Ad Reinhardt, Charles Reznikoff, Adrienne Rich, Gertrude Stein, Wallace Stevens, John Taggart, Rosmarie Waldrop, and William Butler Yeats.

those three general paths persist with the addition of other methodologies.[144] Together, these two critical genealogies (which are as comprehensive as possible) underscore a robust diversity of interpretations that have become increasingly interwoven and interdisciplinary—all in the spirit of the dynamic hybridity of Howe's work.

If all of the readers who have most thoroughly studied *Articulation* have done so from blended methodological perspectives, each writer has also emphasized certain themes more than others. In that spirit, I will chart those topics as I find them addressed by the critics and scholars from my second genealogy in order to provide a vivid context for my argument. Because Howe's writing is so richly generative for and resistant to interpretive work, each approach risks co-creative overdetermination (which is certainly true of my efforts here as well). At some point in the writing process, strong interpretations—especially theoretically driven arguments—can overtake what should be the top priority for any reader/writer: paying close attention to what the literary work has to say on its own terms within the context of each manifestation of the material. (Yes, there's an argument here for the value of close reading in dialogue with the equally contingent, constitutive agencies of chance and intuition, historicism and materialism among other synergistic dynamics.) One of the distinctive features in this legacy of interdisciplinary and inter-/intra-textual criticism concerning *Articulation*—especially for those few critics who have professed their devotion to history and historiography—is that methodological priorities have distracted scholars away from a cluster of concrete particulars that have been hiding in plain sight among Howe's source texts as well as among the poem's para-textual materials: documents, facts, and consequential significations which, like loose threads, prompt an unraveling of interpretations in this field concerning Hope Atherton's story and the poem's openwork historiographic critique.

---

[144] Some of those other theoretical perspectives include: cartography, chaos theory, cognitive poetics, image/text studies, memory studies, narratology, negative dialectics, phenomenology, post-processual archaeology, post-structural anthropology, schema theory, and trauma writing.

One of the first topics examined by readers of *Articulation* investigates psycho-geographic relationships between language and landscape: "*Hope Atherton's Wanderings*" thus leads the poem's words into the woods and back again, as Hope's survival quest guides the poet's etymological/existential search and the poem's wilderness of inter-/intra-textual contexts and forms, styles and subjects. George F. Butterick tracks Howe "over a rough terrain, a stumbling through language, like Atherton's staggering forth to surrender himself," and characterizes the poem as "a report as from under hypnosis, [...] a wave-scan of linguistic activity, from the subliminal to the sublime" (320, 321). For Marjorie Perloff, the poem's "extraordinarily taut sound structure" underscores "not so much Hope's [breakdown] as that of language itself" (1990: 304, 307) shaped by the poet's deconstruction of the lyric voice that emerges from "a chronicle in shards or fragments, as if retrieved from a fire or flood and collaged together with other particles" (1991: 52). Peter Nicholls reads *Articulation* as an archive "from which knowledge of a historical wilderness can now be drawn" and as a resource for resisting "dialectical and discursive structures" (589, 600).

Although Brian Reed, David Clippinger, and Kathleen Crown also engage this psycho-geographic theme, their essays respectively emphasize material/visual textuality, self/Other critiques, and traumatic witnessing (to be addressed below). Stephen Collis interprets the poems collected in *Singularities* vis-à-vis *anarcho-scholastic* inter-/intra-textuality, emphasizing the tropes of emblem and enclosure. *Articulation* thus amplifies disjunctive tensions embedded within "signal words [...], which are really emblematical maps of the linguistic wilderness of New England" that limn "hinging juxtaposition[s] of two terms: enclosure and escape" (47, 52). Elisabeth W. Joyce offers the most insightful and thorough study of *Articulation* as a work of trespass into layers of wilderness, history, and memory; she argues that Howe, following Hope, "becomes a part of self-creation, culture creation, and especially, an integral force in the creation of history, that sedimentation laid down through centuries of memory that infuses the landscape" (167). Nancy Gaffield investigates the poem's linguistic landscapes via cognitive poetics and schema theory, characterizing *Articulation* as a "phenomenological project" in which "Howe constructs a dialectic of 'perceptual meaning' versus 'language meaning'" that "fractures and recontextualizes the discourse of dominance in order to insert oppositional perspectives" (282, 283).

Two interrelated themes have received consistent attention since the appearance of the Awede (1987) and Wesleyan (1990) editions of *Articulation*: linguistic fragmentation/poetic indeterminacy; and material/visual textuality. These perspectives have also informed related methodologies, such as chaos theory, deconstruction, narratology, phenomenology, and postlinear poetics. Bruce Campbell describes *Articulation* as "writing which continuously tests its own limits of truth and expression," as "a sequence without plot" that generates "wordless meaning [...] only because it is, itself, the first in a chain of signifiers" (89, 92). John Palattella follows the Wesleyan edition, emphasizing René Thom's notion of the singularity for his reading of the poem's "typographic turbulence" in each word square that "challenges one to consider how and why distinct particulars emerge under certain cultural and historical conditions" (89, 91). Peter Middleton challenges one of the prevailing views in the field—that Howe's disjunctive language in *Articulation* escapes or at the very least resists normative language rules—arguing that the poem's syntactical incompleteness and textual disruptions engender "a range of propositionality evident in statements that the poem fully affirms, partially affirms, or fails entirely to affirm" (2010: 640). Gaffield's blending of cognitive poetics, phenomenology, and schema theory investigates the fractures in *Articulation* that "reveal what has been hidden [in historical] discourses that place primacy on coherence" (276).

Although Perloff (1991, 1997) and Palattella briefly address the significance of material/visual textuality in *Articulation*, Brian Reed presents one of the most compelling studies of Howe's dynamic inter-/intra-textuality within the context of her training as a visual artist, her early WORD DRAWINGS, and her long-standing admiration of abstract minimalism (especially in works from kindred artists, Ian Hamilton Finlay, Ad Reinhardt, and Agnes Martin). For Reed, "Howe's word-grid seems to present a primordial matrix somehow *just prior* to historical narrative, a condition in which, although the 'past' is still no more than a heterogeneous collection of words, it is nonetheless *poised* to emerge from gross quiddity into intelligibility" (Reed, np). Collis's anarcho-scholastic attunement to Howe's "word-collages" in *Articulation* also underscores abstract-minimalist "grids made from Europe's mind" juxtaposed within and against "a world which must think differently" (47). Joyce's psycho-cartographic mapping of linguistic strata considers image/text *word shards* to be the "poem's prime example" of Howe's (and Hope's) stumbling and stuttering through the landscape (178). Will Montgomery's investigation of *Articulation* primarily concerns the poem's connection to captivity narratives (such as Mary Rowlandson's), prophetic speech (such as Anne Hutchinson's), and Howe's "structural analogy between antinomianism and radical poetics" (82), yet he also underscores the "decontextualizing energies of collage and the rootedness of historical particulars in place that most strongly situates Howe in the post-Olsonian line of historical poetics" (93-94).

Since the appearance of *Singularities* (1990), *The Birth-mark* (1993), and *The Nonconformist's Memorial* (1993), interpretations of *Articulation* have emphasized a cluster of complementary topics, including: boundary/frontier writing, dialectical self/Other critiques, and deconstructions of colonization and conquest in North America; captivity narratives, New England historiography, and antinomian/nonconformist poetics. Middleton reads the poem as a challenge to Kristeva's notion of the semiotic *chora* because, as he asserts, Howe's purportedly disjunctive, revolutionary discourse explores and also recapitulates "what is never clearly text nor clearly other, only a history of boundaries, captures, escapes, genocides and glimpses of something 'seen once'" (1991: 93). Hank Lazer sees *Articulation* as "a contemporary version of the Puritan journal" within "an American literary tradition of frontier writing [...] understood as both a physical and textual place" (66, 68). For Linda Reinfeld, Atherton's story serves as an allegory concerning a fundamental incommensurability between language and experience; *Articulation* thus enacts "a poetics of wreckage and of exile" (125). Howe appropriates Hope's "text as a space for the writing of her own journey" (134) which (in the spirit of contested captivity narratives, violent boundary crossings, and Adorno's negative dialectics) underscores "the knowledge of extinction haunting the history of our time" (147). Similar concerns with reading the poem's deconstruction of lyric voice as signs of protest against "historical authority" (97), of "resistance to conceptuality and dialectic" (597), of "the loss of history into chaos" (172), and of the poet's rebuke against "the sense of entitlement that Manifest Destiny has conferred" (271) respectively inform Palattella's, Nicholls's, Joyce's, and Gaffield's perspectives. Montgomery, however, cautions against counter-hegemonic readings of *Articulation*, arguing that such "interpretations risk muffling the force of Howe's writing by being too quick to name the negativity that informs it" because "the poetry is not primarily carrying out a work of redress" (85).

Conflicted figures and forms of agency in *Articulation* shape James McCorkle's, Kathleen Crown's, Susan M. Schultz's, and David Clippinger's arguments concerning self/Other dynamics inflecting the poem's challenges against the legacy of colonialism in North America. McCorkle sees Atherton as "a liminal figure" who "occupies borders and becomes a specter from regions of otherness," thereby "encapsulate[ing] the poet's passage into the otherness of history" (np). Crown reads *Articulation* as a documentation of "Hope's trauma and wilderness-wandering" that attempts to "restore agency to that traumatized subjectivity by allowing its language" to bear witness to its own deconstruction (np). Schultz argues that Howe's *reverse epic* dismantles "the central ideologies that separate Puritan theology from the [N]ative American context in which they found themselves," thereby returning "to a point where the story can begin again, where it can be more inclusive" (2001: np). Clippinger places Howe's writing within a legacy of works by historically-minded poets (including Pound, Reznikoff, Williams, Olson, and Rosmarie Waldrop), asserting that *Articulation* "confronts the abyss of history in order to search out the trace of the real and the ghost of the Other—the people and texts that have been erased in order to maintain the façade of cultural order" (197). Rachel Back argues that "the encounter with the Other changes Hope to such a degree" (39-40) that (in the spirit of Levinas via Howe's *The Birth-mark*) the poem documents a "'*movement of the Same towards the Other which never returns to the Same*'" (40).[145] Atherton's "wild rantings of a madman" thus underscore "Howe's response to the conquerors' and settlers' early language practices, which continue to haunt the American literary tradition" (44). In Atherton's existential and textual disintegration, Elisabeth A. Frost reasons that "Howe finds an allegorical figure for the de-gendering her own text enacts—its disjunctive language and broken narratives" (119), which deconstruct the "trope of feminized soul [that] allows the Puritan male to appropriate what he codes as feminine in contemplating the next world while legitimizing women's subjugation in this one" (133). Within and against the grain of Puritan historiography, which equates and subordinates "the language of ecstatic prophecy" (134) to the conquest of wilderness, *Articulation* therefore juxtaposes a "feminist tradition" of antinomian poetics "from Hutchinson and Rowlandson through Dickinson, Stein, and H. D."—a nonconformist tradition that also includes Melville, Olson, and Duncan (134).

As these reflections upon the field of criticism (1987-2015) demonstrate, the combined influence of *Singularities*, *The Birth-mark*, and *The Nonconformist's Memorial* has amplified Howe's deft, deviant, and (some would argue) definitive critiques of literary and cultural history—*unsettling the wilderness*—as incisive ways of placing *Articulation* within and against contexts of emerging, contested forms of captivity narratives; colonial and early modern New England history and historiography; prayers, prophecies, and protests; and editorial interventions among archives and artifacts, manuscripts and methodologies. This nexus of perspectives, of course, is also central for *My Emily Dickinson* (1985) as well as for some of Howe's early volumes of poetry, critical essays, and interviews, including *Secret History of the Dividing Line* (1978), "Childe Emily to the Dark Tower Came" (1983), "The Captivity and Restoration of Mrs. Mary Rowlandson" (1985), and her *Talisman*

---

[145] *The Birth-mark* (1993): 37.

interview (1990). The contextual, historiographic passages accompanying *Articulation* as revised and republished in *Singularities*, and Howe's reflections (in the 1990 *Talisman* interview as well as in *The Birth-mark*, 1993) upon her research process and critical perspective have sharpened her readers' manifold concerns with such matters. However, no critical study has yet engaged with the arc of these materials and methods from the Awede text of *Articulation* (1987) to *The Quarry* (2015). That open-work sequence, as I shall argue, elaborates Howe's reading/writing against the grain of Hope Atherton's legacy, and engages the poem's challenge to colonial and early modern New England historiography.

Perloff, Reinfeld, and Nicholls interpret *Articulation* vis-à-vis these aforementioned topics and perspectives, connecting the poem to Howe's research concerning Rowlandson's captivity narrative, Hutchinson's legacy of prophecy and protest, Atherton's uncanny story, and a tradition of antinomian enthusiasm that escapes dialectical systems of capture and control. For Perloff, Rowlandson's disjunctive text and voice shape Howe's pursuit of Atherton's "'untraceable wandering'" (1990: 300) that culminates in his "failure-to-understand what the other is saying" (303), which "becomes Howe's point of departure in *Articulation*" (303). Reinfeld argues that the inherently conflicted, hybrid discursive forms of the captivity narrative resonate with Howe's "capacity for appropriation [which] is at least as great as her capacity to identify with those who suffer as a consequence of having been unfairly appropriated" (136). Contradictions and interruptions in Rowlandson's and Hutchinson's texts signify, for Nicholls, "a language which is radically antimetaphorical" (592) in *Articulation*: an antinomian poetics "of 'spirit' or enthusiasm" in which "words do not become figures for things but remain stubbornly themselves, marks and letters" that "block any displacement from an original (lost) object" (592). McCorkle, Crown, and Schultz elaborate and complicate these perspectives, adding new emphasis to forms of ecstatic prophecy, traumatic witnessing, and textual recovery/rescue in *Articulation*. McCorkle claims that Hope's exilic wanderings prefigure "the [prophetic] lineage of Rowlandson, Dickinson, and Melville" with which Howe identifies: "a patrimony from which she has been excluded" and which has, in turn, shaped their shared "non-authoritative, anonymous, positioning [...] outside the margins" (1999: np). Crown reads the poem as a documentarian work of "ecstatic historiography" that "makes partially intelligible the other's experience, while preserving," through Howe's "disjunctive writing style[,] the shock of its unintelligibility and untranslatability" (2000: np). For Schultz, Rowlandson's and Hutchinson's narratives inform Howe's cross-thinking, *stuttering* "entry into the wilderness [which] makes the poet into a scout or a captive" (2001: np) as well as "an editor, or a reviser" (2005: 143) who deconstructs the patriarchal discourse of colonialism.

Back also underscores the influence of Rowlandson's narrative and Hutchinson's testimony, which "generate the content and influence the poetic praxis" (38) in *Articulation* that documents Hope's "journey back to origins, to first places—linguistic, geographic, historical, and psychological" (41). The poem's psycho-geographic landscape thus participates "in varying forms of deception and subterfuge" (42) emanating from Rowlandson's and Hutchinson's "desire[s] and struggle[s] to define for [themselves] and [their] accusers 'the meaning of knowing'" (48). In Howe's "recovery of textual resistance" (107), Frost locates "a historical and a theoretical project [...] emblematic of an avant-gardist's paradoxical pursuit of the past" that begins with "Hutchinson's unbecoming blasphemy" (115). For Collis, Rowlandson's narrative is "replete with the language and story of enclosure" (52) and thus formatively shapes the "scattering of phonemes" (53) across wilderness landscapes in *Articulation*. Montgomery asserts that Howe "attempts a historicization of the category of the outside in American culture and proposes a literary resistance to the marginalization" (84) of Hutchinson's antinomian legacy. Although Joyce does not emphasize either Rowlandson's narrative or Hutchinson's testimony, her reading of Atherton's story embeds the discourses of captivity and of prophecy in the poem's psycho-geographic wilderness of strata that mix language, memory, history, and time: "Howe's poetic goal is to turn toward memory and events of the past in the effort to take these tangible repositories in the layers of sedimentation and rethink the present" (181). Gaffield argues that Howe "engages with the materiality of the word" in *Articulation*, interrogating "the discourses in which her poetry is shaped, particularly history" (271). The poem's disjunctive inter-/intra-textuality therefore "fractures the myth that history conceals and reveals the hidden voices" (282) of Hutchinson, Rowlandson, Atherton, and presumably others in the seventeenth-century New England phenomenological wilderness of "pre-reflective experience" (283).

In these various arguments—formatively shaped, as they are, by the Wesleyan texts of *Singularities* and *The Birth-mark* (among other poetry volumes and individual essays by Howe published before and since 1990)—Nicholls, Crown, Schultz, and Montgomery also emphasize the role of editorial praxis in *Articulation*, invoking key passages from Howe's evaluative and/or methodological statements, such as: "Hope's literal attributes. Effaced background dissolves remotest foreground. Putative author, premodern condition, presently present what future clamors for release?"[146] And: "The issue of editorial control is directly connected to the attempted erasure of antinomianism in our culture. Lawlessness seen as negligence is at first feminized and then restricted or banished."[147] And: "By choosing to install certain narratives somewhere between history, mystic speech, and poetry, I have enclosed them in an organization, although I know there are places no classificatory procedure can reach, where connections between words and things we thought existed break off."[148] Howe's capacious research context of literary, historical, and philosophical/theoretical materials (especially in *The Birth-mark*) also guides these editorial discussions along paths of historiographic reflection.

Nicholls claims that, for Howe, "the pursuit of historical veracity is one with the desire for editorial accuracy, since both seek to extirpate what seems arbitrary, unrelated, directionless" (591). For Crown, Howe's agency is "active, even salvational [...] in selecting, collecting,

---

[146] *Singularities*, 4.
[147] *The Birth-mark* (1993): 1.
[148] *The Birth-mark* (1993): 45.

and arranging [historical] material" and yet also conflicted, wary of "getting in the way" by "filtering, editing, and reordering" such material (2000: np). Schultz presents incisive studies of this relationship between editorial praxis and historical authority, placing Howe's poetics within the context of influential historicist, new historicist, and post-structural works from Caldwell, Cronon, Greenblatt, Kibbey, Kristeva, Lang, and Slotkin (among others) which are also engaged by the essays collected in *The Birth-mark*.[149] Schultz argues that, as an editor, Howe "does not seek to purify her source texts, but to re-complicate them, implicate them in the 'wilderness' that was overrun by European immigrants, as by white male editors" (1994: np); that Howe's "authority as a poet enables her to revise history, while her authority as a revisionary editor allows her to turn historical documents into poetry" (2001: np); and that Howe's "generic blurring of poetry, narrative, and history" (2005: 158) emerges

---

[149] In her *Acknowledgments* (ix-xiii), Howe underscores the importance of the following works for her research and writing. See respectively Patricia Caldwell, *The Puritan Conversion Narrative: The beginnings of American expression* (Cambridge: Cambridge University Press, 1983); William Cronon, *Changes in the Land: Indians, Colonists, and the Ecology of New England* (New York: Hill and Wang, 1983); Stephen Greenblatt, *Renaissance Self-Fashioning: From More to Shakespeare* (Chicago: University of Chicago Press, 1980); Anne Kibbey, *The Interpretation of Material Shapes in Puritanism* (Cambridge: Cambridge University Press, 1986); Julia Kristeva, *Powers of Horror: An Essay on Abjection*, trans. Leon S. Roudiez (New York: Columbia University Press, 1982); Amy Schrager Lang, *Prophetic Woman: Anne Hutchinson and the Problem of Dissent in the Literature of New England* (Berkeley: University of California Press, 1987); and Richard Slotkin, *Regeneration Through Violence: The Mythology of the American Frontier, 1600-1860* (New York: Harper, 1973). See also F. O. Matthiessen, *American Renaissance: Art and Expression in the Age of Emerson and Whitman* (Oxford: Oxford University Press, 1941); Perry Miller, *Errand Into the Wilderness* (Cambridge: Harvard University Press, 1956); Michael McGiffert, ed., *God's Plot: The Paradoxes of Puritan Piety, Being the Autobiography and Journal of Thomas Shepard* (Amherst: University of Massachusetts Press, 1972); Sacvan Bercovitch, *The American Jeremiad* (Madison: University of Wisconsin Press, 1978); Hayden White, *Tropics of Discourse: Essays in Cultural Criticism* (Baltimore: Johns Hopkins University Press, 1978); Mitchell Robert Breitwieser, and Kenneth Silverman, *The Life and Times of Cotton Mather* (New York: Harper and Row, 1984); and Michel De Certeau, *The Writing of History*, trans. Tom Conley (New York: Columbia University Press, 1988).

directly in response to new historicist methodologies (from the 1970s and 1980s). Montgomery situates Howe's editorial praxis as a liberating force between historical authority (covenant of works) and poetic inspiration (covenant of grace as embodied by the "antinomian current in American literature") that "runs from the banishment of Anne Hutchinson [...] through Emily Dickinson to the marginalization of the poetic avant garde in the late twentieth century" (82).

*   *   *

In these various critical discussions, resonant passages from Howe's essays are often engaged, including these lines from "Encloser"—lines which I've quoted above in this volume, yet in a more abbreviated form. Here is the full passage:

> This tradition that I hope I am part of has involved a breaking of boundaries of all sorts. It involves a fracturing of discourse, a stammering even. Interruption and hesitation used as a force. A recognition that there is an other voice, an attempt to hear and speak it. Its this brokenness that interests me. I see a contemporary American practice that isn't what necessarily gets into the canon and has trouble getting published. It is an echo of an undervoice that was speaking from the beginning and is peculiarly American. This voice keep on speaking *against* the grain.[150]

Given Howe's priorities in *The Birth-mark*—juxtaposing narratives among history, mystic speech, and poetry; engendering connections without connectives—and in this passage from "Encloser"—fracturing discourse in order to hear and speak an echo of an undervoice—as well as throughout *Articulation*—"stuttering out mask or trick" as a means for telepathically transmitting an "aria out of hearing // Sound through cult annunciation / sound through initiation Occult" that contradicts and

---

[150] "Encloser," 192. In this passage, notice how *Its* and *keep* perform the fracturing of syntax under discussion.

evades "Enunciate barbarous jargon / fluent language of fanaticism"— our priorities should likewise be to read and write *against the grain* of the poem's field of action, including the poem's contextual and historical source documents, following the poet's deft engagement with those materials from 1987 to 2015. Such a cross-genre, trans-discursive reading of *Articulation* would provoke an unsettling of the critical wilderness in this field: a complex terrain patiently and respectfully mapped in the above notes and paragraphs that present a capacious, critical literature review. My work here emulates Howe's kindred spirit, whose words she echoes: "There is no document of civilization which is not at the same time a document of barbarism [...] A historical materialist therefore dissociates himself from it as far as possible. He regards it as his task to brush history against the grain."[151]

By *dissociation*, Benjamin does not imply disregard; for the historical materialist, documents are spatio-temporal configurations shaped by existential and ideological tensions. Reading, speaking, and writing against the grain of history (for Benjamin and also for Howe) engenders the promise of revolutionary time—the prophetic time of now, of *kairos*—that may "blast a specific era out of the homogeneous course of history—blasting a specific life out of the era or a specific work out of the lifework" (Benjamin, 263).[152] Kindred spirits with a subtle yet sig-

---

[151] Walter Benjamin, "Theses on the Philosophy of History," 256-257.

[152] If *chronos* time is measurable by clocks and therefore objective, ordinary, and to some degree empty, then *kairos* time is, by contrast, subjective, extraordinary, and full of transformative potential. "Kairic time is made up of discontinuous and unprecedented occasions, instead of identical moments ... [and therefore] marks opportunities that might not recur, moments of decision" (Benedikt, 226). See Amélie Frost Benedikt, "On Doing the Right Thing at the Right Time: Toward an Ethics of Kairos," *Rhetoric and Kairos*, ed. Phillip Sipiora, and James S. Baumlin (Albany: SUNY Press, 2002) 226-235. Although these exact terms do not appear as such in *Articulation*, I invoke them here in the spirit of Kermode's memorable discussions of poetic *(as if)* forms of temporality *(chronos, kairos, aion, pleroma)*, of the interval between *tic* and *tock*, and of concord fictions. See Frank Kermode, *The Sense of an Ending* (Oxford: Oxford University Press, 2000) 39-64. Compared with the theological connotations for kairos that Kermode underscores, Howe's "Green hour" in *Taking the Forest*

nificant difference concerning temporality and transcendence: for Benjamin (as Arendt and Zohn note) *blasting a specific life or a specific work out of the lifework* carries a minimal trace of the Hegelian dialectic of *aufheben* "in its threefold meaning: to preserve, to elevate, to cancel" (263).[153] (I will return, later in this essay, to this complex moment in Benjamin's text, and will also engage with Arendt's refutation of Hegelian dialectics therein.) "As a result of this method," continues Benjamin, "the lifework is preserved in this work *and at the same time canceled*; in the lifework, the era; and in the era, the entire course of history" (263) [italicized for emphasis]. For Howe, "Hegelian becoming" informs "Patriarchal prophesy at heels of hope / Futurity"—that is, sacrificial cycles of homogeneous, teleological, and ultimately transcendent time that obliterate (through their binary, dialectical turning/overturning) heterogeneous languages and particularized lives along a "Migratory path to massacre" devised and defended by "Sharpshooters in history's appledark". Howe's telepathic transmission of the undervoice speaks against the grain of Hegelian systems in ways that would have been astonishingly resonant for Benjamin to encounter.

---

signals a regenerative, inter-/intra-textual, secular temporality engendered by the countless points of figurative resonance within and among, against and through the poem's disjunctive elaborations from *Articulation* to *The Quarry*.

[153] "The result of this process is then that Spirit, in rendering itself objective and making this its being an object of thought, on the one hand destroys the determinate form of its being, on the other hand gains a comprehension of the universal element which it involves, and thereby gives a new form to its inherent principle [...] The principles of the successive phases of Spirit that animate the Nations in a necessitated gradation, are themselves only steps in the development of the one universal Spirit, which through them elevates and completes itself to a self-comprehending *totality*." Georg Wilhelm Friedrich Hegel, *The Philosophy of History*, trans. J. Sibree (New York: Dover Publications, Inc., 1956), 78. It is fundamentally against Hegel's apocalyptic, teleological/transcendental, universal history that Adorno positions his much celebrated and contested argument that "to write poetry after Auschwitz is barbaric." Theodor Adorno, "Cultural Criticism and Society," *Prisms* (Cambridge: MIT Press, 1983), 34. See also Anna-Verena Nosthoff, "Barbarism: Notes on the Thought of Theodor W. Adorno," *Critical Legal Thinking* (15 October 2014): http://criticallegalthinking.com/2014/10/15/barbarism-notes-thought-theodor-w-adorno/[.]

For example, consider the celebrated and contested (un-paginated) double-helical facing pages, where Howe's inter-/intra-textuality imbricates and intercalates *kairic* space-time in polyvocal, strophic assemblages that deconstruct dialectical principles of elevation and cancelation, of possession through loss:

possess remote so abstract life are lost spatio-temporal hum

//

HumTemporal-spatioLostAreLifeAbstractSoRemotePossess

Howe's "Collision or collusion with history"—that is, the poem's historical figuration from *Articulation* to *The Quarry*—engages such radical contingency as a means of listening/reading, speaking/writing within and against, across and through the work's facing pages of collaged archives and artifacts. Such a poetics and praxis recovers, remediates, and releases (in each instance of contiguity and contrariety) languages and lives without elevation/transcendence or cancellation/oblivion (which are brutally crucial factors in the Hegelian dialectic, as noted above). Howe's "archaic hallucinatory laughter" dispels teleological, universal narratives—"Meditation of a world's vast Memory // Predominance pitched across history"—and devises a nonconformist's "dim mirror Naught formula" that diverts dialectical systems of "Kneel[ing] to intellect in our work" and of "Chaos cast[ing] cold intellect back". Throughout this poem's facing pages and openwork sequence from *Articulation* to *The Quarry*, Howe reads and writes through and across, against and within the work's embodied grains of history's "Five senses of syntax". On all of these dimensions, the poem celebrates the heterogeneousness of "what one might know, which in turn is always less than what language might say."[154] Reading *Articulation* against the grain (and in the spirit of Lyn Hejinian's notion of the *open text*) would therefore maximally excite all

---

[154] Lyn Hejinian, *The Language of Inquiry* (Berkeley: University of California Press, 2000), 48.

of the constitutive, tropological elements in the poem's openwork sequence encountered as an activity of critical interventions into the manifold field of literary texts, theoretical methods, and historical documents that shape Howe's on-going, collaborative and constructivist process.

In Howe's 1990 *Talisman* interview, she discusses these matters and priorities while reflecting upon *My Emily Dickinson*, emphasizing the importance of neither explaining nor translating the material, but "meet[ing] the work with writing—you know, to meet in time, not just from place to place but from writer to writer, mind to mind, friend to friend, from words to words" (17). This mode of historical figuration (as a gesture of friendship between kindred spirits) engages "In and against" (17) history encountered as "an actuality" (17) of infinitely unfolding, non-chronological "forms in space and time and in apparent chaos" (30). For Benjamin, such kairic encounters are "shot through with chips of Messianic time" (263) that invoke apocalyptic, future-oriented signification; for Howe, they are *singularities*, a mathematical principle (of radically contingent, networked realities) that she adapts from René Thom. In her conversation with Edward Foster—republished in *Postmodern Poetry* (1994) as well as in *The Birth-mark* (1993 and 2015)—Howe elaborates upon this pivotal choice of *Singularities* as the title for her 1990 Wesleyan volume:

> The singularity (I think Thom is saying) is the point where there is a sudden change to something completely else. It's a chaotic point. It's the point chaos enters cosmos, the instant articulation. Then there is a leap into something else. Predation and capture are terms he uses constantly. I thought this was both a metaphor for Europeans arriving on this continent where a catastrophic change then had to happen—a new sense of things on the part of the original inhabitants and the emigrants, and to the land as well. And it seemed to be a way of describing these poems of mine. They are singular works on pages, and grouped

together, they fracture language, they are charged. "Singularity" was a word dear to the Puritans for other reasons. (1990: 30-31)

In this passage, Howe first connects Thom's "theory of singularity unfolding"[155] to her studies of captivity narratives and the European colonization of New England, then sharply contrasts her concerns with *Singularity* against a Puritan understanding that God's chosen people are specially favored (by their singularities) for election/elevation and translation/transcendence.[156] The word has many other meanings as well.[157] Within the context of this discussion, Howe emphasizes the notions of "a point at which a function takes an infinite value" and of "a region in space-time at which matter is infinitely dense"[158] because the poems collected in *Singularities* (in the spirit of *a bibliography of the king's book; or, eikon basilike*) engender "catastrophes of bifurcation" (1990: 31) of infinitely unfolding, densely juxtaposed radical contingencies.[159]

In such dynamic landscapes of imbricated/intercalated archives and artifacts, the polyphonic undervoice is neither canceled nor elevated, but recovered, remediated, and returned to the linguistic wilderness through the poem's regenerative factual telepathy. Or, to echo Derrida: "*L'autre*

---

[155] Peter Tsatsanis, "On René Thom's Significance For Mathematics and Philosophy," *Scripta Philosophiae Naturalis* 2 (2012): 221.

[156] Steven R. Pointer, "The Emmanuel College, Cambridge, Election of 1622: The Constraints of a Puritan Institution," *Puritanism and Its Discontents*, ed. Laura Lunger Knoppers (Newark: University of Delaware Press, 2003), 107.

[157] Such as: "[…] singleness of aim or purpose; a single or separate thing or entity; the quality or fact of being one in number or kind; the fact or condition of being alone or apart from others; solitariness; private or personal profit or gain; special excellence; the fact or quality of differing or dissenting from others or from what is generally accepted; individuality or eccentricity; a distinctive, noteworthy, or curious thing; a peculiar, exceptional, or unusual feature […]." *Oxford English Dictionary*: http://www.oed.com/[.]

[158] "Singularity." *Oxford English Dictionary*: http://www.oed.com/[.]

[159] See also Howe's discussion of Thom's notion of *singularity* in her essay, "Encloser," 191.

appelle à venir et cela n'arrive qu'à plusieurs voix."[160] Hope Atherton's story is a collage of contested, nested other voices that call [upon the poet and the poem's readers] for a future to arrive through many articulations of sound forms in time.

In all of these ways, Howe's historical figuration amplifies the powers of language to construct a work that does not merely represent reality (*mimesis*) but which constitutes an autonomous reality (*simulacrum*) that actualizes an embodied potentiality (*entelechy*) within a context of radically contingent temporality (*kairos*) that sparks the reader's and the writer's and the work's lyrical and social engagement through the world of the poem's making.[161] (Those are precisely the dynamics at stake in my formulations of *immanent/imminent* and *imbricate/intercalate* in this essay.) Howe's poetics and praxis thereby engender substantial forms of action.

To echo Howe from her 1990 *Talisman* interview, "the mystery is time" (21) because poetry and history live one-inside-the-other (22) in the omni-presence of a past that is not past—that is, the immanence/imminence of the poet's radically contingent encounters with the voices and material traces of Others. "**EF:** Well, how then are poems related to history? // **SH:** I think the poet opens herself like Spicer says. You open

---

[160] Jacques Derrida, in conversation with the author, *Applied Derrida / Derrida Applied*: July 20, 1995, University of Luton, England. "The Other calls [to come/to the future] for that which shall yet arrive through many voices/votes."

[161] This formulation draws upon the crux of Mazzoni's theory of the poetic simulacrum from his treatise, *Della difesa della Commedia di Dante*, first published in 1572: "But yet I say that the language of history and the arts and sciences does not use poetic imitation, and that the poet who treats either of history or of the arts or sciences will use poetic imitation, which we have above called similitudinousness (*similitudinaria*). According to the understanding of those who ought to know […] the idol is that which has no other use in itself but to represent and resemble […] So we can conclude that the historian and the poet who has history for the subject of his poem are different in that the historian will recount things in order to leave behind a memory of the truth, but the poet will write to imitate and leave behind a simulacrum, insofar as it is a simulacrum, of the truth." For this translation by Robert L. Montgomery, see Hazard Adams, ed., *Critical Theory Since Plato* (New York: Harcourt Brace Jovanovich, 1971), 183. For the original text and corresponding pages for this passage, see Jacopo Mazzoni, *Della difesa della Commedia di Dante*, III (Cesena, 1587) 564-65.

yourself and let language enter, let it lead you somewhere" (23). In this conversation, Howe emphasizes her view (30) that history is an open book of lives and stories (including Atherton's) awaiting kairic, telepathic recovery, remediation, and regenerative release:

> Once I was driving to Buffalo alone, moving up there for the winter to teach. It was me and my car, and the mountains. I had a tape of *Articulation* from a reading I had done, and I thought I would turn it on as this was near where Hope had been wandering after the raid—and it was a wonderful feeling because the sounds seemed to be pieces still in the air there. I felt I was returning them home as I drove away from home. They don't belong to me. I didn't originate them. They go back. (1990: 30)

In her essay, "Encloser," Howe recognizes that the mystery of time depends entirely upon perspective. From a chronological view, she "can't *really* bring back a particular time" (194). And yet, Howe swiftly counters that statement: "what if then *is* now. I hope my work here and elsewhere demonstrates something about the mystery of time" (194). Howe's poetics and praxis engages an open field of "traces of *real* events" (194) embedded in the work's historical figuration that "sets words free" (195).

These telepsychological priorities may be found nested among Howe's poems and prose works across the scope of her archives and artifacts, performances and publications. "We have always been in contact with one another, keeping on never letting go, no distance as to time, nothing such as liberty because we are in the field of history."[162] These animist-materialist-vitalist principles of radical contingency, historical figuration, and factual telepathy challenge, evade, reconfigure, subvert, and transfigure established notions about space and time, "slipping from known to utmost bound". And yet, even if such mercurial elements and forces in Howe's works should escape critical discourses and theoretical methodologies, that does not mean that Howe's work escapes history:

---

[162] "Preface," *Frame Structures*, 25.

"our human spirits being partly immaterial at that prefigured time though we didn't know then how free will carries us past to be distance waiting for another meeting a true relation. // Historical imagination gathers in the missing" (*Frame Structures*, 3). We are always already in the field of history which is the poem's kairic, imbricate/intercalate articulation (of sound forms in time).

*   *   *

As many critics and scholars have observed, *Articulation* engages a legacy of modernist and postmodernist concerns for *poems including history*; and yet, the singularity of Howe's historical figuration has been subordinated to literary historical paradigms and theoretical methodologies—priorities that have also diminished the agency of the poem's historiographic source materials. Fundamental questions about the poem's openwork sequence (from 1987 to 2015) remain (as yet) unasked and unanswered, such as: how and why does the work engage in a reading/writing against the grain of Howe's source documents? How and why does each disjunctive adaptation of the poem (from *Articulation* to *The Quarry*) elaborate that historiographic critique? Even among Howe's most historically attuned readers—Perloff (1990), Reinfeld (1992), Palattella (1995), Lazer (1996), Nicholls (1996), McCorkle (1999), Crown (2000), Clippinger (2001), Schultz (2001, 2005), Back (2002), Frost (2003), Collis (2006), Joyce (2010), Montgomery (2010), and Gaffield (2015)—no one has yet even considered the possibility that Howe's engagement with the poem's historical sources engenders a critical reading of those very documents (of which there are more than a few).[163] Howe's readers instead have surprisingly taken her dynamic collage of archives and artifacts as a relatively straightforward summary of

---

[163] Howe's primary sources for the Hope Atherton story include: George Sheldon, *A History of Deerfield, Massachusetts: the times when the people by whom it was settled, unsettled and resettled: with a special study of the Indian wars in the Connecticut valley, With genealogies*, 2 Vols. (Deerfield, MA: E. A. Hall & Co., 1895-1896), [Greenfield, MA: Press of E. A. Hall & Co.]; Sylvester Judd, *History of Hadley: Including the Early History of Hatfield, South Hadley,*

events, as if their reconfiguration were not also a mode of deft disruption. Moreover, no one has yet considered *Articulation* as a critical reading of Atherton's involvement in the garrison's attack (commanded by Captain William Turner) upon a peaceful gathering of Native Tribes at Peskeompscut (Great Fall) at daybreak of May 19, 1676.

Why indeed was the Rev. Atherton there at all? How and why has his true relation of events been adapted, edited, and republished? And by whom, when and why? Furthermore, why has Howe given us particular artifacts and documents from those contested, nested captivity narratives

---

Amherst and Granby Massachusetts (Springfield, MA: H. R. Hunting & Co., 1905); and Daniel White Wells and Reuben Field Wells, *A History of Hatfield, Massachusetts, in Three Parts* (Springfield, MA: F. C. H. Gibbons, 1910). Howe discusses these texts in her subsequent publications noted above: *Talisman* 4 (1990): 14-38; *The Birth-mark* (1993): 155-181; *Postmodern Poetry* (1994): 48-68; *Souls of the Labadie Tract* (2007): 11-19; *The Sound of Poetry/The Poetry of Sound* (2009): 199-204; *The Birth-mark* (2015): 155-181; and *The Quarry* (2015): 49-56. Howe's sources for the larger historical context also include works that were themselves sources for these historiographic narratives by Sheldon, Judd, Wells & Wells, including: Increase Mather, *A Brief History of the War with the Indians in New-England*, 2nd ed. (London, 1676); William Hubbard, *The present state of New-England: being a narrative of the troubles with the Indians in New-England, from the first planting thereof in the year 1607 to this present year 1677, but chiefly of the late troubles in the two last years 1675 and 1676: to which is added a discourse about the war with the Pequods in the year 1637* (London: Printed for Tho. Parkhurst, 1677); John Williams, *The Redeemed Captive, Returning to Zion* (Boston: Printed by B. Green, for Samuel Phillips, 1707); and John Winthrop's notebooks, which were first published as *A journal of the transactions and occurrences in the settlement of Massachusetts and the other New-England colonies, from the year 1630 to 1644: written by John Winthrop, Esq; first governor of Massachusetts: and now first published from a correct copy of the original manuscript*, Books 1-2, ed. Noah Webster (Hartford: Printed by Elisha Babcock, 1790); subsequently appearing in a more complete, revised edition as *The history of New England from 1630 to 1649 by John Winthrop, from his original manuscripts; with notes to illustrate the civil and ecclesiastical concerns, the geography, settlement, and institutions of the country, and the lives and manners of the principal planters by James Savage*, Books 1-3, ed. James Savage (Boston: Little, Brown, 1825-1826, 1853). Winthrop's journals were thereafter usually republished under the title, *The History of New England from 1630–1649*. Among these many historiographic sources, John Williams's *The Redeemed Captive, Returning to Zion* plays a key role in *Articulation* through the editorial agency of Stephen Williams.

100

(and their historiographies) as framing devices for the poem's disjunctive sequence? No one has yet asked these key questions concerning the nexus of biographical, cultural, economic, historical, literary, military, political, religious, and textual factors that (in my interpretation of the poem's historiographic counter-paths) compelled Hope Atherton to accompany Captain Turner's garrison, to witness the massacre, to disobey orders, to flee into the wilderness, and to return with his nonconformist, cautionary tale. More than just an anomaly or a contradiction, a paradox or a mere symptom of colonialism and conquest—as the poem's many readers have surmised—Hope's experience and legacy live "In all of us" (*Talisman*, 1990: 30). Just as Howe takes up Atherton's so-called excursion "for an emblem foreshadowing a Poet's abolished limitations in our demythologized fantasy of Manifest Destiny" (*Singularities*, 4), the poetics and praxis of *Articulation* invokes the ongoing work of restorative justice as a constitutive, co-creative agent in the poem's openwork sequence of reading/writing against the grain.

Many of the aforementioned readers of *Articulation* from Butterick (1987) to Gaffield (2015) have, at the very least, summarized the uncanny story of Hope Atherton for their interpretations of the poem, and have done so by way of surprisingly uncritical readings of Howe's sagacious engagement with archives and artifacts, discourses and documents that frame, in their own distinctive ways, the Atherton story within the context of the poem's recursive concerns with the legacy of the Peskeompskutt massacre (from *Articulation* to *The Quarry*). In this field of criticism and scholarship, examples abound of this tendency toward summarizing without critically reading Howe's source documents, such as: "Howe is preoccupied less with the witnessing of actual events occurring in the past than with the method by which historical repression and recovery operate and by which a 'recollection' of those events is undertaken;"[164] and "the poem confronts the abyss of history in order to search out the trace of the real and the ghost of the Other—the people and texts that have been erased in order to maintain the façade of cultural

---

[164] Crown, http://www.scc.rutgers.edu/however/v1_3_2000/current/readings/crown.html[.]

order;"[165] and despite the poem's "apparently straightforward outline, exactly what transpired on [Atherton's] mission remains elusive in any historical record" because "Howe cites a letter composed over one hundred years after the incident, which in turn summarizes another."[166]

Some readers have even advanced rigorous arguments about the poem's historiographic concerns yet without offering any direct evidence from the poet's source texts, such as: after "reinventing the chaos of [Atherton's] divagations [...], Howe loses Hope to the calamitous conditions of his own restoration;"[167] and "Howe writes an American epic in reverse, in which she endeavors to undo the story told to us by the Puritans," aiming "to get back to a point where the story can begin again, where it can be more inclusive;"[168] and such "simultaneous commitment to the decontextualizing energies of collage and the rootedness of historical particulars in place [...] most strongly situates Howe in the post-Olsonian line of historical poetics."[169]

Few of the poem's readers have acknowledged the relevance of even one or two of Howe's historical source documents (usually only Sheldon's *History of Deerfield* and/or *A History of Hatfield* by Wells & Wells) for the work's composition and context, following the poet's notations (from essays and interviews) in those directions. Even fewer have taken preliminary steps toward reading the poem vis-à-vis Howe's sources, but have turned back from that path, mistakenly concluding that, as *Articulation* becomes increasingly "fragmented, gnomic, [and] enigmatic," the poem becomes less concerned with Hope's (existential and historiographic) breakdown than with "that of language itself;"[170] that Howe appropriates her source texts "as a space for the writing of her own journey" which underscores *not* the persistence of *historical imagination*

---

[165] Clippinger, 197.
[166] Frost, 119.
[167] Palattella, 92.
[168] Schultz (2001): http://www.scc.rutgers.edu/however/v1_6_2001/current/readings/encounters/schultz.html[.] Accessed January, 2003.
[169] Montgomery, 93-94.
[170] Perloff, *Poetic License*, 307.

that gathers in the missing, but "a consciousness of self as a consciousness of perceptual loss" and "the refusal of narrative;"[171] that "Howe has no desire to send us back to her sources, or, indeed, to encourage us to read them;"[172] that "Howe does not mean for the source-text to stand in as an authoritative interpreter" because she "must have [only] stumbled across" such documents "while searching for information for her [1985 *Temblor*] essay on [Mary] Rowlandson;"[173] that "Howe composed her linguistic collage by a method of chance operations that seems precisely *not* to point us toward the historical relevance of any of [her] original sources"[174]; and that *Articulation* "quickly [casts] off historical discourse" because ultimately "the work is not about history."[175]

These curious turnings away from history and historiography signify key moments of misrecognition when critical and/or theoretical methodologies have overtaken the writer's patient attunement to the work. (I'll return to these matters and noted texts.) Of course, such moments are inevitable for any critic, scholar, or theorist; my best efforts here certainly also have their own strengths and weaknesses, blindness and insight. The dedicated pursuit of inextricable particulars—"'Rigor of beauty is the quest'"[176]—is endless: my goal here is to emulate the poem's whirlwind spirit of collage and contingency, recovery, remediation, and regenerative release.

Which of Howe's source documents might we hear echoing across and between, within and through the poem's complex sound scape? This essay investigates *Articulation* through Howe's critique of the poem's historical sources; through her studies of the captivity narrative which informed that critique; through new historical evidence concerning the so-called excursion of Rev. Hope Atherton; and through the arc of the poem's elaborations (from 1987 to 2015) which further Howe's critique

---

[171] Reinfeld, 134.
[172] Nicholls, 596.
[173] Back, 193 n.28.
[174] Frost, 121.
[175] Gaffield, http://dx.doi.org/10.1080/09574042.2015.1069141[.]
[176] Williams, *Paterson*, 3.

of the historiography of Atherton's experience and legacy. In each remediation of these materials and methods from *Articulation* to *The Quarry*, Howe has offered numerous clues as to why "Hope Atherton is lost in the great world of nature";[177] yet the complexity of his erasure from and persistence within the very documents that narrate his story has not yet been imagined or tracked by Howe's readers/writers.

How does the poet's radical contingency and historical figuration engage such a dynamic poetics and praxis? Howe's deft reading/writing against the grain of her sources concerning Atherton's experience documents and deconstructs his strategic erasure from those very narratives. The poem's fundamental, generative aporia is that Hope's story is not his alone: his voice is polyvocal; his narrative, a nested, contested palimpsest that has supplanted his nonconformist experience with heroic accounts of others who would falsely claim authority over his own true relation.

Why indeed did "the Rev. Hope Atherton, the first minister of Hatfield," accompany a garrison of soldiers "against the Indians at the falls above Deerfield, in May, 1676"?[178] Why did no one believe his testimony? Why did he become "a stranger to his community" and die "soon after the traumatic exposure that has earned him poor mention in a seldom opened book"?[179] "Inarticulate true meaning // lives beyond thought / linked from beginning // Pilings of thought under spoken". Who else did and did not accompany Atherton in his flight through the wilderness after the massacre? Why does the Awede text of *Articulation* include the "*EXTRACT from a LETTER (dated June 8th, 1781,) of Stephen Williams to President Styles*" as that work's singular historical text? What has Howe given us to consider, if we compare that document against the poet's sources? How and why does Howe's transcription of this radically contingent extract (from a letter referring to a copy of a paper of an account of a related account of an experience related in a copy of a paper

---

[177] *Souls of the Labadie Tract*, 17; *The Sound of Poetry/The Poetry of Sound*, 203; and *The Quarry*, 55.

[178] "EXTRACT from a LETTER (dated June 8th, 1781,) of Stephen Williams to President Styles," *Articulation* (1987), np.

[179] *Singularities*, 4.

lost and then found among other papers) shape the Atherton story in contested, nested directions? How and why has Hope's narrative been adapted and adopted, transcribed and transfigured? Whose stories and which texts have been edited and substituted, circulated and published; and by whom and why, or why not?

*   *   *

Questions such as these are imperative given the factual telepathy at the heart of *Articulation*—that is, the work's embedded "Planctus of Rachel"—which I hear, see, and feel as an unremitting work of resistant and resilient mourning for everyone involved in the "massacre of Tribal refugees gathered near the falls at Peskeompskutt, at the bend in the Pocumtuc region of the great river, below the upper village of Wissatinnewag and its terraces."[180] The Peskeompskutt massacre—also known as *The Falls Fight* or the Battle of Swamscot Falls/Turner's Falls or the Great Falls massacre[181]—occurred on May 19, 1676 and shapes

---

[180] Doug Harris of the Narragansett Indian Tribal Historic Preservation Office, letter to Walter Ramsey (5 January 2016), re: "Battle of Great Falls / Phase II Support,"
http://www.montague.net/Pages/MontagueMA_News/0237FD5D000F8513.2/Narragansett_Tribal_Statement.pdf[.] Accessed May 10, 2017. That document has subsequently been either moved elsewhere within or removed from the Town of Montague website. See also the major reports from Dr. Kevin McBride, David Naumec, Ashley Bissonnette, and Noah Fellman, "Battle of Great Falls / Wissantinnewag-Peskeompskut," Mashantucket Pequot Museum & Research Center (April 2016),
https://www.montague-ma.gov/files/Battle_of_Great_Falls_Phase_I_Final_Technical_Report.pdf[;] and Kevin McBride, David Naumec, Ashley Bissonnette, Noah Fellman, and Michael Derderian, "The Battle of Great Falls / Wissantinnewag-Peskeompskut," Mashantucket Pequot Museum and Research Center (January 2017),
https://www.montague-ma.gov/files/Battle_of_Great_Falls_Phase_II_Final_Technical_Report.pdf[.]

[181] According to Francis Jennings: "Over 150 mounted men assembled at Hadley [Massachusetts] to attack [a peaceful gathering of Algonquian Tribes at their Peskeompscut (Great Fall) fishing grounds] at daybreak of May 19, 1676. By their own report [the Englishmen] poked their guns inside the unguarded wig-

the "Migratory path to massacre" documented and deconstructed by Howe's *Articulation*. Howe's sources for the poem are narratives written by colonialists and nationalists; as such, those early modern texts embody the undervoices of those who have been silenced in the "struggle for the Americas."[182] The poem's reading/writing against the grain of those shared yet disjunctive histories and meta-histories draws upon a vast and vital lexicon that invokes, without speaking for, Native *survivance* stories that would renounce tragedy and victimry.[183] The co-presence, within the poem's polyvocal landscape, of echoes of Native words—such as *amonoosuck* and *uncannunc*—and mispronounced, stuttered Tribal names—*Nipnet Ninep Ninap*—underscore their incommensurable, persistent otherness that resists the discourse of colonization and conquest.

Howe acknowledges the precarious co-presence of such irreducible alterities. Her abiding care and concern for the ineluctable, inscrutable

---

wams and shot sleeping Indians [many of whom were women, children, and elders]. Of those who waked and fled to the river, many were shot in the water, and others were swept over the falls. When warriors attacked from the opposite shore, the English turned and themselves fled in utter panic, which is the more notable because there probably were no more than 70 warriors on *both* sides of the river to stand up against the 150 Englishmen. In the rout 37 English were killed, whereas only one had died in their dawn attack. Jennings, *The Invasion of America: Indians, Colonialism, and the Cant of Conquest* (New York: Norton, 1975), 319. Increase Mather observed that "to the great dishonor of the English, a few Indians pursued our Soldiers four or five miles, who were in number near twice as many as the Enemy" (30). Casualties among the Squakeags, Nipmunks, Pokomtucks, and Mahicans are estimated to have been as high as 400; among the colonists, as high as 42. Sheldon, Vol. 1, 152-171; Wells & Wells, 85. See also William Hubbard, I: 106, 233, 237; II: 76, 221.

[182] Thomas King, *The Truth About Stories: A Native Narrative* (Minneapolis: University of Minnesota Press, 2003), 77.

[183] See Gerald Vizenor, ed., *Survivance: Narratives of Native Presence* (Lincoln and London: University of Nebraska Press, 2008). As Vizenor observes, the meanings and resonances of *survivance* are various. "Survivance is, of course, related to the word survival, and the definition varies by language [...] 'Survivance is an active sense of presence, the continuance of native stories, not a mere reaction, or a survivable name [...] Survivance means the right of succession or reversion of an estate, and in that sense, the estate of native survivancy'" (19).

facticity of manuscripts respects these complex and nuanced encounters. For example, the numerous archival materials assembled in *Spontaneous Particulars* engender contiguous radical contingencies, such as: the photographically reproduced (6) and typographically transcribed (7) fragmentary manuscript page of Jonathan Edwards, Jr.'s prayer in Mahican (c. 1765); that text's English translation (71) by Carl Masthay; and the accompanying note (71) which deftly critiques Edwards's appropriation of such encounters as evidence of the 'Lost Tribes' theory. Howe's historical figurations and reconfigurations thus present and provoke ethical intersections among cultural, historical, linguistic, political, and textual registers embedded within her work's archival/artifactual, dialethic facing pages.

Howe's poetics and praxis in *Articulation* amplifies the contradictions and cross-outs, sub-texts and sutures signifying sites of encounter, conflict, and violence in cultural, literary, and historical narratives that "all too often relegate Native peoples and their subjectivities to the margins [...], reducing them to little more than mute metaphors and tragic footnotes to American history."[184] Through the poem's inter-/intra-textual fabric, these conflicted and contested *articulations of sound forms in time* call upon Howe's audience to bear witness to this "Rash catastrophe" by reading widely, listening closely, and contributing to the work of restorative justice. Following the "Burying The Hatchet/Tomahawk" ceremony led by Elder Narragansett Medicine Man Running Wolf on May 19, 2004, which included "the smoking of the pipe of peace with the Montague Select Board and Town Administrator at Unity Park,"[185]

---

[184] Billy J. Stratton, *Buried in Shades of Night: Contested Voices, Indian Captivity, and The Legacy of King Philip's War* (Tucson: The University of Arizona Press, 2013), 16. For foundational studies, like Stratton's, that challenge Pilgrim-centric historiographies of New England, see Annette Kolodny, *In Search of First Contact: The Vikings of Vinland, the Peoples of the Dawnland, and the Anglo-American Anxiety of Discovery* (Durham: Duke University Press, 2012); Christine M. DeLucia, *Memory Lands: King Philip's War and the Place of Violence in the Northeast* (New Haven: Yale University Press, 2018); and Lisa Brooks, *Our Beloved Kin: A New History of King Philip's War* (New Haven: Yale University Press, 2019).

[185] Doug Harris, letter to Walter Ramsey,

that on-going process of education and healing continues. Such regenerative work (which encompasses many communities across the ancestral lands of the Pocumtuck people) has been facilitated and documented by Ted Timreck, Peter Frechette, and Doug Harris of the Narragansett Indian Tribal Historic Preservation Office.[186] A recent presentation and panel discussion at Turners Falls High School[187] was dedicated to ongoing Tribal and archaeological efforts to protect sacred sites integral to Peskeompskutt's legacy within the context of a vast and vital Native landscape.[188]

As someone who grew up in New England (in a family descended from English and Irish, French and German immigrants), I recognize my role in this shared story "More than language can express". With the poet-historian as my guide, I also find my ancestors and their struggles in this landscape: "These are the old home trees […] Still we call bitterly bitterly / Stern norse terse ethical pathos". The poem's opening two lines—"from seaweed said nor repossess rest / scape esaid"—have been haunting me since the Awede text of *Articulation* found me at Powell's Books in Portland, Oregon in 1991. That was my first point of contact with Susan Howe's writing—working in the small press/journals section at the Burnside Store. Every time I've returned to these materials—the

---

http://www.montague.net/Pages/MontgueMA_News/0237FD5D000F8513.2/Narragansett_Tribal_Statement.pdf[.] Accessed May 10, 2017.

[186] See the film, *Great Falls: Discovery, Destruction and Preservation in a Massachusetts Town*, directed and edited by Ted Timreck, produced by Ted Timreck and Peter Frechette (Oley, PA: Bullfrog Films, 2011).

[187] "The Land Speaks: New Perspectives on the Falls Fight / A presentation by Archaeologists and Tribal representatives," Thursday, November 16, 2017: http://www.montague.net/n/31/The-Land-Speaks-New-Perspectives-on-the-Falls-Fight[.]

[188] Peskeompskutt dwells in the center of a sacred celestial geography connecting Native peoples from New England to the Ohio valley. See the film noted above, *Great Falls* (2011); and also James W. Mavor, Jr., and Byron E. Dix, *Manitou: The Sacred Landscape of New England's Native Civilization* (Rochester, VT: Inner Traditions International, Ltd., 1989); and Mary Ann Levine, Kenneth E. Sassaman, and Michael S. Nassaney, eds., *The Archaeological Northeast* (Westport: Bergin & Garvey, 1999).

poem's dynamic embeddedness; the legacy of the Peskeompskutt massacre; the uncanny, haunting story of the Rev. Hope Atherton—I alternate between obsessing over the smallest details placed within multiple contexts and/or abandoning myself and the work altogether to the persistent presence of what ultimately cannot be told as such through the poem's "Surging and separating // Flame choristers shuddering flame".[189]

*   *   *

Articulation serves as critical witness to the Peskeompskutt massacre and the Hope Atherton story in the spirit of kindred documentarian volumes that variously invoke the ethos of Objectivist poetics and praxis as a modality for integrating aesthetics, lyric subjectivities, radical contingency, historical figuration, and social activism within and beyond academia.[190] Howe's work resonates distinctively within and against a vital legacy 'after' Objectivism that arguably includes a capacious field from Muriel Rukeyser's *The Book of the Dead* (1938), Lorine Niedecker's *North Central* (1968), and Rachel Blau DuPlessis' *Drafts* (1986-2013) to Charles Reznikoff's *Testimony* (1934-1978), William Carlos Williams' *Paterson* (1946-1958), and George Oppen's *Of Being Numerous* (1968); from Charles Olson's *The Maximus Poems* (1950-1970), Robert Hayden's *Words in the Mourning Time* (1970), and Nathaniel Mackey's *Eroding Witness* (1985), to C. D. Wright's *One Big Self* (1988), Erica Hunt's *Local History* (1993), James Thomas Stevens's *a bridge dead in the water* (2007), M. NourbeSe Philip's *ZONG!* (2008), Myung Mi Kim's *Penury* (2009), Claudia Rankine's *Citizen* (2014), and

---

[189] Here and in other discrete instances throughout this book, I choose to deviate from stylistic conventions (concerning the placement of punctuation marks inside of quotation marks) in order to represent Susan Howe's language exactly as it appears in her works.

[190] See W. Scott Howard and Broc Rossell, "'After' Objectivism: sincerity, objectification, contingency," *Poetics and Praxis 'After' Objectivism*, ed. W. Scott Howard and Broc Rossell (Iowa City: University of Iowa Press, 2018), 1-20; 181-189.

Fred Moten's *The Little Edges* (2015) among numerous poems including history that challenge and complicate, reconfigure and even refuse a line of historical poetics *after* Objectivism. (In these articulations, I wish to amplify a multiplicity of meanings for the word "after" through contrasting typographic gestures: the single quotes ['after'] imply against, post-, resistant to; and the italics [*after*] imply behind or following or shadowing, as in an afterimage. Such nuances underscore tropological and temporal complexities embedded within and against sequentialist methodologies concerning relationships among past, present, and future works—relationships that should be read/written against the grain anew in terms of the difficulties of the present. To echo Howe: what if then *is* now.)

As I outline this inclusive (albeit disjunctive) genealogy of poets and works 'after'/*after* Objectivism, I wish to celebrate a living tradition of artistic change and transformation, influence and transgression from writer to writer and also through the field, which is, itself, a charged medium of poetics and praxis at the center and circumference of each work. I also offer these reflections in the spirit of the robust heterogeneity of artists and writers, schools and methods assembled in the February 1931 'Objectivists' volume of *Poetry*.[191] In fact, one of the most remarkable

---

[191] *Poetry* 37.5 (1931). The table of contents includes, in the following order: poems by Carl Rakosi, Louis Zukofsky, Howard Weeks, Robert McAlmon, Joyce Hopkins, Charles Reznikoff, Norman Macleod, Kenneth Rexroth, S. Theodore Hecht, George Oppen, Harry Roskolenkier, Whittaker Chambers, Henry Zolinsky, Basil Bunting, and Jesse Loewenthal; two poems from Arthur Rimbaud translated by Emanuel Carnevali; poems by John Wheelwright, Richard Johns, Martha Champion, and William Carlos Williams; and Zukofsky's two statements on Objectivist poetics, "Program: 'Objectivists' 1931" and "Sincerity and Objectification: With Special Reference to the Work of Charles Reznikoff." The collection then presents a multifaceted *Symposium*—a dialogic assemblage of paratexts from Zukofsky, Parker Tyler, Charles Henri Ford, and Réné Taupin—concluding with a discussion of André Salmon's poetry translated by Taupin and Zukofsky. This formative context becomes even more complex in light of Zukofsky's essay, "Program: 'Objectivists' 1931," which examined the work of several contemporaries—Ezra Pound, Williams, Marianne Moore, T. S. Eliot, E. E. Cummings, Wallace Stevens, McAlmon, and Reznikoff—who, along with *all* of the "contributors to this [issue of *Poetry*]" have "written in accordance with the principles heading this note." By "this note," Zukofsky was referring to

features in that celebrated volume is the range of disagreements with (and even within) Zukofsky's two programmatic essays, his commentaries and notes (in the *Symposium* documents) concerning the artistic principles ostensibly shared by all of the contributing artists and writers (as noted above). Echoing the dialogic, oppositional tensions at work in the *Symposium* texts and the key arguments made therein by Parker Tyler, Charles Henri Ford, Réné Taupin, and Louis Zukofsky concerning sincerity, objectification, and contingency,[192] Martha Champion's strophic "POEM" offers a direct challenge to Zukofsky's mantra of *thinking with the things as they exist*: "There are places we will not go: / Where yellow birds fly— / And the high hum of their voices / Is like the whir of sewing-machines."[193] (I hear an echo from these lines over to Lorine Niedecker. After reading the February 1931 volume of *Poetry*, Niedecker wrote enthusiastically (yet not without critique) to Zukofsky and enclosed some poems, including "When Ecstasy is Inconvenient,"[194] which (perhaps inspired by Champion's rebuke) delivers a deft riposte to Zukofsky's notion of *rested totality*: "who knows— / flight's end or flight's beginning / for the resting gull?").[195]

Despite such inherent diversity, this complex international and interdisciplinary legacy has often been mistakenly reduced (in the fields of literary criticism and literary history) to the works of four American poets (Zukofsky, Reznikoff, Rakosi, Oppen) plus one British poet (Bunting) and just one (American) woman poet (Niedecker).[196] Genealogical

---

his essay's epigraph: "*An Objective: (Optics)—The lens bringing the rays from an object to a focus. (Military use)—That which is aimed at. (Use extended to poetry)—Desire for what is objectively perfect, inextricably the direction of historic and contemporary particulars.*" See Louis Zukofsky, "Program: 'Objectivists' 1931," Poetry 37.5 (1931): 268.

[192] See Howard and Rossell, 1-20.

[193] "POEM," *Poetry* 37.5 (1931): 265.

[194] Jenny Penberthy, "Life and Writing," *Lorine Niedecker: Collected Works*, ed. Jenny Penberthy (Berkeley: University of California Press, 2002), 3.

[195] "When Ecstasy is Inconvenient," *Lorine Niedecker: Collected Works*, ed. Jenny Penberthy (Berkeley: University of California Press, 2002), 25.

[196] There are, of course, notable exceptions to this statement. Andrew Mcallister builds his anthology around the works of Zukofsky, Oppen, Reznikoff, Rakosi, and also Niedecker, Rexroth, Muriel Rukeyser, and Bunting. See *The*

historicism are also vital networks that may be visualized disjunctively, holistically, oppositionally, synergistically, etc. In my reading/writing against the grain of these narratives, the poetics and praxis of documentation and critical witnessing emerges 'after'/*after* Objectivism as a dynamic mode for poems including history—among other artistic methods that have also been formatively shaped by this dynamic (if sometimes discontinuous and/or disparate) Objectivist legacy, such as: linguistic and cultural-material forms of subjectivity and objectivity; sequential and cross-genre forms of attentive dialogic making; sonic and image/text collage, pastiche, and parody; archival appropriation and remediation; interdisciplinary and multi-modal realisms; concrete-lyrical appositions, discursive reconfigurations, and disjunctive conceptualisms. Howe's poems and essays, collaborative artist books and sonic/visual performances engage the field in all of those ways. Her poetics and praxis destabilizes chronologies with kairic time, which reconfigures the problems of 'legacy' and 'tradition' via the work's imbricate/intercalate moments of dialogic attention radiating within and against, through and across the poem's radical contingency, historical figuration, and factual telepathy, all of which engender the immanent/imminent now. To echo Mackey echoing Creeley echoing Zukofsky: "we write one poem all our lives" of *lower limit speech* and *upper limit song*.[197] Or, invoking Howe yet once more: *we are in the field of history*.

Objectivists, ed. Andrew Mcallister (Hexham, Northumberland: Bloodaxe, 1996). DuPlessis and Quartermain complement these frameworks by shaping *Nexus* around their foundational six poets—Bunting, Niedecker, Oppen, Rakosi, Reznikoff, and Zukofsky—within a diversified field of modernist and postmodernist aesthetics, poetics, and praxis from Europe to the US, UK, and Canada. See Rachel Blau DuPlessis and Peter Quartermain, "Introduction," *The Objectivist Nexus: Essays in Cultural Poetics*, ed. Rachel Blau DuPlessis and Peter Quartermain (Tuscaloosa: University of Alabama Press, 1999), 1-22; 319-320.

[197] "AN INTERVIEW WITH NATHANIEL MACKEY by Charles H. Rowell," (conducted by telephone between Charlottesville, Virginia, and Santa Cruz, California, February 21, 1997): https://vdocuments.site/nathaniel-mackey-a-special-issue-an-interview-with-nathaniel-mackey-58823471d8984.html [.] Accessed January 24, 2018. See also Nathaniel Mackey, *Paracritical Hinge: Essays, Talks, Notes, Interviews* (Madison: University of Wisconsin Press, 2005), 308, 329-330, 335-336, 190.

If we were to place Howe's "Personal Narrative" concerning her process of writing *Articulation* in conversation with foundational statements on Objectivist poetics and praxis (from the February 1931 volume of *Poetry*, for example) we would find convergences with and also divergences from Zukofsky's priorities for "thinking with the things as they exist, and of directing them along a line of melody;"[198] for "sincerity, [...] rested totality, [... and] objectification—the apprehension satisfied completely as to the appearance of the art form as an object [...] inextricably the direction of historic and contemporary particulars—A desire to place everything—everything aptly, perfectly, belonging within, one with, a context— [...] A poem."[199] (In this assemblage of lines, readers familiar with Zukofsky's evolving discourse will recognize the co-presence of two very different texts—"Sincerity and Objectification: With Special Reference to the Work of Charles Reznikoff" (1931) and "An Objective" (1967)—which emerge from a fluid context of intermittent editing and revision (from 1931 to 1967) that includes other essays.)[200]

Howe reflects that, during the 1980s, she "wanted to transplant words onto paper with soil sticking to their roots—to go to meet a narra-

---

[198] "Sincerity and Objectification," *Poetry* 37.5 (1931): 273.

[199] "An Objective," *Prepositions + The Collected Critical Essays*, ed. Mark Scroggins (Hanover: Wesleyan University Press, 2000), 12-15. "An Objective" was first published in Zukofsky's volume, *Prepositions: The Collected Critical Essays* (London: Rapp & Carroll, 1967; and New York: The Horizon Press, 1967), 20-26.

[200] In addition to the two programmatic essays (noted above) included in *Poetry* 37.5 (1931), Zukofsky also published the following texts, all of which informed the many changes that would eventually shape the 1967 form and substance of "An Objective": "Recencies in Poetry," *An "Objectivists" Anthology*, ed. Louis Zukofsky (Le Beausset, Var, France: To, Publishers, 1932), 9-25; "Program: 'Objectivists' 1931" and "Sincerity and Objectification: *With Special Reference to the Work of Charles Reznikoff*" and "Recencies in Poetry," *5 Statements for Poetry* (San Francisco: San Francisco State College, 1958). See Mark Scroggins's insightful discussion of these various documents (and their nested, contested editorial/textual legacy) in *Prepositions + The Collected Critical Essays*, ed. Mark Scroggins (Hanover: Wesleyan University Press, 2000), 177-224. See also Howard and Rossell, 1-20.

tive's fate by immediate access to its concrete totality of singular interjections, crucified spellings, abbreviations, irrational apprehensions, collective identities, palavers, kicks, cordials, comforts."[201] For Zukofsky, the *poem as object* emphasizes literal signification more than figurative; concerns the linguistic remediation of objects of attention to material, sonic, and visual details within their contingent contexts; and presents concrete things not as vehicles for either abstract concepts or interpretations, but as field compositions resulting from *suggested* structural relationships: "A poem. The context based on a world— [...] A poem. This object in process—" ("An Objective," 12-13). For Howe, the poem as *transplanted words onto paper with soil sticking to their roots* is a dynamic organism emphasizing animist-materialist-vitalist synergy among literal and figurative, textual and contextual, material, sonic, and visual details encountered as field compositions resulting from dynamic aleatory [i.e. chance] and structural relationships. Howe's radical contingency meets *a narrative's fate by immediate access to its concrete totality* of singular features; her collaborative agency shapes the conditions for a poetics and praxis of recovery, reconfiguration, and regenerative return. Howe adds to the passage quoted above that she wanted "jerky and tedious details to oratorically bloom and bear fruit as if they had been set at liberty or ransomed by angels" (16).

The differences between Zukofsky's priorities and Howe's, within the context of this limited comparative reading, are slight yet significant. If Zukofsky places the poem's emergence among intrinsic vitalist forces—"yet certainly it arose in the veins and capillaries, if only in the intelligence"—he also emphasizes (yet not without equivocation) "the materials which are outside (?) the veins and capillaries—The context— The context necessarily dealing with a world outside of it" ("An Objective," 15). In Howe's radical contingency and historical imagination, there is no *world outside of it* because the poem is an endlessly embedded inter-/intra-textual wilderness of "Font-voices" that "can be reanimated by appropriation" (*Souls*, 15; *The Quarry*, 53). Both poets emphasize *the direction of historic and contemporary particulars*, but they differ on

---

[201] *Souls*, 16.

this key principle of factual telepathy. For Zukofsky, the poem embodies "A desire to place everything—everything aptly, perfectly, belonging within, one with, a context" ("An Objective," 15); for Howe, "the telepathic solicitation of innumerable phantoms [...] in this forest of letters, theories, and forgotten actualities" (*Souls*, 14; *The Quarry*, 52). Rather than prioritizing a writerly *desire to place the poem within a context*—key idioms in Zukofsky's discourse that suggest gestures of craft and control—Howe's poetics and praxis emphasizes *attentive dialogic close listening* to archival materials that, themselves, call out for artifactual recovery and remediation through the poet's collaborative work.

M. NourbeSe Philip's *ZONG!* provides a striking comparison and contrast with Zukofsky's and Howe's poetics and praxis (albeit within the limited scope of these representative works from all three writers). If Zukofsky's essays (through their various changes between 1931 and 1967) emphasize the poem as an *object in process*, they also generally avoid questions as to how the poem engenders or invokes meaning as part of that constructivist process; the qualities of sincerity and objectification concern intransitive totalities that resist interpretation and predication. Although Philip shares Zukofsky's and Howe's abiding attunement to and care for *the direction of historic and contemporary particulars*, she balances *ZONG!* on the precarious edge between confronting that work's human, linguistic, and material disaster[202] (through the discourse of the poem's historical sources) and conjuring immaterial, extralinguistic significations from the evidence that may be interrogated. In "Notanda," one of the book's concluding sections, Philip articulates this difficulty:

---

[202] "In 1781 a fully provisioned ship, the *Zong*, captained by one Luke Collingwood, leaves the West Coast of Africa with a cargo of 470 slaves and sets sail for Jamaica [...] Instead of the customary six to nine weeks, this fateful trip will take some four months on account of navigational errors on the part of the captain. Some of the *Zong's* cargo is lost through illness and lack of water; many others, by order of the captain are destroyed." M. NourbeSe Philip, *ZONG!* (Wesleyan University Press, 2008), 189.

> The not-telling of this particular story is in the fragmentation and mutilation of the text, forcing the eye to track across the page in an attempt to wrest meaning from words gone astray. […] In the discomfort and disturbance created by the poetic text, I am forced to make meaning from apparently disparate elements—in so doing I implicate myself. The risk—of contamination—lies in piecing together the story that cannot be told. And since we have to work to complete the events, we all become implicated in, if not contaminated by, this activity.[203]

Like Philip, Howe encountered innumerable contradictions between the poem she began assembling—"Body perception thought of perceiving (half-thought"—and the poem that had to be disassembled in order to release the untelling of the impossible story that cannot be told yet which must tell itself: "chaotic architect repudiate line Q confine lie link realm". Howe's work on *Articulation* navigated charged paradoxical territories between scattered facts—"our always fragmentary knowledge"—and spiritual forces, as she observes in her reflections upon encountering Hope Atherton's story in the "sleeping wilderness" of Yale's Sterling Library, where she "felt the telepathic solicitation of innumerable phantoms."[204]

Such inter-/intra-textual "BETWEENNESS"[205] engenders the factual telepathy at work throughout Howe's reconfigurations of the poem from *Articulation of Sound Forms in Time* to *The Quarry*, adding charged variables in each instance to her remediation of Hope's story as well as to her own kindred "Personal Narrative." By "*factual telepathy*,"[206] Howe means that her writing dwells among animist, linguistic, and vitalist forces embedded in the radical contingency of her materials and methods: "Font-voices summon a reader into visible earshot" […]

---

[203] *ZONG!* (Wesleyan University Press, 2008), 198.
[204] "Personal Narrative," *Souls of the Labadie Tract*, 14.
[205] Susan Howe, "Re: Edited Transcription," e-mail to the author (February 10, 2015); and W. Scott Howard, "Archives, Artifacts, Apostrophes: Susan Howe's *Spontaneous Particulars*," *Denver Quarterly* 50.3 (2016): 103.
[206] "Sorting Facts" (1996): 91.

because "ghosts wrapped in appreciative obituaries" may be recovered and reanimated through remediation (*Souls*, 15). And like Philip, who acknowledges the immanent/imminent possibilities of becoming "implicated in, if not contaminated by" the activity of "piecing together the story that cannot be told," Howe is viscerally aware of the risks and responsibilities involved in her relationships with the dead, in her reanimation of their stories by appropriation. Howe acknowledges that she "take[s] [her] life as a poet from their lips, their vocalisms, their breath" which, she admits, "may suggest vampirism" (*Souls*, 16). (Such nuanced, ethical self/Other considerations of the poet's responsibility to rescue, remediate, and release the direction of historic and contemporary particulars do not quite figure so prominently in Zukofsky's priorities for *thinking with the things as they exist*.)

ZONG! differs considerably from *Articulation*. While Howe and Philip both risk assembling their stories "that cannot be told" through forms of discourse and figuration perhaps "already contaminated, possibly irrevocably and fatally" (*ZONG!*, 199), Philip's methodology of case analysis stages "a careful sifting" between legal principles (*ratio decidendi*) and marginal concerns (*obiter dicta*) which "is what the Africans on board the *Zong* become—*dicta*, footnotes, related to, but not, the *ratio*" (199). *ZONG!* includes several rhetorical framing devices—multiple personae and prefaces, annotations and appendices, voices and variables—that signify the poet's complex role as both censor and magician, either constraining speakers or conjuring spirits from varying proximities to the disaster. Through the volume's polysemous and polyvocal immersive intensity, Philip amplifies the lyrical, social, and political power of *ZONG!* as a rite of passage and ritual performance dedicated to the ongoing work of restorative justice.[207]

As Howe notes in her 1990 *Talisman* interview, *Articulation* also lives as a performative work: the public reading releases "the articulation that represents life" (30). Her working papers for the poem (c. 1982-1987) include notes from several readings, each of which shaped changes

---

[207] For documents and photos from Philip's collective readings/performances of *ZONG!*, see http://www.nourbese.com/zong/[.]

to the typescripts.[208] Although certainly more condensed than *ZONG!*, the polysemous and polyvocal sound forms in *Articulation* are no less capacious or captivating in their lyrical, social, and political registers. By minimizing rhetorical distinctions among and distances between layers of radical contingency and historical figuration, Howe implicates her readers in the work's embodied pursuit of "Mr. Atherton's story Hope Atherton" alongside the poet's "Marching and counter marching / Danger of roaming the woods at random". Whereas *ZONG!* amplifies such contrasts through the volume's discursive, methodological sections, the Awede text of *Articulation*—especially the first section, "*Hope Atherton's Wanderings*"—amplifies *betweenness* in every line in each woven, strophic sonicimagetext, thereby embedding the reader in the work's "*whirlwind handwritten*"—that is, in the poem's five-fold telepathic transmission of the disaster's recovery, remediation, and regenerative release. In her subsequent elaborations upon and companions to the Awede text, Howe has provided additional layers of autobiographical, figurative, historical, rhetorical, and visual framing, each time sustaining and yet also discursively subverting the work's asymmetrical escapes. Such is the precarity in any poetics and praxis concerned with *the direction of historic and contemporary particulars.*

But how, exactly, does this poet manage these things? How does the poem's radical contingency, historical figuration, and factual telepathy rescue voices on the brink of oblivion within and against the grain of documents written by the victors without accommodating such alterity to the subversion/containment dialectic? Without speaking for or over the victims and survivors? As several of the poem's readers have cogently argued, *Articulation* recovers, reconfigures, and regenerates the antinomian legacies of Anne Hutchinson and Mary Rowlandson within and against, between and through the poem's unsettling of their nested,

---

[208] Susan Howe Papers, 1942-2002, MSS 0201, Box 2, Folder 17; Box 3, Folders 1-5; and Box 42, Folders 7-9; Geisel Library, Special Collections and Archives, UC San Diego:
http://libraries.ucsd.edu/speccoll/findingaids/mss0201.html[.]

contested narratives. But how, really, does the poem represent their singular lives and losses through those various sources and stories without, as Montgomery incisively reflects, conflating "such incommensurable models of otherness" (84) vis-à-vis the poem's documentarian methods and modes? Similar critiques could also be raised with regard to the numerous cross-genre and cross-disciplinary arguments that have been advanced in the field thus far concerning the poem's transgressive agency—precisely, I would argue—because *Articulation* relentlessly escapes and evokes, shapes and subverts interpretive work. If that assertion may stand, then how does the poem actually engage distinctively and meaningfully with the historiography of the Peskeompskutt massacre and of Hope Atherton's nonconformist experience?

The answers to such challenging and relevant questions are to be found through the poem's transformative encounters with Howe's shaping context of source materials that are specific to each work's radical contingency, historical figuration, and factual telepathy. In the case of *Articulation*, Howe's groundwork amplifies the nested contradictions that shape the poem's historiographic counter-paths: "From the first, New England legend and myth, based on rigid separation of race, concentrated on abduction, communion, war, and diabolism. Contradiction is the book of this place."[209] In these discrete confrontations with contested legacies, how do Howe's methods deconstruct the ideology of colonialism that "has always-already interpellated individuals as subjects"?[210] If, as Louis Althusser has argued, ideology has a material existence, then Howe's writing dwells among manuscripts and printed texts in order to amplify their animist-materialist-vitalist, polysemous and polyvocal agencies: "W'ld bivouac by vineyard / Eagle aureole elses thend". Howe's poetics and praxis echoes Kristeva's affirmation that "there is

---

[209] *My Emily Dickinson* (1985), 45.

[210] Louis Althusser, "Ideology and Ideological State Apparatuses (Notes towards an Investigation)," *Lenin and Philosophy and Other Essays*, trans. Ben Brewster (London: New Left Books, 1971), 164.

within poetic language [...] a *heterogeneousness* to meaning and signification."[211] Each of Howe's poems including history rescues, regenerates, and returns such artifactual heterogeneousness to the archival wilderness of languages and materials that witness and thereby engender the *movement of the Same towards the Other which never returns to the Same*.

By granting priority to texts as *deictic* (demonstrative), *haptic* (tactile), *hylic* (material), *ludic* (playful), *noetic* (intuitive), *syntactic* (predicative), and *thetic* (propositional) articulations of sound forms in time, the poem's radical contingency shapes the most chaotic and transformative forces of tropological constitutive poetics.[212] Howe's historical figuration—lyrical and social, strophic, polyvocal and praxical—stages elegiac inter-/intra-textual interventions among and between, through and within the poem's various counter-paths 'after'/*after* Hope Atherton. In those dynamic ways, *Articulation* contributes to the cultural work of the postmodern elegy that critiques teleological, transcendental historical narratives through linguistic and materialist resistance to closure and consolation.[213]

Howe's subsequent elaborations upon these materials and methods from *Articulation* to *The Quarry* reveal the emergence and development of her key trope of factual telepathy, which recovers voices on the brink of oblivion by amplifying and remediating the contradictions among and between source documents. Following the Awede text, Howe would reflect upon her telepathic connection to Hope Atherton[214] that profoundly

---

[211] *Desire in Language*, 133.

[212] This seven-fold formulation draws upon Kristeva's thought from two books: *Desire in Language* (1980), 124-147; and *Revolution in Poetic Language*, trans. Margaret Waller (New York: Columbia University Press, 1984), 25-67. See also W. Scott Howard, "*WYSIWYG* Poetics: Reconfiguring the Fields for Creative Writers & Scholars," *The Journal of Electronic Publishing*, ed. Aaron McCollough 14.2 (2011):
http://dx.doi.org/10.3998/3336451.0014.204[.]

[213] See Howard, "'The Brevities'" (2002); "Landscapes of Memorialisation" (2003); and "'Fire harvest: harvest fire'" (2006).

[214] See "An Interview With Susan Howe," *Talisman* (1990): 25, 30; "Personal Narrative," *Souls*, 11-19; "Writing *Articulation of Sound Forms in Time*,"

changed her work in ways that anticipated her attunement to the "visual and acoustic shock"[215] she would encounter (c. 2005) in the *Diary* of Hannah Edwards Wetmore (as transcribed by her daughter, Lucy Wetmore Whittelsey) in the "vast collection of Edwards family papers" at the Beinecke Library.[216] *Articulation* and *Frolic Architecture* (2010) are, in this regard, kindred breakthrough works for Howe; both are inter-/intra-textual collages of factual telepathy. Hope's undervoice first guided the poet's understanding that "language attaches to and envelops its referent without destroying or changing it—the way a cobweb catches a fly" (*Souls*, 14; *The Quarry, 31*).

These affinities not only suggest methodological connections and differences among works decades apart, but also underscore the abiding influence of captivity narratives in Howe's poetics and praxis. Since *Articulation* and the other poems collected in *Singularities* (1990), some of Howe's other books that also engage the forms and tropes of the captivity narrative include *The Nonconformist's Memorial* (1993), *Kidnapped* (2002), *The Midnight* (2003), *Souls of the Labadie Tract* (2007), and especially *TOM TIT TOT* (2014). *TTT* alludes to and plays with an English variant of the German *Rumpelstilzchen* story collected by Joseph Jacobs in *English Fairy Tales* (1890) in which these words—"Nimmy Nimmy Not / Your Name's TOM TIT TOT"—break the spell.[217] Whereas the spinning of flax into skeins weaves the folktale's plot, here, in *TTT*, the collaging of "words from images twi[sted] / [f]rom their original source / [h]istory scattered to the fou[r] [winds]" (2014, np) shapes Howe's transfiguration of texts into letterpress pages of concrete poems resembling textiles or wordwhorls. In fact, *TOM TIT TOT* may be Howe's most ambitious, collaborative, dynamic, and playful inter-/intra-textual engagement with captivity narratives; the work collages language from at

---

The Sound of Poetry/The Poetry of Sound (2009): 199-204; and "Personal Narrative," *The Quarry* (2015): 49-56.

[215] *Spontaneous Particulars*, 52.
[216] *The Quarry*, 36.
[217] Joseph Jacobs, *English Fairy Tales*, Illustrated by John D. Batten (London: David Nutt, 1890), 8.

least twenty-one source texts, and was composed by an ensemble of artists, bookbinders, printers, typographers, and publishers (as the colophon to the MoMA edition relates). The various fonts and languages on stage in each sonicimagetext amplify the polyvocality in these palimpsests. *TOM TIT TOT* includes echoes from *Articulation*, and is deeply informed by Howe's methods in *Frolic*. These connections were underscored during the premier exhibition of *TTT* at the Yale Union gallery in Portland, OR in 2013. Selected photograms by James Welling from The Grenfell Press edition of *Frolic* hung on the walls surrounding the table-top presentation of facing pages from *TOM TIT TOT*.

In all of these works shaped by her continued fascination with captivity narratives, Howe simultaneously assembles language from both sides of the page from several documents; *abbreviating, pushing, padding, subtracting, riddling, interrogating, re-writing, pulling texts through texts*. All of those linguistic swatches and threads travel on their own journeys through space and time, interlacing the charged multi-modal multi-directionality that shapes Howe's chance synergies. Although her compositional practices have changed somewhat along with changes in technology since the 1970s, this singular, multifaceted, arti-factual/archival gesture dwells among all of Howe's books from *Hinge Picture* (1974) to *Debths* (2017): writing between pages; folding language within, against, and through language; collaging/painting/staging inter-/intra-texts. The poet simultaneously composes through both sides of the page as well as between facing pages.

Such a dialetheic and dialogic poetics and praxis engenders concrete lyrical/social polyvocal strophic assemblages amplifying "mystery, metaphor, and metamorphosis"[218] in aleatory fusions of form and content, figure and ground. That resilient arc of integrated materials and methods also connects Howe's first published essay, "The End of Art" (1974),

---

[218] "The End of Art" (1974): 3.

which celebrates abstract minimalism, with her recent homage to Wallace Stevens, "Vagrancy in the Park" (2015): "a blaze of artifice reflected in earthly elements composing it."[219]

*   *   *

The poetics and praxis of *Articulation* resides in the radical contingency of documents, ghosts, materials, silences, and voices closest to Howe's historical imagination and Hope's nonconformist experience.

> from seaweed said nor repossess rest
> scape esaid

The Awede text begins with an utterance on the verge of intelligibility and legibility because all eight words dwell among and between, within and across the cipers and deciperings of those who returned from Peskeompskutt (Great Falls) to tell their stories. These are neither Howe's nor Hope's words alone; they are common among those Colonists who fled the massacre, which (through a combination of errors) led to "a panic amongst the exhausted [military] men," then to a "retreat [that] became a rout" (Sheldon, 1:158). The poem's haunting, uncanny opening words are also common among the colonial and early modern historians who endeavored, in their meta-narratives, to accommodate such potentially subversive 'true' relations of escape (from the military rout) to the ideology and rhetoric of the emerging form of discourse that was to become popularly known as the captivity narrative. Hope Atherton's story, in that regard, contributes to some of the early narratives that not only preceded but which, critically, deviated from the narrative patterns and tropes epitomized by Mary Rowlandson's *The Soveraignty &*

---

[219] "Vagrancy in the Park," unpublished typescript and e-mail to the author (March 5, 2015).

Goodness of God, together, with the Faithfulness of His Promises Displayed (1682).[220] In tandem with the poem's unsettling of Rowlandson's story and of Anne Hutchinson's trial, as several of Howe's readers have convincingly argued, *Articulation* also reads/writes against the historiographic grain of the Peskeompskutt massacre and Hope Atherton's legacy.

The poem's transgressive, polyvocal lexicon may be found nested among and between the many contested inter-/intra-texts from Howe's historical and meta-historical sources. This is precisely what the poet and poem signify through the dialetheic passage on the other side of the opening two lines in the Awede text: "*EXTRACT from a LETTER (dated June 8th, 1781,) of Stephen Williams to President Styles*". (We are always-already in the field of history. 1781 is also the year of the Zong's fateful journey. Such kairic synergy links Philip's and Howe's poems including history through their shared engagement with the ongoing work of restorative justice.) Howe's deft and deviant gestures here speak volumes; the least sound counts in every line on each page. The following details have been hiding in plain sight; once noticed, their factual telepathy regenerates the work's radical contingency and historical figuration as modes for documentation and critical witnessing of "lives beyond thought / linked from beginning".

---

[220] *The soveraignty & goodness of God, together, with the faithfulness of his promises displayed; being a narrative of the captivity and restauration of Mrs. Mary Rowlandson. Commended by her, to all that desires to know the Lords doing to, and dealings with her. Especially to her dear children and relations, / written by her own hand for her private use, and now made publick at the earnest desire of some friends, and for the benefit of the afflicted* (Cambridge [Mass.]: Printed by Samuel Green, 1682). An edition was also published in London during the same year: *A true history of the captivity & restoration of Mrs. Mary Rowlandson, a minister's wife in New-England wherein is set forth the cruel and inhumane usage she underwent amongst the heathens for eleven weeks time, and her deliverance from them / written by her own hand ... ; whereunto is annexed a sermon of the possibility of God's forsaking a people that have been near and dear to him, preached by Mr. Joseph Rowlandson ... it being his last sermon* (London: Printed first at New-England, and re-printed at London, and sold by Joseph Poole, 1682).

The *"EXTRACT from a LETTER"* that haunts Howe's epigraph/invocation to the Awede text of *Articulation* concerns one passage in a sequence of correspondence between Stephen Williams[221] (son of Rev. John Williams[222]) and Ezra Stiles (seventh president of Yale College).[223] Howe's typographic interventions here should catch our eyes and ears, prompting our attunement to her reading/writing against the grain of George Sheldon's *History of Deerfield, Massachusetts*, which compiles a legacy of captivity narratives that shape and support a teleological historiographic quest for providential nationalism.[224] Before addressing the

---

[221] Stephen Williams (1694-1782), First Congregational Minister of Longmeadow, MA., was the second son of the Reverend John Williams of Deerfield, MA. and Eunice Mather Williams, daughter of the Rev. Eleazar Mather of Northampton, MA. Stephen is best remembered as a Boy Captive of the Raid on Deerfield, MA, which took place on February 29, 1704, when approximately 40 French soldiers and 200 Abenaki, Huron and Mohawk Indians from Montreal attacked the inhabitants of Deerfield. Stephen, his father, and his sister, Eunice, were taken captive; his mother, Eunice, and his siblings, John Jr. and Jerusha, were killed. Approximately 112 survivors were marched into Canada. The Rev. John Williams eventually returned from Quebec (with Stephen and approximately 60 of the Deerfield captives) first to Boston (on November 21, 1706) and then to Deerfield. For a detailed account of this complex event and legacy, see Evan Haefeli and Kevin Sweeney, *Captors and Captives: The 1704 French and Indian Raid on Deerfield* (Amherst: University of Massachusetts Press, 2003). See also *Raid on Deerfield: The Many Stories of 1704*: http://1704.deerfield.history.museum/home.do[.]

[222] John Williams (1664-1729), a New England Puritan minister, was best known for *The redeemed captive returning to Zion or, A faithful history of remarkable occurrences in the captivity and deliverance of Mr. John Williams, Minister of the Gospel in Deerfield* (1707), which recounts his narrative of captivity and return following the Deerfield Massacre. John Williams's nephew "was the pastor and theologian, Jonathan Edwards. John Williams's first wife, Eunice Mather, was related to Rev. John Cotton; she was a niece of Rev. Increase Mather and a cousin of Rev. Cotton Mather." *Dictionary of Canadian Biography*, Vol. 2 (1701-1740):
http://www.biographi.ca/en/bio/williams_john_1664_1729_2E.html[.]

[223] Ezra Stiles (1727-1795) was a Congregationalist minister, an educator, theologian and author. Stiles served as president of Yale College (1778-1795), and was one of the founders of the College of Rhode Island (Brown University) in 1764. *Encyclopedia.Com*: http://www.encyclopedia.com/people/philosophy-and-religion/protestant-christianity-biographies/ezra-stiles[.]

[224] Sheldon's *History of Deerfield*, as he writes in his "Preface," proposes a "careful study of the Indian relics found in our valley […] relating to the history

dynamic interplay among inter- and intra-texts in Sheldon's and Howe's remediations of the Peskeompskutt massacre and of Hope Atherton's story, a few reflections upon the singularity of this extract from Rev. Stephen Williams's letter are warranted.

As Perloff observes, Howe consulted *A History of Hatfield* (1910) by Daniel White Wells and Reuben Field Wells for Atherton's story: this "and various other histories entered her poem" (1990, 343, n. 4). Beyond this solitary endnote citation, none of Howe's other readers have engaged with Wells & Wells (despite the poet's noted tracks through that volume). Howe also consulted *History of Hadley* (1905) by Sylvester Judd and *The redeemed captive returning to Zion* (1707) by John Williams, in addition to the other historical and meta-historical texts which I've invoked in this essay to illustrate the poem's dynamic inter-/intra-textuality and Howe's robust dialogue with archives and artifacts. None of Howe's readers have considered either Judd's or Williams's texts as key sources for the poem's historiographic critique. Each of Howe's historical and meta-historical sources lends different nuances and incongruities to Atherton's story; that radically contingent "mosaic pattern" of "Summary succession of spectators twisted // away" could be followed endlessly. Some of those imbricate echoes, however, resonate more compellingly than others.

As noted earlier (and as also invoked & embodied through other essays in this collection) my work here follows an openwork sequence in the spirit of Howe's journey from *Articulation* to *The Quarry*. My 2006 essay, "Literal/Littoral Crossings: Re-Articulating Hope Atherton's

---

of the Pocumtuck Indians" with particular attention given to the "times of Philip's War [...], Queen Anne's War, and other contests with the French and Indians" as framed by two foundational mythologies: "the alleged appearance of Gen. Goffe as the deliverer of Hadley, and the romance of the Bell of St. Regis" (v) which respectively provide narrative closure to and consolation for the Indian raids on Hadley (1675) and Deerfield (1704). Both of those events, in turn, frame Sheldon's historiography of the Peskeompskutt massacre and Hope Atherton's nonconformity.

Story After Susan Howe's *Articulation of Sound Forms in Time*,"[225] offered preliminary steps along the path that my work here amplifies. I will revisit some of those first steps within the context of this essay's concluding passages.

The only historical source text for *Articulation* that has received any substantive consideration thus far in the field is George Sheldon's *A History of Deerfield* (1895-1896). Only four of the poem's readers—Nicholls (1996), Back (2002), Frost (2003), and Gaffield (2015)—have engaged with Sheldon's volumes (albeit in the most minimal ways, except for Nicholls); and yet, each has dismissed Sheldon's relevance—not because of what was there to be found, but because of what they did not recognize due to the dominance of their respective methodological and theoretical priorities (which I'll address, below). None of the poem's readers have noticed the following details which illuminate the roles of radical contingency, historical figuration, and factual telepathy at work in *Articulation* as a reading/writing against the grain.

Within the context of the poem's primary and secondary historical sources addressed thus far, the *"EXTRACT from a LETTER (dated June 8th, 1781,) of Stephen Williams to President Styles"* may be found *only* in Sheldon's *A History of Deerfield* (vol. 1:168-169). A close reading of Sheldon's typographic transcription and narrative framing of the extract reveals much when compared against Howe's disruptive re-transcription, which turns contextual archive into radically contingent artifact. Howe's sagacious adaptation of this contested, nested extract (from a letter referring to a copy of a paper of an account of a related account of an experience related in a copy of a paper lost and then found among other papers) unsettles the historiographic wilderness that has, in fact, supplanted Hope's nonconformist story—"Corruptible first figure"—with the legacy of Jonathan Wells, "boy hero of the Turners Falls

---

[225] I should note that, during 2017, EServer initiated a comprehensive migration to new workstations for all of their open access journals. That process is currently scheduled for completion in September, 2018. For those reasons, my citations to my 2006 essay refer to the Internet Archive's *Wayback Machine*: https://web.archive.org/web/20110726035138/http://reconstruction.eserver.org/063/howard.shtml[.]

fight,"[226] whose celebrated legacy is central to Stephen Williams's subversion/containment of the Peskeompskutt massacre and the subsequent, disorderly military retreat. Sheldon, as we shall see, claims that he can trace both Williams's letter and Atherton's narrative "directly back to the hands of the author" (1:168), thereby revealing the generative contradiction/paradox at the heart of his sources for (and contextualizing of) both documents. One of those key source texts of historiographic subversion/containment for Sheldon is John Williams's *The redeemed captive returning to Zion*; through the edited, embedded presence (in Sheldon's text) of John Williams's—that is, Stephen's father's—narrative of captivity and return, we will find the crux of Howe's reading/writing against the grain in *Articulation*.

It is for these reasons that *Articulation* includes numerous vocalizations from other speakers (who were also fleeing the massacre and military rout) embedded within Jonathan Wells's narrative (as progressively remediated by John and Stephen Williams) that collectively disrupt and disperse Atherton's story. The poem (from the Awede text to *The Quarry*) dramatizes the process and politics of Hope's historiographic erasure and of his legacy's recovery, reconfiguration, and regenerative release through Howe's poetics and praxis: "My retrospective excursions follow the principle that ghosts wrapped in appreciative obituaries by committee members, or dedications presented at vanished community field meetings, can be reanimated by appropriation."[227] Howe's deft, deviant adaptations (in both the Awede and Wesleyan texts of *Articulation*) of Stephen Williams's letter deconstruct—through ironic exaggeration—the subversion/containment of Atherton's "incoherent inaccessible muddled inaudible // Speech was a cry for action // erroneous proof /

---

[226] "Jonathan Wells, 4 son of Thomas and Mary (Beardsley) Wells, was born in 1659. He was a boy hero of the Turners Falls fight. He married Hepzibah Colton of Springfield, Mass.; the couple had two sons, one of whom died in infancy." *Guide to the Wells Family Papers*: https://deerfield-ma.org/wp-content/uploads/2013/10/Wells-Family-Papers.pdf[.] See also Pocumtuck Valley Memorial Association: https://deerfield-ma.org/[.]

[227] Howe, *Souls*, 15; and *The Quarry*, 53.

erroneous choice". These details and facts have been embedded in the extract's (and the poem's) radical contingency, historical figuration, and factual telepathy.

In order to present these disruptive inter-/intra-texts, I will first transcribe the language verbatim from Sheldon's *A History of Deerfield*, which surrounds Stephen Williams's narrative in quotation marks, thereby amplifying the palimpsests at play in this meta-history:

> "In looking over my papers I found a copy of a paper left by the Rev. Hope Atherton, the first minister of Hatfield, who was ordained May 10th, 1670. This Mr. Atherton went out with the forces (commanded by Capt. Turner, captain of the garrison soldiers, and Capt. Holyoke of the county militia) against the Indians at the falls above Deerfield, in May, 1676. In the fight, upon their retreat, Mr. Atherton was unhorsed and separated from the company, wandered in the woods some days and then got into Hadley,* which is on the east side of Connecticut River. But the fight was on the west side. Mr. Atherton gave account that he had offered to surrender himself to the enemy, but they would not receive him. Many people were not willing to give credit to his account, suggesting that he was beside himself. This occasioned him to publish to his congregation and leave in writing the account I enclose to you. I had the paper from which this is copied, from his only son, with whom it was left. The account is doubtless true, for Jonathan Wells, Esq., who was in the fight and lived afterward at Deerfield and was intimately acquainted with the Indians after the war, did himself inform *me* that the *Indians* told *him* that after the fall fight, that a little man with a black coat and without any hat, came toward them, but they were afraid and ran from him, thinking it was the Englishman's God, etc., etc." (1:168-169)

The above passage appears in the Awede text of *Articulation* with curious changes compared with Sheldon's text, alterations that should catch our eyes and ears. Firstly, the omissions of the asterisk after Hadley,* as well as of the accompanying note[228] that, for Sheldon, explains away a probable impossibility (which Howe's text amplifies: "Gone and signal through deep water / Mr. Atherton's story Hope Atherton"). Secondly, and most critically, the deletion of "[…] , **with whom it was left. The account is doubtless true, for** […]," which results (in Howe's text) in a key splicing of sentences that engenders the uncanny substitution of Jonathan Wells, Esq. for Hope Atherton's *only son*—a deft and deviant, entangled, and precarious intervention on Howe's part that demonstrates a keen reading/writing against the historiographic grain. The Awede text's reconfiguration of these sentences reads thus: "This occasioned him to publish to his congregation and leave in writing the account I enclose to you. I had the paper from which this is copied, from his only son Jonathan Wells, Esq., who was in the fight and lived afterward at Deerfield […]." Howe's subsequent (and even more subtle) changes to Williams's letter in the Wesleyan text of *Articulation* (to be addressed, below) amplify this ironic critique of Hope's displacement (by the Jonathan Wells legacy) and eventual disappearance from his own story. The poem's radical contingency, historical figuration, and factual telepathy thus confront Atherton's historiographers with a "dim mirror Naught formula" of disruptive "archaic hallucinatory laughter".

According to Arthur Holmes Tucker, Hope Atherton married Sarah Hollister (of Weathersfield, CT) in 1674, and they had three children: "Hope junior and Joseph—twins, born Jan. 7, 1675;" and "Sarah—Born Oct. 26, 1676."[229] Hope, Jr. died young. Tucker has nothing more to say about either Sarah Hollister Atherton or Sarah Atherton. He does note, however, that the "Hatfield records are missing for the four years 1673-1677" which "was the active period of Hope Atherton's ministry" (9).

---

[228] "* This conclusion does not seem warranted by the text." Sheldon, 1: 168. In a most curious instance of genealogical and geographical synergy, Howe's paternal grandmother's mother, Helen Huntington Quincey, grew up in Hadley and was friends with the Dickinsons. See Susan Howe and Marta Werner, "Transcription and Transgression," *The Networked Recluse: The Connected World of Emily Dickinson* (Amherst: Amherst College Press, 2017), 123.

[229] *Hope Atherton and His Times*, 8.

In a sermon to his congregation at Hatfield (on May 28, 1676) Hope recounted his improbable experience, which began on Thursday, May 18, 1676, when "the company of one hundred and fifty or more men, [...] passed along the narrow trail which led northward, toward the 'Great Fall' about twenty miles distant" (Tucker, 63). According to Tucker, after the military attack and chaotic retreat on May 19, Hope was lost in the wilderness, "roving here and there without food" (66) before inexplicably returning to Hadley on Monday, May 22.[230] Tucker observes that Joseph Atherton was, at the time of his father's death (June 8, 1677), the "only living son of Hope" (71).

Howe's other historical sources corroborate these known details about Hope Atherton, his years in Hatfield, and his family life, but, as the Williams letter intimates, Hope's solitary experience in the wilderness and his uncanny return across the Quinetucket/Connecticut River were (for his congregation) and would remain (for his historiographers) problematic.[231] *Articulation* amplifies the convergences and divergences

---

[230] According to James Russell Trumbull, Hope Atherton's sermon "does not name the town into which he came" (1: 335) after emerging from the wilderness. See Trumbull, *History of Northampton, Massachusetts: From Its Settlement in 1654*, 2 vols. (Northampton, MA: Gazette Printing, 1898 – 1902).

[231] Geography is its own palimpsest. Riparian boundaries and river depths will vary with the seasons and over years. And the river of today is not the river of 1676. However, spring runoff "from melting snow in the northern mountains" typically brings the Connecticut River to "seasonally high levels in April and May." Richard W. Garvine, "Physical Features of the Connecticut River Outflow During High Discharge," *Journal of Geophysical Research* 79.6 (1974): 831. Local residents affirm the probable impossibility of Hope's journey during mid-May across Quinetucket. "My home [sits] on a hillside across the valley from where Mary Rowlandson was held captive by King Philip. Behind [the house] is Mt. Grace, named for Rowlandson's infant daughter, whom she is said to have buried there. A few miles to the south are the falls, now named for Capt. Turner. I can't tell where Atherton crossed the river, but perhaps he and the militia had crossed earler at Cheapside, not far south of where the attack occurred. Otherwise, that part of the narrative doesn't make sense to me; the Connecticut itself is very broad and very deep south of Cheapside, especially during the spring snow melt." Edward Foster, e-mail to the author (May 25, 2019). I am grateful to Edward Foster, Christopher Sawyer-Laucanno, and David Brule for their perspectives on the Peskeompskutt legacy and

among these parallel streams of stories: "'Deep water' he *must* have crossed over".

This poignantly ironic, inter-/intra-textual substitution of Jonathan Wells for Hope Atherton's 'only son' in Howe's remediation of the "*EXTRACT from a LETTER*" has astonishingly escaped attention (scape esaid) not only in the field of Howe criticism and scholarship, but also in the field of seventeenth-century New England captivity narratives *before* the first American edition of Mary Rowlandson's *The Soveraignty & Goodness of God, together, with the Faithfulness of His Promises Displayed* (1682).[232] These spliced lines in Howe's disruptive transcription underscore the co-presence of contested, nested narratives echoing within and against, among and through Hope's 'true' relation, including the stories of Thomas Reed, Stephen Belding, John Jones, Jonathan Wells, Experience Hindsell, Benjamin Waite, William Howard, and Captain William Turner among the others who fled the Peskeompskutt massacre—*none of whom* accompanied Atherton on his counter-allegorical journey through the wilderness and across the Quinetucket/Connecticut River (Sheldon, 1: 152-171). "Omen of stumbling / Great unknown captaincy".

Although Stephen Williams's letter observes that Atherton was "unhorsed and separated from the company," his subordination of Hope's aberrant narrative to the heroic story of Jonathan Wells's redeemed return—*the account is doubtless true, for Jonathan Wells, Esq., who was in the fight and lived afterward at Deerfield*—engenders a cluster of resilient myths: that Wells and Atherton were comrades; that Wells rescued Atherton during the military rout; that Wells's narrative corroborates Atherton's story; and that Wells became the custodian of Atherton's transcribed sermon—all of which, critically, shaped Williams's (and subsequently Sheldon's) convoluted claims of authoritative access

---

for their recommendations for further research (which have been added to my notes and bibliography).

[232] See Kathryn Zabelle Derounian-Stodola, and James Arthur Levernier, *The Indian Captivity Narrative, 1550-1900* (New York: Twayne Publishers, 1993), 21. Derounian-Stodola and Levernier do not mention the captivity narratives of either Hope Atherton or Jonathan Wells.

directly back to the hands of the author. Howe's reading/writing against the grain of the poem's historical sources amplifies the "sonic grid of homely minutiae fallen away into posterity" that "carries trace filaments" and "Tumbled syllables" of "bolts and bullets from the blue" (*Souls*, 13; *The Quarry*, 51).

The many voices in *Articulation* emerge from this dynamic inter-/intra-textuality, which, as critics and scholars in the field have cogently shown, also includes other nonconformists, such as Anne Hutchinson and Mary Rowlandson. Most directly and most significantly (for the purpose of my argument) Howe's radical contingency, historical figuration, and factual telepathy deconstruct the dominance of Jonathan Wells's narrative that has eclipsed Atherton's legacy in Sheldon's meta-history (as well as in the poem's other historical sources) because of Sheldon's allegiance[233] to his purportedly original sources for Stephen Williams's letter, Jonathan Wells's story, and Hope Atherton's narrative—sources that all go back to Stephen Williams, his father (the Rev. John Williams), their shared experience in the 1704 attack on Deerfield, and (most critically for the historiography of Atherton's story and legacy) their collaborative authorship, editing, and publishing of *The redeemed captive*.

*   *   *

The Rev. John Williams, his wife Eunice, his sons John Jr. and Stephen, his daughters Eunice and Jerushah, and his African slave Parthena

---

[233] George Sheldon (1818-1916) was born in Deerfield, MA, educated at Deerfield Academy, and worked as a farmer. He is perhaps best remembered for his *History of Deerfield*, as well as for his dedicated service to the Pocumtuck Valley Memorial Association, which he founded in 1870 and over which he presided until his death. In 1844, he married Susan Stewart Stearns of Dummerston, Vermont. He was appointed Justice of the Peace at Deerfield in 1857; was elected as a representative to the General Court of the state legislature of Massachusetts in 1867; and, in 1872, was elected state senator. His first wife died in 1881. In 1897, he married the scientist and historian, Jennie Maria Arms. In 1870, Sheldon and others commemorated the place where Eunice Williams, the wife of John Williams, was killed during the 1704 Deerfield Massacre. That commemorative action also inaugurated the Pocumtuck Valley Memorial Association. See Haefeli and Sweeney, 114, 222, 274.

were all taken captive following an attack on Deerfield, Massachusetts that began on February 29, 1704 orchestrated by French Canadian and Native American forces (under the command of Jean-Baptiste Hertel de Rouville).[234] John Jr., Jerushah, and Parthena were slain "at that time in or near the town."[235] Williams's wife, Eunice, died en route to Quebec. (In 1870, George Sheldon and his second wife, the scientist and historian Jennie Maria Arms, designated the site of Eunice Williams's death as a place of historical remembrance—the first public commemorative action taken by the Pocumtuck Valley Memorial Association over which Sheldon presided until his death in 1916.)[236] The Rev. John Williams eventually returned from Quebec (with Stephen and approximately sixty of the Deerfield captives) first to Boston (on November 21, 1706); subsequently to Deerfield. John Williams narrated their collective stories in *The redeemed captive returning to Zion or, A faithful history of remarkable occurrences in the captivity and deliverance of Mr. John Williams, Minister of the Gospel in Deerfield* (1707), one of the most popular aggregations of captivity narratives following Mary Rowlandson's *The Soveraignty & Goodness of God* (1682).

The Redeemed Captive is a key source for Sheldon and also for Howe. Compared to Sheldon's text, *The Redeemed Captive* performs an

---

[234] See Zabelle and Levernier, 7, 11, 158-166; and especially Haefeli and Sweeney (2003).

[235] Rev. John Williams, *The redeemed captive returning to Zion or, A faithful history of remarkable occurrences in the captivity and deliverance of Mr. John Williams, Minister of the Gospel in Deerfield; who, in the desolation which befel that plantation, by an incursion of French and Indians, was by them carried away, with his family and his neighbourhood, into Canada. Drawn up by himself. Annexed to which, is a sermon, preached by him upon his return. Also, an appendix, by the Rev. Mr. Williams, of Springfield. Likewise, an appendix, by the Rev. Mr. Taylor, of Deerfield. With a conclusion to the whole, by the Rev. Mr. Prince, of Boston* (Boston: Samuel Hall, 1795): https://archive.org/stream/redeemedcaptive00willrich/redeemedcaptive00willrich_djvu.txt[.]

[236] See Margaret M. Bruchac, "Revisiting Pocumtuck History in Deerfield: George Sheldon's Vanishing Indian Act," *Historical Journal of Massachusetts* (Summer 2011): http://www.westfield.ma.edu/mhj/pdfs/Revisiting%20Pocumtuck%20History.pdf[.]

even more blunt and thorough subordination of Atherton's experience to the heroic legend of Jonathan Wells, the boy captive, "then a youth in his iyth year, [who] was afterwards a gentleman improved in publick life, and sustained a worthy character."[237] Howe's other primary historical sources—Sheldon (1895-1896), Judd (1905), Wells & Wells (1910)—that narrate Atherton's story follow these discursive patterns of subversion and containment established by Rev. John Williams in *The Redeemed Captive* and later amplified by his son, Stephen, who edited, revised, and produced at least four subsequent editions of that popular compilation of captivity narratives. The collection was published twice (1707, 1720) before the death of John Williams (1729); then four times (1758, 1773, 1774, 1776) before the death of Stephen Williams (1782); and then in numerous editions and printings going forward (1793, 1795, 1800, 1833, 1853, 1908, 1969, 1972, 1987). An edition of *The Redeemed Captive* published in 1811 combined the stories of John Williams, the Williams family, and Mary Rowlandson.[238] In 1908, George Sheldon wrote an introduction to the sixth edition, which was his annotated text based upon Rev. John Taylor's 1793/5 edition that "included a valuable appendix by Rev. Stephen Williams." In that introduction, Sheldon, critically, underscored the importance of Taylor's edition as "the most satisfactory edition which we have met with."[239] The legacy of the Williams

---

[237] Williams (1795): https://archive.org/stream/redeemedcaptive00willrich/redeemedcaptive00willrich_djvu.txt[.]

[238] *The captivity and deliverance of Mr. John Williams, pastor of the church in Deerfield, and Mrs. Mary Rowlandson, of Lancaster: who were taken, together with their families and neighbors, by the French and Indians, and carried into Canada. Written by themselves* (Brookfield, MA: Printed by Hori Brown, from the press of E. Merriam & Co., September 1811).

[239] Sheldon's introduction includes a brief narrative on the textual history of *The Redeemed Captive*, in which may be found these lines: "A third edition, commonly called the 'Prince edition', was published in Boston, 1758. This included a valuable appendix by Rev. Stephen Williams, D. D., of Longmeadow, himself a 'Boy Captive'. In [1793 and 1795] this edition was faithfully reproduced by Rev. John Taylor of Deerfield, with an appendix by himself which contains a brief account of the Indian depredations in the Valley until the conquest of Canada. This is called the 'Taylor edition'. It is on the whole the most satisfactory edition which we have met with." George Sheldon, "Introduction,"

family has continued to be a source of fascination and provocation for modern writers and readers.[240] Kindred to Reznikoff's archaeological reading/writing (360-361) against the grain of John Williams's narrative, Howe's *Articulation* disrupts this historiography of colonization and conquest, captivity and redemption: "splitting nature's shadow / splitting the world".

The "*EXTRACT from a LETTER*" that Howe includes in the Awede and Wesleyan texts of *Articulation* bears the date of June 8th, 1781, which signals a key moment in Stephen Williams's efforts to annotate, edit, and republish what would have been the seventh printing (during his lifetime) of *The Redeemed Captive*, which (in all editions and printings) includes excerpts from his own journals that recount his experience as a boy captive. When Stephen Williams wrote to President Styles, he was, as Sheldon's history observes, "then preparing his valuable 'Appendix' to the 'Redeemed Captive'" (1:168). In that version of the Appendix—first published (after Stephen's death) in the Taylor edition of 1793/5—Williams continued his effort (as expressed in the 1758 and subsequent printings (1773, 1774, 1776) of the text during his lifetime) to accommodate to the colonialist ideology of captivity and redemption two deviant, problematic stories: that of his sister, Eunice Williams, and

---

(Springfield, MA: H.R. Hunting Co., 1908), Rpt. 6th ed., Rev. John Williams, *The redeemed captive returning to Zion or, A faithful history of remarkable occurrences in the captivity and deliverance of Mr. John Williams, Minister of the Gospel in Deerfield; who, in the desolation which befel that plantation, by an incursion of French and Indians, was by them carried away, with his family and his neighbourhood, into Canada. Drawn up by himself. Annexed to which, is a sermon, preached by him upon his return. Also, an appendix, by the Rev. Mr. Williams, of Springfield. Likewise, an appendix, by the Rev. Mr. Taylor, of Deerfield. With a conclusion to the whole, by the Rev. Mr. Prince, of Boston* (Boston: Samuel Hall, 1795):
https://archive.org/stream/redeemedcaptive00willrich/redeemedcaptive00willrich_djvu.txt[.]

[240] See, for example, Catharine Maria Sedgwick, *Hope Leslie* (1827); Charles Reznikoff, "The Good Old Days: Recitative Historical Episodes" (1977), *The Poems of Charles Reznikoff 1918-1975*, ed. Seamus Cooney (Boston: David R. Godine, 2005), 359-368; John Demos, *The Unredeemed Captive* (New York: Vintage, 1994); and Mary P. Wells Smith, *The Boy Captive of Old Deerfield* (Dallas: Gideon House Books, 2016).

that of the Rev. Hope Atherton. That sequence of micro-edits and revisions reveals the desired, progressive erasure of his sister's story, and the parallel subordination of Hope's problematic experience to the heroic legend of Jonathan Wells. This is the precise *in medias res*—the dynamic, contested, nested *betweenness*—that Howe's sagaciously selected and adapted *"EXTRACT from a LETTER"* sets in motion for her poem's reading/writing against the grain. Because he could not save his sister, Williams substituted Jonathan Wells as the hero (i.e. captor) for Hope's uncanny return.

Eunice Williams (also known as Marguerite Kanenstenhawi Arosen) was adopted by a Catholic Mohawk family of Kahnawake (on the south shore of the St. Lawrence River, near Quebec, Canada); was subsequently married into the Tribe, and eventually became a transculturated woman, thus replacing "her role as dutiful daughter in the Williams family with her new role as dutiful Indian wife" (Derounian-Stodola, and Levernier, 160). Contrary to popular opinions (which were shaped by popular narratives of captivity, suffering, and providential return to colonial life, such as those edited stories compiled in *The Redeemed Captive*), Eunice was permitted to visit her white relatives in Deerfield, and did so on three occasions: August 1740, July 1741, and June 1761 (Derounian-Stodola, and Levernier, 161). After each of these visits (which were traumatic for the Williams family and which generated local legends) Eunice freely returned to her Mohawk family.

For his part, as Derounian-Stodola and Levernier note, Stephen Williams "continued to hope that his sister would reconvert to Puritanism" and rejoin her colonial family, but eventually abandoned all hope of Eunice's return sometime between his last known letter to her (dated September 19, 1761) and Eunice's last known letter to him (dated March 12, 1771) which Stephen did not answer (161). When Stephen Williams wrote to President Styles on June 8th, 1781, he was, as Sheldon notes, "then preparing his valuable 'Appendix' to the 'Redeemed Captive'" (1:168) in which Eunice's story was entirely omitted; and in which Hope Atherton was mentioned only once, as "a gentleman of publick spirit" who "accompanied the army." Stephen Williams's subversion, containment, and eventual erasure of his sister's successful transculturation shaped his parallel subordination of Atherton's nonconformist story to that of Jonathan Wells, another boy captive (like Stephen) who returned redeemed (while his sister did not). This comparative, family systems reading (of triangulated trauma and the politics of race and ethnicity) signals nested, contested escapes among several other transculturated early modern individuals whose remarkably complex lives warrant further study.[241]

Sheldon's source for the letter that Howe disruptively adapts, and for the narratives concerning Jonathan Wells and Hope Atherton, are manuscripts "from which some vandal has cut the signature, but clearly in the handwriting of Steen, son of Rev. John Williams, dated 'Springfield, L. M., [Long Meadow,] Feb. 1, 1731-2'" (1:161). After deciphering the handwriting of Steen/Stephen, Sheldon then invokes another source and other hands/figures involved in this swerving transmission of papers and documents from person to person across time: "The substance of this was published by Rev. John Taylor, in an appendix to the 'Redeemed Captive', in 1793; but as it is intimately connected with our narrative, it seems fitting to give the entire paper in this place. Mr. Taylor prefaces the story by saying it was 'the substance of an attested copy of the account, taken from his own mouth'." That is: verbatim *from the mouth* of Jonathan Wells as attested (through Sheldon's narrative framing) by Rev. John Taylor's 1793/5 preface to the story's publication (in Stephen Williams's Appendix to *The Redeemed Captive*) in which Taylor describes the story as *the substance of an attested copy of the account*. In this meta-historical preface to the embedded narrative, "Escape of Jonathan Wells," Sheldon thus traces a path of inter-/intra-textual transmission: from Jonathan Wells's verbal account to Stephen Williams's manuscript of that story, which Williams then progressively edited and revised in subsequent publications of his Appendix to *The Redeemed Captive*, which (following Stephen Williams's death in 1782)

---

[241] See Derounian-Stodola, and Levernier, 158-166.

Rev. Taylor then edited and republished in 1793/5. As we shall see, Sheldon claims, critically, his own direct connection to the Williams papers, which are among his primary palimpsests for the Jonathan Wells and the Hope Atherton narratives.

Sheldon continues: "At the date of this manuscript, Mr. Wells, the hero in fact and name, was living in Deerfield, where he died January 3rd, 1738-9" (1:161). Stephen Williams's letter to President Styles is dated June 8th, 1781. In this preface to the Wells story, Sheldon establishes key contradictions and paradoxes at the circumferential center of this convoluted path of textual transmission: an ostensibly direct connection between Stephen Williams and Jonathan Wells; and Wells's heroic stature as the boy captive (who reputedly rescued Hope Atherton among others escaping from the military rout). Sheldon then concludes this paragraph by proleptically invoking a "tradition elucidating one point in the story"—that is, Stephen Williams's letter that will be placed several pages later as a concluding subversion and containment of Hope Atherton's narrative: "To this paper will be added some statements connected with it, from other manuscript[s] in the same handwriting, together with a tradition elucidating one point in the story" (1:161).

Sheldon's meta-history then presents "Escape of Jonathan Wells" as a typographic transcription *from the mouth* of Wells (as edited and republished by John Williams, Stephen Williams, and Rev. Taylor). Wells's narrative tells the story of his struggle, during the military rout following the Peskeompskutt massacre, to protect his comrades, including John Johns (who was seriously wounded during the military action and later abandoned in the forest by Wells) and Stephen Belding (whose life was saved by Wells). Wells's story of his time in the wilderness, however, makes no mention of Hope Atherton. That curious detail is consistent among all of the historical sources that include a true relation of the "Escape of Jonathan Wells."

The supreme irony in that sequence (from J. Wells to J. Williams to S. Williams to Taylor to Sheldon to Judd to Wells & Wells) is that Atherton's nonconformist experience, his narrative, and his legacy are progressively subverted and contained by the emerging discourse of the heroic captivity narrative that, critically, informs the providential, teleological historiography of colonization and conquest during the early modern and modern eras. The first seven word squares in *Articulation* (pages 6-9 in the Wesleyan text) collage a wilderness of phonemes and phrases, texts and transcriptions adapted from Jonathan Wells's narrative among so many others (including the stories of Thomas Reed, Stephen Belding, John Jones, Experience Hindsell, and Benjamin Waite) as they are all co-presently embedded within and interpolated throughout the poem's historical source documents, engaged precisely and precariously in the subversion and containment of transgressive agency. "Deep generations of the old pass over / Surging and separating". Howe's strophic, polyvocal assemblages in *Articulation* amplify the dissonance among all of those inter-/intra-texts in order to release the undervoice from a kindred dissenter.

*   *   *

The *tradition elucidating one point in the story* to which Sheldon refers is precisely the crux of the matter that Howe's reading/writing against the grain disrupts. To echo *Articulation*, these manuscripts and printed texts from Stephen Williams are contested, nested, unstable adaptations from transcriptions based upon 'true' relations of accounts of "fleeting communication // Carried away before a pursuer / Demonstration[s] in a string of definitions". Sheldon sets all of this in motion as a preface to the embedded narrative, "Escape of Jonathan Wells" (1:161-166), which (in Sheldon's sequence of inter-/intra-texts) precedes "Mr. Atherton's Story" (1:166-168), which, in turn, is interrupted and concluded by Stephen Williams's letter to President Styles (1:168-169), which subordinates Atherton's experience not only to Wells's reputed heroism during the rout (as if Hope had also been saved by Wells) but also, critically, to Wells's supposed proximity to Atherton's published narrative: as if Wells had been given *the paper from which this is copied*; and/or as if Wells had received that document directly from Joseph

Atherton; and/or as if Wells could either be mistaken (or could become a surrogate) for Atherton's *only son*.

Sheldon's meta-history concerning the transmission of Hope's story also follows a similar (yet even more tenuous) convoluted path compared to the genealogy for Jonathan Wells's narrative. After Wells's story (1:161-166) Sheldon introduces Atherton's transcribed, edited text by way of his (that is, Sheldon's) highly mediated access to the Williams papers, which articulate their own purportedly direct access to Hope's story:

> On another paper Mr. Williams refers "to an account of the wonderful providence of God towards the Rev. Mr. Hope Atherton, who was likewise in the expedition. He was unhorsed, lost & left & would have surrendered himself to the [I]ndians, but they would not receive him but ran from him. He got over the Great River and got safe into Hadley. This account was drawn up by himself, and signed by himself, but the account would be too long to insert in this extract, &c." (1:166)

Here, Stephen Williams simultaneously affirms—*this account was drawn up by himself, and signed by himself*—and also undermines the integrity of this claim of direct access to Atherton's original account of his ordeal, which *would be too long to insert in this extract, &c.*. Sheldon then explains away any lingering doubts: "When Mr. Williams wrote the above meagre abstract, the original MS. was in his possession. A copy of this follows:—" (1:166). In these curious lines, Sheldon asserts, critically, that Stephen Williams had *in his possession* Hope Atherton's original manuscript, but chose to include only a transcribed excerpt in his Appendix to *The Redeemed Captive*. Also in this passage, which introduces "Mr. Atherton's Story," Sheldon charts his own path of mediated access to the 'original' Atherton narrative by way of the Williams papers, *a copy of which follows*.

After presenting Hope's narrative, Sheldon outlines the trail of inter-/intra-textual palimpsests, a path that inadvertently (and tellingly) undermines his claim of direct access to Hope's original manuscript (among the Williams papers):

> This interesting narrative has been long lost and sought for. At length it has been discovered, and can now be traced directly back to the hands of the author. Mr. Atherton never recovered from the effects of his terrible experience, and died June 4th, 1677. His only surviving son, Joseph, settled in Deerfield. The paper was loaned by him to Lieut. Timothy Childs, and was seen in his hands by Ebenezer Grant, who, by leave of Atherton, sent it to Rev. Stephen Williams, who was then preparing his valuable "Appendix" to the "Redeemed Captive." Mr. Williams made a copy of this, and doubtless sent back the original to the owner, according to the conditions of the loan. Who among the Athertons has the *original*? (1:168)

According to this relation, Hope's manuscript traveled from him to his son, Joseph, who then loaned it to Lieut. Timothy Childs; those papers, in the hands of Childs, were witnessed by Ebenezer Grant, who was given permission by Joseph Atherton to send the manuscript to Stephen Williams, who then made a copy *and doubtless sent back the original to the owner, according to the conditions of the loan*. In these lines, Sheldon reveals that he only has access to Williams's edited copy of Atherton's story, and that the original manuscript has not actually been discovered, but in fact continues to be *long lost and sought for*. "Who among the Athertons has the *original*?"

Notwithstanding these embedded contradictions and paradoxes, Sheldon continues, in the next paragraph, with his genealogy of textual transmission, claiming direct access to the original Atherton manuscript while also amplifying the many layers of remediation involved in his edited adaptation of "Mr. Atherton's Story" as subverted and contained by the historiography of Jonathan Wells's heroic journey through the wilderness:

> In 1781, Mr. Williams sends his copy to Pres. Ezra Stiles; and in 1857, Dr. Henry R., son of Ezra Stiles, sends it to Sylvester Judd, and J. R. Trumbull of Northampton has recently found it in the Judd collection of MSS. Mr. Trumbull has kindly sent me a *verbatim* copy, which it seems fitting to print, with the accompanying letter. The story of Jonathan Wells confirms the correctness of Atherton's narrative. (1:168)

Sheldon's version of Hope Atherton's story thus emerges from Trumbull's *verbatim* copy of Stephen Williams's edited adaptation of the narrative (produced within the context of his ongoing work with *The Redeemed Captive*) which Trumbull found in the Judd collection of manuscripts and then sent to Sheldon. Judd's document was given to him by Henry R, son of President Styles to whom Stephen Williams sent his edited excerpt of the Atherton narrative which, as his letter of June 8th, 1781 recounts, emerges from a copy of a paper of an account of a related account of an experience related in a copy of a paper lost and then found among other papers. This is precisely the nested and contested, ideological and discursive basis of Sheldon's claim that the Atherton manuscript has *been discovered, and can now be traced directly back to the hands of the author*. Sheldon's concluding sentence in this paragraph underscores yet once more the subversion/containment dialectic of colonization and conquest: "The story of Jonathan Wells confirms the correctness of Atherton's narrative." The next paragraph in Sheldon's text introduces the *"EXTRACT from a LETTER"* that subordinates Atherton's story to that of Wells. Howe's radical contingency, historical figuration, and factual telepathy in *Articulation* unsettle this palimpsestic genealogy of teleological heroism, this inter-/intra-textual "Summary of fleeting summary / Pseudonym[s] cast across empty // Peak proud heart".

Sheldon's meta-discourse thus navigates a labyrinth of materials in order to accommodate Atherton's nonconformist experience to the logic and rhetoric of the *peak proud heart* captivity narrative as exemplified by Jonathan Wells, "the hero in fact and name [...] then aged 16 years and 2 or 3 months who was in the action [at the Falls Fight, May 19th]" (1:161-162). In Sheldon's narrative concerning "Turners Falls Fight" (1:152-171), "Escape of Jonathan Wells" not only precedes "Mr. Atherton's Story" but, critically, interrupts and then supersedes Hope's account by way of Stephen Williams's letter that subverts/contains Atherton's experience via Wells's reputed authority to which Williams adds not only his approval—"The [Atherton] account is doubtless true, for Jonathan Wells, Esq., who was in the fight and lived afterward at Deerfield"—but, critically, his dubious claims of direct access to the original documents. Sheldon recapitulates those micro-narratives that amplify the many contested, nested layers of remediation involved in these complex networks of textual exchange and erasure.

*   *   *

Howe's disjunctive openwork sequence of materials and methods from *Articulation* to *The Quarry* ironically amplifies and thereby deconstructs all of these contradictions and paradoxes, engaging modalities and tropes from early modern captivity narratives and embedded inter-/intra-texts (from the palimpsests of her meta-historical source texts) in order to recover, remediate, and release Hope Atherton's erasure from those very narratives that subordinate his story to the ideology and historiography of colonization and conquest (as exemplified by Jonathan Wells's heroic narrative and legacy). Howe's poetics and praxis reads/writes history against the grain, dehiscing linguistic seeds of regenerative sound forms in time, assuming "Hope Atherton's excursion for an emblem foreshadowing a Poet's abolished limitations in our demythologized fantasy of Manifest Destiny" (*Singularities*, 4).

In "The Falls Fight," which in *Singularities* (4) precedes the *EXTRACT*, Howe includes language from Stephen Williams's Appendix (199) to *The Redeemed Captive* (1795) that amplifies the myth of Atherton's military service alongside Jonathan Wells: "The Rev. Hope Atherton, minister of the gospel, at Hatfield, a gentleman of publick spirit, accompanied the army. The pilots were Messrs. Benjamin Wait, and Experience Hinsdale."[242] The post-Williams historiographies from Sheldon (1895-1896), Judd (1905), and Wells & Wells (1910) each narrate, in varying degrees, these contrasting and increasingly conflated views of Atherton's role as both minister and soldier. Howe's deft, deviant adaptations of Stephen Williams's letter (in different ways in both the Awede and Wesleyan texts of *Articulation*) spark these disruptive interventions, illuminating a network of documents, manuscripts, and texts that shape these conflicting views of Atherton's agency at Peskeompskutt.

    from seaweed said nor repossess rest
    scape esaid

The following details (which are consistent among all of the above-noted historiographies) are especially revealing: Jonathan Wells and Hope Atherton were, in fact, not together in the forest at any time as they fled the aftermath of the massacre. Their journeys were parallel, but their paths did not cross.

None of the historiographies document Atherton's participation in the military action; furthermore, Hope's printed narrative (as presented within the texts from Sheldon, Judd, Wells & Wells, and also Tucker) makes no mention whatsoever of his readiness to fire a weapon or his having done so. Hope's narrative does not mention Jonathan Wells; likewise, Wells's story (about his own escape) makes no mention of Atherton. The only account given by Wells concerning Atherton may be found in Stephen Williams's letter in which (as Williams narrates) Wells does not include Atherton in his own story of rescue and return, but rather mocks Hope afterwards by way of hearsay: "the *Indians* told *him* [i.e. Wells] that after the fall fight, that a little man with a black coat and

---

[242] John Williams (1908): https://archive.org/stream/redeemedcaptive00willrich/redeemedcaptive00willrich_djvu.txt[.]

without any hat, came toward them, but they were afraid and ran from him, thinking it was the Englishman's God, etc., etc.." Stephen Williams's account of this rumor forms the basis for the subsequent historiographies from Sheldon to Judd to Wells & Wells: "Many people were not willing to credit the story of the escape, suggesting that [Atherton] was beside himself [...] The truth of his account is confirmed by the statement of Jonathan Wells [...]."[243] Reading/writing against the grain, following *Articulation*, we thus find an "Impulsion of a myth of beginning / The figure of a far-off Wanderer".

Atherton's role at Peskeompskutt was problematic: for the soldiers, especially during the rout; for his community's reception of his unbelievable and undesirable story; and for his historiographers who would rather sing praises of Jonathan Wells than acknowledge the unfortunate demise of Hatfield's first minister. *The Redeemed Captive* thus initiates what Sheldon (1:161) describes as "a tradition [of] elucidating" these troublesome details through the subversion and containment of Atherton's nonconformist story via the myth that Wells was Hope's comrade-in-arms: *in this action was also the Rev. Mr. Atherton*. In "The Falls Fight," Howe sagaciously tracks Atherton's curiously abrupt disappearance from the soldiers: "Except for Hope Atherton and seven or eight others who were somehow separated from their fellows. These Christian soldiers soon found themselves lost" (4). The sentences that immediately follow in this paragraph from *Singularities* have nothing further to say about Atherton (which is precisely Howe's point) but rather relate details from Jonathan Wells's narrative—that is, the story that has supplanted Hope's. Howe's radical contingency here ironically stages and thereby critiques Atherton's historiographic erasure, as the text concludes several sentences later on the same page: "Hope's literal attributes. Effaced background dissolves remotest foreground. Putative author, premodern condition, presently present what future clamors for release?" (4).

---

[243] Wells & Wells (1910): http://www.archive.org/stream/ahistoryhatfiel00wellgoog/ahistoryhatfiel00wellgoog_djvu.txt[.]

Jonathan Wells's narrative of escape, in fact, makes no mention of Atherton; likewise, Hope's story has nothing whatsoever to say about the heroism of Jonathan Wells during Atherton's flight through the wilderness. These details and omissions are consistent across all of the historical source texts that shaped Howe's research and writing process from *Articulation* to *The Quarry*.

Also consistent among those historiographies that reproduce Atherton's narrative are the following uncanny remarks about his experience during the chaotic moments that sparked his solitary journey: "I was in eminent danger through an instrument of death: a gun was discharged against me at a small distance, the Lord diverted the bullet so that no harm was done me. When I was separated from the army, none pursued after me [...]" (Sheldon, 1:166-167; Tucker, 67-68).

Atherton interprets this provocation and his subsequent abandonment as justified punishment (for what, exactly, he does not say): "[...], as if God had given the heathen a charge, saying, let him alone he shall have his life for a prey." A common refrain among Puritan colonists would draw upon Psalms 2.8: "Ask of me, and I shall give *thee* the heathen *for* thine inheritance, and the uttermost parts of the earth *for* thy possession."[244] The word *heathen* appears numerous times in Sheldon's *History of Deerfield*, and only once in Hope Atherton's true relation (which is a printed transcription from his sermon to his congregation after his return). Such language of systemic prejudice[245] contrasts with

---

[244] The Holy Bible: King James Version (New York: Meridian, 1974), 466.

[245] During the seventeenth century, the discourse of colonization and conquest in North America strategically engaged the word *savage* to signify both *nonperson* and *nonland*. See, for example, John Smith, *The generall historie of Virginia, New-England, and the Summer Isles with the names of the adventurers, planters, and governours from their first beginning. an0: 1584. to this present 1624. With the procedings of those severall colonies and the accidents that befell them in all their journyes and discoveries Also the maps and descriptions of all those countryes, their commodities, people, government, customes, and religion yet knowne. Divided into six bookes. By Captaine Iohn Smith sometymes governour in those countryes & admirall of New England* (London: Printed by I[ohn] D[awson] and I[ohn] H[aviland] for Michael Sparkes, 1624), 68, 144-145; and Samuel Purchas, *Hakluytus Posthumus or Purchas his pilgrimes. Contayning a history of the world, in sea voyages & lande-travells, by Englishmen*

Hope's subsequent statement that his gestures of surrender were denied without force or violence: "They accepted not the tender which I made, when I spake, they answered not, when I moved toward them they moved away from me. I expected they would have laid hands upon me, but they did not" (Sheldon, 1:167; Tucker, 68). Perhaps amplifying Atherton's ambivalent feelings of gratitude and shame, those minimal acknowledgments of shared humanity find their unequivocal predication through Hope's invocation of divine agency: "Enemies cannot do what they will, but are subservient to over-ruling providence of God."

Where the historiographers (beginning with Stephen Williams) relate that "Mr. Atherton was unhorsed and separated from the company," Howe reads/writes against the grain, listening closely to the absent presence of "bullets from the blue" (*Souls*, 13; *The Quarry*, 51). Who fired a gun at Hope Atherton *at a small distance*, and for what reason? By accident, or accidentally on purpose? None of the historical texts that include Hope's narrative comment upon this most troublesome detail in Atherton's testimony despite that fact's persistence among all of the texts that reproduce Hope's story. That explosive silence speaks volumes through Howe's poetics and praxis: "Bright armies wolves warriors steers // scorned warning captive compulsion".

(I will return to this matter after further reflections, in this essay's following sections, upon the cultures of colonization and conquest that shaped early modern New England captivity narratives, land acquisition economics and politics, and the business of the Atherton family—all of

---

& others. Wherein Gods wonders in nature & providence, the actes, arts, varieties, & vanities of men, with a world of the worlds rarities, are by a world of eywitnesse-authors, related to the world. Some left written by M. Hakluyt at his death. More since added. His also perused & perfected. All examined, abreviated with discourse. Adorned with pictues and expressed in mapps. In fower parts. Each containing five bookes (London: by W. Stansby for H. Fetherstone, 1625), Vol. IV, 1814. Neither the Geneva Bible nor the King James Bible use the word *savage*. The word appears countless times, however, in Sheldon's *History of Deerfield*, and not once in Hope Atherton's narrative. See also Jennings for a rich, deconstructive genealogy of the myth of savagery (6-12, 15-16, 31, 46, 59, 60-61, 73-74, 76, 77-78, 80-81, 109-110, 119-120, 127, 146, 154-155, 158-159, 160, 299, 334).

which, in my reading of the evidence, compelled Hope Atherton to accompany the military, to abandon the Peskeompskutt massacre, and consequently to be fired upon and abandoned by the military.)

Why was Hope's story not believed? And how did his ordeal shape his final days? According to Howe's text in *Singularities*, "No one believed the Minister's letter. He became a stranger to his community and died soon after the traumatic exposure that has earned him poor mention in a seldom opened book" (4). In the eyes of his fellow villagers, Hope had returned home as a coward; his feelings of shame must have been beyond measure.

In his letter to President Styles, Stephen Williams underscores his interpretation of the elements in Atherton's story that were most vexing for his congregation: becoming separated from (or deserting) the military; claiming to have crossed the Connecticut River from west to east (thanks to divine intervention); and embellishing his unsuccessful efforts to surrender himself. Williams then concludes that "Many people were not willing to give credit to his account, suggesting that he was beside himself" (Sheldon 1:168-169). According to Tucker, "after the terrible physical and nervous ordeal" (which was compounded by a subsequent, retaliatory Indian attack upon the settlement of Hatfield on Tuesday, May 30) Hope "lived for more than a year" but "never recovered" (70) and died on June 8, 1677. According to Wells & Wells: "He never recovered from the exposure [...] The story of his remarkable escape was read by him to his congregation after his sermon on Sunday, May 28" (85). Judd is especially critical of Atherton's claims and state of mind: "Some persons, in those days, imagined that Mr. Atherton had been partially deranged, and had deceived himself. He did not admit this" (173). According to Sheldon, "Mr. Atherton never recovered from the effects of his terrible experience, and died June 4th, 1677" (1:168).

All of these historical source texts[246] follow the narrative and rhetorical strategies established by John Williams and then amplified by

---

[246] At least one of Atherton's nineteenth-century historiographers expresses an awareness of the degree to which John and Stephen Williams emend Hope's story to their own purposes. See Trumbull (1: 335).

Stephen Williams in their many editions of *The Redeemed Captive*. In the legacy of the Peskeompskutt massacre, Jonathan Wells emerges as the heroic figure—the boy captive who saved others during the rout and returned redeemed—whose narrative subverts and contains Hope Atherton's nonconformist experience: "Mr. Wells arrived at Hatfield on the Sabbath, between meetings, and was received with inexpressible joy, as one having arisen from the dead" (Stephen Williams, Appendix, 207).

Atherton's historiographers deploy these narrative strategies in order to gloss over those aspects of Hope's sermon that were antithetical to the ideology and rhetoric of the captivity narrative: that he was fired upon by someone in the army; that he was subsequently abandoned by the militia; that he was neither harmed nor taken captive by Indians despite his repeated efforts to surrender himself; and that he was either protectively borne by Native peoples across the Quinetucket River, or providentially buoyed from west to east. These details in Hope's account made his sermon unbelievable and undesirable for his community (and his historiographers) because, in these troubling ways, his narrative was deviating from the emerging story lines for the captivity narrative and other related forms of discourse (such as the conversion narrative and the true relation). Furthermore, in my reading of the evidence (which I will discuss, below) there were other pressing matters compelling and conflicting Hope's presence at Peskeompskutt, all of which amplified the dynamics that shaped his community's rejection of his experience.

*   *   *

Atherton's historiographers accommodate his nonconformity to the emerging standards of the captivity narrative, one of which concerns the documentation of a genealogy for the narrative's transmission *from the mouth* and/or *from the hands of the author* directly to the custodians, editors, and publishers of the story—that is, a sequence of textual adaptations, each foregrounding the palimpsest's *immediacy through remediation* (Derounian-Stodola, and Levernier, 8-15). Such meta-narratives thereby establish the vexed authenticity and reproducibility of Hope's story (subverted/contained by Wells's story) as evidence for the teleological, providential unfolding of colonization and conquest. In these important ways, the radical indeterminacy of Atherton's narrativized subordination to Wells's legendary heroism performs, in the wake of the military rout, the ideological and discursive reification of the colonial encounter with threatening, uncontainable otherness.

To echo Stratton's incisive syncretic reading, the "essential power of the prevailing system of colonial representation lies in its capacity to synthesize and maintain the seemingly incongruous attributes" of recalcitrant, recirculated, and reputed discursive stability, which is, itself, the product of violent confrontations with (and subordinations of) irremediable alterity.[247] After the military rout, the progressive historiographic subversion and containment of Atherton's nonconformist experience was profoundly informed by the triangulation of colonial desire for a sacrificial victim—in this case, a local and deeply conflicted sacred/secular exemplar of what René Girard[248] theorizes as the *monstrous double*—to substitute for the threatening otherness of Native survivance that, following Gerald Vizenor's articulation (19), renounces tragedy and victimry. As Girard (165) and Bhabha (66) also discern, these moments of hegemonic reification engender reproducible ruptures (linguistic/textual, bodily/visceral) in subjectivities and negations of identities that perpetuate cycles of reciprocal violence.

As we have seen, Stephen Williams claims to have a verbatim transcription of this heroic story *from the mouth* of Jonathan Wells, a claim

---

[247] *Buried in Shades of Night*, 16. See also Edward Said, *Orientalism* (New York: Vintage, 1978), 58; Homi Bhabha, *The Location of Culture* (London: Routledge, 1994), 66; and Jacques Derrida, "Signature Event Context," *Margins of Philosophy*, trans. Alan Bass (Chicago: University of Chicago Press, 1982), 313.

[248] *Violence and the Sacred*, trans. Patrick Gregory (Baltimore: The Johns Hopkins University Press, 1977). "Under the heading *monstrous double* we shall group all the hallucinatory phenomena provoked at the height of the crisis by unrecognized reciprocity. The monstrous double is also to be found wherever we encounter an 'I' and an 'Other' caught up in a constant interchange of differences" (164).

that is recapitulated by Rev. John Taylor and the subsequent historiographers (Sheldon, Judd, Wells & Wells) who amplify Wells's heroism as a foil to Atherton's unbelievable and undesirable claims. This dialectical strategy of subversion and containment engenders a cluster of mythologies in the historical source texts: that Wells and Atherton were comrades during and after the military action; that Wells either protected or rescued Atherton; that Atherton transmitted his story to Wells; and that Wells's story corroborates (and thereby supersedes) Atherton's narrative. The Awede text of *Articulation* amplifies and thereby critiques these nested, contested mythemes through the uncanny substitution (in Howe's adaptation of Stephen Williams's letter) of Jonathan Wells, Esq. for Hope Atherton's *only son*: "This occasioned him [Hope Atherton] to publish to his congregation and leave in writing the account I enclose to you. I had the paper from which this is copied, from his only son Jonathan Wells, Esq., who was in the [Great Falls] fight and lived afterward at Deerfield […]."

Both the Awede and Wesleyan texts omit, critically, "The account is doubtless true" (which appears in Williams's letter as represented by Howe's source texts), thereby dismantling any claims, in the remediated *EXTRACT*, to accuracy and ownership (concerning the Atherton narrative) from J. Wells, J. Williams, S. Williams, Taylor, Sheldon, Judd, and Wells & Wells. In the Wesleyan text of *Articulation*, Howe furthers these incisive readings/writings against the grain by altogether deleting "his only son" from Williams's *EXTRACT*, thereby amplifying the text's radically contingent erasure of Hope's "only surviving son, Joseph, [who] settled in Deerfield" (Sheldon, 1:168)—who was, in fact, the first custodian of his father's narrative—and thereby also deconstructing (through exaggerated irony) the myth of Jonathan Wells's role as rightful curator of Atherton's narrative: "I had the paper from which this is copied, from Jonathan Wells, Esq." (*Singularities*, 5).

If the Awede text prompts a nexus of critical reflections—*who transcribed and published Atherton's sermon? how did Stephen Williams acquire the document? why would Jonathan Wells be misrecognized as Hope's only son? why would Atherton give his narrative to Wells? how and why did Hope's story change in each stage of the document's transmission? how and why do the poem's historical source texts narrate these textual exchanges and erasures?*—then the Wesleyan text amplifies those questions and concerns.

Howe's Awede and Wesleyan texts of *Articulation* thus dramatize these embedded contradictions and paradoxes among inter-/intra-texts, which, if left unchecked, would perpetuate the subversion and containment of Hope's story within the fold of captivity narratives that have been transcribed, edited, collected, and transmitted in the service of bolstering the ideology and historiography of Manifest Destiny, which Howe's radical contingency and historical figuration dismantle within and against the grain of Hope's narrativization: "Scion on a ledge of Constitution / Wedged sequences of system // Causeway of faint famed city / Human ferocity". Whereas Atherton's historiographers delineate the networked frames of reference among and between these vexed inter-/intra-texts, thereby establishing a meta-narrative that accommodates deviant stories to the logic of colonization and conquest, Howe's *Articulation* ironically exaggerates, exposes, and explodes those lines of textual demarcation, ideological reification, and teleological momentum. Howe's disjunctive sequence of materials and methods from *Articulation* to *The Quarry* thereby confronts us with the transformative forces of constitutive tropological poetics and praxis, hurling the reader into the poem's telepathic transmission of the disaster's typographic and spatio-temporal immanence/imminence. Across and between, within and against the discourse of colonization and conquest that would interpolate (and thereby capture) encounters with irremediable otherness as providential *signs taken for wonders*, Howe's methods deconstruct those deeply embedded contradictions through gestures of recovery, remediation, and regenerative release: "Rugged solacing on surge sheltering".

These are some of the facts from what must be untold through counter-factual means, through the poem's disruptive openwork articulations of the story that cannot be told as such. Atherton's historiographers attempted to contain the alterity of his experience by substantiating their reputed direct access to Hope's sermon through his story's successive adaptations and subordinations to Jonathan Wells's heroic legacy: "Gone and signal through deep water / Mr. Atherton's story Hope Atherton". Howe's poetics and praxis destabilizes and dispels these discursive and ideological forms of colonization and conquest as "infinite miscalculation[s] of history". *Articulation* speaks truth to power.

*　　　*　　　*

Few of the poem's readers have taken any steps toward engaging Howe's historical sources; those who have considered such a path have dismissed the significance of those texts for the poem's primary concerns. None of the poem's readers have yet observed the critical intersection of historiographic points addressed in this essay; none have yet considered the degree to which *Articulation* reads/writes those historiographies of "Patriarchal prophesy at heels of hope / Futurity" against the grain—that is, how the poem deconstructs colonialist and nationalist discourses that have supplanted Hope Atherton's nonconformist story with heroic narratives that reaffirm providential and teleological paradigms; and none have yet studied the poem's progressive critique, informed by the rhetoric of captivity narratives, across the work's disjunctive, sequential elaborations from the Awede text of *Articulation* to *The Quarry's* "Personal Narrative."

In the following sections, this essay will amplify those aspects of my argument (from *Articulation* to *The Quarry*) vis-à-vis comparative readings of Howe's embedded inter-/intra-texts that destabilize the poem's source documents; through methodological counter-readings of the works of Nicholls (1996), Back (2002), Frost (2003), and Gaffield (2015) among others who have turned away from Howe's source materials; and via contextualized investigations of the cultures of colonization and conquest that shaped early modern New England captivity narratives, land acquisition economics and politics, and the business of the Atherton family—all of which, in my reading of the evidence, compelled Hope Atherton to accompany the militia and to abandon the Peskeompskutt massacre.

> from seaweed said nor repossess rest
> scape esaid

In this charged, tropological field of echoes and erasures, Hope's words are not his alone; they are deeply embedded among the various inter-/intra-texts remediated through the poem's meta-historiographic sources. Howe's disruptive, intersectional methods amplify the innumerable contradictions and paradoxes involved among those palimpsests in the progressive subversion and containment of Atherton's experience, narrative, and legacy. The poem's openwork counter-paths from 1987 to 2015 rescue, remediate, and release Hope's story within and through, between and across this archival/artifactual wilderness: "True wildness is like true gold; it will bear the trial of Dewey Decimal."[249]

In the 2009 presentation of those lines, Howe counters their propitious resonance by concluding her essay, thus: "Kneel to intellect in our work / Chaos cast cold intellect back" (204). In each instance of the poem's sequential forms, Howe integrates such deft, disruptive variations: as illustrated by the more overt (and, in some ways, quite problematic) adaptations of *Articulation* from the Awede to the Wesleyan text; as well as by the more subtle (and yet also significant) remediations of "Personal Narrative" in 2007, 2009, and 2015. Howe's reading/writing against the grain of her many historical source documents liberates Atherton's legacy from historiographic subversion and containment, thereby regenerating the languages of our shared experience *in the field of history*. The poem's disjunctive reconfigurations chart a trans-generational project of immanent/imminent recovery, remediation, and regenerative release through the articulation of sound forms in time:

> If I were to read aloud a passage from a poem of your choice, to an audience of judges in sympathy with surrounding

---

[249] "Personal Narrative," *Souls of the Labadie Tract*, 19; "Writing *Articulation of Sound Forms in Time*," *The Sound of Poetry/The Poetry of Sound*, 204; and "Personal Narrative," *The Quarry*, 56.

library nature, and they were to experience its lexical inscape as an offshoot of Anglo-American modernism in typographical format, it might be possible to release our great-great-grandparents, beginning at the greatest distance from a common mouth, eternally belated, some coming home through dark ages, others nearer to early modern, multitudes of them meeting first to constitute certain main branches of etymologies, so all along there are new sources, some running directly contrary to others, and yet all meet at last, clothed in robes of glory, offering maps of languages, some with shining tones. (*The Quarry*, 56)

For Howe, such inter-/intra-textual encounters are physical events "of immediate revelation" (*The Birth-mark*, 1) that telepathically transmit, through a "space-time phenomenon", "other people's struggles and their voices", their sounds and spirits "(ghosts if you like)" which "leave traces in a geography [...] of the spirit of the place" (*The Birth-mark*, 156). Howe's radical contingency imbricates/intercalates the spiritual and temporal, geographic and typographic manifestations of language "so intimately ... that it seems permissible to discover everywhere [their] chance correspondences"[250] yet without invoking even the slightest trace of elevation/transcendence and cancellation/oblivion.

Howe's poetics and praxis, in this regard, differs slightly yet significantly from Benjamin's. Howe and Benjamin agree that "Historical ma-

---

[250] Susan Howe, "The Poet and the World of Her Influences: Lyn Hejinian, Susan Howe, Myung Mi Kim," Mills College, Oakland, October 11, 1993; cited in Simpson, *Poetic Epistemologies*, 186. As Simpson insightfully notes, in these lines, Howe echoes Arendt's introduction to Benjamin's *Illuminations*: "The theoretical aspect that was bound to fascinate him was the doctrine of the superstructure" which Benjamin used "only as a heuristic-methodological stimulus" without any serious interest "in its historical or philosophical background. What fascinated him about the matter was that the spirit and its material manifestation were so intimately connected that it seemed permissible to discover everywhere Baudelaire's *correspondences*, which clarified and illuminated one another if they were properly correlated, so that finally they would no longer require any interpretative or explanatory commentary" (11).

terialism wishes to retain that image of the past which unexpectedly appears" as "singled out by history at a moment of danger;" and that in "every era the attempt must be made anew to wrest tradition away from a conformism that is about to overpower it" (255). They differ, critically, in terms of their respective methods for encountering "a historical subject [...] as a monad" (263). For Benjamin, such encounters signal a "revolutionary chance in the fight for the oppressed past," and call for "blasting a specific life out of the era or a specific work out of the lifework" (263)—a counter-method that (as Arendt and Zohn observe) minimally retains a trace of the Hegelian dialectic of *aufheben* "in its threefold meaning: to preserve, to elevate, to cancel" (263). Although this singular footnote from Arendt and Zohn provides such acknowledgment, Arendt, in her introduction to *Illuminations*, refutes the relevance of dialectical materialism in Benjamin's poetic thinking: "That such thinking should ever have bothered with a consistent, dialectically sensible, rationally explainable process seems absurd" (13).

Arendt's incisive discussions of Benjamin's celebrated tropes of the *flâneur* and of the *angel of history* underscore the significance, for his thought, of non-dialectical fusions of "word and thing, idea and experience" coinciding in the smallest of objects that "could contain in the most concentrated form everything else" (12). In those respects, Benjamin and Howe are kindred spirits. However, Arendt's meditation on the *flâneur's* "final transfiguration" (13) in the angel of history (which Benjamin saw in Klee's celebrated "Angelus Novus") offers a telling contrast with Howe's radical contingency, historical figuration, and factual telepathy in *Articulation*. For Arendt, Benjamin's trope of the angel—which is to say, his comparative interpretation of Klee's 1920 monoprint and Gerhard Scholem's "Gruss vom Angelus"—"does not dialectically move forward into the future" but "is blown backwards into the future by the storm of progress" (12-13). Noticeably absent from Arendt's discussion is any reflection upon Scholem's poem, which expresses the futility of staying *"timeless time"* (257) that finds an echo in Benjamin's lines: "a storm is blowing from Paradise; it has got caught in his wings with such violence that the angel can no longer close them" (257-258).

Whether facing backward or forward, Benjamin's angel cannot quite yet escape the teleological momentum—the timeless time—of the storm that "we call progress" which "irresistibly propels him into the future [...,] while the pile of debris before him grows skyward" (258). This ineluctable apocalyptic force in Benjamin's thought in his "Theses on the Philosophy of History" echoes the dialectical teleology of Hegel's transcendental system.

There is no such apocalyptic angel in Howe's *Articulation*; no such inescapable teleological catastrophic force against which the poem tragically strives to "make whole what has been smashed" (Benjamin, 257). Howe's poetics and praxis across this work's disjunctive sequence from the Awede text to *The Quarry's* "Personal Narrative" subverts origins and endings, deconstructing the works of the "historians themselves who have transformed narrativity from a manner of speaking into a paradigm of the form that reality itself displays to a 'realistic' consciousness" (White, 24). Howe reads/writes the poem's historiographic sources against the grain, amplifying the contradictions and paradoxes embedded in their "empty frame[s] of a linear succession which formally answers to questions on *beginning* and to the need for *order*" (De Certeau, 12). Within and against the discursive field of subversion and containment that would, if left unchecked, perpetuate an "invisible power that is invested in [the] dehistoricized figure of Man" narrativized and thereby constituted "at the cost of those 'others'—women, natives, the colonized, the indentured and enslaved—who, at the same time but in other spaces, were becoming the peoples without a history" (Bhabha, 282), Howe's historical figuration recovers, remediates, and releases the poem's "Cries open to the words inside them / Cries hurled through the Woods" between and within, through and across the work's centripetal and centrifugal, *kairic* articulation of sound forms in time.

Within and against such a syncretic counter-historiographic methodology, however, more nuanced critical and ethical differentiations are warranted, especially at the level of Howe's polyvocal word squares in *Articulation* that collage word roots and cognates from a dizzying range of languages, including Greek and Latin; French and German; Anglo

Saxon, Old Irish, and Old Norse; and Algonquian and Iroquoian. In reading/writing against the grain of the poem's historiographic sources—that is, to echo Benjamin, *documents of barbarism*—Howe's poetics and praxis encounters a fundamental contradiction/paradox similar to and yet significantly different from Philip's realization that the story that cannot be told "is locked within the text of those individuals […] who were themselves an integral part of a system that engaged in the trade in humans" (199). In her struggle to assemble *ZONG!*—the story that cannot be told, but which must tell itself as (and through) the impossibility of its own telling—Philip engaged a multifaceted, dynamic method of "fragmentation and mutilation of the text, forcing the eye to track across the page in an attempt to wrest meaning from words gone astray" (198) combined with a hermeneutics of "simultaneously censoring the activity of the reported [legal] text while conjuring the presence of excised Africans, as well as their humanity" (199).

Howe's poetics and praxis questions "every proof of authority and power"—incisively mindful that "records are compiled by winners" and that "scholarship is in collusion with Civil Government"—because she hopes to find "some trace of love's infolding through all the paper in the libraries" that her works and readers encounter (*Birth-mark*, 1993:4). Through the limited presence of Algonquian and Iroquoian words, *Articulation* does not attempt to conjure or to speak for the humanity of the hundreds of Native peoples (many of whom were women and children) who lost their lives during the Peskeompskutt massacre. And yet, the linguistic co-presence of Native words within the discourse of the poem's historiographic texts (which mispronounce and stutter their alterity) amplifies their incommensurable persistence within the context of Howe's word squares. Within and against, across and through these constraints, *Articulation* recognizes the "essential *untranslatability* from […] subaltern discourse[s] to imperialist discourse,"[251] thereby intimating a story of Native survivance that ultimately cannot be told by the

---

[251] Rey Chow, "Where Have All the Natives Gone?," *Displacements: Cultural Identities in Question*, ed. Angelika Bammer (Bloomington and Indianapolis: Indiana University Press, 1994), 132.

poem, but which must nonetheless be told as such through discrete aporetic linguistic and textual/contextual encounters that fold the discourse of colonization and conquest against itself, amplifying the contradictions and paradoxes therein, speaking truth to power.

A more discerning analysis would also account for the nuanced ways in which Howe's poetics and praxis in *Articulation* engages the co-presence of each cultural/linguistic tradition differently and distinctively. Such an incisive macro-/micro-exploration (which has not yet been attempted in the field) lies beyond the scope of my primary concern here with Howe's reading/writing against the grain of Hope Atherton's erasure from his own legacy, which includes his problematic witnessing of the Peskeompskutt massacre, his vexed escape from the military rout, and his uncanny return to Hadley across Quinetucket: "Untraceable wandering / the meaning of knowing // Poetical sea site state / Abstract alien point".

*   *   *

In such dynamic, transformative, and tropological landscapes of imbricated/intercalated archives and artifacts, the polyphonic undervoice in *Articulation* returns anew to the linguistic wilderness of the poem's historiographic sources, disrupting their logic of teleology and providential transcendence. Howe's collagist critiques of the progressive meta-historical subordination of Atherton's nonconformity to Wells's heroic legacy therefore exaggerate the submersion of Hope's voice beneath the literal/littoral surface of Jonathan's narrative, which itself embodies a confluence of other colonial subjects and speakers, defenders and dissidents who also fled into the wilderness.

For example, these two dialetheic passages appear respectively in the Awede text of *Articulation* on recto and verso pages, the first in a sequence of concrete, strophic, polyvocal social lyrics in the poem's first section, "*Hope Atherton's Wanderings*":

Prest try to set after grandmother   Clog nutmeg abt noon

revived by and laid down left ly	scraping cano muzzell
little distant each other and fro	foot path sand and so
Saw digression hobbling driftwood	gravel rubbish vandal
forage two rotted beans & etc.	horse flesh ryal tabl
Redy to faint slaughter story so	sand enemys flood sun
Gone and signal through deep water	Danielle Warnare Servt
Mr. Atherton's story Hope Atherton	Turner Falls Fight us
	Next wearer April One[252]

---

[252] Many echoes from Sheldon's text may be heard in *Articulation*; in these two strophic, polyvocal word squares, tracks may be followed from the nested, contested stories of Stephen Belding, John Jones, and especially of Jonathan Wells, which dominates Sheldon's narrative of those colonists who fled the massacre: "{In this fight for life, as appears by another scrap of our manuscript, he stopped and took up behind him Stephen Belding, a boy companion of sixteen years, who thus escaped.} […] They then separated again & had about ten men left with him, and his horse failing considerably by reason of his wound, & himself spent wth bleeding, he was left with one John Jones, a wounded man likewise. […] These two men were unacquainted wth ye woods, & without anny track or path. J. W. had a gun & J. J. a sword. J. J. represented ye badness of his wounds, & made his companion think they were certainly mortall, and therefore when y^y separated in order to find the path, J. W. was glad to leave him, lest he sh^d be a clog or hindrance to him. Mr. W. grew faint, & once when ye Indians prest him, he was near fainting away, but by eating a nutmeg, (which his grandmother gave him as he was going out) he was revivd. […] Ab^t noon this, & at ab^t sun an hour high at n^t, being disturbed by ye flies, he stopd ye touch hole of his gun & struck fire, & set ye woods on fire […]" (Sheldon, 1:162). In this passage, language surrounded by { } signifies Sheldon's meta-narrative that comments upon his source texts; the rest of the passage derives from Sheldon's transcription of those sources. In Sheldon's narrative (1:153) Danielle Warnare is listed among the men of Hadley, MA, who were prepared to serve alongside Major Savage in the upcoming fight at Peskeompskutt; Sheldon's source for this information is a letter

Although the Awede and Wesleyan texts differ considerably in their respective reconfigurations of *Articulation*—significant differences that will be addressed—both editions emphasize the importance of reading Howe's inter-/intra-textual assemblages within and against, among and between one another, following echoes through the poem's openwork sequence of reading/writing against the grain. For example, in these two word squares (as well as in the poem's subsequent facing pages) Howe's radical contingency imbricates/intercalates words and phrases—*sound forms in time*—from the voices of Stephen Belding, John Jones, Danielle Warnare, Jonathan Wells, and Hope Atherton (among others, including Thomas Reed) whose narratives are entangled among and within the genealogy of historical sources (from J. Wells, J. Williams, S. Williams, Taylor, Sheldon, Judd, Wells & Wells) that subvert and contain Atherton's nonconformist story through the heroic legacy of Jonathan Wells, the boy captive who saved other lost soldiers and returned redeemed.[253] Atherton's voice and narrative thus submerge into the poem's field of archival/artifactual factual telepathy—"Gone and signal through deep water / Mr. Atherton's story Hope Atherton"—reemerging with new emphasis several pages later in this section's closing page: "Loving Friends and Kindred:— / When I look back / So short in charity and good works / We are a small remnant / of signal escapes wonderful in themselves / We march from our camp a little / and come home / Lost the beaten track and so".

At every instance of its utterance throughout *Articulation*, Atherton's *undervoice* speaks within and against, alongside and through many other embedded texts and voices. For example, in this passage at the close of "*Hope Atherton's Wanderings*," the words "Loving Friends &

---

from Savage (April 29, 1676) to the General Court. Thomas Reed escaped captivity and on May 15 "came into headquarters and gave a full account of the unwarlike conditions of affairs up the river" (1:154).

[253] To follow those strophic, polyvocal word squares from the Awede text of *Articulation* [unpaginated pages 7; 8-9; 10-11; 12-13; 14-15; 16] over to Sheldon's *History of Deerfield*, see respectively in Sheldon, volume one, pages 49, 162, 163, 169; 163, 165; 187, 274-275; 140, 580; 357; 89.

Kindred" are, in fact, not from Atherton, but from Benjamin Waite (Sheldon, 1:185); "We are a small remnant" emerges from a petition dated April 30, 1678 from "Dearfield's poor inhabitants" (Sheldon, 1:189); "signal escapes" are indeed from Hope's sermon on Sunday, May 28, 1676 (Sheldon, 1:166); "We marched from our camp a Little" appear in neither Jonathan Wells's nor Hope Atherton's narratives, but in Captain Benjamin Wright's journal (Sheldon, 1:445); and so on. Some key words, such as *signal* and *escape*, are ubiquitous among Howe's historical sources and their innumerable embedded speakers and scribes, transcribers and textual editors.

However, across all of Howe's historical sources, **signal escapes** appear together only (and only once) within the context of Hope's transcribed sermon/narrative. At this most discrete level of imbricate/intercalate *kairos*—that is, the articulation of sound forms in time most singularly immanent and imminent for Hope's legacy—Howe's radical contingency, historical figuration, and factual telepathy return Atherton's words to the historiographic wilderness in a gesture of recovery, remediation, and regenerative release that emulates the imagination's triumphant escape in *Paterson*, Book 5: "It is the imagination / which cannot be fathomed. / It is through this hole / we escape   .
          " (210).

The most dominant captivity narratives woven into the poem's first section, *"Hope Atherton's Wanderings"*, however, are the contiguous stories of Hope Atherton, Stephen Belding, John Jones, and especially Jonathan Wells. Throughout the poem, Howe's poetics and praxis engages multiple, co-present texts within and against their historiographic contexts alongside the work's kindred concerns with the narratives and legacies of Anne Hutchinson and Mary Rowlandson.

These imbricated polyvocalisms and palimpsests concerning Hope Atherton's story and legacy have been hiding in plain sight since the publication of the Awede text in 1987 and, long before that, since the publication of Howe's source documents (1895-1896, 1905, 1910). However, these radical contingencies in *Articulation* have not yet received attention in the field as such, and they reveal Howe's historical imagination at work among and between, through and across her articulation of sound forms in time that resist closure and consolation. "Historical imagination gathers in the missing".[254] "L'Imagination historique se rassemble dans le manque".[255] These numerous inter-/intra-textual gestures engage a poetics and praxis—a factual telepathy—that exaggerates and thereby deconstructs the discursive and generic/modal characteristics of the Indian captivity narrative that informed Howe's research and writing process (c. 1982-1985) leading up to her work on *Articulation*. Howe's strophic, polyvocal, dialethic passages and pages amplify the background noise within and against those contexts: "Knowledge narrowly fixed knowledge / Whose bounds in theories slay". In the many narratives covering and recovering Hope Atherton's experience and vexed legacy, Howe found a kindred nonconformist captivity captive calling out for rescue, reconfiguration, and regenerative release.

*   *   *

Only two of the poem's readers—Peter Nicholls (1996) and Rachel Back (2002)—have noticed the contradictory/paradoxical presence of Jonathan Wells's narrative within the fabric of *Articulation*; yet both dismissed (on methodological grounds) the significance of the poem's historiographic concerns, and neither began to consider the multiple, co-present stories at stake in Howe's reading/writing against the grain of the poem's source documents. In his interpretation of the above two word squares—emphasizing keywords such as *clog, prest, nutmeg, grandmother,* and *revived*—Nicholls suggests that Perloff (1990) and Reinfeld (1992) also detected the co-presence of Jonathan Wells's narrative. However, their texts, in fact, do not engage with any of the embedded historiographic narratives to be found among Howe's sources. To be sure, Nicholls is the first to identify the co-presence, in the poem's sequence of dialethic word squares, of Jonathan Wells's narrative from Sheldon's *History of Deerfield*: "When we refer to this source we are in

---

[254] *Frame Structures*, 3.
[255] *Deux et*, 11.

for a surprise, for the main passage used by Howe for her first six stanzas is headed 'Escape of Jonathan Wells'; it has nothing at all to do with Hope Atherton!" (595). Nicholls was on the right path, but followed no further and did not begin to sense the *debths* of Howe's deft, deviant concerns with reading/writing against the grain of the narratives that have subverted and contained Hope Atherton's story and legacy. He did not consider Sheldon's meta-history as a palimpsest shaped by many layers of colonial and early modern narratives, and therefore did not imagine the dynamic historiographic critiques embedded in Howe's disruptive, tropological language throughout *Articulation*. Nor did he consider Howe's presentation of Stephen Williams's letter (in both the Awede and Wesleyan texts) and of the other historical narratives included in the Wesleyan edition to be dynamically adapted/edited critiques of those very source texts and contexts. These decisive turns in Nicholls's argument consequently informed the critical paths followed by Back (2002), Frost (2003), and Gaffield (2015).

Giving priority to his deconstructive methodology—strongly inflected by Derrida's critique, in *Glas*, of Freud's thoughts on mourning and melancholia—Nicholls turned away from history and historicity: "Howe has no desire to send us back to her sources, or, indeed, to encourage us to read them" (596) because her "selection of items actually tends to block" emergent narratives, substituting "molecular opacity for the integrative movements of narration" (596-597). Such a deconstructive turn (against dialectical thought) supports Nicholls's placement of *Articulation* within the context of Howe's methods of hesitation and stammering kindred with her radical antinomian tradition that includes Anne Hutchinson, Mary Rowlandson, and Emily Dickinson (597). Thus, Nicholls emphasizes subsequent claims: Howe's disruptive "failure to speak fluently" embeds resistance and violence "at the heart of poetic language;" shatters "language into bits and pieces" which subvert intelligibility while foregrounding the materiality of "graphic and phonic elements;" and thereby "jettison[s] historical narrative" while also refusing "to let go of the past" (597). Following Nicholls's argument, Howe's nonconformist enthusiasm therefore transmits "a language intermittently 'stripped to its *un*translatability' ("*Difficulties* Interview," 19), in which 'truth' appears less as the product of moral judgment than as a force by which the past possesses the subject" (597).

As compelling as this interpretation may be within the context of Nicholls's deconstructive methodology (which subordinates agency to indeterminacy), contradictions and paradoxes abound when we recall Howe's priorities in *Articulation* (and, arguably, throughout her works) to rescue, remediate, and release voices and lives, materials and documents that have been silenced or suppressed. If "exaggerated history is poetry" (*Birth-mark*, 96) "because we are in the field of history" (*Frame Structures*, 25), and if "Poetry shelters other voices" (*Birth-mark*, 47) because "We have always been in contact with one another, keeping on never letting go, no distance as to time" (*Frame Structures*, 25), then surely "This is [our] historical consciousness" and "[We] have no choice in it" because Howe's poetics and praxis "tenderly lift[s] from the dark side of history, voices that are anonymous, slighted—inarticulate" (*The Europe of Trusts*, 13-14). In my reading of these vitally important lines, the phrase, *tenderly lift from*, does not mean *disconnect*, or *remove* from history, but rather to gather and give back; or, as I have often written here: to recover, to remediate, and to release words and voices to the linguistic wilderness of our shared experience.

Back, Frost, and Gaffield are the only other critics in the field (to the best of my knowledge) who have acknowledged the presence of George Sheldon's *History of Deerfield* within the fabric of *Articulation*; Nicholls's argument formatively shaped their paths of inquiry and subsequent disregard for the relevance of Howe's historical source documents for the poem's concerns with Hope Atherton's story and legacy. In an endnote to her volume, Rachel Back argues that "Howe does not mean for the source-text to stand in as an authoritative interpreter or master narrative of her poetry" because "Nicholls shows how Howe's 'selection of items' from the Sheldon text 'tends to block [an] emergent narrative' and that she is at all times more interested in the individual word, its sound and shape on the page" (193). Elisabeth Frost also overlooks the significance of Sheldon's text: "Nicholls's account reveals that

Howe composed her linguistic collage by a method of chance operations that seems precisely *not* to point us toward the historical relevance of any of Howe's original sources. And yet this arbitrary mode of construction suits Hope's wanderings, which appear in ironic fragments suggesting the breakdown of the masculine order of the state" (121). In her interpretation of the polyvocal word squares and dialogic facing pages throughout *Articulation*, Nancy Gaffield claims that the "individual poems in both sections […] quickly cast off historical discourse" because "the work is not about history" but rather "about how language has been misappropriated by history/his story. Hovering between sense and nonsense, the fractures reveal what has been hidden in those discourses that place primacy on coherence" (276). Gaffield does not search further than this in Sheldon's text for hidden information concerning Atherton, although she does find within *Articulation* the kindred co-presence of Anne Hutchinson and Mary Rowlandson because "Hope as a captive evokes other captivity narratives" (281).

Notwithstanding these curious swervings away from Sheldon's text (and more broadly from the ever-present historical agency of Howe's poetics and praxis), Gaffield, Frost, and especially Back build compelling, valuable arguments concerning Howe's reading/writing against the grain of Anne Hutchinson's and Mary Rowlandson's stories and legacies. In that regard, they also amplify and challenge some of Nicholls's incisive readings. Nicholls was first in the field to follow the opening sequence of seven word squares in *Articulation* back to Sheldon's representation of Jonathan Wells's narrative; and, at the micro-level, Nicholls was also first in the field to connect the presence, in *Articulation*, of "the mysterious 'M' and 'R' of stanzas 3 and 4" (596) to the co-presence of Mary Rowlandson's narrative.[256] The enigmatic lines in which these initials appear are quite distinctive: "who was lapd M as big as any kerchief / as like tow and beg grew bone and bullet"; and "Who was lapt R & soe

---

[256] See also Ann Vickery, *Leaving Lines of Gender: A Feminist Genealogy of Language Writing* (Hanover: Wesleyan University Press, 2000), 185; and Gaffield, 277.

grew bone bullet / as like tow and as another scittuation / Stopt when Worshp Steven boy companion".

To the best of my knowledge, none of the poem's readers have yet considered Sheldon's *History of Deerfield* as one of the sources for these lines and initials.[257] As noted here, these lines directly echo a passage from Sheldon's representation of Jonathan Wells's narrative that recounts how he was struck by a bullet in his "thigh in a place which before had been broken by a cart wheel & never set but the bones lapd & so grew together […]." *Articulation* uses both "lapd" and "lapt" (which does not appear in Sheldon's text). According to Noah Webster, "lapped" means "turned or folder over;" and "lappet" means "a part of a garment or dress that hangs loose."[258] Within the context of Howe's lines, their counter-reading of Sheldon's text echoes the co-presence therein (1:162) of lapped/lappet bodies and bones, garments and gestures, words and wounds entangled within Wells's transcribed and edited narrative, including the co-presence of John Jones (whom Wells did not save) and of Stephen Belding (whom Wells rescued).

A close reading of Sheldon's representation of Wells's narrative reveals that his own survival, in fact, owes a debt to John Jones (1:162) who "represented ye badness of his wounds, & made his companion think they were certainly mortall," which convinced Wells to leave Jones behind (so that he might be free to save himself and consequently also Stephen Belding). Sheldon's text indicates (1:159) that Jones survived, but does not say how.

---

[257] "He was with the 20 men y^t were obliged to fight wth the enemy to recover their horses; after he mounted his horse a little while, (being then in the rear of ye company) he was fird at by three Indians who were very near him; one bullet passd so near him as to brush his hair another struck his horse behind a third struck his thigh in a place which before had been broken by a cart wheel & never set but the bones lapd & so grew together so y^t altho one end of it had been struck and the bone shatterd by ye bullet yet the bone was not wholly lossd in ye place where it had knit. Upon receving his wound he was in danger of falling from his horse, but catching hold of ye horse's maine he recovered himself" (Sheldon, 1: 162).

[258] Noah Webster, *American Dictionary of the English Language*, 1828 edition online: http://webstersdictionary1828.com/[.]

168

In these astonishing ways, Sheldon's text elucidates Howe's radical contingency and historical figuration: these incisive lines in *Articulation*—"who was lapd M" and "Who was lapt R & soe grew bone bullet"—signify, via factual telepathy, the poem's disturbance of the dominance of MR JW's heroic narrative that has lapped/lappet not only Hope Atherton's story, but also the embedded story of John Jones. Howe's enigmatic initials M and R thus invoke a field of contiguous narratives and legacies alongside the co-presence of Mary Rowlandson—whose "presentation of truth severed from Truth is a rude effraction into a familiar American hierarchical discourse of purpose and possession" (*TEMBLOR* 2, 1985: 116)—and of Anne Hutchinson, "the rose at the threshold" of the "primordial struggle of North American literary expression" (*Birth-mark*, 1993:21, 4).

Many convincing arguments have been made in this field for the significance of Mary Rowlandson's and Anne Hutchinson's foundational legacies within the context of *Articulation*. For example, Back finds the narratives of Rowlandson and Hutchinson to be "crucial to our understanding" of respectively the first and second parts of *Articulation*, "as their stories seem to generate the content and influence the poetic praxis of the work" (38). Whereas Back sees Rowlandson's *Narrative* as informing much of the first section, "Hope Atherton's Wanderings", she encounters Anne Hutchinson as the "second Puritan female figure wandering through" (44) *Articulation* who, critically, acts as the "single constant figure" (48) in the poem's second section, "Taking the Forest". Frost argues that "Howe's tale of origins begins with Hutchinson's unbecoming blasphemy" (115) because *Articulation* invokes a feminist tradition (including Rowlandson, Dickinson, Stein, and H. D. as well as Melville, Olson, and Duncan) that challenges Puritan theology, which, "despite its seemingly fluid gender constructions […,] reinforces a difference that reveals male privilege and shackles women" (134). Gaffield's blending of cognitive poetics and schema theory "connects Hope's story to a female entity or entities," especially Rowlandson and Hutchinson (281).

However, none of the poem's many readers from 1987 to present have yet considered the work's collage of archival materials (beginning with Stephen Williams's *EXTRACT* in the Awede edition) as a sequence of constitutive artifacts underscoring Howe's reading/writing against the grain of the poem's meta-historical context concerning the Peskeompskutt massacre and Hope Atherton's story and legacy. For example, Back reads the "three-page prose opening" in the Wesleyan edition as a dry catalog "of the savagery of the white settlers toward the Indians and of the Indians toward the white settlers" (40); Frost follows "The Falls Fight" from *Singularities* as an "apparently straightforward outline" (120); and Gaffield summarizes the text as an historical "account" through which "Howe announces her aim" for the poem, which, ultimately, "is not about history" (276). Such turnings away from history (as charted in this essay's literature reviews and critical discussions) underscore the force of methodological and theoretical priorities, which also have their discrete and definitive moments in time amidst the ever-shifting politics of literary discourse.

*   *   *

Elisabeth W. Joyce reads *Articulation* as "the clearest manifesto" (166) for Howe's work because "it is only through becoming a part of the landscape [...] that the poet becomes a part of self-creation, culture creation, and especially, an integral force in the creation of history" (167). My own multifarious paths here through the poem's historiographic landscape underscore Howe's decisive engagements with a diversified tradition of undervoices that individually and collectively unsettle the wilderness; and which, critically, amplify our attunement to Howe's telepathic connection to Hope Atherton's story across the poem's openwork sequence from *Articulation* to *The Quarry*. And, I would emphasize, that synergistic network of methods and materials arguably also includes: poems that appeared individually in journals (c.

1982 and after)[259] that eventually found their way into the Awede text; "Childe Emily to the Dark Tower Came" (1983); a series of lectures on Dickinson (1984-1985); "Statement for the New Poetics Colloquium" (1985); and "The Captivity and Restoration of Mrs. Mary Rowlandson" (1985)—among other published and unpublished works; lecture notes[260] and working papers—all of which informed Howe's dynamic, transformative research and writing process that shaped *My Emily Dickinson*, *Articulation, a bibliography of the king's book; or, eikon basilike,* and *The Birth-mark* among other collections. In all of those ways, *Articulation* escapes every time, and such innumerable *scapes esaid* authenticate the work.[261]

For example, the single unnumbered page [twenty-six] from the Awede text of *Articulation* that does not appear in the Wesleyan edition engenders a destabilizing and regenerative absent presence—lines from which this essay variously invokes: "Light inaccessible as darkness / Irradiation of infinite // Principles judgements must connect / Soul lying awake in sleep // Parabolic scholar / Follower".

---

[259] The Awede edition of *Articulation of Sound Forms in Time* notes that some of the poems therein "first appeared in *Conjunctions, Sulfur, Acts, Ironwood, Boundary, Luna Tack, Hambone,* and *Io*." A micro-study of those publications would reveal many changes and omissions compared with the Awede text. For example, in the sequence of "Six Poems" published in *Sulfur* 9 (1984): 88-94, the first twenty-four lines do not appear in any of the subsequent printings of *Articulation of Sound Forms in Time*. The majority of the rest of these poems and pages from *Sulfur* 9 (1984) do appear in the Awede text, except for these lines: "Wound doe and hind / Wounded errors wound others" (91); "Offering or gesture of offering / Imagery and imagery // Jig green revelry" (92); and "Clay and country / merry and making merry // merry and making Captive" (93).

[260] In *The Birth-mark*, Howe notes: "An early draft of the essay on Mary Rowlandson was originally presented as part of three lectures on Emily Dickinson I gave at New College in San Francisco, 1984. Another draft was presented at the New Poetics Colloquium of the Kootenay School of Writing at the Emily Carr College of Art and Design, Vancouver, British Columbia, August 1985" (1993: xii).

[261] "That is, the poem escapes the poem. Or the poem escapes the poet. Or is it, the poem escapes the poetics? With the simultaneity of making and a sense of loss, something escapes inside the work. This 'escape' authenticates the work." Rachel Blau DuPlessis, *Surge: Drafts 96-114* (Cromer, UK: Salt, 2013), 15.

I read *Articulation* as a clear manifesto for Howe's radical contingency, historical figuration, and factual telepathy. The disjunctive, dynamic sequence of the poem's intermittent development and transformation from c. 1982 to 2015 includes numerous changes to the work—many of which engage the most discrete levels of line edits; many others, with macro-levels of book design and reformatting (as in the Wesleyan edition). A comprehensive assessment of those many adaptations to the whole poem—which I've described as an 'openwork sequence'; or as a 'synergistic network'; or as a 'centripetal and centrifugal disjunctive collage'; and/or via other kindred articulations herein—would be a fitting subject for descriptive bibliographic investigation (far beyond the scope of my limited, selective efforts here). Indeed, this field of criticism and scholarship would benefit greatly from such meticulous attention to the mediation and remediation of Howe's published works and public performances (electronic and print, manuscript and typescript, video and vinyl). In all of those ineluctably various ways, the works escape the work and vice versa. Howe's swerving remediations of these materials and methods emulate kindred revisions of poems and pages (c. 1982 and after) that would contribute to her reconfigurations of *Articulation* from the Awede text (1987) to the Wesleyan text in *Singularities* (1990) and to the subsequent adaptations of "Personal Narrative" in 2007, 2009, and 2015.

In addition to those elements in the poem's transformations already addressed in this essay, I will now engage with some of the more notable features in the poem's disjunctive journey from *Articulation* to *The Quarry*. At each step along the way, those micro- and macro-modifications to *Articulation* further Howe's reading/writing against the grain of the poem's historical source documents concerning the co-present legacies of Anne Hutchinson, Mary Rowlandson, Hope Atherton, and the others whose stories and voices (from literary and cultural history) echo within and against the poem's nested undervoices. The contested forms and tropes of discourse particular to captivity narratives were, in these dynamic ways, foundational for Howe's methods of radical contingency, historical figuration, and factual telepathy.

In her 1990 *Talisman* interview, Howe reflects that she was (c. 1982-1984) "up in the stacks at [Yale's] Sterling Library searching for information on various Indian raids near Deerfield and Hadley during the French and Indian wars", turning the pages "of a history of Hadley", when Hope's name "just caught" her:

> It was the emblematical name. Here was this person. A man with a woman's name. He had this borderline, half-wilderness, half-Indian, insanity-sanity experience. He was a minister accompanying an army. The enemy thought he might have been God. Was he telling the truth? Had he been hiding or marching? I went home and quickly wrote the abstract pieces at the beginning. Usually I work very, very slowly, but this time the sections came fast. So then there was that section and Hope's name, and the whole thing took on a different form. (25)

In this passage, Howe refers to Judd's *History of Hadley* (1905), which does not play a role in either *My Emily Dickinson* or *The Birth-mark*, or in any of Howe's other works published between c. 1982-1993—despite numerous echoes among those texts within the openwork fabric of *Articulation*. On page 127 in *Souls of the Labadie Tract* (2007), Howe notes, for the first time in her publications, another historical source text for her work on *Articulation*—Sheldon's *A History of Deerfield* (1895-1896)—which she also found in the Sterling Library in the course of her research concerning Dickinson, Rowlandson, and Hutchinson. Sheldon's volume, likewise, does not play a role in any of Howe's other publications outside the scope of *Articulation*, which (alongside the co-presence of Judd's volume plus the other historical sources already addressed in this essay) therefore illustrates a distinctive path for this poem's reading/writing against the grain of Hope Atherton's story—that is, a singularly disjunctive openwork counter-path (from *Articulation* to *The Quarry*) within and across, between and through intersections among Hutchinson's, Rowlandson's, and Dickinson's co-present legacies in those other publications by Howe within the context of the years noted above.

173

The macro-counter-path that *Articulation* shares with Howe's other works that engage with Hutchinson's and Rowlandson's legacies concerns the complex and deeply vexed historiographies of King Philip's War (also known as Metacomet's War and/or as Pometacomet's Rebellion, 1675-1678) and of the Raid on Deerfield (1704) which respectively have so often been deployed (within the poem's historical and historiographic documents) in order to frame the Peskeompskutt massacre (1676) within a providential, teleological narrative that includes Atherton's subordination to the heroic legacy of Jonathan Wells. Howe's openwork sequence of reconfiguring Hope's inter-/intra-textual subversion and containment should therefore be followed vis-à-vis those larger frames of historical and historiographic engagement. This is precisely what Howe's progressive changes to the poem have given us to encounter from *Articulation* to *The Quarry* as evidence of her deft, artifactual disruptions of the archival wilderness.

The many differences between the Awede and the Wesleyan editions thus constitute radically contingent, contiguous works that underscore Howe's persistent unsettling of the poem's meta-historical engagement. Howe's edits to and revisions of *Articulation* across and within these two very different editions of the poem also illustrate the work's changing contexts of mediation and remediation. Notwithstanding Howe's lingering ambivalence about the challenges she encountered during the poem's adaptation and production by Wesleyan—frustrations also expressed in her 1995 interview with Lynn Keller—the volume's woodcut images amplify the poem's cultural, historiographic, and political critiques. And yet, as such, these disturbing images have escaped critical attention in the field. The Wesleyan edition's untitled woodcuts (by an unknown artist from Kachergis Book Design of Pittsboro, NC) appear prominently on the book's cover, title-page, and inter-title pages (1, 39, 61). The cover image and its two subsequent reconfigurations within the pages of *Articulation* limn powerful critiques of the Peskeompskutt massacre. These depictions of overwhelming aggression against a peaceful gathering of Native Tribes exaggerate and thereby unmask the fantasy of Manifest Destiny that led the colonial militia to

Peskeompskutt and that subsequently shaped the legacy of providential, teleological historiography. Such amplified, artifactual portraits of "antecedent terror stretched to a whisper" speak truth to power, constituting the radically contingent archival grounding within and against which Howe articulates the poem's disruptive historical figuration and regenerative factual telepathy.[262]

In the first published instance (2007) of direct reference to Sheldon's *A History of Deerfield*, Howe calls our attention to three pages in *Souls* (12, 13, and 17) that include photographic reproductions of excerpts from pages 299, 166, 165 in volume one of Sheldon's text—pages that respectively document: an excerpt from "An Account of what was lost by the souldeirs" (1:299) who took part in a fight against Native forces at "Dearfield Medow on the last of Febewarey, 1703-4" (1:298) submitted by Jonathan Wells and Ebenezer Wright; an excerpt from Atherton's sermon to his congregation (1:166); and an excerpt (1:165) from Jonathan Wells's narrative that informs the polyvocal strophic assemblages—that is, the first seven dialethic word squares—in the Awede text of *Articulation*. Howe deftly alters the presentation of these artifacts in subsequent adaptations of her "Personal Narrative": in the 2008 text, "Writing *Articulation of Sound Forms in Time*," the photographic reproduction of "An Account" does not appear; in the 2015 text, "Personal Narrative," that excerpt from Wells & Wright returns (49). In those instances (2007 and 2015) of appearance, this particular excerpt from Sheldon's representation of the account from Wells and Wright amplifies the subordination of the Peskeompskutt massacre and of Atherton's legacy to the macro-historiographic narratives concerning a providential, teleological progression from Metacomet's War to the Raid on Deerfield; in the one instance (2008) where "An Account" does not appear, Howe's text amplifies the micro-historiographic subordination and containment of Hope's story by the heroic legacy of Jonathan Wells within the more

---

[262] All of the historical sources engaged by *Articulation* agree that there was no English settlement at Great Fall prior to the massacre. The woodcut image thus depicts a monstrous cathexis: a colonial building and a Christian flag under attack, as if we are viewing the moment through the typological, teleological perspective of Manifest Destiny.

limited scope of the Peskeompskutt massacre. All three adaptations of Howe's "Personal Narrative" underscore the poem's entangled and precarious openwork readings/writings against the historiographic grain: "Hope Atherton is lost in the great world of nature. No steady progress of saints into grace saying Peace Peace when there is no peace" (2008: 203).

Howe composed "Personal Narrative" for presentation on a panel at the 2006 MLA convention; the essay was first published in *Souls of the Labadie Tract* (2007) and thereafter revised and reprinted in *The Sound of Poetry/The Poetry of Sound* (2009) and in *The Quarry* (2015). The narrative's sequential transformations engender a poetics and praxis of radical contingency and historical figuration specific to each volume's context. Each of Howe's works is simultaneously centric and eccentric, deviant and divinatory; all texts share close affinities shaped by accidental incidents and subjunctive conditions across time beyond anticipation or plan; and yet each poem also destabilizes the field of disjunctive synergy among and between all immanent/imminent texts within and against, through and beyond their individual forms and fields of emergence: "Quicksand swallows the bottom // Leaf carried out of invisible hearing / Accoustic signature // prefiguration".

*   *   *

The fact that Howe claims these passages of poetic prose as a "Personal Narrative" underscores the significance of Hope Atherton's story and legacy in the development of her work across decades, as I have charted and discussed. The discursive forms and tropes distinctive to North American captivity narratives amplified that resonance for Howe's poetics and praxis (from c. 1982-2015). Within the context of those adaptations of the openwork sequence of *Articulation* that find their respective placements within and against the grain of *Souls of the Labadie Tract*, *The Sound of Poetry/The Poetry of Sound*, and *The Quarry*, Howe reflects upon her chance discovery of Sheldon's *A History of Deerfield*:

> I vividly remember the sense of energy and change that came over me one midwinter morning when, as the book lay open in sunshine on my work table, I discovered in Hope Atherton's wandering story the authority of a prior life for my own writing voice [...] I felt the spiritual and solitary freedom of an inexorable order only chance creates [...] In Sterling's sleeping wilderness I felt the telepathic solicitation of innumerable phantoms. The future seemed to lie in this forest of letters, theories, and forgotten actualities. I had a sense of the parallel between our always fragmentary knowledge and the continual progress toward perfect understanding that never withers away. (*Souls*, 13-14)

Atherton's undervoice struck a deeply personal chord. In her reading/writing against the grain of Hope's nested, contested historiography, Howe encountered *the authority of a prior life for [her] own writing voice.*

The thirteen lines of poetry on the unpaginated page [43] in the Awede text (page 34 in the Wesleyan text) may also be found on pages 13 and 14 of "THERE ARE NOT LEAVES ENOUGH TO CROWN TO COVER TO CROWN TO COVER" (1990 and 1992), lines that echo powerfully within and against, across and through the disjunctive sequence of disappearances and appearances for that prose poem from *Pythagorean Silence* (1982)—in which that text does not appear as such—to *Jimmy and Lucy's house of 'K'* 5 (1985) and to *The Europe of Trusts* (1990 and 2002)—which includes the work as a preface to a reconfigured *PYTHAGOREAN SILENCE*—to *American Women Poets in the 21st Century* (2002) and to *The Quarry* (2015). Within the context of those contingent, contiguous passages in "THERE ARE NOT LEAVES," those thirteen lines (which appear without revisions from 1985 to 2015) are respectively introduced and concluded by reflections upon Howe's father's letters during World War II—which "were a sign he was safe" (1990: 13)—and by the poet's abiding concern with historical figuration:

177

"This is my historical consciousness I have no choice in it. In my poetry, time and again, questions of assigning *the cause* of history dictate the sound of what is thought [...] Poetry brings similitude and representation to configurations waiting from forever to be spoken" (1990:13-14).

The co-presence of these thirteen lines from *Articulation* (1987, 1990) within the context of these kindred passages (1985, 1990, 1992, 2002, 2015) from "THERE ARE NOT LEAVES" further amplifies the inclusion of both "Personal Narrative" and "There Are Not Leaves Enough to Crown to Cover to Crown to Cover" in *The Quarry*—the first time for these companion works from the openwork sequence of *Articulation* to appear together in the same volume. Their co-present resonance echoes the poet's wish to "tenderly lift from the dark side of history, voices that are anonymous, slighted—inarticulate" (1990: 14). In these deft and powerful ways, *The Quarry* thus illuminates the complete arc of Atherton's *telepathic solicitation.* Howe's poetics and praxis across the openwork sequence of *Articulation* rescues, remediates, and releases Hope's undervoice to the linguistic wilderness of our shared experience in the field of history.

Just as Hope's sound forms in time found Howe by chance on a midwinter morning in the Sterling Library, the poem's openwork sequence from *Articulation* to *The Quarry* returns Atherton's *sounds still in the air* to their home: *they go back.* "prefiguration without premeditation // migratory odd scrap trilogy".

*   *   *

The alternating titles for these cross-genre passages—"PERSONAL NARRATIVE" (2007), "Writing *Articulation of Sound Forms in Time*" (2009), "Personal Narrative" (2015)—place the poem's openwork compositional process within contexts that were, for Howe, personal as well as cultural and historiographic. During the course of her research (c. 1982 and afterwards) concerning Dickinson, Rowlandson, and Hutchinson, Howe encountered an archive of intersecting colonial and early modern discursive/literary forms of documentation and witnessing, of prophecy and protest—such as the *personal narrative*, the *true relation*, the *conversion narrative*, the *true account*, the *report and plea*, the *vindication*, and the *captivity narrative* (among other modalities)—that were emerging on both sides of the Atlantic during tumultuous centuries of colonization and conquest, reform and revolution.[263]

Captivity narratives first emerged as products of the "crusading mentality" when the "nation states of Europe" and their representative "invaders of strange continents assumed an innate and absolute superiority over all other peoples because of divine endowment" (Jennings, 5). Within and against that global scope from early medieval Europe throughout the early modern and modern eras, captivity narratives became popular and readily reproducible, vexed instruments of racial and spiritual prejudice as well as vital forms of resistance against cultural, economic, linguistic, military, and political hegemony.[264] Captivity narratives were (and still are) among the most foundational discursive and ideological forms for colonial, neocolonial, and postcolonial historiography as well as for the emergence of a range of literary forms, especially the novel. These complex networks of textual production and circulation

---

[263] For foundational studies of these emergent forms of cultural and literary expression, see Slotkin (1973); Caldwell (1983); Kibbey (1986); Harry S. Stout, *The New England Soul: Preaching and Religious Culture in Colonial New England* (New York and Oxford: Oxford University Press, 1986); Lang (1987); Elspeth Graham, Hilary Hinds, Elaine Hobby, and Helen Wilcox, eds., *Her Own Life: Autobiographical Writings by Seventeenth-Century Englishwomen* (London: Routledge, 1989); Phyllis Mack, *Visionary Women: Ecstatic Prophecy in Seventeenth-Century England* (Berkeley: University of California Press, 1992); Derounian-Stodola and Levernier (1993); Helen Ostovich and Elizabeth Sauer, eds., *Reading Early Modern Women: An Anthology of Texts in Manuscript and Print, 1550-1700* (New York: Routledge, 2004); Stratton (2013); and W. Scott Howard, "Prophecy, Power, and Religious Dissent," *A History of Early Modern Women's Writing*, ed. Patricia Phillippy (Cambridge: Cambridge University Press, 2018), 315-331.

[264] See, for example, Marc Falkoff, ed., *Poems From Guantánamo: the Detainees Speak* (Iowa City: University of Iowa Press, 2007); Benjamin Mark Allen, and Dahia Messara, eds., *The Captivity Narrative: Enduring Shackles and Emancipating Language of Subjectivity* (Cambridge: Cambridge Scholars Publishing, 2012); and Billy J. Stratton, "Captivity Narratives," *The Oxford History of Popular Print Culture*, ed. Ronald J. Zboray and Mary Saracino Zboray (Oxford: Oxford University Press, 2019), 189-203.

have received much critical attention (especially in recent decades)[265] yet much more work remains to be done, especially at the foundational levels to grow and manage archives for North American Indian, Afro-American, Afro-Caribbean, Asian-American, and Latinx primary materials.[266] In their vast scholarly study, Wilcomb E. Washburn and Alden T. Vaughn examine hundreds of narratives from the Edward E. Ayer Collection of the Newberry Library, Chicago.[267]

Shaped by their many sites of contested authority, documentation, editing, remediation, and transmission, North American colonial and early modern captivity narratives underscore dynamically unstable forms of conflict, subversion, and containment. From John Smith's *Generall Historie of Virginia* (1624) to John Williams's *The redeemed captive returning to Zion* (1707) to Elizabeth Hanson's *God's Mercy Surmounting Man's Cruelty* (1728) to Charlotte Alice Baker's *True Stories*

---

[265] In addition to the works already noted, see Alden T. Vaughn, and Edward W. Clark, *Puritans among the Indians: Accounts of Captivity and Redemption 1676–1724* (Cambridge, MA: Belknap Press of Harvard University Press, 1981); Francis Roe Kestler, ed., *The Indian Captivity Narrative: A Woman's View* (New York: Garland, 1990); Colin G. Calloway, *North Country Captives: Selected Narratives of Indian Captivity From Vermont and New Hampshire* (Hanover, NH: University Press of New England, 1992); Evan Haefeli, and Kevin Sweeney, *Captive Histories: English, French, and Native Narratives of the 1704 Deerfield Raid* (Amherst: University of Massachusetts Press, 2006); and Daniel E. Williams, Christina Riley Brown, Salita S. Bryant, et al., eds., *Liberty's Captives: Narratives of Confinement in the Print Culture of the Early Republic* (Athens, GA: University of Georgia Press, 2006).

[266] See, for example, these libraries and digital resources: Yale's Native American History Primary Sources collection, http://guides.library.yale.edu/c.php?g=295897&p=1972892[;] the Newbery Library's Edward E. Ayer Collection, https://www.newberry.org/american-indian-and-indigenous-studies[;] The Givens Collection at University of Minnesota, https://www.lib.umn.edu/givens[;] Yale's collections for South Asia: Orientalism from the 17th-20th centuries, http://guides.library.yale.edu/c.php?g=296361&p=1974988[;] and the collections in African American History and Latin American Studies at University of Delaware, http://guides.lib.udel.edu/c.php?g=85389&p=548467[.]

[267] Wilcomb E. Washburn, and Alden T. Vaughn, *Garland Library of Narratives of North American Indian Captives*, 112 vols. (Westport, CT: Garland, 1976–1983).

of New England Captives (1897), these dramatized recapitulations of European colonization and conquest are deeply "interwoven into the very fabric of early American culture" (Derounian-Stodola and Levernier, 8). George Sheldon reflects that "Mrs. Howe is known as the 'Fair Captive', a prominent character in romantic history" (1:638). In *The Birth-mark*, Susan Howe describes the captivity narrative as "both a microcosm of colonial imperialist history and a prophecy of our contemporary repudiation of alterity, anonymity, darkness" (1993:89).

Among, between, and through the polyvocalisms that inform Hope's undervoice, Howe encountered a kindred nonconformist whose story (within the context of numerous other early narratives) precedes Mary White Rowlandson's *The Soveraignty & Goodness of God* (1682) and deviates from the rhetorical characteristics of the heroic captivity narratives that Atherton's historians would employ as foundational allegories of providential, teleological historiography. Atherton's story also, critically, deviates from the paradigmatic status given to Rowlandson's narrative by Richard Slotkin, whose work was foundational for Howe's research in addition to the numerous other volumes of criticism, scholarship, and theory she underscores in *The Birth-mark*. According to Slotkin, in a captivity narrative

> a single individual, usually a woman, stands passively under the strokes of evil, awaiting rescue by the grace of God. [...] The captive's ultimate redemption by the grace of Christ and the efforts of the Puritan magistrates is likened to the regeneration of the soul in conversion. [...] Through the captive's proxy, the promise of a similar salvation could be offered to the faithful among the reading public, while the captive's torments remained to harrow the hearts of those not yet awakened to their fallen nature. (94-95)

This oft-cited passage presents a compelling sequence of interpretive claims and tropes—all of which support Slotkin's mythopoetic argument that underscores the pivotal significance (for his methodology) of Rowlandson's narrative as expressing "an archetype of the American experience" specific to "the Puritans' anxieties about their social and spiritual position" (98). Echoing Slotkin's charismatic perspective, other scholars have claimed that Rowlandson's narrative was so popular that all available copies of the volume's first edition were literally read to pieces.[268]

Foundational myths (especially those in the field of literary studies that emphasize *anxiety* as a key trope) are as elusively nested and contested as they may also be resiliently precarious and prejudiced; and, to be sure, Slotkin's work followed the path set forth by his predecessors, including Perry Miller. Slotkin locates this ideological shift (for the Puritans' increasing *anxieties about their social and spiritual position*) within the years of 1689-1692—the context for and legacy of King William's War—when "a series of dramatic events compelled the Puritans to look to the captivity narrative for their mythological sustenance" (116). Miller, however, finds such heightened anxiety distinctive to second and third generation Puritans, whose election sermons express "a deep disquietude [of] troubled utterances" because something fundamental "has gone wrong" (2). From John Higginson's *The Cause of God and His People in New-England* (1663) to Samuel Danforth's *A Brief Recognition of New England's Errand into the Wilderness* (1670) to Increase Mather's *A Discourse Concerning the Danger of Apostasy* (1677), the jeremiads of the 1660s and 1670s inform Miller's study of the apocalyptic literary tradition for which the wilderness signifies redemption and ruin as exegetical pretexts for conversion and catastrophe (239). Miller's book is dedicated to Susan Howe's parents. In *The Birth-mark*, Howe chides Miller's prejudices: how "could he have written so many books and essays, one of them called *Errand into the Wilderness* and have left out the [Native] inhabitants?" (1993:161). She also underscores

---

[268] See Frank Mott, *Golden Multitudes: The Story of Best Sellers in the United States* (New York: Macmillan, 1960), 303; and Jill Lepore, *The Name of War: King Philip's War and the Origins of American Identity* (New York: Alfred A. Knopf, 1998), 149. See Stratton's incisive critiques of Slotkin's and Lepore's foundational readings of Rowlandson's narrative: respectively, pages 24-25, 57, 107, 137; and 19, 65, 69, 108, 110, 125-129, 141, 147.

therein her own abiding care for and concerns with North American history and historiography: "I am trying to understand what went wrong when the first Europeans stepped on shore here [...] There are things that must never be forgotten" (1993:164).

Slotkin's interpretation of the captivity narrative's defining characteristics continues to hold paradigmatic status in the field of literary studies despite (or perhaps due to) that bias given to one exemplary text (Rowlandson's narrative) within a field of primary documents "so numerous that the full corpus of texts has yet to be identified" (Derounian-Stodola and Levernier, 8). (That complex, compelling story challenges the foundations of American literary history beyond the scope of this essay's primary concerns with Howe's reading/writing against the grain of the historical sources for *Articulation* that most directly pertain to Atherton's experience at Peskeompscut, his escape from the military and flight into the wilderness, his uncanny return, his unfortunate demise, and the subordination of his story to the heroic legacy of Jonathan Wells.) Atherton's true relation anticipated some of the emerging rhetorical motifs of captivity narratives, including: typological interpretations of decisive, inexplicable events; causal relationships among the workings of Christ's grace, God's special providence, and the captive's sufferings; and analogies between the captive's return and the consequent promise of salvation for the faithful among the reading public.[269]

And yet, fundamental questions about this paradigm should be engaged, such as: for whom are these foundational discursive markers inclusive or exclusive, protective or prejudicial? Atherton's narrative threatened the logic of the status quo in his congregation and community at Hatfield, advancing claims both dishonorable—that he was fired upon and abandoned by the military; that he tried repeatedly and yet in vain to surrender himself—and audacious, especially his autotelic application of Isaiah 43:2 ("When thou passest through the waters, I will be with thee;

---

[269] Richard Slotkin and James K. Folsom, eds., *So Dreadfull A Judgment: Puritan Responses to King Philips's War, 1676-1677* (Middletown: Wesleyan University Press, 1978), 301-314.

and through the rivers, they shall not overflow thee")[270] to his purported passage across Quinetucket.[271] In the concluding lines of his narrative, as represented in the note herein, Atherton expressed his self-awareness that he may *have spoken beyond what is convenient.*

*   *   *

As many of the poem's readers have argued, *Articulation* invokes a tradition that includes, for Howe's work, the foundational figures of Anne Hutchinson and Mary Rowlandson. My interpretation places Hope Atherton in their kindred, nonconformist company. Considering the competing power relations that shaped his life and times, and based upon my reading of the historical and historiographic evidence, I believe that Atherton was compelled to accompany the militia to Peskeompscut on May 19, 1676 in order to represent the Atherton Company—his family's land acquisition group—that was in crisis (following the death, in 1661, of Hope's father, Major General Humphrey Atherton) and fierce competition with other business and military interests along the eastern and

---

[270] The Holy Bible: King James Version (New York: Meridian, 1974), 580.

[271] "Two things I must not pass over that are matter of thanks-giving unto God: the first is, that when my strength was far spent, I passed through deep waters and they overflowed me not, according to those gracious words of Isa. 43, 2; the second is, that I subsisted the space of three days & part of a fourth without ordinary food. I thought upon those words "Man liveth not by bread alone, but by every word that proceedeth out of the mouth of the Lord." I think not to too much to say, that should you & I be silent & not set forth the praises of God thro' Jesus Christ, that the stones and beams of our houses would sing hallelujah. I am not conscious to myself that I have exceeded in speech. If I have spoken beyond what is convenient, I know it not. I leave these lines as an orphan, and shall rejoice to hear that it finds foster Father's & Mother's. However it fare amongst men, yet if it find acceptance with God thro' Christ Jesus, I shall have cause to be abundantly satisfied. God's providence hath been so wonderful towards me, not because I have more wisdom than others (Danl 2, 30) nor because I am more righteous than others; but because it so pleased God. H. A. Hatfield, May 24th, 1676" (Sheldon 1:167-168).

western banks of Quinetucket situated within and against the wider context of Metacomet's War (1675-1678). My 2006 article introduced and documented some of those comparative readings.[272]

This current essay amplifies those preliminary insights within a more capacious, dynamic research context including new evidence concerning Atherton's experience, story, and legacy; the critical reception of *Articulation* from 1987 to present; and the poem's openwork sequence (c. 1982-2015). Considering the poem's historical source documents, as I have discussed at length in this essay, I also believe that Hope was so horrified by what he witnessed at Peskeompscut that he disobeyed orders, was fired upon and then abandoned by the military; and that his dissent, his uncanny survival and return to Hadley, his outlandish claims and unfortunate demise were consequently subverted and contained by heroic captivity narratives in the historical and historiographic texts going forward from J. Wells, J. Williams, S. Williams, Taylor, Sheldon,

---

[272] See Howard (2006): https://web.archive.org/web/20110726035138/http://reconstruction.eserver.org/063/howard.shtml[.] For that essay's historiographic engagement (in dialogue with my readings therein of *Articulation*, *Singularities*, and *The Birth-mark*) see respectively the following texts: Eric B. Schultz and Michael J. Tougias, *King Philip's War: The History and Legacy of America's Forgotten Conflict* (Woodstock, VT: The Countryman Press, 1999), 1-57, 143-233; Francis Jennings, *The Invasion of America: Indians, Colonialism, and the Cant of Conquest* (New York: Norton, 1976), 82, 254-326; George Madison Bodge, *Soldiers in King Philip's War: Being a Critical Account of That War with a Concise History of the Indian Wars of New England From 1620-1677* (Boston, 1906), 242, 244-247; Douglas Edward Leach, *Flintlock and Tomahawk: New England in King Philip's War* (New York: W.W. Norton & Co. Inc., 1958), 14-29, 199-207; Increase Mather, *A Brief History of the Warr with the Indians in New-England* (Boston, 1676), 30; William Hubbard, *A Narrative of the Troubles with the Indians in New-England* (Boston, 1677), 230-231; William Moore, *Indian Wars of the United States From the Discovery to the Present Time* (Philadelphia: J. & J. L. Gihon, 1852), 131; James D. Drake, *King Philip's War: Civil War in New England, 1675-1676* (Amherst: University of Massachusetts Press, 1999), 133, 234 n. 56; Arthur Holmes Tucker, *Hope Atherton and His Times* (Deerfield: Pocumtuck Valley Memorial Association, 1926), 1-9, 49, 62-72; Richard Slotkin and James K. Folsom, eds., *So Dreadfull A Judgment: Puritan Responses to King Philips's War, 1676-1677* (Middletown: Wesleyan University Press, 1978), 301-314; Jill Lepore, *The Name of War* (1998), 149.

Judd, and Wells & Wells. Some readers may disagree with these claims and conclusions, of course, and I fully acknowledge their radical contingency, historical figuration, and factual telepathy. Howe's artifactual reading/writing against the grain of *Articulation* has been my guide through the archival wilderness.

The Birth-mark includes one moment (1990:121) of reflection upon Humphrey Atherton, who "was the chief military officer in New England" at the time of his death in 1661. In that passage, Howe also notes that while John Winthrop, Jr. was serving (from 1659-1676) as governor of the Connecticut colony, he "became a partner in the Atherton Company"; that the Company "consisted of a group of land speculators whose double dealings with the Narragansetts made them into wealthy landowners"; that Humphrey Atherton mocked Mary Dyer's body after her execution, saying "'She hangs there as a flag'"; and that James Savage (who edited John Winthrop's *The History of New England from 1630 to 1649*) described Humphrey Atherton as deserving "'much honor in our early annals'."

Arthur Holmes Tucker's *Hope Atherton and His Times* (1926) found me by chance at Powell's Books in 1993 (as I relate in this collection's opening essay) at a time when I was preparing to present a 'new historicist' reading of *Articulation* at a conference at the University of Oregon. Howe did not have access to Tucker's volume during the years and decades of her openwork engagement with Atherton's story and legacy; none of her publications between 1982 and 2015 reference *Hope Atherton and His Times*.

Tucker's volume observes that Captain William Turner (who led the militia to Peskeompscut) "was long a resident of Dorchester and had served with Humphrey Atherton in various town duties" (63). Jennings (254-326) and Leach (14-29) offer detailed accounts of the Atherton Company's various dealings and many shareholders (which included John Winthrop, Jr. and Captain Turner). According to the Yale Indian Papers Project, Humphrey Atherton (1608-1661) began his "land speculation venture" in 1659 with the support of "influential shareholders in

186

the colonies" who promoted methods "of gaining control over vast quantities of Indian land."[273] John Frederick Martin's *Profits in the Wilderness* provides extensive coverage of the Atherton Company's history.[274] Martin notes (66) that Simon Bradstreet, the future Massachusetts governor, became a shareholder in 1660.

According to Martin, "a secular, business organization for the purpose of holding, managing, and developing wilderness land" was first necessary to found a town, and that "this organization was distinct from the church and congregation" (145). In the majority of the sixty-three early New England towns within the scope of Martin's research, land corporations were formed before towns were settled and churches gathered; and (although "the incompleteness of records bars certainty") probably none of the founders of the first forty-one towns even procured "a part-time minister to preach to the churchless settlers during the first year of settlement" (146). One of Howe's source documents, *A History of Hatfield, Massachusetts*, records a group of farms purchased in 1659 by a "company of proprietors" that included Hope's father, who took his land "elsewhere to accommodate the new town" of Hatfield (Wells & Wells, 27). Following those transactions, the "land for the town of Hatfield was secured in three purchases" beginning on July 10, 1660. Martin observes that there were "several other father-son relationships involving [land] speculators and ministers" (126).

After Hatfield was founded in 1660, the northern territories along the western and eastern banks of Quinetucket were fiercely contested sites of competing land claims and military conflicts that prepared the ground for the Peskeompskut massacre in 1676 within the much larger context of Metacom's War. "While returning home in the dark after reviewing his troops on Boston Common," Humphrey Atherton's "horse

---

[273] Yale Indian Papers Project: http://yipp.yale.edu/bio/bibliography/atherton-humphrey-1608-1661[.] Accessed June 8, 2017.

[274] John Frederick Martin, *Profits in the Wilderness: Entrepreneurship and the Founding of New England Towns in the Seventeenth Century* (Chapel Hill and London: University of North Carolina Press, 1991), 33, 54-55, 62, 64, 66-73, 82-83, 89-91, 124-125, 227, 261.

was struck by a stray cow. In the collision[,] he was thrown and killed. Sept. 16, 1661" (Tucker, 7). Following the accident, several investors, governing officials, and lawyers representing New York, Massachusetts, Connecticut, and Rhode Island competed for control of the Atherton Company, which, as Martin's extensive research shows, encountered "troubled years" (82) during the 1670s. Howe's *Articulation* tells us that Hope Atherton was "'the first minister of Hatfield, who was ordained May 10th, 1670'."

All of these entangled, precarious factors (among so many others) shaped the circumstances that compelled Hope Atherton to be present at Peskeompskut and to dissent.

According to Sheldon, in 1743, Hope's son, Joseph, and Jonathan Wells, Esq. were proprietors of, respectively, forty; and two hundred and three acres in the "second division" of lands beginning at Green River and running "along the seven-mile line to the Long Hill wood lots"—tracts that were "afterwards known in records and deeds as the 'First' and 'Second Divisions of Inner Commons'"—lines of division between the lots north of Deerfield that "all ran 'West, nineteen degrees North'" (1:506-507).

Through the telepathic promptings of Hope's undervoice, Susan Howe encountered *the authority of a prior life for [her] own writing voice*. "We are a small remnant / of signal escapes wonderful in themselves".

Accidental Purpose:
Chance and Discipline from *My Emily Dickinson* to *Debths*

Between storms on consecutive Sunday afternoons in January, 2015, Susan Howe and I talked about her recently published *Spontaneous Particulars: The Telepathy of Archives*, which we considered from a variety of perspectives (including manuscript studies and textual scholarship, visual arts and dramatic performance). We discussed her work's abiding engagement with the poetry of Emily Dickinson, William Carlos Williams, and Wallace Stevens; with the philosophy of C. S. Peirce, the primacy of archival research, and the dynamics of sonic and textual collage. While the sleet and snow annotated the woods and roads in Guilford, CT, we talked in her second-floor studio over cups of tea and in the company of books and working papers. *Spontaneous Particulars* draws upon decades of Howe's research, writing, and teaching, so we connected this curatorial assemblage of "visual and verbal textualities and textiles"[275] to a range of her print and digital works from *My Emily Dickinson* to *Debths*.

This interview text also places those conversations and their transcriptions within the context of our correspondence from October 2013 to August 2017—that is, from the exhibition of *TOM TIT TOT* at Yale Union Gallery in Portland, OR through the publication of three books—*Spontaneous Particulars, TOM TIT TOT,* and *The Quarry*—two studio recordings with the composer, David Grubbs—*WOODSLIPPERCOUNTERCLATTER* (their fourth CD) and a vinyl reissue of *Thiefth* (their first CD)—and a sequence of lectures, readings, gallery exhibitions, musical performances, interviews, podcasts, one visit to Ireland during the summer of 2015, and the emergence of *Debths*.[276]

---

[275] *Spontaneous Particulars*, 21.
[276] Some of these events and works include: Susan Howe, "from *Debths*," *Academy of American Poets: poem-a-day* (September 19, 2013): https://www.poets.org/poetsorg/poem/debths[;] "Susan Howe, TOM TIT TOT" (Portland, OR: Yale Union, October 5–December 1, 2013):

189

Our Sunday afternoon meetings were animated by Susan Howe's generous intensity, by reading aloud and discussing, by looking closely at works of art, and by agreeing to disagree on a few matters. During a time when she was obviously in the midst of many things—including the final stages of writing "Vagrancy in the Park"—Susan made me feel welcomed, engaged, and provoked at the same time. As Maureen McLane observes: "Howe's attention is fierce yet friendly. She has a darting wit. Howe is in person both delicate and formidable; so, too, her work."[277]

---

http://yaleunion.org/susan-howe/[;] "Susan Howe," *Whitney Biennial* (New York: Whitney Museum of American Art, 21014):
http://whitney.org/Exhibitions/2014Biennial/SusanHowe[;] Susan Howe and R. H. Quaytman, *TOM TIT TOT* (New York: The Museum of Modern Art, 2014); Susan Howe, Dee Morris, Nancy Kuhl, and Al Filreis, "There it was (PoemTalk #83)," *Jacket2* (December 29, 2014):
http://jacket2.org/podcasts/there-it-was-poemtalk-83[;] Catherine Halley, "Detective Work," [Interview with Susan Howe], *Poetry Foundation* (January 14, 2015): http://www.poetryfoundation.org/features/articles/detail/70196[;] Susan Howe, "from *Tom Tit Tot*," *Hambone* 21 (2015): 50-9; Susan Howe and David Grubbs, *WOODSLIPPERCOUNTERCLATTER* (Chicago: Blue Chopsticks, 2015); ---, *THIEFTH* (New York: ISSUE Project Room, 2015); Susan Howe, "Vagrancy in the Park" (2015):
http://www.thenation.com/article/vagrancy-in-the-park/[;] and *The Quarry* (2015).

Susan Howe's *Debths* (2017) includes adapted passages from this interview, which will be noted below. "I have finished the material for my new book which will come out in spring/summer 17. It has Tom Tit T and a series I made from the TTT 2 series now called Periscope. I spent months on the rather brief Foreword but included a bit of material about Yeats edition and Secret Languages that I had in our interview. Differently but the same. Once it is finally proofed and a few glitches fixed it I can send you a pdf. But ND's final proof reader may take a month or so to get to it." (Susan Howe, e-mail to W. Scott Howard, November 20, 2016.)

Note on archives, databases, and websites: unless otherwise specified, materials in the Susan Howe Papers collections at the Geisel Library, UC San Diego, and at the Beinecke Library, Yale University were respectively consulted during March, 2013, October, 2015; and January, 2015. Unless otherwise noted, all databases and websites were consulted during August, 2017.

[277] McLane, "Susan Howe, The Art of Poetry,"
https://www.theparisreview.org/interviews/6189/susan-howe-the-art-of-poetry-no-97-susan-howe[.]

After our talks, I took long walks leaning into the weather and wrote for days.

I've often reflected upon the essays her students contributed to the volume, *I Have Imagined A Center // Wilder Than This Region*, each of which rings true to my memorable visits. Susan Howe embodies a late-modernist antinomian "vigilance *now* for what action must attend"[278] together with "a will to show, rather than profess how works make their way into the world; how words work together on the page; and how words work through and across generations and material permutations moving from one context to another."[279] In that spirit of dialogue and inter-/intra-textuality—of collecting, recomposing, weaving[280]—this interview juxtaposes our conversations and correspondence with the "echo of the library's multitude of voices […]."[281]

*   *   *

---

[278] Thom Donovan, "O Fling Without A Sleeve: Susan Howe and the Pedagogy of Enaction," *I Have Imagined A Center // Wilder Than This Region: A Tribute to Susan Howe* (Cuneiform Press, 2007), 52.

[279] Kyle Schlesinger, "Sparks in the Library," *A Center // Wilder*, 87.

[280] The process of transcribing and then transforming our January, 2015 conversations from their audio recordings into draft typescripts followed many paths that were often interrupted—sometimes by our work and travel schedules or by health and/or family matters, but also especially when our e-mails and attached documents introduced new threads, texts, and tangles. Between January, 2015 and August, 2017, we exchanged and revised at least nine working drafts of this interview text, which progressively incorporated language from our e-mail correspondence (going back to October, 2013) plus new questions and replies, edits and revisions along the way. This edition (appearing for the first time, here) celebrates the spirit of those dynamic exchanges; my subtext occasionally includes excerpts from alternate passages from our conversations and correspondence. Dates and references in those instances are approximate. I am grateful to Susan Howe for her generosity and patience with this collaborative commitment to what Jerome J. McGann might call an "impossible truth." Jerome J. McGann, "Exceptional Measures: The Human Sciences in STEM Worlds," *Scholarly Editing: The Annual of the Association for Documentary Editing* 37 (2016): http://scholarlyediting.org/2016/essays/essay.mcgann.html.

[281] Barbara Cole, "The Absent Center Is The Ghost Of A ~~King~~ Queen: On Susan Howe's Buffalo," *A Center // Wilder*, 39.

191

WSH: Which books or works of art have been most interesting and important to you in recent years, and why?

Howe: Anything by Henry James. Henry, and Alice also. For years and years. But if you are referring to specific events and to works that have directly affected my writing since *That This*, my husband's sudden death from a pulmonary embolism on January 3rd, 2008 changed everything.[282] During the harrowing months that followed, I visited the major exhibition, *Poussin and Nature: Arcadian Visions* at the Metropolitan.[283] At the museum bookstore, I chanced on T. J. Clark's *The Sight of Death*.[284] I bought it at once because I was attracted by the title and admire his art criticism. Clark structures his book around two of Poussin's greatest landscape paintings: *Landscape with a Calm*, and *Landscape with a Man killed by a Snake*. In January 2000, they were exhibited face-to-face in a small square room at the Getty Museum, where he was on a fellowship. The *Snake* landscape, normally exhibited at the National Gallery in London, was already a favorite. Here, in relation to *Calm*, he noticed new elements. He began by making a series of diary notations during morning visits—morning after morning, reregistering the details of light, local weather, weather in the paintings, what one told about the other. Clark's "experiment in art writing" explores the myriad emotions great paintings evoke, the personal associations they carry, ways in which they instigate, and crystallize various ranges of experience. Seeing Poussin's late paintings at the Met among a host of other landscapes and

---

[282] Peter H. Hare (1935-2008). "Through his writings and teachings, Hare left an indelible impact upon the history of American philosophy, having helped to draw the works of Charles Peirce, George H. Mead, William James, Alfred North Whitehead and John Dewey into central positions in international philosophy." Patricia Donovan, "Peter Hare, 72, Distinguished Philosophy Professor," University at Buffalo, *News* (January 8, 2008):
http://www.buffalo.edu/news/releases/2008/01/9064.html[.]

[283] *Poussin and Nature: Arcadian Visions* (New York: The Metropolitan Museum of Art, February 12 – May 11, 2008):
http://www.metmuseum.org/press/exhibitions/2008/poussin-and-nature--arcadian-visions[.]

[284] *The Sight of Death: An Experiment in Art Writing* (New Haven and London: Yale University Press, 2006).

biblical scenes, with signage providing too much information and a constant flow of viewers was another experience completely. Because I had just experienced the actual sight of death the winter morning I found Peter, Poussin's *Snake* painting struck home. Clark's cover image expresses the suspension of a future tense in the running man's gesture as he raises his hand to make a sign. *The Sight of Death* influenced the form of my essay, "The Disappearance Approach"[285] which opens *That This*, and also to some extent, "Vagrancy in the Park."[286]

Over the past few years, Daniel Heller-Roazen's books—most of all *Echolalias*, and also *Dark Tongues*[287]—encouraged and inspired the progress of lectures I was working on that became *Spontaneous Particulars*. We share a delight in puns, definitions, riddles, single letters and phonemes, chance and coincidence. I only wish I had his linguistic brilliance. What Daniel can do with the etymology of the English word *dove*, or *roam*, or with the weirdly contrasted relationship between *casual* and *casualty* is terrific. He suggested I read *The Secret Languages of Ireland*, by the Irish archaeologist R. A. Stewart Macalister.[288] The lure of Bog-Latin, Shelta and Bēarlagair na Sāer, of Ogham and cryptology may feel superannuated or fatally picturesque to some; not to Daniel and not to me. *The Secret Languages* was published the year I was born, so maybe

---

[285] "The actors I encounter in Poussin's world have names ingrafted from myth and scripture. At the dawn of thought river gods are keeping watch." *THAT THIS*, 26.

[286] "In the future general progress of things will Manhattan be a field of ruins like the ruins near Rome in Poussin's late landscapes? All canvases turned face inward toward the wall in a room filled with poems that take the place of mountains now turned face down in the cosmic dust of history?" "Vagrancy in the Park," (Susan Howe, PDF typescript and e-mail to W. Scott Howard, March, 2015), 16; and *The Quarry*, 13.

[287] Daniel Heller-Roazen, *Echolalias: On the Forgetting of Language* (New York: Zone Books, 2008); and
Dark Tongues: The Art of Rogues and Riddlers (New York: Zone Books, 2013).

[288] R. A. Stewart Macalister, *The Secret Languages of Ireland With Special Reference to the Origin and Nature of The Shelta Language partly based upon Collections and Manuscripts of the late John Sampson, Litt. D. Sometime Librarian of the University of Liverpool* (Cambridge: Cambridge University Press, 1937).

it's a mystic connection. I love my particular edition published by Craobh Books.[289] It has a plain light blue jacket over the paper board, with text normally reserved for the inside flap in simple serif typeface on the cover, so the effect is both dryly pedagogical and rebellious. You learn from this first impression that the volume will investigate secret dialects, thieves' cant, the Irish underworld—comparative vocabularies included. According to Macalister, the work is based on a random collection of loose sheets, letters, manuscript notebooks, scraps of paper, dictionary slips—"relics of the industry of the late lamented John Sampson, known to all as one of the greatest of the world's authorities on the Gypsies, their origin, history, manners, customs, folklore, and language."[290] *Secret Languages* is wonderfully littered with etymological particulars, diacritical characters, hieroglyphs, wordlists, oblique slashes.[291] In its attention to detail and surprise it reminds me of Thoreau's journals. Letting words go down to their smallest diameter. To distances and great meadows on the paper side. These are philological wilderness encounters. I keep *Secret Languages* on my desk now with other books essential for gleaning. I used pieces of one chapter heading, "The Vagrants of Ireland," in *TOM TIT TOT*. Possibly the word "vagrant" popped into my head when I titled my essay on Wallace Stevens' late poetry "Vagrancy in the Park." I thought I was punning on his late poem, "Vacancy in the Park," but who can tell?

Vagrants can be vandals.

Another vagrant soul who's been on my mind is the artist Paul Thek. In 2011, I saw the retrospective exhibition of Paul Thek's work, *Diver*, on its closing day at the Whitney[292] and was overwhelmed by the power of his later works, particularly the series of small bronze sculptures titled

---

[289] *Secret Languages* (Armagh, Northern Ireland: Craobh Rua Books, 1997).
[290] *Secret Languages* (1937), ix.
[291] See *Debths*, 21.
[292] *Paul Thek: Diver, A Retrospective* (New York: The Whitney Museum of American Art, October 21, 2010-January 9, 2011): http://whitney.org/Exhibitions/PaulThek[.]

The Personal Effects of the Pied Piper.[293] I love the way single words or phrases scrawled across strokes of color over sheets from newspapers transformed these so-called art objects into poems. Being unable to return to the exhibition, I pored over the catalogue.[294] *Diver* was crucial to my long poem—or the series of word drawings I call *TOM TIT TOT*—which, in a way, echoes Thek's small sculptures.[295]

I've also been trolling through two of the Yeats editions from Cornell University Press, *New Poems: Manuscript Materials* (which is edited by J. C. C. Mays) and *Last Poems: Manuscript Materials.*[296] *New Poems* was the last collection published in Yeats's lifetime. I am in awe of the editions certain textual scholars have accomplished. I am not one myself, but stumbled into the field due to my fascination with the problems Emily Dickinson's manuscripts raise. I enjoy facsimile editions of poets whose manuscripts have a strong visual component; the editorial transcriptions are of particular interest to me, because they convey dogged efforts to translate into typeface what dictates the hand when it comes into contact with paper.[297] It will always be imperfect. All the awkward typographical effects—letters, acrostic signals, strokes, crossouts, changed meanings—can't match the hand's gestures, the human touch.[298] One of the delights of having access to a great library like Ster-

---

[293] Paul Thek, "The Personal Effects of the Pied Piper" (New York: Whitney Museum of American Art, 2010): http://whitney.org/WatchAndListen/Tag?context=curators&play_id=332[.]

[294] Elisabeth Sussman and Lynn Zelevansky, eds., *Paul Thek: Diver, A Retrospective* (New York: Whitney Museum of American Art, 2010).

[295] See *Debths*, 11-12.

[296] W. B. Yeats, *New Poems: Manuscript Materials*, ed. J. C. C. Mays and Stephen Parrish (Cornell: Cornell University Press, 2001); and W. B. Yeats, *Last Poems: Manuscript Materials*, ed. James Pethica (Cornell: Cornell University Press, 1997).

[297] See *Debths*, 22.

[298] "Howe: You have to tie them down somewhere in type. But the odd thing is that in the end, what I'm most interested in is not the original, but the copy. In a way, that's what *TOM TIT TOT* is all about." (Interview typescripts and e-mails to W. Scott Howard, April, 2016; May, 2016; June, 2016.) For Howe's remarkable drawings of and reflections upon Dickinson's manuscripts, see Susan Howe Papers, YCAL MSS 338, Series III, Notebooks and Diaries, 1984-2007, Box 12,

ling (at Yale) is the access it provides to such expansive collected editions I couldn't afford to own. The Cornell Yeats volumes are ideal because his work is visionary in the widest, wildest sense, and because his spelling is so appalling, single words carry an uncanny charge.

WSH: Could you tell me more about J. C. C. Mays and his work's importance to you?

Howe: James Mays's six-volume *Collected Works of Samuel Taylor Coleridge* (part of the great multi-volume Coleridge edition from the Bollingen Princeton series)[299] has been an inspiration. There are many ways I use it. Many. It is invaluable for all sorts of reasons. Mays also has an interest in contemporary experimental poetry, has a large collection of small press publications, and wrote a book called *Coleridge's Experimental Poetics*.[300] Importantly, this aspect of Coleridge's writing—including his sense of mischief—never gets lost throughout the six volumes with their myriad footnote trails, chronological tables and typographical ornaments, such as swelled rules and dropped initials. Most recently, Mays's 800-page *Coleridge's Father*[301] shows the lengths one can go to when following traces of a loved author through ever widening circles of the real world they grew out of. STC is Jim Mays's Walden Pond. Under the surface may be trunks of trees and log canoes from another age. He and Jerome McGann (whose many works, especially *The Romantic Ideology*, *The Textual Condition*, and *Dante Gabriel Rossetti:*

Folder 24, Notebook: Dickinson Material (Spring 2001), Beinecke Library, Yale University:
http://drs.library.yale.edu/fedoragsearch/rest/[.]

[299] Samuel Taylor Coleridge, *The Collected Works*, Vol. 16, Part 1, *Poems: Reading Text*, ed. J. C. C. Mays (Princeton: Princeton University Press, 2001); and Samuel Taylor Coleridge, *The Collected Works*, Vol. 16, Part 2, *Poems: Variorum Text*, ed. J. C. C. Mays (Princeton: Princeton University Press, 2001).

[300] *Coleridge's Experimental Poetics* (New York: Palgrave, 2013).

[301] *Coleridge's Father: Absent Man, Guardian Spirit* (Bristol: The Friends of Coleridge, 2014).

A Hypermedia Archive, are crucial)[302] were encouraging and supportive of my early theories relating to the editorial history of Emily Dickinson's manuscripts. Their work has taught me ways in which the seemingly dry-as-dust field of textual scholarship can be subversive in the best sense, the revolutionary sense—patient recovery, a painstaking search for truth through particulars. The search is what matters. McGann's recent essay, "Exceptional Measures: The Human Sciences in STEM Worlds," was published in *The Annual of the Association for Documentary Editing*.[303] One might wonder, with a journal titled like that—who needs readers? But what a mistake!

WSH: In *Spontaneous Particulars* you address a question you've been following for many years and which seems even more urgent today. Why are manuscripts not taken with more seriousness in some academic circles?[304]

Howe: This whole matter has had a hold on me since my work on Dickinson. Textual scholarship—*this* kind of interest—such obsessively detailed errands into manuscript wildernesses were blithely ignored in the academy during the glory days of Critical Theory. I too was inspired and influenced in all my writing by developments in psychoanalytic thought, Deconstruction, the New Historicists. In a bookstore during the eighties and nineties, rather than heading for the Poetry section, I went straight to the Theory aisles—lured by titles such as *The Wolfman's*

---

[302] Jerome J. McGann, *The Romantic Ideology: A Critical Investigation* (Chicago: University of Chicago Press, 1983); *The Textual Condition* (Princeton: Princeton University Press, 1991); *Dante Gabriel Rossetti: A Hypermedia Archive* (NINES, 2008): http://www.rossettiarchive.org/[.]

[303] *Scholarly Editing: The Annual of the Association for Documentary Editing* 37 (2016): http://scholarlyediting.org/2016/essays/essay.mcgann.html[.]

[304] "Why are manuscripts so underestimated in all academic disciplines?" Susan Howe Papers, YCAL MSS 338, Series II, Writings, [1994]-2007, Box 9, "Work for Ether/Either, Fall, 1996," Beinecke Library, Yale University, http://drs.library.yale.edu/fedoragsearch/rest/[.]

Magic Word, or *Marine Lover of Friedrich Nietzsche*.[305] But the enigmas Dickinson's manuscripts raise in terms of final intentions, those ways in which editorial intervention can work to create the Icon carried aloft in the crowd, showed me the limits of grand conclusions without close attention to particulars—even the New Historicists seemed more interested in general theories than particular material documents.[306]

In this century, information is shaped by the evolution of electronic technologies. We believe everything can be data mined, and myriad forms of textual reproduction and presentation, data-based approaches and premises are now at play in the theory and practice of text editing. And this is a wonderful thing, in terms of opening access to common readers as well as scholars. *The Online Concordance to Wallace Stevens' Poetry*[307] was essential for my work on "Vagrancy in the Park."[308] I love concordances, and I'm more accustomed to running them down in printed forms in major libraries. Online, they encourage unboundedness. But there is a sadness and even danger in such immediacy. These hardcover facsimile editions represent a dedicated allegiance to accuracy. McGann calls it a faith in "impossible truth."[309]

WSH: There's something quite singular about how *Spontaneous Particulars* taps into these phenomena. It's a sort of hybrid of prose poetry, gallery exhibition, annotated notebook, and collage. How did this work come about?

---

[305] Nicolas Abraham and Maria Torok, *The Wolfman's Magic Word: A Cryptonymy*, trans. Nicholas Rand (Minneapolis: University of Minnesota Press, 1986); Luce Irigaray, *Marine Lover of Friedrich Nietzsche* (New York: Columbia University Press, 1991).

[306] "I will never be able to explain why manuscripts are so underestimated in all academic disciplines even including linguistics and semiology." Susan Howe, "Ether Either," 122.

[307] John Serio and Greg Foster, *The Online Concordance to Wallace Stevens' Poetry*: http://www.wallacestevens.com/concordance/WSdb.cgi[.]

[308] This essay first appeared in *The Nation* (October 15, 2015): http://www.thenation.com/article/vagrancy-in-the-park/[.]

[309] "Scholars pledge allegiance to that impossible truth." McGann, "Exceptional Measures": http://scholarlyediting.org/2016/essays/essay.mcgann.html[.]

Howe: It began several years ago when the Academy of American Poets asked me to give a lecture at their annual meeting.[310] When they asked me for a title, I vaguely said, "Poetry and Telepathy." I don't think I had the words "spontaneous particulars" when I first started working on the lecture, but over time I changed the title to "Spontaneous Particulars of Sound,"[311] a line from Wallace Stevens's poem, "The Creations of Sound."[312] I wanted to emphasize the supreme importance of the ear in prose and poetry. The hard thing was to translate the slide lecture to paper because I collaged the slides—without explaining why they were in the order I had arranged them, nor describing where they came from, thus leaving the audience to make their own associations. PowerPoint can vary dramatically from what one sees on one's own computer, as the public presentation depends on whatever may have been happening on a particular day, the quality of the projector, screen, darkness of the room, a script, and the voice reading the script. A lecture is a performance. Many things can go wrong and they usually do. It is a variable situation. To translate the lecture and images into book form, I had to subtract some illustrations because printing costs and page layout necessitated another arrangement. So, in all of those ways, the lecture and the book are different animals.

WSH: There are so many evocative passages. This page, for example:

---

[310] "NYU to Host Fifth Annual Poets Forum—Oct. 20-22," New York University, *News* (September 23, 2011): http://www.nyu.edu/about/news-publications/news/2011/september/nyu-to-host-fifth-annual-poets-forumoct-20-22-.html[.]

[311] "The Spontaneous Particulars of Sound," *The Lionel Trilling Seminar*, Columbia University, *Events* (December 1, 2011): http://heymancenter.org/events/the-spontaneous-particulars-of-sound/[.]

[312] "They do not make the visible a little hard // To see nor, reverberating, eke out the mind / On peculiar horns, themselves eked out / By the spontaneous particulars of sound." Wallace Stevens, "The Creations of Sound," *The Collected Poems* (New York: Vintage Books, 1990), 311.

> Poetry has no proof nor plan nor evidence by decree or in any other way. From somewhere in the twilight realm of sound a spirit of belief flares up at the point where meaning stops and the unreality of what seems most real floods over us [...] It's a sense of self-identification and trust, or the granting of grace in an ordinary room, in a secular time.[313]

Howe: Well, yes, that's *it* for me. That's what it's all about. I pulled this paragraph from another essay that began as a lecture on Wallace Stevens and Jonathan Edwards, "Choir Answers to Choir," that was in the *Chicago Review* a few years ago.[314] In spite of myself, I suppose I'm a believer. A negative believer. I keep George Herbert's "Prayer" pinned to the wall over my writing table: "Church-bells beyond the stars heard, the soul's blood, / The land of spices; something understood."[315] That's how I feel when looking at a single Hart Crane worksheet for the "Cape Hatteras" section of *The Bridge*.[316]

WSH: *Spontaneous Particulars* covers a lot of ground and opens so many doors and windows.

Howe: I think of it as a collaborative effort. It wouldn't exist without Barbara Epler at New Directions, who partnered with Christine Burgin, the gallerist and publisher, and Leslie Miller, who has already designed and published several editions of my work at The Grenfell Press.[317] The

---

[313] *Spontaneous Particulars*, 63.

[314] "Choir answers to Choir: Notes on Jonathan Edwards and Wallace Stevens," *Chicago Review* 54.4 (2009): 51-61. For this noted passage, see page 58. On the relationship between these two paragraphs within the context of Howe's abiding engagement with Wallace Stevens' poetry, see Howard, "Archives, Artifacts, Apostrophes," 99-107.

[315] George Herbert, "Prayer (I)," *The Complete English Poems*, ed. John Tobin (London: Penguin, 1991), 46.

[316] *Spontaneous Particulars*, 61 and 78.

[317] These volumes include: Robert Mangold and Susan Howe, *The Nonconformist's Memorial* (New York: TheGrenfell Press, 1992); and Susan Howe and James Welling, *Frolic Architecture* (New York: The Grenfell Press, 2010). *TOM TIT TOT* (MoMA, 2014) was hand-printed at The Grenfell Press by Brad Ewing

four of us had such a good time, figuring out what to add, what to subtract in terms of affordability and layout. Ideally *The Midnight*[318] would have been published the same way, with color photographs, but it was a trade book and that makes a difference as to what is possible in terms of printing costs. *Spontaneous Particulars* falls halfway between poetry book and artist's book.

WSH: That was such a different time in terms of collaboration and technology. I've been looking through the Beinecke folders[319] that gather the groundwork for *The Midnight*, and what I see happening there is intense remediation: photographs of books, of letters, of fabrics, of newspapers, of images; photos of photos; photocopies of those photos; photocopies of photocopies—family history, textual legacy, meta-archives, all in a *whirlwind*.

Howe: Not a whirlwind to me. It was formally arranged. *The Midnight* has an emphasis on photographs because Peter loved books as ob-

---

and Leslie Miller, who designed the volume with Howe and her daughter, R. H. Quaytman. "The printmaker Brett Groves worked closely with Quaytman to produce all of the images, which include the frontispiece, 'The Temple of Time,' printed as a six-color silkscreen at Axelle Editions; digitally at the Lower East Side Printshop; and by letterpress at The Grenfell Press." *Spontaneous Particulars* and *TOM TIT TOT* are perhaps Howe's most thoroughly collaborative books of poetry yet achieved. See Howard, "'TANGIBLE THINGS / Out of a stark oblivion',"
https://dulibraries.wordpress.com/2015/08/05/tangible-things-out-of-a-stark-oblivion-spellbinding-tom-tit-tot/[.]

[318] *THE MIDNIGHT* (New York: New Directions, 2003). Some of these artifactual materials were reproduced with remarkable care and clarity in *KIDNAPPED* (Tipperary, Ireland: CORACLE, 2002). My copy (number 159 of 300) includes a detached bookmark fragment, "The collarbone / of a hand" in the hand of the poet, which also appears in one of the photographed books pictured in this unpaginated small press edition.

[319] Susan Howe Papers, YCAL MSS 338, Series II, Writings, [1994]-2007, Boxes 5, 6, 9; and Series IV, Professional Papers, 1961-2007, Box 14, Beinecke Library, Yale University:
http://drs.library.yale.edu/fedoragsearch/rest/[.]

jects and he loved taking photographs. We were beginning our relationship. I had moved into his house in Buffalo. I felt welcomed, and at home after years and years of mourning David's death[320] and feeling like an outsider in that border city. Peter set up a workroom for me—we got large tables, the kind I always need for thinking, doors on file cabinets or plumber's pipes—and the house (being the house of a philosophy professor) was already filled with books. Though I met Peter after writing *Pierce-Arrow*,[321] and while he was the co-editor of *The Transactions of the Charles Sanders Peirce Society*,[322] the Philosophy Department at UB was located in a different building on that brutalist 60s campus, and the split between Philosophy and Critical Theory over in the English Department building was fraught (to say the least). While working on *Pierce-Arrow*, I had been warned by my colleague Charles Bernstein not to even approach Peter Hare! How wrong he was. We both were. Peter couldn't have been more tolerant: he introduced me to other Peircean scholars; he guided me to philosophers whose ideas I had never heard of. He was also a great editor. I look back on those days of working on *The Midnight*—both in Buffalo, and later in Guilford—and realize, my God, even though the book was an elegy for my mother[323] who died only the year before I

---

[320] David von Schlegell (1920-1992). "David von Schlegell, an abstract sculptor and painter who was also a professor emeritus at the Yale University School of Art, […] had his first one-man show of sculpture in New York City at the Royal Marks Gallery in 1965, and in 1966 his work was included in "Primary Structures" at the Jewish Museum, an exhibition that helped establish Minimalism." Roberta Smith, "David von Schlegell, Abstract Artist, Is Dead at 72," *The New York Times* (October 6, 1992):
http://www.nytimes.com/1992/10/06/arts/david-von-schlegell-abstract-artist-is-dead-at-72.html[.]

[321] *Pierce-Arrow* (New York: New Directions, 1999).

[322] *The Transactions of the Charles Sanders Peirce Society*: http://peircesociety.org/transactions[.]

[323] Mary Manning Howe Adams (1905-1999). "Dublin-born and raised, Mary Manning had been associated both with the Abbey Theatre, where she had been a pupil in Sara Allgood's acting class, and as a writer for the Gate Theatre in the era of MacLiammoir and Edwards […] Ms Manning was a prolific playwright and novelist, and adapted the novel, *Guests of the Nation*, for a film directed by Denis Johnston […] In 1935, Molly came to Boston, and married Mark

met Peter, I felt more at peace composing, arranging, and re-arranging all the elements involved than I had for a long, long time.

WSH: In those typescripts, I especially enjoyed the pages where you're portraying your grandfather's speech—manipulating the page, then overtyping to get that Moiré effect.[324]

Howe: Oh, yes. His stutter. Peter reminded me of Grandpa. Not that he stuttered, but in his loyalty and trust. He was a gentleman of the old school.

WSH: When did you make the shift, in your writing practice, from typewriter to computer? Is there a book in particular that captures this transition?

Howe: It was a big thing for me to shift, in my poetry, from typewriter to computer. Before, I would constantly cut and paste and erase. It was in the late-80s up at Buffalo—*Melville's Marginalia*,[325] I think,

---

DeWolf Howe, a Harvard Law School professor […] She was one of the founders of the Poets' Theatre in Cambridge, which brought some of the country's most distinguished poets and poet dramatists to its stage." *The Irish Times* (Thursday, July 8, 1999): http://www.irishtimes.com/opinion/mary-manning-howe-adams-1.204225[.] For a recording of Mary Manning Howe reading poems by W. B. Yeats, visit Christina Davis, Susan Howe, and Fanny Howe, "Invocation," *VOCARIUM* (Harvard University, c. 1940s):
http://hcl.harvard.edu/poetryroom/vocarium/recordings/catalyst_howe.cfm[.]

[324] "[…] some phonetic chiaroscuro of disorder, Or the way if a match is scraped fire results […] GRANDPA: (laboring to get a civil first syllable straight)." Susan Howe Papers, YCAL MSS 338, Series II, Writings, [1994]-2007, Box 5, "Work on Preterient," Beinecke Library, Yale University: http://drs.library.yale.edu/fedoragsearch/rest/[.] See also "Ether Either," 123.

[325] Susan Howe Papers, YCAL MSS 338, Series II, Writings, [1994]-2007, Box 9, "Notes and Ideas while writing *Melville's Marginalia* (1989)," Beinecke Library, Yale University:
http://drs.library.yale.edu/fedoragsearch/rest/[.] Susan Howe, "Melville's Marginalia," *The Nonconformist's Memorial* (New York: New Directions, 1993), 91-159; see also Susan Howe, *Marginalia de Melville*, trans. Susan Howe, Bénédicte Vilgrain, Richard Sieburth, and Bernard Rival (Paris: Théâtre Typographique,

shows the transition—but I made this shift first in my prose. *My Emily Dickinson*[326] was all typewriter, but the essays in *The Birth-mark*[327] were done on one of the old chunky Apple desktop computers. To this day, I never trust anything until I see it run through my printer. The idea of merely trusting the screen image doesn't exist for me. I clung to the typewriter for poems into the late-80s. With the poetry it was just somehow the tactile *thing*, which brings it all around to touch, to acoustics—because it's a ritual. For quite a few years, I produced poetry programs on the radio (at WBAI in the 70s)[328] and I edited tape and I loved doing it—the materiality, the *slash*, the cutting with the razor—and I became so sensitive because every single poet has a verbal tic. And what do you do—how far do you go in editing?[329] It was a very big transition for my poetry. *Melville's Marginalia* was where I crossed over.

1997), which was the first publication of *Melville's Marginalia* as a single volume book. On this edition, Howe reflected: "I had to change line breaks in the translation of the poem as I couldn't bear the way lengths of lines became straggly or too short in translation! [...] Have just given lectures at Stanford and Notre Dame [... and am now] at work on a new [manuscript] and very taken up with Charles Sanders Peirce—" (Susan Howe, letter to W. Scott Howard, April 24, 1997). "Melville's Marginalia" was also adapted into a musical performance by Susan Howe and David Grubbs that was published as their first CD, *THIEFTH* (Chicago: Blue Chopsticks, 2005) and then republished on vinyl, *THIEFTH* (New York: ISSUE Project Room, 2015). See also "Susan Howe and David Grubbs," PennSound:
http://writing.upenn.edu/pennsound/x/Howe-Grubbs.php[.]

[326] *My Emily Dickinson* (Berkeley: North Atlantic Books, 1985). See also Susan Howe Papers, YCAL MSS 338, Series IV, Professional Papers, 1961-2007, Boxes 14, 15, 16, 17, Beinecke Library, Yale University:
http://drs.library.yale.edu/fedoragsearch/rest/[.]

[327] *The Birth-mark: unsettling the wilderness in American literary history* (Hanover and London: Wesleyan University Press, 1993). See also Susan Howe Papers, 1942-2002, MSS 0201, Boxes 51, 52, 53, Geisel Library, Special Collections and Archives, UC San Diego:
http://libraries.ucsd.edu/speccoll/findingaids/mss0201.html[.]

[328] Susan Howe, "Poetry Programs, WBAI-Pacifica Radio," *PennSound*:
http://www.writing.upenn.edu/pennsound/x/Howe-Pacifica.php[.]

[329] Anyone who has had the pleasure of talking with Susan Howe knows how delightfully various her speech patterns can be. Transposing those polyvocal scores to this typescript's sonic register has been challenging.

WSH: In your *Pierce-Arrow* typescripts,[330] several pages have these vibrant strokes and annotations made with a rainbow pencil: circlings, arrows, numerations, underlinings, revisions. I don't recall seeing any of these markings in your papers at UCSD.[331] Can you tell me about rainbow pencil?

Howe: Oh, yes. I use a particular rainbow pencil to mark my scripts for readings. They are black and don't have a brand name so the multi-colored tips are like little lights. I found them years ago at Bob Slate Stationers in Harvard Square, a wonderful store. Since my mother's death, I seldom go to Cambridge. The nibs are softer and the colors more brilliant than any others I know of. These final two are worn down to stubs! I started marking my reading scripts with regular pencils years ago, probably for reading *Thorow*.[332] I love it that Thoreau was an early American pencil manufacturer.

Increasingly, with the scripts I use for performances with David Grubbs, I've found these colored marks I once considered to be acoustic signals also produce a visual pleasure-effect—so each of these pages[333]

---

[330] Susan Howe Papers, YCAL MSS 338, Series II, Writings, [1994]-2007, Boxes 5, 9, 10; and Series IV, Professional Papers, 1961-2007, Boxes 14, 15, Beinecke Library, Yale University:
http://drs.library.yale.edu/fedoragsearch/rest/[.]

[331] Susan Howe Papers, 1942-2002, MSS 0201, Boxes 55, 56, Geisel Library, Special Collections and Archives, UC San Diego:
http://libraries.ucsd.edu/speccoll/findingaids/mss0201.html[.]

[332] This work first appeared in *Temblor* 6 (1987): 3-21; was republished in *Singularities* (Hanover and London: Wesleyan, 1990), 39-59; then translated, appearing as "Passe-Thoreau" and "Thorow" in *Thorow*, trans. Bernard Rival (Paris: Théâtre Typographique, 2002), 7-32, 49-76; and then adapted, appearing as the first track in the first studio CD by Howe and David Grubbs, *THIEFTH* (Chicago: Blue Chopsticks, 2005), which was reissued on vinyl, *THIEFTH* (New York: ISSUE Project Room, 2015). See also Susan Howe Papers, 1942-2002, MSS 0201, Box 9, Folder 11, Geisel Library, Special Collections and Archives, UC San Diego:
http://libraries.ucsd.edu/speccoll/findingaids/mss0201.html.

[333] Annotated typescript pages for *WOODSLIPPERCOUNTERCLATTER*, which premiered October 25, 2013 at ISSUE Project Room. "Veering away from the stuttering, profoundly fragmented séance of *Frolic Architecture* (2011), Howe and Grubbs present a sound-work that germinates from new, unpublished

could almost be drawings. Most colored strokes and scribbled notes are there to catch timed silences, emphasis, word order. When I'm in the moment, actually reading to an audience, I'm too nervous to notice them. I almost never read a book without having a pencil nearby for making marginal marks. I need to have a pencil beside me at my readings—in case of what? I do not know. Maybe for luck. Not pens. Pens are too final. Pencil can always be erased. I save the marked scripts and re-use them so they have other signs of wear and tear. The rainbow effect is crucial. These odd prismatic marks—sometimes singular and clear, sometimes smudged—create a sound-sign territory of accidental purpose. I enjoy the way the colors *float* on the page.

WSH: They're sound forms in time, and also notation / floatation devices.[334] You've got the timing marked here, *3 sec.*, and here, *15 sec.*

Howe: This is because David has timed sections using his acoustic effects—piano, electronic music, field recordings, slivers of speech. I mark how many seconds separate each sequence before I begin. After all, this is collaboration, and his acoustic effects are as important as my spoken words.[335] There's a thrill in the discipline of timing. David is more relaxed about accidents than I am. On the scripts, you can also see I have other written directions—*don't rush / lower / wait // pause / quiet / wait*—stage directions to myself.

Susan Howe text collages (Tom Tit Tot, Childe Roland, Paul Thek, W. B. Yeats, etc.) blended with the resonant sounds and represented spaces of a grand piano and field recordings made in Boston's Gardner Museum." "David Grubbs & Susan Howe," *ISSUE Project Room*:
http://issueprojectroom.org/event/david-grubbs-susan-howe[.]

[334] This phrase, *notation / floatation devices*, echoes one of Catherine Halley's comments in the text of her interview with Susan Howe, "Detective Work": http://www.poetryfoundation.org/features/articles/detail/70196[.]

[335] Susan Howe and David Grubbs, *WOODSLIPPERCOUNTERCLATTER* (New York: ISSUE Project Room, October 25, 2013): https://vimeo.com/138668754[.]

206

WSH: Digital media are shaping new ways of listening and seeing. Have you ever thought about making a film?

Howe: No. I loved writing the essay on Chris Marker.[336] And I have loved watching films all my life. Far more than going to the theater, because as André Bazin wonderfully said, "There are no wings to the screen."[337]

WSH: In recent years, your work has engaged collaboratively with digital sound and video, open access web cultures, and galleries. How are these media—these differently charged spaces—informing or suggesting what's next for your work?

Howe: I recently read *Sound Unseen* by Brian Kane.[338] He begins with a meditation on a mysterious noise coming from deep underground in Moodus, Connecticut. Nobody can explain its source. Scientists have offered theories, First Peoples had their explanations, settlers had theirs, current residents have theirs, but really, it's simply unknowable. It's a sound unseen. Like the Oracle, or the *akousmatikoi* and Pythagoras's veil.[339]

---

[336] "Sorting Facts" (1996): 295-343.

[337] André Bazin, *What is Cinema?*, 2 vols., trans. Hugh Gray (Berkeley: University of California Press, 1973). "The screen is not a frame like that of a picture but a mask which allows only a part of the action to be seen. When a character moves off screen, we accept the fact that he is out of sight, but he continues to exist in his own capacity at some other place in the décor which is hidden from us. There are no wings to the screen. There could not be without destroying its specific illusion, which is to make of a revolver or of a face the very center of the universe. In contrast to the stage the space of the screen is centrifugal" (vol. 1, 105).

[338] *Sound Unseen: Acousmatic Sound in Theory and Practice* (Oxford: Oxford University Press, 2014).

[339] Kane investigates the Iamblichan account of Pythagorean disciples that divides the school into two groups "separated by a veil: The *mathematikoi*, seated inside the veil close to Pythagoras, were not only able to see the master lecturing but were entitled to witness demonstrations of this theories; the *akousmatikoi*, seated outside the veil, were only entitled to hear the master's propositions and were not given the privilege of seeing the demonstrations […] The *akousmatikoi*,

I don't know yet where I will go next in terms of my writing. *TOM TIT TOT* broke my poetry, opened a new path to follow that began with the poems in *Frolic Architecture*[340] and has been encouraged in acoustic directions while working on collaborations with David.[341] Working with Leslie Miller and her openness to printing whatever strange word collage I present her with—solving the crossover between scanning and letterpress—has had an equally strong effect. I still felt somehow that *Frolic* was anchored-down to some material, a document or fact—to Hannah Edwards's original text[342]—whereas *TOM TIT TOT* tosses chance and discipline together in a more kaleidoscopic way—seeing the Paul Thek show and then my experience of living at the Gardner Museum in Boston on a fellowship.[343] You could say, on one level, that *TOM TIT TOT* is written by a retired Professor who takes her notes and tosses them into the air and lets them fall down where they may.[344] In terms of the internet, I feel like a barbarian at the gates. I wish I knew how to make use of

---

or exoteric disciples, are typically described as religious Pythagoreans [...] In contrast, the *mathematikoi*, or esoteric disciples, are characterized as scientific Pythagoreans, often identified as the genuine disciples of the group" (55-56).

[340] Susan Howe and James Welling, *Frolic Architecture* (New York: The Grenfell Press, 2010); Susan Howe, "Frolic Architecture," *THAT THIS*, 37-95; Susan Howe and David Grubbs, *Frolic Architecture* (Chicago: Blue Chopsticks, 2011).

[341] Susan Howe and David Grubbs, *Frolic Architecture* (Boston: Harvard University, November 2, 2011):
https://www.youtube.com/watch?v=xR6cfDFTL8Q[.]

[342] "That this book is a history of / a shadow that is a shadow of // me mystically one in another / Another another to subserve" (*THAT THIS*, 39). See also *Spontaneous Particulars*, 44-45. Hannah Edwards Wetmore, "Diary" and "Diary fragments," Jonathan Edwards Collection, GEN MSS 151, Series IV, Edwards Family Writings, 1704-1904, Box 24, Folders 1378, 1379, 1380, 1381, 1382, Beinecke Library, Yale University:
http://drs.library.yale.edu/fedoragsearch/rest/[.]

[343] "Susan Howe" (Boston: Isabella Stewart Gardner Museum, 2012): http://www.gardnermuseum.org/contemporary_art/artists/susan_howe[.]

[344] "[...] Scattered marks and loop / off words from images twi / from their original source / history scattered to the fou / of a page it was *you* playn, / [...]." *TOM TIT TOT* (MoMA, 2014), unpaginated. "The way Ricky Jay shuffles his cards. But of course this is a wild exaggeration because I do work carefully over the collaged fragments." (Susan Howe, e-mail to W. Scott Howard, August 18, 2017.) See also the epigraph to Edward Clodd's *TOM TIT TOT*, which draws

208

the wonders of this new world and could manipulate InDesign, or Photoshop. But you can't teach an old dog new tricks. I use scissors, tape, and a simple Canon copier to construct or break up the collaged elements in my work. Leslie takes it from there.

WSH: *TOM TIT TOT* is a spellbinding collage of "TANGIBLE THINGS / Out of a stark oblivion."[345] Would you agree that bibliographies are curious poems in their own right?

Howe: For me they often are. All my life, I've loved fairy tales, and the magic appearance of those three monosyllabic three-letter words as both name and title, Tom Tit Tot, reminded me of Thek's *Personal Effects of the Pied Piper*, which led me back to Browning's wonderful poem, "Childe Roland to the Dark Tower Came."[346] I began *My Emily Dickinson* with "Childe Roland."[347] So, at the very beginning of my work and now here so many years later in *TOM TIT TOT*—via Thek, Browning, even Yeats, who also made use of Browning's "Childe Roland"—I have circled through spontaneous particulars (fable and folklore) ending with the beginning.[348]

---

from John Florio's 1603 translation of Montaigne's essay, "Of Names": "What diversitie soever there be in herbs, all are shuffled up together under the name of a sallade. Even so, upon the consideration of names, I will here huddle up a gallymafry of diverse articles." Edward Clodd, *Tom Tit Tot: an essay on savage philosophy in folk-tale* (London: Duckworth & Co., 1898), epigraph. Michel de Montaigne, "Of Names," *The Essayes of Michael Lord of Montaigne*, trans. John Florio (London: George Routledge and Sons, Ltd., 1894), 136.

[345] *TOM TIT TOT* (MoMA, 2014), unpaginated. See also *TOM TIT TOT* (New York: The Museum of Modern Art, 2014):
https://www.moma.org/learn/resources/library/council/howequaytman[.]

[346] Robert Browning, "Childe Roland to the Dark Tower Came," *The EServer Poetry Collection*, http://poetry.eserver.org/childe-roland.html.

[347] "Both 'Childe Roland to the Dark Tower Came' and 'My Life had stood—a Loaded Gun—,' written in the latter half of the nineteenth century, are triumphantly negative poems. Their authors, alien explicators of ruin after the Tablets of the Law were broken, live on in archaic time beyond future" (*My Emily Dickinson*, 69).

[348] In the recorded conversations and also in earlier drafts of this typescript, this passage leads to an exchange that underscores Howe's poetics and praxis of

WSH: How do you find the right balance between chance and discipline when you're writing?

Howe: I recently heard the stage magician and actor Ricky Jay give a lecture at Yale.[349] I think it was for various departments—Art History, Drama, English—so the audience consisted of a wide variety of listeners. The way he described performing his card tricks was a metaphor for the way I write essays. It struck me as being so Peircean—in that it all depends on chance, spontaneity, discipline, habit—in a word, *tychism*. To get his tricks to work, Ricky Jay has to shuffle, practice, shuffle, practice—for hours and hours, days and weeks. When I'm writing an essay, I obsessively cut and paste, cut and paste, erase, shift, print out, look, shift, erase. Put this in someplace else. Move that somewhere else. Shuffling cards speaks to all of this—you reach spontaneity through habit, through discipline.

What I'm trying to figure—this miracle about it—takes me back to how Cézanne's work is an obsession of dots, colors, and strokes. And also to Peirce's idea of *synechism*[350]—how connections happen without

---

contingency: "WSH: Your work seems to happen in the dynamic *midst* of things. Howe: Yes, it's *betweenness*—always, always. Always between. Always, between." (Interview typescript and e-mail to W. Scott Howard, February, 2015; and May, 2016.) See also Howard, "Archives, Artifacts, Apostrophes," 103; and Howe, *Debths*, 18.

[349] *From the World Wide Website of Ricky Jay*:
http://www.rickyjay.com/[.]

[350] "Synechism, as a metaphysical theory, is the view that the universe exists as a continuous whole of all of its parts, with no part being fully separate, determined or determinate, and continues to increase in complexity and connectedness through semiosis and the operation of an irreducible and ubiquitous power of relational generality to mediate and unify substrates. As a research program, synechism is a scientific maxim to seek continuities where discontinuities are thought to be permanent and to seek semiotic relations where only dyadic relations are thought to exist. Synechism and pragmatism mutually support each other: synechism provides a theoretical rationale for pragmatism, while use of the pragmatic maxim to identify conceivable consequences of experimental activity enriches the content of the theory by revealing and creating relationships."

connectives—*in*sight unseen. Stein says the same thing differently in several of her writings and lectures, such as "Composition as Explanation,"[351] or "Henry James." They might seem repetitive and random, but they are, in fact, right on the money, revelatory and extremely precise. Ricky Jay says the danger of all this shuffling is not knowing when to stop, rather than stopping to allow the right thing to happen.

WSH: As if the cards were acting on their own. Is Ricky Jay's shuffling a form of *factual telepathy*?[352]

Howe: Exactly. Can the cards be controlled? That's the question. To see Jay shuffle the pack and then throw a card into the air and it somehow comes down in the exact place appears to be miraculous. It's the same way a word lands in a line in the right place. Or what unseen power brings two lines together. Procedure, randomness, chance, and habit. You have to keep practicing. Using everything. It's the trick of the trade.

Joseph Esposito, "Synechism," *The Digital Encyclopedia of Charles S. Peirce*: http://www.digitalpeirce.fee.unicamp.br/[.]

[351] "It is very likely that nearly every one has been very nearly certain that something that is interesting is interesting them. Can they and do they. It is very interesting that nothing inside in them, that is when you consider the very long history of how every one ever acted or has felt, it is very interesting that nothing inside in them in all of them makes it connectedly different. By this I mean this. The only thing that is different from one time to another is what is seen and what is seen depends upon how everybody is doing everything. This makes the thing we are looking at very different and this makes what those who describe it make of it, it makes a composition, it confuses, it shows, it is, it looks, it likes it as it is, and this makes what is seen as it is seen. Nothing changes from generation to generation except the thing seen and that makes a composition." Gertrude Stein, "Composition as Explanation," *Poetry Foundation*:
http://www.poetryfoundation.org/resources/learning/essays/detail/69481[.]

[352] On the emergence of this key trope of *factual telepathy* in Howe's writing, see "Sorting Facts" (1996): 297; and Susan Howe Papers, YCAL MSS 338, Series II, Writings, [1994]-2007, Box 9, "Work for Ether/Either, Fall, 1996," Beinecke Library, Yale University:
http://drs.library.yale.edu/fedoragsearch/rest/. "If love hovers telepathically in far-fact nostalgia listen at flash instants […]." On the significance of Howe's factual telepathy in *The Quarry*, see Howard, "Art in Art / Stone on Stone," http://talismanarchive3a.weebly.com/howard-howe.html[.]

211

WSH: In *Sorting Facts*, you describe Dickinson's manuscripts (by quoting Vertov) as "Drawings in motion. Blueprints in motion. Plans for the future."[353] When you're collaging paragraphs and lines, are you listening and watching for intuition?

Howe: Well, that sort of intuition is predestined. I can work and work and work for days on crafting one paragraph. Suddenly a word jumps out. It doesn't look right or it sounds wrong. Stevens ends "The Creations of Sound" this way: "We do not say ourselves like that in poems. / We say ourselves in syllables that rise / From the floor, rising in speech we do not speak."[354] Fundamentally—who knows?

WSH: *TOM TIT TOT* is like a kaleidoscope of drawings in motion. If, as you said earlier, *TOM TIT TOT* 'broke' your poetry, how did it shape *The Quarry*?

Howe: After finishing *TOM TIT TOT*, a work that balances on a line between poetry and visual art, I returned to an essay concerning Stevens that I had worked and re-worked for years. In a way, *TOM TIT TOT* led to "Vagrancy in the Park."[355] Even if "Vagrancy" is now the first essay

---

[353] *Sorting Facts: or, Nineteen Ways of Looking at Marker* (New York: New Directions, 2013), 48; and *The Quarry*, 126.

[354] *The Collected Poems*, 311.

[355] "Howe: I've been wondering if together they might someday form one book." (Interview typescript and e-mail to W. Scott Howard, January, 2015 and April, 2016.) These reflections illustrate Howe's creative process betwixt and between the publications of *Spontaneous Particulars* (2014), *TOM TIT TOT* (MoMA, 2014), *The Quarry* (2015): and the emergence of *Debths* (2017), all four of which were synergistically woven into her working papers, typescripts, galley proofs, notes and sketches for her work's new directions. "WSH: Have you published all of the work that went into *TOM TIT TOT*? // Howe: Well, [walking away] this [files opening, pages turning] is what, really [walking back] … this is just what all of it together would be—someday hopefully. This would be [pages turning] *debths*—that's from *Finnegan's Wake*. Isn't that wonderful—*debt* and *depths*—by just that *b* … So, there's a whole prose section [pages turning] and then there would be *TOM TIT TOT*, which is the one with Becky, and then there's this other section … which is poems like this [pages turning] so

in *The Quarry*, I think of it in certain ways as a long poem—just as I sometimes think of *TOM TIT TOT* as a collaged essay on Yeats's late poetry.[356]

WSH: *TOM TIT TOT* premiered as a gallery installation and performance with David Grubbs at Yale Union[357] in 2013. Are these multimedia collaborations taking you back, in new ways, to your roots in dramatic performance and visual arts?

Howe: On some level, I think of the space of a page as a stage with word characters moving across. Growing up during the 1940s and 50s in Cambridge, Mass, I acted in Brattle Theatre and Poets' Theatre productions whenever a child actor was needed. As my mother's daughter, the theatre has always seemed more real than real life. The Brattle was an attempt at a Repertory Theatre on the English model, while the Poets' Theatre, though wildly free, wasn't method acting. The playwright's words were foremost. I was in the crowd scene of *The Playboy of the Western World* at the Brattle with the great Irish actress Sara Allgood,[358] who took me under her wing. She was an old woman then, but I've never forgotten her power. Around the same time, at the Poets' Theatre, I was one of the possessed girls during the Salem witchcraft hysteria in Lyon Phelps' three-act verse drama, *The Gospel Witch*. I remember having to suddenly stand up and shout out "Mother, mother, who is, what is, where

---

there's three elements ... But let me show you ... [walking away, walking back, book opening] ... This is the MoMA edition of *TOM TIT TOT* [pages turning] ... this is the whole thing. It's really beautifully done." (Interview typescript and e-mail to W. Scott Howard, January, 2015 and February, 2015.)

[356] See *Debths*, 21.

[357] "Susan Howe, TOM TIT TOT" (Yale Union): http://yaleunion.org/susan-howe/. For photographs from that event, visit Howard, "Spellbinding *TOM TIT TOT*," https://dulibraries.wordpress.com/2015/08/05/tangible-things-out-of-a-stark-oblivion-spellbinding-tom-tit-tot/[.]

[358] *Theatre Arts* 34 (1950): 55.

213

is, God?"[359] I've never been able to get that silly line out of my head. Later, when I was probably sixteen, I was the boy who leads an old blind man around the stage in *The Trojan Horse* by Archibald MacLeish.[360] Checking Google, I see that Paul Brooks, in a note[361] accompanying the first edition, ties the play to the McCarthy era. According to Brooks, the script was intended more generally to explore in myth the sense of deception the poet had perceived in his own century. These were the Cold War years. FBI agents were all over Cambridge and Boston, asking questions. My father[362] was a friend of Alger Hiss and his brother Donald—they all clerked for Oliver Wendell Holmes at the end of his long life.[363] Both my parents believed Hiss was innocent. I can remember many dinner table discussions over how to help what to do and daddy's bewilderment and anger. I am glad he died before the real story came out. If it is the real story. I still have my doubts. In our family, Whittaker Chambers

---

[359] William Lyon Phelps, "Autumn" (un-published). See also John R. W. Small, "The Playgoer: At the Christ Church Parish House," *The Harvard Crimson* (April 26, 1951):
http://www.thecrimson.com/article/1951/4/26/the-playgoer-pit-was-a-sadly/[.]

[360] "Mary Manning Howe, an Abbey Theatre actress married to law professor Mark DeWolfe Howe, directed *The Trojan Horse* for the Poets' Theatre, in a double bill with *This Music*. The Howes' daughter Susan played the part of the [youth] very effectively, and won Archie's enduring affection." Scott Donaldson and R. H. Winnick, *Archibald MacLeish: an American Life* (New York: Houghton Mifflin, 1992), 429.

[361] "Archibald MacLeish," *Poetry Foundation*:
http://www.poetryfoundation.org/poems-and-poets/poets/detail/archibald-macleish[.]

[362] Mark De Wolfe Howe (1906-1967) was a member of the Harvard Law School Faculty and the biographer of Justice Oliver Wendell Holmes. See "Mark De Wolfe Howe Dies; Lawyer, Historian Was 60," *The Harvard Crimson* (March 1, 1967): http://www.thecrimson.com/article/1967/3/1/mark-de-wolfe-howe-dies-lawyer/[.]

[363] Mark De Wolfe Howe wrote a two-volume biography of Justice Oliver Wendell Holmes: *The Shaping Years, 1841-1870* (Harvard: Harvard University Press, 1957); and *The Proving Years, 1870-1882* (Harvard: Harvard University Press, 1957). In her October 28, 2016 conversation with Marta Werner, Howe reflects: "We all blamed Holmes for driving him to an early grave." See Susan Howe and Marta Werner, "Transcript and Transgression," *The Networked Recluse: The Connected World of Emily Dickinson* (Amherst: Amherst College Press, 2017), 125.

seemed as shifty and diabolical as Iago. How we loathed him. Years later, when I discovered that he was a friend of Louis Zukofsky, I was shocked. Before that, the suicide of F. O. Matthiessen in 1950 was an event I will never forget. To think now—he was only 48 at the time. He was one of my parents' closest friends. I would have been 12—those were the years when the Brattle was a real theater. So, politics and theatre were all one—after all, my mother had grown up in Dublin during the Easter Rising and the Civil War years, the years of Yeats and Maud Gonne, of Pádraig Pearse, the Abbey and Gate Theatres—drama and politics were united even if Ireland wasn't.

I was cast as Everyman in the 15th-century morality play of that name when I was a tenth grader in a girl's school in Brookline. As I learned his speeches and spoke them aloud onstage, I felt a profound connection—a sort of conversion experience. It scared me. What started as pride at having been chosen to play the lead role in a new school yielded to foreboding born from the demands of the words I was reciting. I began to feel they managed me. I recently borrowed a copy of the book from the Guilford Library, and wonder all these years later: what a strange play to have teenage girls memorize and perform! The grim accounts of the pain of hell and purgatory. The restless revolution of wheels. The souls of the proud to grasp the mysterious blank at the center. What was the Beaver Country Day School thinking?

At one point Death says to Everyman: *"On thee thou must take a long journey: / Therefore thy book of count with thee thou bring; / For turn again thou can not by no way, / And look thou be sure of thy reckoning* [...].[364] Now it seems prophetic in terms of my life since. Because if you are an artist, you go in a direction—a coalescence of religious and secular maybe, but it is a journey. There is no other way and there will be a reckoning.

---

[364] *Everyman*, ed. Ernest Rhys (Project Gutenberg, 2006), public domain, http://www.gutenberg.org/files/19481/19481-h/19481-h.htm[.]

WSH: How do you celebrate a mystery without betraying it? Or, is a certain transgression necessary in the reckoning? In which of your works was this journey most exciting and exacting?

Howe: Each series of poems and almost every essay I write involves an obsession. This obsessive-compulsive curiosity hasn't changed, though the form of the work changes. I follow one word, fact, event, interest, or trace that leads to another. Coincidences and connections egg me on: a single word (thorow), or a name (Tim Tit Tot), or spotting an odd book (*Bibliography of the King's Book*,[365] or *Melville's Marginalia*[366]), or a misspelling, or an archaic term, or a word or line crossed-out. Years ago, I chanced on the word "thorow" for "through" in an eighteenth-century letter by Sir William Johnson, an Anglo-Irish fur trader, in the historical section of a small local library in Lake George, New York that set me off on a series work I titled *Thorow*. I plundered that edition of Johnson's papers,[367] oddly spelled words, their blunt letter subtractions, and the sense of immediate violence they evoked for me. More recently, I chanced on a volume titled *Tom Tit Tot*[368] in the folklore section of The Butler Library at Columbia while I was looking for something else. I always think the current poem or essay I am working on is the most exciting and that all my previous work has led to it. I don't think of crossing a line between esoteric and exoteric wonder or anything like that while I'm working on something, but some work falls more one way than the other. With each series, I am totally engrossed in the subject at hand, with no final intention, though I am very conscious of the way

---

[365] Edward Almack, *A Bibliography of the King's Book or Eikon Basilike* (London: Blades, East & Blades, 1896).

[366] Wilson Walker Cowen, "Melville's Marginalia," dissertation (Boston: Harvard University, 1965); and *Melville's Marginalia*, 2 vols. (New York: Garland, 1987). See also *Melville's Marginalia Online*: http://melvillesmarginalia.org/m.php?p=policies[.]

[367] *Sir William Johnson Papers*, revised edition (New York State Library, 2015), http://www.nysl.nysed.gov/publications/johnsoncd.htm[.]

[368] Edward Clodd, *Tom Tit Tot: an essay on savage philosophy in folk-tale* (London: Duckworth & Co., 1898).

elements on facing pages mirror one another. Line by line, one stanza speaking to and mirroring the other.

The sense of transgression and reckoning enters because what I make of these finds involves disruption, quotation, omission—you might say plagiarizing. At the same time, I am collecting, recomposing. It's a process akin to weaving or embroidering in that it involves pinning something down, but it could also be called *acousmatic listening*.[369] Ventriloquism. Because, after all, this concerns other voices, voices of the dead. Near the end of *Paterson*, Williams frames this encounter as a hunt, in which you capture—and kill the thing you desire:

> The Unicorn roams the forest of all true lovers' minds. They hunt it down. Bow wow! sing hey the green holly![370]

Emerson, in "The American Scholar," reverses the paradox:

> It was dead fact; now, it is quick thought. It can stand, and it can go. It now endures, it now flies, it now inspires. Precisely in proportion to the depth of mind from which it issued, so high does it soar, so long does it sing.[371]

Probably the most exciting and transgressive work of mine I can think of is *Frolic Architecture*, which changed everything for me. There,

---

[369] "As an alternative to the aesthetic approach to acousmatic sound, I take the position that acousmatic listening is a shared, intersubjective practice of attending to musical and nonmusical sounds, a way of listening to the soundscape that is cultivated when the source of sounds is beyond the horizon of visibility, uncertain, underdetermined, bracketed, or willfully and imaginatively suspended. The term 'acousmatic listening' should be understood as a rubric intended to capture a set of historically situated strategies and techniques for listening to sounds unseen" (Kane, *Sound Unseen*, 7).

[370] William Carlos Williams, *Paterson (Book Five)* (New York: New Directions, 1958), unpaginated.

[371] Ralph Waldo Emerson, "The American Scholar," *Digital Emerson: A Collective Archive*:
http://digitalemerson.wsulibs.wsu.edu/exhibits/show/text/the-american-scholar.

I moved into an acoustic relationship with the print source material. I thought I was making word drawings based on my typographic transcription of Lucy's Wetmore Whittelsey's eighteenth-century handwritten transcription of her mother Hannah's private journal.[372] I cut into passages from my transcription with scissors, turned and adjusted them, taped sections onto sections, ran them through the copier, then re-worked and folded over the results.[373] The mirroring effect leads me on. And yet, in what seems to be random and yet chance at the same second, and even as I may think I am the one doing the composing, there is also another composer: Hannah. There is still Hannah's *acousmatic voice*.[374] So, the first-person pronoun, the *I*, is really a shifter, depending on context and speaker. By cutting into my photocopies of those transcribed pages—that's where the light is. This was a departure for me, in the sense that what I constructed with my hands—those collaged sections—had also occurred as parts of other poems.

Echoes. It's all about echoes.

---

[372] *Spontaneous Particulars*, 53. Hannah Edwards Wetmore, "Diary, 1736-39, copy in the hand of Lucy Wetmore Whittelsey, with commentary," Jonathan Edwards Collection, GEN MSS 151, Series IV, Edwards Family Writings, 1704-1904, Box 24, Folder 1377, Beinecke Library, Yale University: http://drs.library.yale.edu/fedoragsearch/rest/[.]

[373] These remediated artifacts appear in The Grenfell Press and New Directions editions of *Frolic Architecture*, in the New Directions edition of *Spontaneous Particulars* (pages 44, 46, 59, 60, 62), and also in the CD insert for *Frolic Architecture* (Chicago: Blue Chopsticks, 2011) by Susan Howe and David Grubbs. See also Howard, "Archives, Artifacts, Apostrophes," 99-107.

[374] Kane, *Sound Unseen*, 193-5, 206-13, 219-22. "The spacing of source, cause, and effect characteristic of acousmatic sound is made perspicuous by the fact that the sonic effect underdetermines attributions of the source or cause. When discussing the acousmatic voice, we might adjust the terms slightly and say that the underdetermination of the source by the voice reveals the structural spacing of the voice and its source. That spacing, rather than encouraging a reduction of the voice *either* to the status of an autonomous entity *or* to the physicality of its source, makes the voice into a site of endless detour or reference. The acousmatic voice directs the listener toward the absent presence or present absence of the source, without ever allowing the completion of that passage" (194-195). See also *Debths*, 18.

WSH: In *Spontaneous Particulars*, you write: "If you are lucky, you may experience a moment *before*."[375] Can you tell me more about this?

Howe: Early this morning I woke with this line running through my mind: "The eye sees the outside." I didn't have a pencil beside my bed so kept running it over and over in that half-asleep state hoping not to forget it. The more I did, the more I felt its relation to marginal marking and how my need to make pencil strokes as acoustic marks is related to this mystery that the eye sees what is *outside* in the landscape or in the form of words or drawings on paper, but before that, *inside*, the slash or mark wells up in that instant gesture from the deepest place, where music before counting hails from.[376] It's that instant of no words—Peirce's definition of *Firstness*.[377] You need *Secondness* and *Thirdness* to express the sensation.[378] Firstness is that *thingness*. I mean—before you kill it by capturing it and yes, *before*. Before you do anything, it has come from an opposite direction. Henry James has the most wonderful story about

---

[375] *Spontaneous Particulars*, 18.

[376] See *Debths*, 22.

[377] "The typical ideas of Firstness are qualities of feeling, or mere appearances [...] independently of its being perceived or remembered [...] The unanalyzed total impression made by any manifold not thought of as actual fact, but simply as a quality as simple positive possibility of appearance is an idea of Firstness." Charles Sanders Peirce, "Letters to Lady Welby," *Critical Theory Since 1965*, ed. Hazard Adams and Leroy Searle (Tallahassee: University Press of Florida, 1986), 639-40. See also *Spontaneous Particulars*, 36-7; and Susan Howe Papers, YCAL MSS 338, Series III, Notebooks and Diaries [1984-2007], Box 11, "Sketch Book Journal, 1995, 1 of 13," Beinecke Library, Yale University: http://drs.library.yale.edu/fedoragsearch/rest/. "Conceivably I mean / the feelings of blue / and red had passed / away but sensation / has two forms [...]."

[378] "The type of an idea of Secondness is the experience of effort, prescinded from the idea of a purpose [...] In regard to its dynamic first, a Second is determined either by virtue of its own intrinsic nature, or by virtue of a real relation to that second (an action). Its immediate second is either a Quality or an Existent [...] Thirdness is the triadic relation existing between a sign, its object, and the interpreting thought, itself a sign, considered as constituting the mode of being of a sign" ("Letters to Lady Welby," 640, 641, 642).

this called "Flickerbridge"—about this house that will be ruined by discovery and publicity.[379] That's what is so great about Dickinson. She escapes capture.

WSH: *"The stroke is a voice / but it is a voice"*—this I remember from your notebook transcriptions of Dickinson's manuscripts.[380] *Spontaneous Particulars* walks a fine line between outside and inside—documenting archival secondness while invoking artifactual firstness—so that the reader might take a leap from here to there.

Howe: Yes, that's right. It's just a leap. But it's a thrilling one.[381]

WSH: Are these leaps across connections without connectives also instances of conversion?

Howe: Well, of course, conversion is also copying—*conversion* in every way. That's why this Webster manuscript in the archives at New York Public Library was such a wonderful chance discovery. And this is all thanks to Christine Burgin. This book owes so much to her sense of design. We looked at endless papers in the Webster archive,[382] and suddenly I saw this fragment—*"Trans // Trans plant // Tran.splen.dent // Trans.port"*—of course, I thought of Stevens's "Transport To Summer"—and then turned the manuscript over: *"the quality of being // may*

---

[379] "So this admirable old house, all time-softened white within and time-faded red without, so everything that surrounds you here and that has, by some extraordinary mercy, escaped the inevitable fate of exploitation: so it all, I say, is the sort of thing that, if it were the least bit to fall to pieces, could never, ah, never more, be put together again." Henry James, "Flickerbridge," *The Ladder: A Henry James Website*, ed. Adrian Dover: http://www.henryjames.org.uk/flick/home.htm[.]

[380] Susan Howe Papers, YCAL MSS 338, Series III, Notebooks and Diaries, 1984-2007, Box 12, Folder 24, Notebook: Dickinson Material (Spring 2001), Beinecke Library, Yale University: http://drs.library.yale.edu/fedoragsearch/rest/[.]

[381] See *Debths*, 22.

[382] The Noah Webster Papers, New York Public Library Manuscripts and Archives Division: http://archives.nypl.org/[.]

be transmitted // sending from one // sending through // one to another, to pass // mission // may be transmitted // susceptibility of // nstance" [.][383] This is exactly what we're talking about. But, what *is* it? Is it something visual or something else?

WSH: And speaking of images, I wanted to ask you about the cover photograph by Thomas Smillie.

Howe: Yes, Christine found that. She has a deep interest in magic and spiritualist books and art objects. Thomas Smillie was an eccentric and the Smithsonian's first photographer.[384] He photographed every single object they had during this turn-of-the-century period, which is the time of Peirce, this period that is so fascinating to me. You could say this is my very *American* book—from Jonathan Edwards Jr.'s Christian prayer in the Mohegan language, which is so ironic, to Captain John Smith's *Generall Historie of Virginia*; from the Webster and Dickinson manuscripts to those from Hart Crane and Lucy Wetmore Whittelsey.

WSH: I love how the book arranges these artifacts without much (if any) explanation so that their firstness sparks creativity and critique while also escaping capture.

Howe: That's right. This is conversion and *conversion*. Well, you know who led me into this sort of thing: William Carlos Williams. I am so profoundly inspired by *Paterson*, particularly the Library section—to search for the beautiful thing. And also, there's a feeling of hostility. He's not comfortable at all in the Library—the smell of must and dead men's souls. The minute he brings in "Beautiful thing," you know:

---

[383] Noah Webster, notes for the word "Transport," in *Spontaneous Particulars*, 64-67, as transcribed on pages 64 and 67 by Susan Howe and Diane Ducharme. See also Howe's notes (on page 79) to pages 64-67.

[384] On the vernacular photographs and readymades of Thomas Smillie, visit Merry Foresta, "The Smithsonian's First Photographer," *Smithsonian Institution Archives* (Washington, D. C., May 14, 2009):
http://siarchives.si.edu/blog/smithsonians-first-photographer.

> Beautiful thing,
> my dove, unable and all who are windblown,
> touched by the fire
>   and unable,
> a roar that (soundless) drowns the sense
> with its reiteration
>   unwilling to lie in its bed
> and sleep and sleep, sleep
>   in its dark bed.[385]

And all those *so be its*. And then, I'm suddenly listening to Dostoyevsky's *so be it, so be it* in *Crime and Punishment*[386] and wondering if that's where Williams got it.

WSH: Or maybe from *Hamlet*?[387]

Howe: Or the Bible. There are so many. I kept rearranging these connections to *Paterson* in *Spontaneous Particulars*. What would I take out? What would I use?

WSH: I also wanted to ask you about the facing pages at the exact center of the book, where you present two of Williams's 'prescriptions'

---

[385] *Paterson (Book Three)* (New York: New Directions, 1949), np.

[386] "No matter, I am not confounded by the wagging of their heads; for everyone knows everything about it already, and all that is secret is made open. And I accept it all, not with contempt, but with humility. So be it! So be it! 'Behold the man!'" Fyodor Dostoevsky, *Crime and Punishment*, trans. Constance Garnett (Project Gutenberg, 2016), part 1, chapter 2: http://www.gutenberg.org/files/2554/2554-h/2554-h.htm[.]

[387] "HORATIO [Within] Heaven secure him! // HAMLET So be it! // HORATIO [Within] Hillo, ho, ho, my lord! // HAMLET Hillo, ho, ho, boy! come, bird, come." William Shakespeare, *Hamlet* (MIT Shakespeare, 1983), act 1, scene 5: http://shakespeare.mit.edu/hamlet/full.html[.]

for "the locust / tree [...] as such / as such [...]."[388] How did this arrangement come about?

Howe: In the whole of this book, these facing pages and the last paragraph on page 63 would be my favorite parts. To see passages of *Paterson* scribbled in pencil on his prescription pads at SUNY Buffalo's Poetry Collection[389] was stunning. I am so happy with these two pages—finally cutting the work down to these two manuscripts and the lines I wrote to accompany them. Here, I don't see the difference between poetry and prose. "Ask the librarian behind the desk for a cardboard box of labeled file folders containing singular whispering skeletons. Place one in my looking-glass hands."[390] Writing two sentences like this, after much shuffling, feels like one of Ricky Jay's card tricks. Gertrude Stein, another great magician, in one of her "Lectures in America" referring to English literature of the sixteenth century, hits the nail on the head: "It was no longer just a song it was a song of words that were chosen to make a song that would sound like the words they were to sing."[391]

WSH: *As such—as such.* This is the moment of chance that abides within the everyday?

Howe: Yes, the miracle of chance. Beauty is chance and there is a rigor in the quest.[392] Frank O'Hara's "In Memory of My Feelings" is dedicated to Grace Hartigan. Midway through the poem, he comes up

---

[388] *Spontaneous Particulars*, 40, 41.
[389] The William Carlos Williams Collection, 1902-1960, The Poetry Collection of the University Libraries, University at Buffalo, The State University of New York: http://library.buffalo.edu/pl/[.]
[390] *Spontaneous Particulars*, 41.
[391] Gertrude Stein, "What Is English Literature," *Lectures in America* (Boston: Beacon Press, 1957), 30.
[392] "'Rigor of beauty is the quest. But how will you find beauty when / it is locked in the mind past all remonstrance?'" *Paterson (Book I)* (New York: New Directions, 1946), unpaginated.

with the line "Grace / to be born and live as variously as possible [...]."[393] I can't write poems quickly. I don't have his gift. But it's the same happiness. Sitting in my room alone, hour after hour, cutting and pasting, printing out, shifting, erasing. Grace is various, as in Anne Hutchinson's sense of the term.[394] It's a gift that comes to you made up of these tychic encounters.

WSH: The regenerative violence—the chance destructiveness—of the library fire in *Paterson* is so important for Williams, but the tenor of *Spontaneous Particulars* is quite different.

Howe: The essays in *The Birth-mark* are violent—but, no, there's not the same kind of violence in *Spontaneous Particulars* and no hostility toward the Library as you find in Williams. Nevertheless, I have built it around that particular section of *Paterson*. So there *is* conflict involved. I love libraries. I am only comfortable, really, with books around me. When I travel, I run to find the local library.

WSH: And sometimes you find the library in nature close to home, as you write of Leetes Island: "Reading *Paterson* reminds me of walking

---

[393] "Grace / to be born and live as variously as possible. The conception / of the masque barely suggests the sordid identifications." Frank O'Hara, "In Memory of My Feelings," Russell Ferguson, *In Memory of my Feelings: Frank O'Hara and American Art* (Los Angeles: University of California Press, 1999), 91.

[394] "Mr. Nowell: How do you know that that was the spirit? Mrs. H.: How did Abraham know that it was God that bid him offer his son, being a breach of the sixth commandment? Dep. Gov.: By an immediate voice. Mrs. H.: So to me by an immediate revelation. Dep. Gov.: How! an immediate revelation. Mrs. H.: By the voice of his own spirit to my soul." Thomas Hutchinson, *The History of the Province of Massachusetts-Bay, From the Charter of King William and Queen Mary; in 1691, Until the Year 1750,* Appendix II, "The Examination of Mrs. Ann Hutchinson *at The court at Newtown, November 1637*" (Boston: Thomas & John Fleet, 1828), 508. See also *The Birth-mark* (1993): 51-55, 74-76, 104-108.

barefoot across a small strip of common land near my house that's littered with beach glass, broken oyster shells, razor clams and kelp."[395] Your sense of place has always been at the center of your work.

Howe: Deeply so. As it is in Williams. One thing we share is an abiding concern with how to express an American spirit of place. To get *home* to the local—to a place for which there is no name. For me, home is this room in Guilford. Or, home is the quarry. It's the rock, as in Stevens. It's the hunter and the hunted. My home for a time was also Buffalo, a city not unlike Paterson. There's something haunted about upper New York State (and also Lake George) that calls to me on a primal level. John Ashbery, who was born in Rochester, has the wonderful poem, "As You Came from / the Holy Land // of western New York State / were the graves all right in their bushings / was there a note of panic in the late August air / [...]."[396] Because I am slightly agoraphobic, I don't often travel, but when I'm in a place, boy do I go into that place.

WSH: I also wanted to ask you about the epigraph from Santayana's *Last Puritan*[397] that opens the Library section in Book Three of *Paterson*.

Howe: Santayana is more or less forgotten now, but he was a crucial figure for a generation that included Williams, Stevens, Eliot, Stein. Even later, Robert Lowell. Stevens was a student at Harvard when Santayana was a popular young philosophy professor there; Williams shared his Spanish background. "To an Old Philosopher in Rome," one of Stevens's most magnificent poems, was of course a tribute to Santayana.

---

[395] *Spontaneous Particulars*, 37.
[396] *Self-Portrait in a convex Mirror* (New York: Penguin, 1976), 6.
[397] "Cities, for Oliver, were not a part of nature. He could hardly feel, he could hardly admit even when it was pointed out to him, that cities are a second body for the human mind, a second organism, more rational, permanent and decorative than the animal organism of flesh and bone: a work of natural yet moral art, where the soul sets up her trophies of action and instruments of pleasure." *Paterson (Book Three)* (New York: New Directions, 1949), unpaginated.

I can't explain why Williams uses the quotation as an epigraph in *Paterson*, but *In The American Grain* has a lot to say, for and against, early New England Puritans.[398]

WSH: I remember your notes, at the Beinecke, from reading Cotton Mather's *Magnalia*[399] among other Puritan texts. You were tracking a motif: how to deny the self-elect and yet embody the denial of the elect self.[400]

Howe: Hutchinson's covenant of grace would say: you never know if you are saved or not. Good works don't make a difference in terms of election. The nothingness that is. *No* is nested inside the word *know*—absence and negation are bound inextricably to knowledge. Stevens is so profoundly the antinomian and the metaphysical poet. "The vivid transparence that you bring is peace."[401] The source is transparence. The isn't.

WSH: *Paterson* looms large in *Spontaneous Particulars*, but what about the presence of Stevens's "The Creations of Sound"? Earlier, you mentioned your slide lecture, "Spontaneous Particulars of Sound," which echoes that poem. And I'm also thinking of "The Course of a Particular," which figures briefly into *Souls of the Labadie Tract*[402] and which plays a more elaborate role in "Vagrancy."[403] How do you see the presence of

---

[398] See, for example, "Cotton Mather's Wonders of the Invisible World," *In The American Grain* (New York: New Directions, 1933), 81-104.

[399] Cotton Mather, *Magnalia Christi Americana* (London, 1702).

[400] "Visible manifestation at premium // Self's personality most radical / invention— / God's grace—speaking on the unspeakable // How to deny the self-elect / & yet embody the denial of / the elect self. // Linguistic gesture intended / to move the audience— / embodiment & self-denial [...]." Susan Howe Papers, YCAL MSS 338, Series III, Notebooks and Diaries [1984-2007], Box 11, "Sketch Book Journal, 1995, 1 of 13," Beinecke Library, Yale University: http://drs.library.yale.edu/fedoragsearch/rest/[.]

[401] "Notes Toward A Supreme Fiction," *The Collected Poems*, 380.

[402] "Today while out walking I experience ways in which Stevens' late poem 'The Course of a Particular' locates, rescues, and delivers what is secret, wild, double, and various in the near-at-hand." *Souls of the Labadie Tract*, 74.

[403] *The Quarry*, 3-17, 20, 24-27.

Stevens in these works compared to that of Williams in *Spontaneous Particulars*?

Howe: Williams and Stevens are both concerned with particulars, local and sonic particulars. Lines come to an edge. Necessity coming to light—differently. What I love about *Paterson* is the stumbling, the bad mixed with the good, the romanticism and the slang. The whole mess of it. I completely identify with the passion and the insecurity and the anxiety to get something about the American voice and history. I think of his great essay "Edgar Allan Poe" as a model for the form. "Poe gives the sense for the first time in America, that literature is *serious*, not a matter of courtesy but of truth." "Method, punctuation, grammar—" What sentences![404] And then I think of Stanley Cavell, speaking of Thoreau: "It is through nature that nature is to be overcome. It is through words that words are to be overcome. (Silence may only be the tying of the tongue, not relinquishing words, but gagging on them. True silence is the untying of the tongue, letting its words go."[405] I love the letting go aspect of *Paterson*. Reading Stevens (particularly the later work) is more soothing. Of course there is rage, as in "The Idea of Order at Key West": "Oh! Blessed rage for order, pale Ramon, / The maker's rage to order words of the sea[.]"[406] But it's a rage for order. *Blessed* has a capital B and you read aloud in your head the three syllable way. Reading Stevens is comforting in the way the Psalms are. It's the sound and sense of speech we do not speak. That thing we're never going to get to—that we don't get to.

WSH: And yet—for me, at least—there's a feeling of controlled revelation in so many of Stevens's poems. "It is as if / We had come to an end of the imagination, / Inanimate in an inert savoir."[407] Right?

---

[404] *In The American Grain*, 216, 227.
[405] *The Senses of Walden* (Chicago and London: University of Chicago Press, 1992), 44.
[406] *The Collected Poems*, 130.
[407] "The Plain Sense of Things," *The Collected Poems*, 502.

Howe: Yes—and no. After all, "savoir" activates "savior" when I see the letters on paper. I feel both reverent and tempted toward transgression when approaching the vast critical edifice built around Wallace Stevens's writings. That's why I was having such a hard time writing "Vagrancy in the Park," which echoes his "Vacancy in the Park"—"March . . . Someone has walked across the snow, / Someone looking for he knows not what"[408]—it's one of his last poems. For some reason, Dickinson's works do not intimidate me in the same way. The critical wall doesn't seem forbidding. I know her in a way I will never know Williams or Stevens.

WSH: What were you looking for in your writing of "Vagrancy in the Park"?

Howe: I don't know. The only time I ever approached another essay with such manic intensity was when I was writing *My Emily Dickinson*. And I was young then. *"And look thou be sure of thy reckoning"*—Death says to Everyman. Maybe I needed to return to those Cold War years—the years when Stevens was writing his last poems. I felt it as almost a sacred obligation. Though I know you can't step in the same river twice. Even the River of Rivers in Connecticut.

WSH: Was there a breakthrough moment?

Howe: Yes. I was obsessing over differences between Williams and Stevens and exploring some ideas about Spinoza I hadn't been able to clarify in my mind. Finally, a book by Jane Bennett[409] did the trick as to what makes Spinoza applicable now—how his ideas are about moving in time. So much of this is about *Articulation of Sound Forms in Time*![410] There is Deleuze's Spinoza (Bennett) and there is Santayana's Spinoza

---

[408] "Vacancy in the Park," *The Collected Poems*, 511.
[409] *Vibrant Matter: a political ecology of things* (Durham and London: Duke University Press, 2010). "Spinoza and vibrant matter (a few notes)," (W. Scott Howard, e-mail to Susan Howe, February 05, 2015.)
[410] *Articulation of Sound Forms in Time* (Windsor, VT: Awede, 1987).

(Stevens) and somewhere between is where I find myself. In comparison to Williams, Spinoza is there with Stevens in a pattern in the old metaphysics. Obviously, for me manuscripts are vibrant bodies. For Stevens, words are vibrant bodies. And then there is the fact that his whole insurance practice as a Surety and Claims lawyer called on him to immerse himself in the vibrant details involved in construction.

Rather than the essay I meant to be writing, "Vagrancy in the Park" turned into a long prose poem or balances on a line between. It follows threads, as in *Souls of the Labadie Tract*. I have quotations from a whole variety of Stevens's lines woven in along with a specific description of Elizabeth Park where he spent so much time walking and thinking. It's also personal, a return through Stevens's correspondence with Jack Sweeney (who was one of my mother's good friends when my father was away in the war). Jack used to take us on weekend picnics in the fields around Belmont and Concord. Memories of the Concord River and the Battleground Bridge and The Old Manse merge with their constant recalling of the matchless beauty of Irish landscapes and how there could be no comparison here. Their delight in Irish writing and their laughter when they were together. I guess I'm eternally trying to unite Ireland and America. The section called "Ring Around the Roses" starts with a rose garden in Elizabeth Park (in Hartford)[411] and ends with Yeats's "The Irish Cliffs of Moher."[412] At my age, I am interested in their late poems,

---

[411] "After the war, we spent the summer [in Ireland], and I used to play in Herbert Park near my grandmother's house on Wellington Place in Dublin. Hartford was Dublin. Home in the world—away in the world—landscape and language threaded." "Vagrancy in the Park," *The Nation*: http://www.thenation.com/article/vagrancy-in-the-park/[.]

[412] In the passage that immediately follows Howe's "landscape and language threaded," the essay includes lines from Wallace Stevens' letter #842 To Barbara Church (September 10, 1952): "'As one grows older, one's own poems begin to read like the poems of someone else. Jack Sweeney (the Boston Sweeney) sent me a post-card from County Clare the other day—the worn cliffs towering up over the Atlantic. It was like a gust of freedom, a return to the spacious, solitary world in which we used to exist'." ("Vagrancy in the Park," *The Nation*: http://www.thenation.com/article/vagrancy-in-the-park/[.]) This tychic intercalation posits the germ for Stevens' "The Irish Cliffs of Moher" in Jack's post card. (*The Quarry*, 21-27).

the connections and radical differences. I think that Stevens couldn't acknowledge it, but he really read Yeats. And that sense of finality is always going to be a great insecurity—a different kind of insecurity compared with Williams's presence in *Paterson*.

WSH: Which of the last Yeats poems interest you most?

Howe: *TOM TIT TOT* became an essay on nearly all of Yeats's last poems. The one poem I'm so obsessed about now is "Cuchulain Comforted" and it's about birds. "Then certain Shrouds that muttered head to head / Came and were gone […] Convicted cowards all by kindred slain" […]. And the final line: "They had changed their throats and had the throats of birds."[413] A less comforting poem I cannot imagine. Stevens's bird song "At the earliest ending of winter" may be only "scrawny cry" but it's "A chorister" surrounded by "choral rings, / Still far away."[414] Yeats and Stevens both end on bird poems—incredibly different bird poems.

WSH: Birds are very important for your work too, from the beginning all the way through.

Howe: Yes, and it's weird—how that is. If you look at the paintings I was doing before switching over to poetry, there are always photos of birds collaged with watercolor washes. Or lists of bird names. In a way, listing the names of birds led me from painting to poetry.[415]

---

[413] "Cuchulain Comforted," William Butler Yeats, *Collected Poems* (Adelaide: University of Adelaide Library, 2014), public domain, https://ebooks.adelaide.edu.au/y/yeats/william_butler/y4c/index.html[.]
See also *The Poems of W. B. Yeats* (New York: Macmillan, 1983), 332.

[414] "No Ideas About The Thing But The Thing Itself," *The Collected Poems*, 534.

[415] Susan Howe Papers, YCAL MSS 338, Series VI, Art Work [1958-73], Boxes 21, 22, 23, 24, 25, 26, 27, 28, 29, 30, Beinecke Library, Yale University: http://drs.library.yale.edu/fedoragsearch/rest/[.]

WSH: From "Vagrancy in the Park" to "The End of Art,"[416] your essays collected in *The Quarry* emerge from a wide range of contexts across decades. How did you make these choices about which prose poems to select, especially considering the hybrid and embedded forms of their previous appearances?

Howe: I can see now that a lot of my work has been like *Paterson*—sequential and mixed forms. For many years, I have worried over this problem of separating my essays from their original books. This is an essential element in all my work. I couldn't bear to do this with *Eikon*[417] nor could I do this with *The Midnight*. And I also feel that my work has been so much both essay and poem that's it hard to say which is which. So that makes it problematical. There were many works I wanted to include—the beginning of *Melville's Marginalia* was one. The first plan for what eventually became *The Quarry* was to pull some essays from *The Birth-mark* to include with others in one volume, but I couldn't bring myself to break up that group because that collection is really a whole work. The selections that bother me most in *The Quarry* are those taken from *Pierce-Arrow*. Those were the most difficult in terms of cutting away other material. But the Stevens essay and "The End of Art" connect in that sense of silence, mystery, and oneness. This surprised me when I confronted them all together. "Vagrancy in the Park" is where all my love, longing, memory, and imagination is buried or roaming. When I was writing the essay, which begins with a section called "Roaming," I never once thought of the word "roam" in connection with Dickinson. And suddenly last night I remembered it's in her Loaded Gun poem:

And now We roam in Sovreign Woods –
And now We hunt the Doe –
And every time I speak for Him

---

[416] "The End of Art," *Archives of American Art Journal* 14.4 (1974): 2-7.
[417] *a bibliography of the king's book; or, eikon basilike* (providence: paradigm press, 1989).

The Mountains straight reply – [418]

"Roam" links *My Emily Dickinson* to *The Quarry*.[419] Maybe I was drawn to that particular poem for reasons I was not aware of, or maybe it is following me. Hard to escape the singular power of singular words. "[…] dont you know that 'No' is the wildest word we consign to Language?"[420] she once wrote in a love letter to Judge Otis P. Lord. Wow.

WSH: You mentioned that *TOM TIT TOT* offers a meditation on 'late' poetry. Apart from *Frame Structures*,[421] which collects some of your first published volumes, do you see any of your books offering a meditation on 'early' poetry?

Howe: *Singularities* and the works collected there.[422] This was before *The Birth-mark* and before Buffalo.[423] Before entering Academia without any discipline and being flung into it because of the Dickinson book—all of which was very good for me. Producing *Singularities* was difficult because Wesleyan had never done that sort of work before. It

---

[418] "My Life had stood - a Loaded Gun (764)," *Poetry Foundation*: http://www.poetryfoundation.org/poems-and-poets/poems/detail/52737[.] See also Emily Dickinson, *The Poems of Emily Dickinson*, ed. R. W. Franklin (Cambridge: Harvard University Press, 1999), 342.

[419] *My Emily Dickinson*, 34; *The Quarry*, 3, 12, 15, 179.

[420] "Letter 562," *Emily Dickinson: Selected Letters*, ed. Thomas H. Johnson (Cambridge and London: Harvard University Press, 1986), 246.

[421] *Frame Structures: Early Poems, 1974-1979* (New York: New Directions, 1996). This volume includes: *Frame Structures* (New Directions, 1995), *Hinge Picture* (Telephone Books, 1974), *Chanting at the Crystal Sea* (Fire Exit, 1975), *Cabbage Gardens* (Fathom Press, 1979), and *Secret History of the Dividing Line* (Telephone Books, 1978).

[422] *Singularities* (Hanover and London: Wesleyan, 1990) includes the following sequential works: *Articulation of Sound Forms in Time*, *Thorow*, and *Scattering As Behavior Toward Risk*. Only the first of these appeared earlier as a chapbook: *Articulation of Sound Forms in Time* (Windsor, VT: Awede Brita Bergland, 1987).

[423] Howe taught for nineteen years (1988-2007) at the State University of New York at Buffalo where she held the Samuel P. Capen Chair in Poetry and the Humanities.

was a different time and there were all these design and layout rules. *Articulation of Sound Forms in Time*—the Hope Atherton book—was a real breakthrough.[424] That was a moment where I made a kind of new language out of old words and yet they were from a person; so I entered into a kind of telepathic communication with Hope Atherton. Much of this was influenced by my correspondence with Norman O. Brown—his hermeticism. As if he were Pythagoras pushing me in a Dionysian direction. He introduced me to Deleuze and Guattari's *Thousand Plateaus*[425] and the multivocality inside someone speaking. But at heart I am a Puritan. He probably was too.

WSH: In terms of book design, are fonts important for you?

Howe: Yes, of course. They're crucial. And the margins and spacing. My poems are like grids. The breathing spaces are so important.

WSH: Does the grid inform a balance between chance and discipline?

Howe: Yes, something flies out of the grid. When using watercolor—perhaps because of its transparency—you can destroy an expensive piece of paper with one wrong dollop of color. But another would work like magic. I wish I could go back to it, but I can't. That obsession was overpowering. And writing is overpowering and I can't be overpowered in two different directions. Some people can, but I can't. *TOM TIT TOT* (despite being inspired by Paul Thek) is all grids but no color. My

---

[424] For Howe's reflections upon her work with the Hope Atherton story, see "Personal Narrative," *Souls of the Labadie Tract*, 11-19; "Writing *Articulation of Sound Forms in Time*," *The Sound of Poetry / The Poetry of Sound*, ed. Marjorie Perloff and Craig Dworkin (Chicago and London: University of Chicago Press, 2009), 199-204; and "Personal Narrative," *The Quarry*, 49-56.

[425] Gilles Deleuze and Félix Guattari, *A Thousand Plateaus: Capitalism and Schizophrenia*, trans. Brian Massumi (Minneapolis: University of Minnesota Press, 1987).

daughter would say those word drawings are still lifes because people won't read them as a series.

TOM TIT TOT is about constant motion. At the Whitney event,[426] that was the question everyone was asking me: *how do you read these?* I like the idea that they're still lifes, but they're *not* because the poems' words that were chosen are moving from page to page. Each one is separate, yes, but they're placed into a mirroring sequence so it's a progress. You need to keep walking and reading. Almost the way in Elizabeth Park you read the labels for each separate plot in the rose garden while pausing to smell the roses.

WSH: I loved the way the Yale Union installation of *TOM TIT TOT* invited that spirit of *bibliodérive*.[427] And speaking of walking poems, I'm remembering your *Jacket2* podcast on Stevens's "The Poem That Took

---

[426] "Susan Howe," *Whitney Biennial* (New York: Whitney Museum of American Art, 2014):
http://whitney.org/Exhibitions/2014Biennial/SusanHowe[.]

[427] On the emergence of the Situationist trope, *dérive*, see the letter from Ivan Chtcheglov to Michèle Bernstein and Guy Debord published in *Internationale Situationniste* #9 (August 1964), trans. Ken Knabb and Reuben Keehan, *Situationist International Online*:
http://www.cddc.vt.edu/sionline/si/letters.html[.] "The *dérive* (with its flow of acts, its gestures, its strolls, and its encounters) was *to the totality* exactly what psychoanalysis (in the best sense) is to language. Let yourself go with the flow of words, says the psychoanalyst. He listens, until the moment he rejects or modifies (one could say *détourns*) a word, an expression or a definition. The dérive is certainly a technique, almost a therapeutic one. But just as analysis unaccompanied by anything else is almost always *contraindicated,* so continual dériving is dangerous to the extent that the individual, having gone too far—not without bases, but without defenses—is threatened with explosion, dissolution, dissociation, or disintegration. And thus the relapse into what is termed 'ordinary life,' that is to say, in reality, into 'petrified life.' In this regard I now take back the *Formulary*'s propaganda for a *continuous dérive*. It could be continual like the poker game in Las Vegas, but only for a certain period, limited to a weekend for some people, to a week as a good average; a month is really pushing it. In 1953-1954 we dérived for three or four months straight. That's the extreme limit. It's a miracle it didn't kill us. We had a constitution—a bad constitution—of iron." See also Sadie Plant, *The Most Radical Gesture: The Situationist International in a Postmodern Age* (New York: Routledge, 1992), 58-59.

the Place of a Mountain."[428] Would you say that archives are your mountains?

Howe: Archives are more like going into the woods. Poems and essays are my mountains. To pull off a line or a page is the mountain. And that takes the place of the traveling I can't do. The mountain is the poem and the poem takes the place of the mountain.

WSH: What's most important to you?

Howe: To keep on working. Often out on late afternoon walks I think of Thoreau. His accurate eye for the smallest detail. The way he notes specific seasonal changes, bird songs, cloud formations. Sometimes when I come in, I check his *Journal* notes for the same day well over two hundred years ago now and marvel at particular sentences. Their distance and presence.[429]

---

[428] Susan Howe, Dee Morris, Nancy Kuhl, and Al Filreis, "There it was (PoemTalk #83)," *Jacket2* (December 29, 2014):
http://jacket2.org/podcasts/there-it-was-poemtalk-83[.]

[429] "Before June 1637 able bodied people preferred to walk the old Indian trail called the Shore Path. When you came to see me in early June the bridal wreath bush at the edge of our woods had just stopped blooming but now mountain laurels take its place. How do we abandon perceptual givens in writing? All the poems I have ever written are in large measure indebted to Leetes Island […] Thoreau begins his journal by writing 'My journal should be the record of my love. I would write in it only of the things I love. My affection for any aspect of the world. What I love to think of'." Susan Howe Papers, YCAL MSS 338, Series II, Writings, [1994]-2007, Box 9, "Work for Ether/Either, Fall, 1996," Beinecke Library, Yale University:
http://drs.library.yale.edu/fedoragsearch/rest/[.]

Archives, Artifacts, Apostrophes:[430]
Spontaneous Particulars

> Sheer verbal artistry can be a force for mercy [...]
> Hit or miss—an arrow into the eye of loving.[431]

This is a book of gifts, wonder, and poetry of the highest order dwelling within everyday acts and materials of attention, intuition, motion, sound, texture, and vision. *Spontaneous Particulars* offers a potent synthesis of Susan Howe's dynamic genius: an exquisite homage to the quest for rigorous beauty thriving in wildernesses sheltered within archives; to the collaborative work required for such vital preservation and public engagement; and ultimately to the pursuit of what escapes capture, conformity, and conversion. In an age of radical transformations for libraries, Howe's "collaged swan song to the old ways" (9) celebrates the necessary angels of serendipity and synergy at the heart of creativity and research. Each page is a poem of liminal image/text transformations of archives, artifacts, and apostrophes on the verge of oblivion, "'Emerging / from / an / Abyss / and / entering / it / again'" (18); each poem limns "'drawers and drawers full of drawings'" (19) arranged in appositional glimpses "'or swim / of things'" (62) along "'peripheries of light / - / doom / etc / -'" (78). As the above allusions and quotations respectively intimate, the works of William Carlos Williams, Wallace Stevens, Emily Dickinson, Gertrude Stein, Hannah Edwards Wetmore, and Hart Crane shape some of the innumerable intra- and inter-textual portals across collections and centuries in Howe's threshold poetics *here*.

Spontaneous Particulars draws upon decades of Howe's reading, writing, and teaching to combine prose, paratexts, and photographs in a festival of collaborative research, discovery, and poetic making. This

---

[430] A shorter version of this essay appeared as "Archives, Artifacts, Apostrophes: Susan Howe's *Spontaneous Particulars*" in *Denver Quarterly* 50.3 (2016): 99-107.

[431] *Spontaneous Particulars*, 51.

book is classic Howe, and yet radically characteristically singular: "originally conceived as a lecture" accompanied by a "slide-show presentation" (9), this mesmerizing tychic performance animates "an occult invocation of verbal links and forces" encountered in "research libraries and special collections" where "words and objects come into their own and have their place again" (59). *My Emily Dickinson* (1985), *The Birthmark* (1993), *Souls of the Labadie Tract* (2007), *That This* (2010), *Sorting Facts* (2013), and *TOM TIT TOT* (2014), for example, also emerge from integrated contexts of Howe's scrupulous-aleatory research, avant-gardist scholarship, and visionary poetics. And *Pierce-Arrow* (1999), *The Midnight* (2003), and Jen Bervin's and Marta Werner's *The Gorgeous Nothings* (2013)—to which Howe contributes a preface—are kindred image/text archival volumes that echo Howe's telepathic synechism here, but *Spontaneous Particulars* conveys a more direct and most stunning treatment of autonomous kinetic artifacts collaged in facing-page sequences of astonishment and chance pareidolia. Here, we find ourselves immersed in a kaleidoscope of Howe's discoveries reconfigured from a slide-lecture more like a documentary of a gallery exhibition where we are invited to explore and co-create at random amidst the interplay of light and shadow, text and context, sound and silence, figure and ground & etc. "This is not a moment for making analogies—Howe's poems are like drawings are like notations are like collages. No. They are poems."[432] Each page is a *w-h-o-l-e* poem of eccentricities; each poem, an apostrophe—"To reach is to touch" (60)—from boundaries between noumena and phenomena: "Things-in-themselves and things-as-they-are-for-us" (18). Howe simultaneously illumines and obscures the crescent—"some parenthesis which darkens the sense" (46)—between archival remediation and artifactual irremediableness, folding and unfolding the seams/seems.

This curatorial assemblage of "visual and verbal textualities and textiles" (21) amplifies the vibrant materiality of artifacts—particulars

---

[432] Anon., "Susan Howe: TOM TIT TOT," *Exhibition Pamphlet* (Portland, OR: Yale Union, 2013): http://yaleunion.org/susan-howe/[.]

spontaneous—that call upon our intuitive pursuit of their ciphers and decipherings mediated through archives "by mystic documentary telepathy" (18) thereby revealing "a literal and mythical sense of life hereafter—" (25). Howe's spiritual quest is, in fact, paramount in all that she does—from her minimalist visual art in the late 1960s to her image/text broadsides from the early 1970s to her first published collection of poems, *Hinge Picture* (1974), to her soundscapes performed and recorded with David Grubbs (*Thiefth*, 2006, *Souls of the Labadie Tract*, 2007, *Frolic Architecture*, 2011, *WOODSLIPPERCOUNTERCLATTER*, 2015)—and that keen attunement sparks her reverential agency in *Spontaneous Particulars*: "When you see the material objects, in all their variety of shapes and surfaces, it's like coming on unexplained spirits singing into air".[433] If Susan Howe's favorite word is *k-n-o-w* because "What you *can't* know now is also *present* in the way you sound [no] in English",[434] then *Spontaneous Particulars* documents perceptible imperceptibilities (*kataphasis/apophasis*) among, between, and within artifacts and archives.

This volume may offer, for some readers, a first point of contact with Hart Crane's typescripts, or Rebekah White's embroidery, or Gertrude Stein's handwriting, or Noah Webster's miscellaneous notes, extracts, and quotations—among many other unique materials imaged with remarkable clarity. Notwithstanding the sensuousness of these multifarious artifactual encounters, the practical magic in *Spontaneous Particulars* resides in the realm of the tangible/intangible split second when the senses are synaesthetically transfigured. "Each collected object or manuscript is a pre-articulate empty theatre where a thought may surprise itself at the instant of seeing. Where a thought may hear itself see" (24).

---

[433] McLane, "Susan Howe: The Art of Poetry," http://www.theparisreview.org/interviews/6189/the-art-of-poetry-no-97-susan-howe[.]
[434] Catherine Halley, "Interview with Susan Howe: Detective Work," *Poetry Foundation* (14 January 2015): http://www.poetryfoundation.org/article/249896[.]

The wild ephemerality here lives in the immanent/imminent realm of wonder and vulnerability before recognition, on the verge of conversion (in every sense of the word):

> Often by chance, via out-of-the-way card catalogues, or through previous web surfing, a particular "deep" text, or a simple object (bobbin, sampler, scrap of lace) reveals itself *here* at the surface of the visible, by mystic documentary telepathy. Quickly—precariously—coming as it does from an opposite direction.
> If you are lucky, you may experience a moment *before*. (18)

These lines articulate the manifold playful wagers in each page of *Spontaneous Particulars*: that the 30+ photographic images might witness artifacts traveling at their own velocities on their several journeys; that the accompanying prose poems might intimate yet not interpret the collection's inherent field of tropological action; that the credits and endnotes might similarly document without defining these ecstatic relationships between archives and artifacts; that the numerous highly-charged erasures, gaps, silences, blank spaces, unnumbered pages, and undocumented materials might invoke the reader's imaginative co-creative engagement; that each page might propel revolving doors among micro-, macro-, and meta-archives. *Spontaneous Particulars* is an open work of "material details" and embedded apostrophes (in every sense of the word) signifying present-absent possessives living still amidst "twill fabrics, bead-work pieces, pricked patterns, four-ringed knots, tiny spangles, sharp-toothed stencil wheels; in quotations, thought-fragments, rhymes, syllables, anagrams, graphemes, endangered phonemes, in soils and cross-outs" (21).

The Library section from Howe's favorite of the "separate limited editions" (33)—Book Three (1949)—of Williams's *Paterson* looms large here: "a Romantic literary Pietist enters the library in the hope of unraveling tangled skeins of evidence. Paterson (he has named himself for his city) rifles through old newspapers and local histories with their genteel accounts of celebrations, picnics, suicides—" (34). Howe's whirlwind poetics emulates the "fire of poetic artifice" (39) from Paterson's library—"'Whirling flames, leaping / from house to house, building to building /// carried by the wind /// The Library is in their path /// Beautiful thing! aflame . /// a defiance of authority'" (39)—and strikes at least one reflection upon the "acquisitive violence, the rapacious 'fetching' involved in [specialized] collecting" (43), but the glow of Howe's "eye of loving" is a recollective "force for mercy" (51) amidst these fragments and animalcules striking inland again (toward Guilford and New Haven) to begin again. She avers: "Reading *Paterson* reminds me of walking barefoot across a small strip of common land near my house that's littered with beach glass, broken oyster shells, razor clams and kelp" (37).

Howe gestures that she will "begin" *Spontaneous Particulars* "with the marvelous opening" (9) from *The Library*, having, of course, already begun our archival tour with the book's cover photograph (4477) by Thomas Smillie (c. 1890) which stages a drama of *toujours-déjà/jamais vu*. Here, we find one of Smillie's 'specimens' *before* Duchamp's readymades. Howe presents this impromptu vernacular composition without commentary, thereby investing Smillie's blue daguerreotype with tropological potential for connections without connectives elsewhere and otherwise, such as: drawers like sentences (19), fabrics like knotted skeins of quotations (31), glimpses of C. S. Peirce's doodled "'dingy *blue*'" (36) and of Crane's pencil-blue annotation, "'*doubt / ful*'" (61). Between the cover and Howe's preface (9) we find an appositional cluster of artifacts limning apostrophes to violence and mercy on the threshold of survivance—Jonathan Edwards, Jr.'s prayer in Mahican (c. 1765) which Howe documents simultaneously in four remediations: one photographic image on page 6; one italicized typographic transcription (with Kenneth Minkema) on page 7; one translation into English (by Carl Masthay) on page 71; and one contextual endnote also on page 71. These opening & closing materials reverberate hauntingly alongside the volume's disjunctive presentation, in the concluding pages, of kindred artifacts: a transcription of Webster's notes for the word "Transport" placed before (64) and after (67) a double-sided photographic reproduction (65-66) of the manuscript fragment; a transcription (78) from Crane's work sheet for the "Cape Hatteras" section of *The Bridge* (c. 1925); a note on Webster's notes (79); and a quotation from Captain John Smith's *The Generall Historie of Virginia* (1624). Such micro-, macro-, and meta-archival juxtapositions animate each and every page in *Spontaneous Particulars*, shaping the volume's conditions for serendipity and synergy from cover to cover.

Howe's works relentlessly problematize chronology, destabilizing origins and endings with a regenerative kairotic indeterminacy—that is: "BETWEENNESS. Always, always, always between. Always between".[435] *Spontaneous Particulars* emerges vividly from a series of slide-lectures and keynote presentations since her 2011 Trilling Seminar at Columbia, "Spontaneous Particulars of Sound," and yet the book also channels Howe's abiding interest in the works of Dickinson and Stevens, for example, which she discusses in the interviews collected in *The Difficulties*, Vol. 3, No. 2 (1989). Compared with the tangible presence of six manuscript fragments from The Emily Dickinson Collection, the co-presence of Wallace Stevens, while perhaps more allusive/elusive/illusive, plays an equally significant role, especially concerning Howe's engagements with Williams's works and also with various materials in the Jonathan Edwards Collection, which this volume respectively arranges in two key moments.

The first (page 34) faces an eighteen-line passage from *The Library* (page 35) and formulates an incisive reading of Stevens's assessment of Williams's developing poetics, c. 1921-49. Howe concludes this prose poem, thus—"Spontaneous sound particulars balance the scale of law with magic" (34)—thereby amplifying this book's resonance with two

---

[435] Susan Howe, "Re: Edited Transcription," e-mail to W. Scott Howard (February 10, 2015). Here and in other discrete instances throughout this book, I choose to deviate from stylistic conventions (concerning the placement of punctuation marks inside of quotation marks) in order to represent Susan Howe's language exactly as it appears in her works.

of Stevens's poems, "The Creations of Sound" (from *Transport to Summer*) and "The Course of a Particular" (omitted from *The Collected Poems*) which receives momentary emphasis in *Souls of the Labadie Tract* (2007) and magnified "neathering" in "Vagrancy in the Park" (2015).[436] The second of these instances (page 63) reconfigures a paragraph from Howe's 2009 essay, "Choir answers to Choir,"[437] where the passage appears amidst reflections upon Stevens's "The Owl in the Sarcophagus," "The Noble Rider and the Sound of Words," and Jonathan Edwards's "A Divine and Supernatural Light":

> Poetry has no proof nor plan nor evidence by decree or in any other way. From somewhere in the twilight realm of sound a spirit of belief flares up at the point where meaning stops and the unreality of what seems most real floods over us. It's a sense of self-identification and trust, or the granting of grace in an ordinary room, in a secular time. (58)

In *Spontaneous Particulars*, this crucial paragraph includes an additional sentence—"The inward ardor I feel while working in research libraries is intuitive" (63)—which adapts an earlier moment in the 2009 essay: "Understanding isn't something that belongs to reason. Understanding comes to pass as an outward sign of inward grace. The feeling of union and bliss I get while reading 'The Owl in the Sarcophagus' is intuitive" (57). The backwards-forwards disjunctive reticulations here accentuate Howe's reverence for poetry of a certain magnitude "running parallel to religious faith" through which "words engender objects in spite of the fact there is no inherent reason a particular one should stand so wrought" ("Choir," 57-58).

The co-presence in *Spontaneous Particulars* of these intra- and inter-textual passages signals Howe's synchronous discoveries (c. 2005):

---

[436] See. Respectively, *Souls of the Labadie Tract*, 25, 74; and "Vagrancy in the Park," http://www.thenation.com/article/vagrancy-in-the-park/[.]

[437] "Choir answers to Choir" (2009): 51-61.

of "the term 'Labadist' in reference to the genealogical research of Wallace Stevens and his wife Elsie Kachel Moll Stevens" (*Souls*, NDP, 23); of Jean de Labadie, the Labadie Tract, and the "'labadie poplar'"[438]; and of "the vast collection of Edwards family papers at the Beinecke Rare Book and Manuscript Library".[439] And this wider & wilder context illuminates a generative nexus of performances, lectures, and publications— further complicating questions of 'origin' and 'ending' for *Spontaneous Particulars [of Sound]*, especially when we recall that *Souls of the Labadie Tract*, the book, includes "Personal Narrative" that returns to the Hope Atherton story from *Articulation of Sound Forms in Time* (Awede, 1987) which echoes the Stevens poems noted above & etc. Balancing law with magic, these multifarious highly-charged appositional silences and gaps among, between, and within Howe's phanopoetic particulars invite "a mysterious leap of love" (25).

Libraries are sheltered wildernesses where sacred and secular realms converge and diverge at thresholds in spacetime: "So it's telepathic though who knows why or in what way" (*Souls*, CD, Insert). Each page in *Spontaneous Particulars* is a polyvocal poem of liminal image/text reconfigurations on the verge of disappearance. Howe's poetics deftly whorls eccentric fusions of archival recovery, artifactual collage, and apostrophic floreate foldingflare:

---

[438] Susan Howe and David Grubbs, Insert, *Souls of the Labadie Tract*, CD (Blue Chopsticks, 2007).

[439] Susan Howe and David Grubbs, Insert, *Frolic Architecture*, CD (Blue Chopsticks, 2011).

```
    , the  .
   as yeu ɔirl cu.
   g moon rent .
   yh hang poised tt,
   rifint air, nor had
   rl at he far reaches
          oth land and
   ?w at id, or swim  e
   .nild , flu of things  o
```

This strophic image/text (page 62) appears apposite to the pivotal prose poem (page 63) discussed above, and is the last in a sequence (pages 44, 46, 59, and 60) of *Hannah doves*,[440] each a high-tech repro-

---

[440] Susan Howe, "Re: How lovely!" E-mail to W. Scott Howard (October 20, 2012). My daughter, Gwendolyn, helped me make several origami birds from photocopied pages from *Frolic Architecture* (2010), one of which I sent (via regular post) to Susan along with a note about the presentation I would soon be giving, "Archive and Artifact: Susan Howe's Poetics," at the *Rocky Mountain Modern Language Association Conference* (October 13, 2012) at the University of Colorado, Boulder. (I gave the rest of the origami birds to those who were there for our panel.) In reply to my letter, Susan wrote (via e-mail): "The little

duction of low-tech photocopied openwork cut & paste foldings/splicings from Howe's typographic transmissions of Lucy Wetmore Whittlesey's manuscript transcriptions of the diary of her mother, Hannah Edwards Wetmore, collaged "with a mix of sources from other conductors and revealers in the thick of things—before" (Anon.). This particular kaleidoscopic soundform also appears in *Frolic Architecture* (The Grenfell Press, 2010), *That This* (New Directions, 2010), and on the cover of Howe's CD with Grubbs, *Frolic Architecture* (2011). "The paper relic rustles when turned. It could almost be a wing" (McLane). Howe's discovery, "One day, by chance," of the folder, "*Wetmore, Hannah Edwards, Diary: in the hand of her daughter Lucy Wetmore Whittlesey*" (52), began with an apostrophe—"'Oh that I had wings like a dove! *for then* would I fly away, and be at rest'"—reaching toward/touching upon other inter-/intra-textual transfigurations of Psalm 55.6. "The visual and acoustic shock of that first exclamatory 'Oh' on paper brown with oxidation, made me think in a rush of Henry James' great novel *The Wings of the Dove* (1902) and the beauty of the King James version" (52).

Howe's skein of Hannah doves in *Spontaneous Particulars* interlaces the artifactual with the archival in gestures of recovery and release—echoing, embracing, emulating, and escaping Jonathan Edwards's *Efficacious Grace*, becoming "'Not wings alone, but rhythmsof spread wings'" (61)—thereby gathering momentum for flight.[441] In an instance of dialetheism shaped by the chance simulacra of remediation, this last image/text defies recognition as such in the opening list of image

---

origami bird arrived today and I love it. The whole thing seems [so] perfect in relation to "Spontaneous Particulars of Sound" with my wings of the dove section. And I have just now been arranging a powerpoint for [a] lecture I have enlarged and changed for Johns Hopkins next week—working on pp images of manuscripts with bird related images! I am going to put my Hannah dove up in my workroom so it is with me in spirit. Thank Gwen. Truly. It's marvelous."

[441] "'Not wings alone, but rhythmsof spread wings'" may be found in the photographic reproduction, in *Spontaneous Particulars*, of the manuscript/typescript page from Hart Crane's work sheet for the "Cape Hatteras" section of *The Bridge*, c. 1925. Howe's typographic transcription of this page also illustrates the ineluctable, animist-materialist-vitalist, inscrutable dynamics among archives, artifacts, and apostrophes "~~riding onward~~" (78).

credits and also in the endnotes where page 62 is absent, having already flown after an immanent/imminent "idea of God, natureless and Nature [in a betweenness where one] almost forgets human words".[442] These craftivist DIY Hannah doves (which also emulate Dickinson's manuscripts) follow other birds in *Spontaneous Particulars*, each an inter-/intra-textual folding/unfolding of archives, artifacts, and apostrophes. Howe's threshold poetics and praxis limns these polysemous *sounds & silences* approaching disappearances on multiple levels throughout the volume, engendering velocities for "'A flock of wild fowl in flight'" (26).

The image of this poet as a 'library cormorant' emerges[443] from *The Birth-mark* and has since reified into a trope for Howe's tenacious hunting for books, as recently underscored by Marjorie Perloff's announcement on the detachable wrapper for *Spontaneous Particulars* as well as by Jonathan Creasy's review. Perloff aptly modifies the figure to suit this "extraordinary *telepathy of archives* [which] is the very opposite of passive absorption," and Creasy turns the metaphor toward "the poet's sense of the library and manuscript archive as untouched wilderness" where the researcher/explorer forges "through guarded, forbidden territory."[444]

The innumerable birds in Susan Howe's works (past and present) are "tender, tangled, violent, august, and infinitely various" (59). There are no cormorants per se in *Spontaneous Particulars*, but there are doves, falcons, nightingales, teals, "winged Sesames" (78) among others lost or found, and one glorious swan.

---

[442] Susan Howe and David Grubbs, Insert, *WOODSLIPPERCOUNTERCLATTER*, CD (Blue Chopsticks, 2015).

[443] *The Birth-mark* (1993): 26.

[444] See, respectively, Perloff, "Announcement," *Spontaneous Particulars*, book wrapper; and Creasy, "Susan Howe's Telepathy," *Los Angeles Review of Books* (20 January 2015): http://lareviewofbooks.org/review/susan-howes-telepathy[.]

Bibliography of Works Cited

Abraham, Nicolas, and Maria Torok. *The Wolfman's Magic Word: A Cryptonymy*. Trans. Nicholas Rand. Minneapolis: University of Minnesota Press, 1986.

Adams, Hazard. *Antithetical Essays in Literary Criticism and Liberal Education.* Tallahassee: Florida State University Press, 1990.

Adorno, Theodor. "Cultural Criticism and Society." *Prisms.* Cambridge: MIT Press, 1983. 17-34.

African American History and Latin American Studies Collections. University of Delaware: http://guides.lib.udel.edu/c.php?g=85389&p=548467 [.]

Allen, Benjamin Mark, and Dahia Messara. Eds. *The Captivity Narrative: Enduring Shackles and Emancipating Language of Subjectivity.* Cambridge: Cambridge Scholars Publishing, 2012.

Almack, Edward. *A Bibliography of the King's Book or Eikon Basilike.* London: Blades, East & Blades, 1896.

Althusser, Louis. "Ideology and Ideological State Apparatuses (Notes towards an Investigation)." *Lenin and Philosophy and Other Essays.* Trans. Ben Brewster. London: New Left Books, 1971. 121-173.

Altieri, Charles. "Some Problems About Agency in the Theories of Radical Poetics." *The Recovery of the Public World: Essays on Poetics in Honour of Robin Blaser*. Ed. Charles Watts and Edward Byrne. Burnaby, BC: Talonbooks, 1999. 411-427.

Anderson, Benedict. *Imagined Communities: Reflections on the Origin and Spread of Nationalism*. London: Verso, 1983.

Andrews, Bruce. "Suture—& Absence of the Social." *The Difficulties: Susan Howe Issue*. Ed. Tom Beckett. Kent, Ohio: Viscerally Press, 1989. 67-70.

Anon. *Theatre Arts* 34 (1950): 55.

---. "Mark De Wolfe Howe Dies; Lawyer, Historian Was 60." *The Harvard Crimson* (March 1, 1967): http://www.thecrimson.com/article/1967/3/1/mark-de-wolfe-howe-dies-lawyer/ [.]

---. "Mary Manning Howe Adams (1905-1999)." *The Irish Times* (Thursday, July 8, 1999): http://www.irishtimes.com/opinion/mary-manning-howe-adams-1.204225 [.]

---. *Everyman*. Ed. Ernest Rhys. Project Gutenberg, 2006: http://www.gutenberg.org/files/19481/19481-h/19481-h.htm [.]

---. "Susan Howe: TOM TIT TOT." *Exhibition Pamphlet*. Portland, OR: Yale Union, 2013: http://yaleunion.org/susan-howe/ [.]

Ashbery, John. *Self-Portrait in a Convex Mirror*. New York: Penguin, 1976.

Atherton, Humphrey. "Humphrey Atherton." *Indian Papers Project*. Yale University: http://yipp.yale.edu/bio/bibliography/atherton-humphrey-1608-1661 [.]

Back, Rachel Tzvia. *Led By Language: The Poetry and Poetics of Susan Howe*. Tuscaloosa and London: The University of Alabama Press, 2002.

Baker, David. *Heresy and the Ideal: On Contemporary Poetry*. Fayetteville: University of Arkansas Press, 2000.

Bazin, André. *What is Cinema?* 2 vols. Trans. Hugh Gray. Berkeley: University of California Press, 1973.

Benedikt, Amélie Frost. "On Doing the Right Thing at the Right Time: Toward an Ethics of Kairos." *Rhetoric and Kairos*. Ed. Phillip Sipiora, and James S. Baumlin. Albany: SUNY Press, 2002. 226-235.

Benjamin, Walter. "The Work of Art in the Age of Mechanical Reproduction." *Illuminations*. Ed. Hannah Arendt. Trans. Harry Zohn. New York: Schocken, 1968. 217-251.

---. "Theses on the Philosophy of History." *Illuminations*. Ed. Hannah Arendt. Trans. Harry Zohn. New York: Schocken, 1968. 253-264.

Bennett, Jane. *Vibrant Matter: a political ecology of things*. Durham and London: Duke University Press, 2010.

Bercovitch, Sacvan. *The American Jeremiad*. Madison: University of Wisconsin Press, 1978.

Bernstein, Charles. "'Passed by Examination': Paragraphs for Susan Howe." *The Difficulties: Susan Howe Issue*. Ed. Tom Beckett. Kent, Ohio: Viscerally Press, 1989. 84-88.

Bhabha, Homi. *The Location of Culture*. London: Routledge, 1994.

Blake, William. *The Marriage of Heaven and Hell*. Ed. Morris Eaves, Robert N. Essick, and Joseph Viscomi. London: Tate Gallery, 1993.

Bodge, George Madison. *Soldiers in King Philip's War: Being a Critical Account of That War with a Concise History of the Indian Wars of New England From 1620-1677*. Boston, 1906.

Breitwieser, Mitchell Robert, and Kenneth Silverman. *The Life and Times of Cotton Mather*. New York: Harper and Row, 1984.

Brooks, Lisa. *Our Beloved Kin: A New History of King Philip's War*. New Haven: Yale University Press, 2019.

Browning, Robert. "Childe Roland to the Dark Tower Came." *The EServer Poetry Collection*: http://poetry.eserver.org/childe-roland.html [.]

Bruchac, Margaret M. "Revisiting Pocumtuck History in Deerfield: George Sheldon's Vanishing Indian Act." *Historical Journal of Massachusetts* (Summer 2011): http://www.westfield.ma.edu/mhj/pdfs/Revisiting%20Pocumtuck%20History.pdf [.]

Burch, Robert. "Charles Sanders Peirce." *Stanford Encyclopedia of Philosophy*. Ed. Edward N. Zalta. Winter, 2014: http://plato.stanford.edu/entries/peirce/#anti [.]

Burt, Stephen. "Close Calls With Nonsense: How to Read, and Perhaps Enjoy, Very New Poetry." *The Believer* 2.5 (2004): http://www.believermag.com/issues/200405/?read=article_burt [.]

Butler, Judith. *Precarious Life: The Powers of Mourning and Violence*. London and New York: Verso, 2004.

Butterick, George F. "The Mysterious Vision of Susan Howe." *North Dakota Quarterly* 55.4 (1987): 312-321.

Caldwell, Patricia. *The Puritan Conversion Narrative: The beginnings of American expression*. Cambridge: Cambridge University Press, 1983.

Calloway, Colin G. *North Country Captives: Selected Narratives of Indian Captivity From Vermont and New Hampshire*. Hanover, NH: University Press of New England, 1992.

Campbell, Bruce. "'Ring of Bodies / Sphere of Sound': An Essay on Susan Howe's *Articulation of Sound Forms in Time*." *The Difficulties: Susan Howe Issue*. Ed. Tom Beckett. Kent, Ohio: Viscerally Press, 1989. 89-96.

Carter, John. *A B C for Book Collectors*. New York: Alfred A. Knopf, 1990.

Caruth, Cathy, ed. *Trauma: Explorations in Memory*. Baltimore: The Johns Hopkins University Press, 1995.

Case, Kristen. *American Pragmatism and Poetic Practice Crosscurrents from Emerson to Susan Howe*. Rochester: Camden House, 2011.

Cavell, Stanley. *The Senses of Walden*. Chicago and London: University of Chicago Press, 1992.

Champion, Martha. "POEM." *Poetry* 37.5 (1931): 265.

Chow, Rey. "Where Have All the Natives Gone?" *Displacements: Cultural Identities in Question*. Ed. Angelika Bammer. Bloomington and Indianapolis: Indiana University Press, 1994. 125-151.

Chtcheglov, Ivan. Letter to Michèle Bernstein and Guy Debord. *Internationale Situationniste* #9 (August 1964). Trans. Ken Knabb and Reuben Keehan. *Situationist International Online*: http://www.cddc.vt.edu/sionline/si/letters.html [.]

Clark, T. J. *The Sight of Death: An Experiment in Art Writing*. New Haven and London: Yale University Press, 2006.

Clements, Arthur. *Poetry of Contemplation*. Albany: State University of New York Press, 1990.

Clippinger, David. "Between the Gaps, the Silence and the Rubble: Susan Howe, Rosmarie Waldrop, and (Another) Pound Era." *Denver Quarterly* 36 1-2 (2001): 189-205.

Clodd, Edward. *Tom Tit Tot: an essay on savage philosophy in folktale*. London: Duckworth & Co., 1898.

Cole, Barbara. "The Absent Center Is The Ghost Of A King Queen: On Susan Howe's Buffalo." *I Have Imagined A Center // Wilder Than This Region: A Tribute to Susan Howe*. Cuneiform Press, 2007. 33-39.

Coleridge, Samuel Taylor. *The Collected Works*. Vol. 16. Part 1. *Poems: Reading Text*. Ed. J. C. C. Mays. Princeton: Princeton University Press, 2001.

---. *The Collected Works*. Vol. 16. Part 2. *Poems: Variorum Text*. Ed. J. C. C. Mays. Princeton: Princeton University Press, 2001.

Collis, Stephen. *Through Words of Others: Susan Howe and Anarcho-Scholasticism*. Victoria: University of Victoria Press, 2006.

Conte, Joseph M. *Unending Design: The Forms of Postmodern Poetry*. Ithaca: Cornell University Press, 1991.

Cooke, Christina. "An Old-School Book Scout: Wayne Pernu." *The New Yorker* (March 9, 2012): http://www.newyorker.com/books/page-turner/an-old-school-book-scout [.]

Cowen, Wilson Walker. "Melville's Marginalia." Dissertation. Boston: Harvard University, 1965.

---. *Melville's Marginalia*. 2 vols. New York: Garland, 1987.

Cowper, William. *The Task*. London, 1785.

Creasy, Jonathan. "Susan Howe's Telepathy." *Los Angeles Review of Books* (20 January 2015): http://lareviewofbooks.org/review/susan-howes-telepathy [.]

Cronon, William. *Changes in the Land: Indians, Colonists, and the Ecology of New England*. New York: Hill and Wang, 1983.

Crown, Kathleen. "Documentary Memory and Textual Agency: H.D. and Susan Howe." *How2* vol.1, no.3 (2000): http://www.scc.rutgers.edu/however/v1_3_2000/current/readings/crown.html [.]

Dante Gabriel Rossetti: A Hypermedia Archive: http://www.rossettiarchive.org/ [.]

Dawson, Edward. *The Practical Methode of Meditation*. London, 1614.

de Certeau, Michel. *The Writing of History*. Trans. Tom Conley. New York: Columbia University Press, 1988.

Deleuze, Gilles, and Félix Guattari. *A Thousand Plateaus: Capitalism and Schizophrenia*. Trans. Brian Massumi. Minneapolis: University of Minnesota Press, 1987.

DeLucia, Christine. *Memory Lands: King Philip's War and the Place of Violence in the Northeast*. New Haven: Yale University Press, 2018.

de Montaigne, Michel. *The Essayes of Michael Lord of Montaigne*. Trans. John Florio. London: George Routledge and Sons, Ltd., 1894.

Demos, John. *The Unredeemed Captive*. New York: Vintage, 1994.

Derounian-Stodola, Kathryn Zabelle, and James Arthur Levernier. *The Indian Captivity Narrative, 1550-1900*. New York: Twayne Publishers, 1993.

Derrida, Jacques. "Signature Event Context." *Margins of Philosophy*. Trans. Alan Bass. Chicago: University of Chicago Press, 1982. 307-330.

Dickinson, Emily. "Letter 562." *Emily Dickinson: Selected Letters*. Ed. Thomas H. Johnson. Cambridge and London: Harvard University Press, 1986. 246-247.

---. *The Poems of Emily Dickinson: Reading Edition.* Ed. Ralph W. Franklin. Harvard University Press, 1999.

---. "My Life had stood - a Loaded Gun (764)." *Poetry Foundation*: http://www.poetryfoundation.org/poems-and-poets/poems/detail/52737 [.]

Donaldson, Scott, and R. H. Winnick. *Archibald MacLeish: an American Life*. New York: Houghton Mifflin, 1992.

Donne, John. "A Valediction: of weeping." *P O E M S, By J. D. WITH E L E G I E S ON THE AUTHORS D E A T H*. London: Printed by M.F. for John Marriot, 1633. 228-229.

---. "The Canonization." *English Seventeenth-Century Verse*. Vol. 1. Ed. Louis Martz. New York: Norton, 1969. 48-50.

---. "A Valediction: of weeping." *English Seventeenth-Century Verse*. Vol. 1. Ed. Louis Martz. New York: Norton, 1969. 58-59.

Donovan, Patricia. "Peter Hare, 72, Distinguished Philosophy Professor." University at Buffalo, *News* (January 8, 2008): http://www.buffalo.edu/news/releases/2008/01/9064.html [.]

Donovan, Thom. "O Fling Without A Sleeve: Susan Howe and the Pedagogy of Enaction." *I Have Imagined A Center // Wilder Than This Region: A Tribute to Susan Howe*. Cuneiform Press, 2007. 51-57.

Dostoevsky, Fyodor. *Crime and Punishment*. Trans. Constance Garnett. Project Gutenberg, 2016: http://www.gutenberg.org/files/2554/2554-h/2554-h.htm [.]

Drake, James D. *King Philip's War: Civil War in New England, 1675-1676*. Amherst: University of Massachusetts Press, 1999.

Duncan, Robert. *A Poet's Mind: Collected Interviews with Robert Duncan, 1960-1985*. Ed. Christopher Wagstaff. Berkeley: North Atlantic Books, 2012.

DuPlessis, Rachel Blau. *The Pink Guitar: Writing as Feminist Practice*. New York: Routledge, 1990.

---. *Surge: Drafts 96-114*. Cromer, UK: Salt, 2013.

DuPlessis, Rachel Blau, and Peter Quartermain. "Introduction." *The Objectivist Nexus: Essays in Cultural Poetics*. Ed. Rachel Blau DuPlessis and Peter Quartermain. Tuscaloosa: University of Alabama Press, 1999. 1-22; 319-320.

Eco, Umberto. *The Role of the Reader: Explorations in the Semiotics of Texts*. Bloomington: Indiana University Press, 1979.

Edward E. Ayer Collection. Newbery Library: https://www.newberry.org/american-indian-and-indigenous-studies [.]

Edwards, Jonathan. *Jonathan Edwards Collection.* GEN MSS 151, Edwards Family Writings, 1704-1904. Beinecke Library, Yale University: http://drs.library.yale.edu/fedoragsearch/rest/ [.]

Eliot, T. S. *The Waste Land: A Facsimile and Transcript of the Original Drafts Including the Annotations of Ezra Pound.* Ed. Valerie Eliot. New York: Harcourt Brace Jovanovich, Inc., 1971.

---. "Tradition and the Individual Talent." *Selected Prose of T. S. Eliot.* Ed. Frank Kermode. New York: Farrar, Straus and Giroux, 1975. 37-44.

---. "The Metaphysical Poets." *Selected Prose of T. S. Eliot.* Ed. Frank Kermode. New York: Farrar, Straus and Giroux, 1975. 60-64.

Emerson, Ralph Waldo. "The American Scholar." *Digital Emerson: A Collective Archive*: http://digitalemerson.wsulibs.wsu.edu/exhibits/show/text/the-american-scholar [.]

Esposito, Joseph. "Synechism." *The Digital Encyclopedia of Charles S. Peirce*: http://www.digitalpeirce.fee.unicamp.br/ [.]

Falkoff, Marc. Ed. *Poems From Guantánamo: the Detainees Speak.* Iowa City: University of Iowa Press, 2007.

Felman, Shoshana, and Dori Laub. *Testimony: Crises of Witnessing in Literature, Psychoanalysis, and History.* New York: Routledge, 1992.

Ferguson, Russell. *In Memory of my Feelings: Frank O'Hara and American Art.* Los Angeles: University of California Press, 1999.

Foresta, Merry. "The Smithsonian's First Photographer." *Smithsonian Institution Archives.* Washington, D. C. (May 14, 2009): http://siarchives.si.edu/blog/smithsonians-first-photographer [.]

Foster, Edward. *Postmodern Poetry: The Talisman Interviews*. Hoboken: Talisman House Publishers, 1994.

Frost, Elisabeth A. *The Feminist Avant-Garde in American Poetry*. Iowa City: University of Iowa Press, 2003.

Gaffield, Nancy. "Susan Howe's Landscapes of Language: *Articulation of Sound Forms in Time* and 'The Liberties'." *Women: A Cultural Review* 26:3 (2015): http://dx.doi.org/10.1080/09574042.2015.1069141 [.]

Gardner, Helen. *The Metaphysical Poets*. Oxford: Oxford University Press, 1961.

Garvine, Richard W. "Physical Features of the Connecticut River Outflow During High Discharge." *Journal of Geophysical Research* 79.6 (1974): 831-846.

Girard, René. *Violence and the Sacred*. Trans. Patrick Gregory. Baltimore: The Johns Hopkins University Press, 1977.

Givens Collection. University of Minnesota: https://www.lib.umn.edu/givens [.]

Goldstein, Laurence. "A Problem for the Dialetheist." *Bulletin of the Section of Logic* 15.1 (1986): 10-13.

Graham, Elspeth, Hilary Hinds, Elaine Hobby, and Helen Wilcox. Eds. *Her Own Life: Autobiographical Writings by Seventeenth-Century Englishwomen*. London: Routledge, 1989.

Greenblatt, Stephen. *Renaissance Self-Fashioning: From More to Shakespeare*. Chicago: University of Chicago Press, 1980.

Grosmann, Uta. *Poetic Memory: The Forgotten Self in Plath, Howe, Hinsey, and Glück*. Madison: Farleigh Dickinson University Press, 2012.

Guide to the Wells Family Papers: https://deerfield-ma.org/wp-content/uploads/2013/10/Wells-Family-Papers.pdf [.]

Haefeli, Evan, and Kevin Sweeney. *Captors and Captives: The 1704 French and Indian Raid on Deerfield.* Amherst: University of Massachusetts Press, 2003.

---. *Captive Histories: English, French, and Native Narratives of the 1704 Deerfield Raid.* Amherst: University of Massachusetts Press, 2006.

Harris, Doug. "Letter to Walter Ramsey (5 January 2016), re: 'Battle of Great Falls / Phase II Support'." MontagueMANews: http://www.montague.net/Pages/MontagueMA_News/0237FD5D-000F8513.2/Narragansett_Tribal_Statement.pdf [.]

Hegel, Wilhelm Friedrich. *The Philosophy of History*. Trans. J. Sibree. New York: Dover Publications, Inc., 1956.

Hejinian, Lyn. *The Language of Inquiry*. Berkeley: University of California Press, 2000.

Heller-Roazen, Daniel. *Echolalias: On the Forgetting of Language.* New York: Zone Books, 2008.

---. *Dark Tongues: The Art of Rogues and Riddlers.* New York: Zone Books, 2013.

Herbert, George. "Prayer (I)." *The Complete English Poems*. Ed. John Tobin. London: Penguin, 1991. 45-46.

The Holy Bible: King James Version. New York: Meridian, 1974.

Homer. *The Iliad*. Trans. Robert Fitzgerald. Garden City, NY: Anchor Books, 1974.

---. *The Iliad*. Ed. Gregory R. Crane. Perseus Digital Library (2017): http://www.perseus.tufts.edu/hopper/text?doc=Perseus:text:1999.01.0133 [.]

Hopkins, Gerard Manley. *The Poems of Gerard Manley Hopkins*. Ed. W. H. Gardner and N. H. MacKenzie. New York: Oxford University Press, 1967.

Howard, W. Scott. "'writing ghost writing': A Discursive Poetics of History; or, Howe's 'hau' in Susan Howe's *a bibliography of the king's book; or, eikon basilike*." *Talisman: A Journal of Contemporary Poetry & Poetics* 14 (1996): 108-130.

---. "Teaching, How/e?: *not per se*." *Denver Quarterly* 35.2 (2000): 81-93. Rpt. *Poetry Criticism*. Vol. 54. Ed. Timothy J. Sisler. Detroit: Gale, Inc., 2004. 118-122.

---. "'The Brevities': Formal Mourning, Transgression & Postmodern American Elegies." *The World in Time and Space: Towards a History of Innovative American Poetry in Our Time*. Ed. Edward Foster and Joseph Donahue. *Talisman: A Journal of Contemporary Poetry and Poetics* 23-26 (2002): 122-146.

---. "Landscapes of Memorialisation." *Studying Cultural Landscapes*. Ed. Iain Robertson and Penny Richards. London: Arnold, Inc., and New York: Oxford University Press, 2003. 47-70.

---. "'roses no such roses': Jen Bervin's *Nets* and the Sonnet Tradition from Shakespeare to the Postmoderns." *Double Room* 5 (2005): http://webdelsol.com/Double_Room/issue_five/Jen_Bervin.html [.]

---. "'Fire harvest: harvest fire': Resistance, Sacrifice & Historicity in the Elegies of Robert Hayden." *Reading the Middle Generation Anew: Culture, Community, and Form in Twentieth-Century American Poetry*. Ed. Eric Haralson. Iowa City: University of Iowa Press, 2006. 133-152.

---. "Literal / Littoral Crossings: Re-Articulating Hope Atherton's Story After Susan Howe's *Articulation of Sound Forms in Time*." *Reconstruction: Studies in Contemporary Culture* 6.3 (2006): https://web.archive.org/web/20110726035138/http://reconstruction.eserver.org/063/howard.shtml [.]

---. "Anglo-American Metaphysical Poetics: Reflections on the Analytic Lyric from John Donne to Susan Howe." *The McNeese Review* 46 (2008): 36-52.

---. "'That Noble Flame': Literary History & Regenerative Time in Katherine Philips's Elegies and Society of Friendship." *Dialogism & Lyric Self-Fashioning: Bakhtin and the Voices of a Genre*. Ed. Jacob Blevins. Cranbury, NJ: Susquehanna University Press, 2008. 136-162.

---. "*WYSIWYG* Poetics: Reconfiguring the Fields for Creative Writers & Scholars." *The Journal of Electronic Publishing*, ed. Aaron McCollough 14.2 (2011): http://dx.doi.org/10.3998/3336451.0014.204 [.]

---. "Apophatic Haecceity: William Bronk & the Analytic Lyric." *William Bronk in the Twenty-First Century*. Ed. Edward Foster and Burt Kimmelman. Greenfield, MA: Talisman House, 2013. 81-91.

---. "'TANGIBLE THINGS / Out of a stark oblivion': Spellbinding *TOM TIT TOT*." University of Denver (2015): https://dulibraries.wordpress.com/2015/08/05/tangible-things-out-of-a-stark-oblivion-spellbinding-tom-tit-tot/ [.]

---. "Archives, Artifacts, Apostrophes: Susan Howe's *Spontaneous Particulars*." *Denver Quarterly* 50.3 (2016): 99-107.

---. "Art in Art / Stone on Stone: Susan Howe's Quarrying." *Talisman: A Journal of Contemporary Poetry & Poetics* 44 (2016): http://talismanarchive3a.weebly.com/howard-howe.html [.]

---. "Prophecy, Power, and Religious Dissent." *A History of Early Modern Women's Writing*. Ed. Patricia Phillippy. Cambridge: Cambridge University Press, 2018. 315-331.

---. Correspondence with Susan Howe (1995-1997). *Susan Howe Papers*. MSS 0201, 1942-2002. Geisel Library, Mandeville Special Collections and Archives, UC San Diego: http://libraries.ucsd.edu/speccoll/findingaids/mss0201.html [.]

---. Correspondence with Susan Howe (1998-2019). Personal collection.

Howard, W. Scott, et al. Eds. "Difficult Praise." *Reconfigurations: A Journal for Poetics & Poetry / Literature & Culture* (November, 2007): http://reconfigurations.blogspot.com/2007/11/difficult-praise.html [.]

Howard, W. Scott, and Broc Rossell. "'After' Objectivism: sincerity, objectification, contingency." *Poetics and Praxis 'After' Objectivism*. Ed. W. Scott Howard and Broc Rossell. Iowa City: University of Iowa Press, 2018. 1-20; 181-189.

Howe, Fanny. *The Wedding Dress: Meditations on Word and Life*. Berkeley and Los Angeles: University of California Press, 2003.

Howe, Mark De Wolfe. *Justice Oliver Wendell Holmes, Volume One: The Shaping Years, 1841-1870*. Harvard: Harvard University Press, 1957.

---. *Justice Oliver Wendell Holmes, Volume Two: The Proving Years, 1870-1882*. Harvard: Harvard University Press, 1957.

*   *   *

Howe, Susan.

Works:

---. *One of Them*. Unpublished (c. 1969). Susan Howe Papers, 1942-2002, MSS 0201, Box 41, Folder 3, Geisel Library, Special Collections and Archives, UC San Diego: https://library.ucsd.edu/speccoll/findingaids/mss0201.html [.]

---. *Circumnavigator*. Unpublished (c. 1970). Susan Howe Papers, 1942-2002, MSS 0201, Box 41, Folder 5, Geisel Library, Special Collections and Archives, UC San Diego: https://library.ucsd.edu/speccoll/findingaids/mss0201.html [.]

---. "The End of Art." *Archives of American Art Journal* 14.4 (1974): 2-7.

---. *Hinge Picture*. Telephone Books, 1974.

---. *Chanting at the Crystal Sea*. Fire Exit, 1975.

---. *Secret History of the Dividing Line*. Cambridge and Somerville, Massachusetts: New England Free Press and Telephone Books, 1978.

---. *Cabbage Gardens*. Fathom Press, 1979.

---. *The Liberties*. Loon Books, 1980.

---. *Pythagorean Silence*. New York: Montemora Foundation, 1982.

---. *Defenestration of Prague*. New York: Kulchur Foundation, 1983.

---. "Part Two: Childe Emily to the Dark Tower Came." *Code of Signals: Recent Writings in Poetics*. Io #30. Ed. Michael Palmer. Berkeley: North Atlantic Books, 1983. 196-218.

---. "Six Poems." *Sulfur* 9 (1984): 88-94.

---. "Statement for the New Poetics Colloquium." *Jimmy and Lucy's house of 'K'* 5 (November, 1985): 13-17.

---. "The Captivity and Restoration of Mrs. Mary Rowlandson." *TEMBLOR: Contemporary Poets 2* (1985): 113-121.

---. *My Emily Dickinson*. Berkeley: North Atlantic, 1985.

---. *Articulation of Sound Forms in Time*. Windsor, VT: Awede Press, 1987.

---. "Thorow." *TEMBLOR: Contemporary Poets* 6 (1987): 3-21.

---. *a bibliography of the king's book; or, eikon basilike*. providence: paradigm press, 1989.

---. "Encloser." *The Politics of Poetic Form: Poetry and Public Policy*. Ed. Charles Bernstein. New York: Roof Books, 1990. 175-196.

---. "Heliopathy." *Temblor: Contemporary Poets* 4 (1990): 42-54.

---. *Singularities*. Hanover: Wesleyan University Press, 1990.

---. *The Europe of Trusts*. Los Angeles: Sun & Moon, 1990.

---. *The Nonconformist's Memorial*. New York: New Directions, 1993.

---. *The Birth-mark: unsettling the wilderness in American literary history*. Hanover and London: Wesleyan University Press, 1993.

---. *Frame Structures: Early Poems, 1974-1979*. New York: New Directions, 1996.

---. "Sorting Facts; or, Nineteen Ways of Looking at Marker." *Beyond Document: Essays on Nonfiction Film*. Ed. Charles Warren. Hanover: Wesleyan University Press, 1996. 295-343.

---. *Marginalia de Melville*. Trans. Bernard Rival. Courbevoie: Théâtre Typographique, 1997.

---. *Deux et*. Trans. Bénédicte Vilgrain and Bernard Rival. Courbevoie: Théâtre Typographique, 1998.

---. "Ether Either." *Close Listening: Poetry and the Performed Word*. Ed. Charles Bernstein. New York and Oxford: Oxford University Press, 1998. 111-127.

---. "Renunciation Is a P[ei]rcing Virtue." *Profession 1998*. Ed. Phyllis Franklin. New York: MLA, 1998. 51-61.

---. "Heterologies: Community of Form in Practice and Imagination." *The Recovery of the Public World: Essays on Poetics in Honour of*

Robin Blaser. Ed. Charles Watts and Edward Byrne. Burnaby, Canada: Talon Books, 1999. 217-220.

---. *Pierce-Arrow*. New York: New Directions, 1999.

---. "There Are Not Leaves Enough to Crown to Cover to Crown to Cover." *American Women Poets in the 21st Century*. Ed. Claudia Rankine and Juliana Spahr. Middletown: Wesleyan University Press, 2002. 325-328.

---. *Thorow*. Trans. Bernard Rival. Courbevoie: Théâtre Typographique, 2002.

---. *The Europe of Trusts*. New York: New Directions, 2002.

---. *KIDNAPPED*. Tipperary, Ireland: CORACLE, 2002.

---. *THE MIDNIGHT*. New York: New Directions, 2003.

---. *My Emily Dickinson*. New York: New Directions, 2007.

---. *Souls of the Labadie Tract*. New York: New Directions, 2007.

---. "Writing *Articulation of Sound Forms in Time*." *The Sound of Poetry / The Poetry of Sound*. Ed. Marjorie Perloff and Craig Dworkin. Chicago: University of Chicago Press, 2009. 199-204.

---. "Choir answers to Choir: Notes on Jonathan Edwards and Wallace Stevens." *Chicago Review* 54.4 (2009): 51-61.

---. *THAT THIS*. New York: New Directions, 2010.

---. "Sorting Facts; or, Nineteen Ways of Looking at Marker." *Framework: The Journal of Cinema and Media* 53.2 (2012): 380-428.

---. *Sorting Facts; or, Nineteen Ways of Looking at Marker*. New Directions Poetry Pamphlet #1. New York: New Directions, 2013.

---. "from *Debths*." *Academy of American Poets: poem-a-day* (September 19, 2013): https://www.poets.org/poetsorg/poem/debths [.]

---. *Spontaneous Particulars: The Telepathy of Archives*. New York: Christine Burgin / New Directions, 2014.

---. "Vagrancy in the Park / The essence of Wallace Stevens: Roses, roses. Fable and dream. The pilgrim sun." *The Nation* (October 15, 2015): http://www.thenation.com/article/vagrancy-in-the-park/ [.]

---. "from *Tom Tit Tot*." *Hambone* 21 (2015): 50-59.

---. *The Quarry*. New York: New Directions, 2015.

---. *The Birth-mark: unsettling the wilderness in American literary history*. New York: New Directions, 2015.

---. *Debths*. New York: New Directions, 2017.

---. *Concordance*. New York: The Grenfell Press, 2019.

Collaborative Works / Books:

Howe, Susan, and Robert Mangold. *The Nonconformist's Memorial*. New York: The Grenfell Press, 1992.

Howe, Susan, and James Welling. *Frolic Architecture*. New York: The Grenfell Press, 2010.

Howe, Susan, and R. H. Quaytman. *TOM TIT TOT*. New York: The Museum of Modern Art, 2014.

---. *TOM TIT TOT*. New York: The Museum of Modern Art, 2014: https://www.moma.org/learn/resources/library/council/howequaytman [.]

Collaborative Works / Interviews:

Howe, Susan, and Tom Beckett. "The Difficulties Interview." *The Difficulties: Susan Howe Issue*. Ed. Tom Beckett. Kent, Ohio: Viscerally Press, 1989. 17-27.

Howe, Susan, and Janet Ruth Falon. "Speaking With Susan Howe." *The Difficulties: Susan Howe Issue*. Ed. Tom Beckett. Kent, Ohio: Viscerally Press, 1989. 28-42.

Howe, Susan, and Edward Foster. "An Interview With Susan Howe." *Talisman: A Journal of Contemporary Poetry and Poetics* 4 (1990): 14-38.

Howe, Susan, and Lynn Keller. "An Interview with Susan Howe." *Contemporary Literature* 36.1 (1995): 1-34.

Howe, Susan, and Jon Thompson. "Interview with Susan Howe." *Free Verse* (2005): https://english.chass.ncsu.edu/freeverse/Archives/Winter_2005/interviews/S_Howe.html [.]

Howe, Susan, and Maureen N. McLane. "Susan Howe, The Art of Poetry No. 97." *Paris Review* 203 (2012): https://www.theparisreview.org/interviews/6189/susan-howe-the-art-of-poetry-no-97-susan-howe [.]

Howe, Susan, Dee Morris, Nancy Kuhl, and Al Filreis. "There it was (PoemTalk #83)." *Jacket2* (December 29, 2014): http://jacket2.org/podcasts/there-it-was-poemtalk-83 [.]

Howe, Susan, and Catherine Halley. "Detective Work." *Poetry Foundation* (January 14, 2015): http://www.poetryfoundation.org/features/articles/detail/70196 [.]

Howe, Susan, and Marta Werner. "Transcription and Transgression." *The Networked Recluse: The Connected World of Emily Dickinson*. Ed. Trustees of Amherst College. Amherst: Amherst College Press, 2017. 123-138.

Collaborative Works / Studio Recordings:

Howe, Susan, Fanny Howe, and Christina Davis. "Invocation." *VOCARIUM*, Harvard University (c. 1940s): http://hcl.harvard.edu/poetryroom/vocarium/recordings/catalyst_howe.cfm [.]

Howe, Susan, and David Grubbs. *THIEFTH.* CD. Chicago: Blue Chopsticks, 2005.

---. *Souls of the Labadie Tract.* CD. Chicago: Blue Chopsticks, 2007.

---. *Frolic Architecture.* CD. Chicago: Blue Chopsticks, 2011.

---. *THIEFTH.* Vinyl. New York: Issue Project Room, 2015.

---. *WOODSLIPPERCOUNTERCLATTER.* CD. Chicago: Blue Chopsticks, 2015.

Howe, Susan, Nathaniel Mackey, and Shannon Ebner. *STRAY: A Graphic Tone.* Amsterdam, Netherlands: Roma Publications, 2019: https://www.printedmatter.org/catalog/52888/ [.]

Exhibitions:

Howe, Susan. *TOM TIT TOT.* Portland, OR: Yale Union (October 5–December 1, 2013): http://yaleunion.org/susan-howe/ [.]

---. *Whitney Biennial.* New York: Whitney Museum of American Art (January 27-April 10, 2014): http://whitney.org/Exhibitions/2014Biennial/SusanHowe [.]

Presentations:

Howe, Susan, Lyn Hejinian, and Myung Mi Kim. "The Poet and the World of Her Influences." Mills College, Oakland, CA (October 11, 1993).

Howe, Susan. "Poetry and Telepathy." *Poets Forum*, New York University (October 20-22, 2011): http://www.nyu.edu/about/news-publications/news/2011/september/nyu-to-host-fifth-annual-poets-forumoct-20-22-.html [.]

---. "The Spontaneous Particulars of Sound." *The Lionel Trilling Seminar*, Columbia University (December 1, 2011): http://heymancenter.org/events/the-spontaneous-particulars-of-sound/ [.]

---. Isabella Stewart Gardner Museum. Artist residency. (2012): https://web.archive.org/web/20131109052615/http://www.gardner-museum.org/contemporary_art/artists/susan_howe [.]

Howe, Susan, and David Grubbs. "Frolic Architecture." Harvard University (November 2, 2011): https://www.youtube.com/watch?v=xR6cfDFTL8Q [.]

---. "WOODSLIPPERCOUNTERCLATTER." Issue Project Room (October 25, 2013): http://issueprojectroom.org/event/david-grubbs-susan-howe [;] and https://vimeo.com/138668754 [.]

Special Collections:

"Susan Howe." PennSound: http://writing.upenn.edu/pennsound/x/Howe.php [.]

"Susan Howe and David Grubbs." PennSound: http://writing.upenn.edu/pennsound/x/Howe-Grubbs.php [.]

"Susan Howe, Poetry Programs, WBAI-Pacifica Radio." *PennSound*: http://www.writing.upenn.edu/pennsound/x/Howe-Pacifica.php [.]

Susan Howe Papers. MSS 0201, 1942-2002. Geisel Library, Mandeville Special Collections and Archives, UC San Diego: http://libraries.ucsd.edu/speccoll/findingaids/mss0201.html [.]

Susan Howe Papers. YCAL MSS 338, 1956-2008. Beinecke Library, Yale University: http://hdl.handle.net/10079/fa/beinecke.howesu [.]

*   *   *

Hubbard, William. *The present state of New-England: being a narrative of the troubles with the Indians in New-England, from the first planting thereof in the year 1607 to this present year 1677, but chiefly of the late troubles in the two last years 1675 and 1676: to which is added a discourse about the war with the Pequods in the year 1637.* London: Printed for Tho. Parkhurst, 1677.

Hutchinson, Thomas. *The History of the Province of Massachusetts-Bay, From the Charter of King William and Queen Mary; in 1691, Until the Year 1750.* Boston: Thomas & John Fleet, 1828.

Irigaray, Luce. *Marine Lover of Friedrich Nietzsche.* New York: Columbia University Press, 1991.

Jackson, Holbrook. *The Anatomy of Bibliomania.* New York: Charles Scribner's Sons, 1932.

Jacobs, Joseph. *English Fairy Tales. Illustrated by John D. Batten.* London: David Nutt, 1890.

James, Henry. "Flickerbridge." *The Ladder: A Henry James Website.* Ed. Adrian Dover: http://www.henryjames.org.uk/flick/home.htm [.]

Jay, Ricky. *From the World Wide Website of Ricky Jay*: http://www.rickyjay.com/ [.]

Jenkins, G. Matthew. *Poetic Obligation: Ethics in Experimental American Poetry After 1945.* Iowa City: University of Iowa Press, 2008.

Jennings, Francis. *The Invasion of America: Indians, Colonialism, and the Cant of Conquest.* New York: Norton, 1975.

Johnson, Mark. *The Poetry Project* (October 27, 2014): https://soundcloud.com/poetry-project-audio/mark-johnson-claire-wilcox-oct-27th-2014 [.]

Joyce, Elisabeth W. *"The Small Space of a Pause": Susan Howe's Poetry and the Spaces Between.* Lewisburg: Bucknell University Press, 2010.

Judd, Sylvester. *History of Hadley, Including the Early History of Hatfield, South Hadley, Amherst and Granby Massachusetts.* Springfield, MA: H. R. Hunting & Co., 1905.

Kane, Brian. *Sound Unseen: Acousmatic Sound in Theory and Practice*. Oxford: Oxford University Press, 2014.

Keller, Lynn. *Forms of Expansion: Recent Long Poems by Women*. Chicago: The University of Chicago Press, 1997.

Kermode, Frank. *The Sense of an Ending*. Oxford: Oxford University Press, 2000.

Kestler, Francis Roe. Ed. *The Indian Captivity Narrative: A Woman's View*. New York: Garland, 1990.

Kibbey, Anne. *The Interpretation of Material Shapes in Puritanism*. Cambridge: Cambridge University Press, 1986.

King, Thomas. *The Truth About Stories: A Native Narrative*. Minneapolis: University of Minnesota Press, 2003.

Kolodny, Annette. *In Search of First Contact: The Vikings of Vinland, the Peoples of the Dawnland, and the Anglo-American Anxiety of Discovery*. Durham: Duke University Press, 2012.

Kristeva, Julia. *Desire in Language: A Semiotic Approach to Literature and Art*. Ed. Leon S. Roudiez. Trans. Thomas Gora, Alice Jardine, and Leon S. Roudiez. New York: Columbia University Press, 1980.

---. *Powers of Horror: An Essay on Abjection*. Trans. Leon S. Roudiez. New York: Columbia University Press, 1982.

---. *Revolution in Poetic Language*. Trans. Margaret Waller. New York: Columbia University Press, 1984.

Lang, Amy Schrager. *Prophetic Woman: Anne Hutchinson and the Problem of Dissent in the Literature of New England*. Berkeley: University of California Press, 1987.

Lazer, Hank. "'Singing into the draft': Susan Howe's Textual Frontiers." *Opposing Poetries*. Vol. 2. Evanston: Northwestern University Press, 1996. 60-69.

Leach, Douglas Edward. *Flintlock and Tomahawk: New England in King Philip's War*. New York: W.W. Norton & Co. Inc., 1958.

Lepore, Jill. *The Name of War: King Philip's War and the Origins of American Identity*. New York: Alfred A. Knopf, 1998.

Levinas, Emmanuel. *Collected Philosophical Papers*. Trans. Alphonso Lingis. Boston: Martinus Nijhoff, 1987.

Levine, Mary Ann, Kenneth E. Sassaman, and Michael S. Nassaney. Eds. *The Archaeological Northeast*. Westport: Bergin & Garvey, 1999.

Lewalski, Barbara. *Protestant Poetics and the Seventeenth-Century Religious Lyric*. Princeton: Princeton University Press, 1979.

Lewis, Joel. "Dreamers That Remain." *American Book Review* 10.1 (1988): 9.

Ma, Ming-Qian. "Poetry as History Revised." *American Literary History* 6.4 (1994): 716-737.

---. "Articulating the Inarticulate: *Singularities* and the Countermethod in Susan Howe." *American Women Poets in the 21st Century*. Ed. Claudia Rankine and Juliana Spahr. Middletown: Wesleyan University Press, 2002. 329-352.

Macalister, R. A. Stewart. *The Secret Languages of Ireland With Special Reference to the Origin and Nature of The Shelta Language partly based upon Collections and Manuscripts of the late John Sampson, Litt. D. Sometime Librarian of the University of Liverpool*. Cambridge: Cambridge University Press, 1937.

---. *The Secret Languages of Ireland With Special Reference to the Origin and Nature of The Shelta Language partly based upon Collections and Manuscripts of the late John Sampson, Litt. D. Sometime Librarian of the University of Liverpool*. Armagh, Northern Ireland: Craobh Rua Books, 1997.

Mack, Phyllis. *Visionary Women: Ecstatic Prophecy in Seventeenth-Century England.* Berkeley: University of California Press, 1992.

Mackey, Nathaniel. *Paracritical Hinge: Essays, Talks, Notes, Interviews.* Madison: University of Wisconsin Press, 2005.

MacLeish, Archibald. "Archibald MacLeish." *Poetry Foundation*: http://www.poetryfoundation.org/poems-and-poets/poets/detail/archibald-macleish [.]

Marker, Chris. *La Jetée / Sans Soleil* New York: Criterion Collection, 2007.

Marsh, Nicky. "'Out of My Texts I Am Not What I Play': Politics and Self in the Poetry of Susan Howe." *College Literature* 24.3 (1997): 124-137.

Martin, John Frederick. *Profits in the Wilderness: Entrepreneurship and the Founding of New England Towns in the Seventeenth Century.* Chapel Hill and London: University of North Carolina Press, 1991.

Martz, Louis. *The Poetry of Meditation.* New Haven: Yale University Press, 1954.

Mather, Cotton. *Magnalia Christi Americana.* London, 1702.

Mather, Increase. *A Brief History of the War with the Indians in New-England.* 2nd ed. London, 1676.

Matthiessen, F. O. *American Renaissance: Art and Expression in the Age of Emerson and Whitman.* Oxford: Oxford University Press, 1941.

Mavor, James W., Jr., and Byron E. Dix. *Manitou: The Sacred Landscape of New England's Native Civilization.* Rochester, VT: Inner Traditions International, Ltd., 1989.

Mays, J. C. C. *Coleridge's Experimental Poetics.* New York: Palgrave, 2013.

---. *Coleridge's Father: Absent Man, Guardian Spirit.* Bristol: The Friends of Coleridge, 2014.

Mazzoni, Jacopo. *Della difensa della Commedia di Dante*, III. Cesena, 1587.

---. Trans. Robert L. Montgomery. *Critical Theory Since Plato.* Ed. Hazard Adams. New York: Harcourt Brace Jovanovich, 1971. 178-191.

Mcallister, Andrew. Ed. *The Objectivists.* Hexham, Northumberland: Bloodaxe, 1996.

McBride, Kevin, David Naumec, Ashley Bissonnette, and Noah Fellman. "Battle of Great Falls / Wissatinnewag-Peskeompskut." Mashantucket Pequot Museum & Research Center (April 2016): https://www.montague-ma.gov/files/Battle_of_Great_Falls_Phase_I_Final_Technical_Report.pdf [.]

McBride, Kevin, David Naumec, Ashley Bissonnette, Noah Fellman, and Michael Derderian. "The Battle of Great Falls / Wissantinnewag-Peskeompskut." Mashantucket Pequot Museum and Research Center (January 2017): https://www.montague-ma.gov/files/Battle_of_Great_Falls_Phase_II_Final_Technical_Report.pdf [.]

McCorkle, James. "Prophecy and the Figure of the Reader in Susan Howe's *Articulation of Sound Forms in Time." Postmodern Culture* 9.3 (1999): https://muse.jhu.edu/article/27712 [.]

McGann, Jerome J. *The Romantic Ideology: A Critical Investigation.* Chicago: University of Chicago Press, 1983.

---. *The Textual Condition.* Princeton: Princeton University Press, 1991.

---. *Black Riders: The Visible Language of Modernism.* Princeton: Princeton University Press, 1993.

---. "Exceptional Measures: The Human Sciences in STEM Worlds." *Scholarly Editing: The Annual of the Association for Documentary Editing* 37 (2016): http://scholarlyediting.org/2016/essays/essay.mcgann.html [.]

McGiffert, Michael. Ed. *God's Plot: The Paradoxes of Puritan Piety, Being the Autobiography and Journal of Thomas Shepard.* Amherst: University of Massachusetts Press, 1972.

Melville, Herman. "Billy Budd, Sailor." *Great Short Works of Herman Melville.* Ed. Warner Berthoff. New York: Harper & Row, 1969. 429-505.

Melville's Marginalia Online: https://web.archive.org/web/20160523095910/http://melvillesmarginalia.org/m.php?p=policies [.]

Menand, Louis. *The Metaphysical Club.* New York: Farrar, Straus and Giroux, 2001.

Merleau-Ponty, Maurice. *Sense and Non-Sense.* Trans. Hubert L. Dreyfus and Patricia Allen Dreyfus. Evanston: Northwestern University Press, 1964.

---. *The Merleau-Ponty Aesthetics Reader: Philosophy and Painting.* Ed. Galen A. Johnson. Trans. Michael B. Smith. Evanston: Northwestern University Press, 1993.

Metcalf, Paul. "The Real Susan Howe." *The Difficulties: Susan Howe Issue.* Ed. Tom Beckett. Kent, Ohio: Viscerally Press, 1989. 52-56.

---. "Hope Atherton's Wanderings" (2010): http://www.english.illinois.edu/maps/poets/g_l/howe/hope.htm [.]

Middleton, Peter. "On Ice: Julia Kristeva, Susan Howe and avant-garde poetics." *Contemporary Poetry Meets Modern Theory.* Ed. Antony Easthope and John O. Thompson. Toronto: University of Toronto Press, 1991. 81-95.

---. "Open Oppen: Linguistic Fragmentation and the Poetic Proposition." *Textual Practice* 24.4 (2010): 623-648.

Miller, Perry. *Errand Into the Wilderness*. Cambridge: Harvard University Press, 1956.

Möckel-Rieke, Hannelore. *Fiktionen von Natur und Weiblichkeit: zur Begründung femininer und engagierter Schreibweisen bei Adrienne Rich, Denise Levertov, Susan Griffin, Kathleen Fraser und Susan Howe*. Trier, Germany: WVT Wissenschaftlicher Verlag Trier, 1991.

Montgomery, Will. *The Poetry of Susan Howe: History, Theology, Authority*. New York: Palgrave, 2010.

Moore, William. *Indian Wars of the United States From the Discovery to the Present Time*. Philadelphia: J. & J. L. Gihon, 1852.

Mott, Frank. *Golden Multitudes: The Story of Best Sellers in the United States*. New York: Macmillan, 1960.

Native American History Primary Sources. Yale University: http://guides.library.yale.edu/c.php?g=295897&p=1972892 [.]

Naylor, Paul. *Poetic Investigations: Singing the Holes in History*. Evanston: Northwestern University Press, 1999.

Nelson, Maggie. *The Argonauts*. Minneapolis: Graywolf Press, 2015.

Nichols, Miriam. *Radical Affections: Essays on the Poetics of Outside*. Tuscaloosa: The University of Alabama Press, 2010.

Nicholls, Peter. "Unsettling the Wilderness: Susan Howe and American History." *Contemporary Literature* 37.4 (1996): 586-601.

Nicolson, Marjorie. *The Breaking of the Circle*. New York: Columbia University Press, 1960.

Niedecker, Lorine. "When Ecstasy is Inconvenient." *Lorine Niedecker: Collected Works*. Ed. Jenny Penberthy. Berkeley: University of California Press, 2002. 25.

Nosthoff, Anna-Verena. "Barbarism: Notes on the Thought of Theodor W. Adorno." *Critical Legal Thinking* (15 October 2014): http://criticallegalthinking.com/2014/10/15/barbarism-notes-thought-theodor-w-adorno/ [.]

Ostovich, Helen, and Elizabeth Sauer. Eds. *Reading Early Modern Women: An Anthology of Texts in Manuscript and Print, 1550-1700*. New York: Routledge, 2004.

Owen, Maureen. "Susan Howe's Poetry." *The Difficulties: Susan Howe Issue*. Ed. Tom Beckett. Kent, Ohio: Viscerally Press, 1989. 57-58.

Oxford English Dictionary: http://www.oed.com/ [.]

Palattella, John. "An End of Abstraction: An Essay on Susan Howe's Historicism." *Denver Quarterly* 29.3 (1995): 74-97.

Paul Thek: Diver, A Retrospective. New York: The Whitney Museum of American Art (October 21, 2010-January 9, 2011): http://whitney.org/Exhibitions/PaulThek [.]

Peirce, Charles S. "Letters to Lady Welby." *Critical Theory Since 1965*. Ed. Hazard Adams and Leroy Searle. Tallahassee: University Press of Florida, 1986. 639-642.

---. *Charles S. Peirce Papers 1859-1913*. Houghton Library, Harvard University: http://oasis.lib.harvard.edu/oasis/deliver/~hou02614 [.]

Penberthy, Jenny. "Life and Writing." *Lorine Niedecker: Collected Works*. Ed. Jenny Penberthy. Berkeley: University of California Press, 2002. 1-11.

Perloff, Marjorie. *Poetic License: Essays on Modernist and Postmodernist Lyric*. Evanston: Northwestern University Press, 1990.

---. *Radical Artifice: Writing Poetry in the Age of Media.* Chicago: University of Chicago Press, 1991.

---. "Textuality and the Visual: A Response." (1997): https://web.archive.org/web/20160409172458/http://marjorieperloff.com/essays/ [.]

---. "Announcement." *Spontaneous Particulars: The Telepathy of Archives.* New York: Christine Burgin / New Directions, 2014. Book wrapper.

Philip, M. NourbeSe. *ZONG!* Wesleyan University Press, 2008.

Pinsky, Robert. "In Praise of Difficult Poetry." *Slate* (Monday, April 23, 2007): http://www.slate.com/id/2164823/pagenum/all/#page_start [.]

Plant, Sadie. *The Most Radical Gesture: The Situationist International in a Postmodern Age.* New York: Routledge, 1992.

Pocumtuck Valley Memorial Association: https://deerfield-ma.org/ [.]

Pointer, Steven R. "The Emmanuel College, Cambridge, Election of 1622: The Constraints of a Puritan Institution." *Puritanism and Its Discontents.* Ed. Laura Lunger Knoppers. Newark: University of Delaware Press, 2003. 106-121.

Pound, Ezra. *Literary Essays of Ezra Pound.* Ed. T. S. Eliot. New York: New Directions, 1954.

Poussin and Nature: Arcadian Visions. New York: The Metropolitan Museum of Art (February 12 – May 11, 2008): http://www.metmuseum.org/press/exhibitions/2008/poussin-and-nature--arcadian-visions [.]

Powell's City of Books: http://www.powells.com/ [.]

Preminger, Alex, et al. Eds. *The New Princeton Encyclopedia of Poetry and Poetics.* Princeton: Princeton University Press, 1993.

Priest, Graham, and Francesco Berto. "Dialetheism." *The Stanford Encyclopedia of Philosophy*. Ed. Edward N. Zalta (Spring 2017): https://plato.stanford.edu/archives/spr2017/entries/dialetheism/ [.]

Purchas, Samuel. *Hakluytus Posthumus or Purchas his pilgrimes. Contayning a history of the world, in sea voyages & lande-travells, by Englishmen & others. Wherein Gods wonders in nature & providence, the actes, arts, varieties, & vanities of men, with a world of the worlds rarities, are by a world of eywitnesse-authors, related to the world. Some left written by M. Hakluyt at his death. More since added. His also perused & perfected. All examined, abreviated with discourse. Adorned with pictues and expressed in mapps. In fower parts. Each containing five books*. London: by W. Stansby for H. Fetherstone, 1625.

Putnam, Hilary. *Realism With a Human Face*. Ed. James Conant. Cambridge: Harvard University Press, 1990.

Quartermain, Peter. "And the Without: An interpretive essay on Susan Howe." *The Difficulties: Susan Howe Issue*. Ed. Tom Beckett. Kent, Ohio: Viscerally Press, 1989. 71-81.

---. *Disjunctive Poetics: From Gertrude Stein and Louis Zukofsky to Susan Howe*. Cambridge: Cambridge University Press, 1992.

Raid on Deerfield: The Many Stories of 1704: http://1704.deerfield.history.museum/home.do [.]

Ramke, Bin. "Elegy as Origin." *Denver Quarterly* 23.3-4 (1989): 33-39.

Rankine, Claudia. *Citizen: An American Lyric*. Minneapolis: Graywolf Press, 2014.

Ratcliffe, Stephen. "Idea's Mirror." *The Difficulties: Susan Howe Issue*. Ed. Tom Beckett. Kent, Ohio: Viscerally Press, 1989. 43-45.

Reed, Brian. "'Eden or Ebb of the Sea': Susan Howe's Word Squares and Postlinear Poetics." *Postmodern Culture* 14.2 (2004): http://pmc.iath.virginia.edu/issue.104/14.2reed.html [.]

Reinfeld, Linda. *Language Poetry: Writing as Rescue*. Baton Rouge: Louisiana State University Press, 1992.

Renwick, Vanessa. *Oregon Department of Kick Ass*: http://www.odoka.org/about/ [.]

Reznikoff, Charles. "The Good Old Days: Recitative Historical Episodes." *The Poems of Charles Reznikoff 1918-1975*. Ed. Seamus Cooney. Boston: David R. Godine, 2005. 359-368.

Rodney, Janet. "Language and Susan." *The Difficulties: Susan Howe Issue*. Ed. Tom Beckett. Kent, Ohio: Viscerally Press, 1989. 46-51.

Rorty, Richard. *Contingency, irony, and solidarity*. Cambridge: Cambridge University Press, 1989.

Rowell, Charles H. "AN INTERVIEW WITH NATHANIEL MACKEY by Charles H. Rowell." (February 21, 1997): https://vdocuments.site/nathaniel-mackey-a-special-issue-an-interview-with-nathaniel-mackey-58823471d8984.html [.]

Rowlandson, Mary. *The soveraignty & goodness of God, together, with the faithfulness of his promises displayed; being a narrative of the captivity and restauration of Mrs. Mary Rowlandson. Commended by her, to all that desires to know the Lords doing to, and dealings with her. Especially to her dear children and relations, / written by her own hand for her private use, and now made publick at the earnest desire of some friends, and for the benefit of the afflicted*. Cambridge [Mass.]: Printed by Samuel Green, 1682.

---. *A true history of the captivity & restoration of Mrs. Mary Rowlandson, a minister's wife in New-England wherein is set forth the cruel and inhumane usage she underwent amongst the heathens for eleven weeks time, and her deliverance from them / written by her own hand ... ;*

whereunto is annexed a sermon of the possibility of God's forsaking a people that have been near and dear to him, preached by Mr. Joseph Rowlandson ... it being his last sermon. London: Printed first at New-England, and re-printed at London, and sold by Joseph Poole, 1682.

---. *Narrative of the Captivity and Restoration of Mrs. Mary Rowlandson.* Project Gutenberg (2009): https://www.gutenberg.org/files/851/851-h/851-h.htm [.]

Said, Edward. *Orientalism.* New York: Vintage, 1978.

Schlesinger, Kyle. "Sparks in the Library." *I Have Imagined A Center // Wilder Than This Region: A Tribute to Susan Howe.* Cuneiform Press, 2007. 85-94.

Schmitz, Neil. "Introduction: The Planctus of Rachel." *I Have Imagined A Center // Wilder Than This Region: A Tribute to Susan Howe.* Cuneiform Press, 2007. 11-17.

Schoenberg, Arnold Schoenberg. *Style and Idea: Selected Writings of Arnold Schoenberg.* Ed. Leonard Stein. Trans. Leo Black. New York: St. Martin's Press, 1975.

Schultz, Eric B., and Michael J. Tougias. *King Philip's War: The History and Legacy of America's Forgotten Conflict.* Woodstock, VT: The Countryman Press, 1999.

Schultz, Susan M. "Exaggerated History." *Postmodern Culture* 4.2 (1994): https://muse.jhu.edu/article/27452 [.]

---. "The Stutter in the Text: Editing and Historical Authority in the Work of Susan Howe." *How2* vol. 1, no.6 (2001): http://www.scc.rutgers.edu/however/v1_6_2001/current/readings/encounters/schultz.html [.]

---. *A Poetics of Impasse in Modern and Contemporary American Poetry.* Tuscaloosa: The University of Alabama Press, 2005.

Sebald, W. G. *The Rings of Saturn*. Trans. Michael Hulse. New York: New Directions, 1998.

Sedgwick, Catharine Maria. *Hope Leslie* (1827).

Serio, John, and Greg Foster. *The Online Concordance to Wallace Stevens' Poetry*: http://www.wallacestevens.com/concordance/WSdb.cgi [.]

Shakespeare, William. *Hamlet*. MIT Shakespeare, 1983: http://shakespeare.mit.edu/hamlet/full.html [.]

Sheldon, George. *A History of Deerfield, Massachusetts: the times when the people by whom it was settled, unsettled and resettled: with a special study of the Indian wars in the Connecticut valley, With genealogies*. 2 Vols. Deerfield, MA: E. A. Hall & Co., 1895-1896. [Greenfield, MA: Press of E. A. Hall & Co.]

---. "Introduction." Rpt. 6th ed. Rev. John Williams. [Boston: Samuel Hall, 1795]. *The redeemed captive returning to Zion [...] With a conclusion to the whole, by the Rev. Mr. Prince, of Boston*. Springfield, MA: H.R. Hunting Co., 1908: https://archive.org/stream/redeemedcaptive00willrich/redeemedcaptive00willrich_djvu.txt [.]

Simpson, Megan. *Poetic Epistemologies: Gender and Knowing in Women's Language-Oriented Writing*. Albany: State University of New York Press, 2000.

Sir William Johnson Papers. Revised edition. New York State Library, 2015: http://www.nysl.nysed.gov/publications/johnsoncd.htm [.]

Slotkin, Richard. *Regeneration Through Violence: The Mythology of the American Frontier, 1600-1860*. New York: Harper, 1973.

Slotkin, Richard, and James K. Folsom. Eds. *So Dreadfull A Judgment: Puritan Responses to King Philips's War, 1676-1677*. Middletown: Wesleyan University Press, 1978.

Small, John R. W. "The Playgoer: At the Christ Church Parish House." *The Harvard Crimson* (April 26, 1951): http://www.thecrimson.com/article/1951/4/26/the-playgoer-pit-was-a-sadly/ [.]

Smith, A. J. *Metaphysical Wit.* Cambridge: Cambridge UP, 1991.

Smith, John. *The generall historie of Virginia, New-England, and the Summer Isles with the names of the adventurers, planters, and governours from their first beginning. an0: 1584. to this present 1624. With the procedings of those severall colonies and the accidents that befell them in all their journyes and discoveries Also the maps and descriptions of all those countryes, their commodities, people, government, customes, and religion yet knowne. Divided into six bookes. By Captaine Iohn Smith sometymes governour in those countryes & admirall of New England.* London: Printed by I[ohn] D[awson] and I[ohn] H[aviland] for Michael Sparkes, 1624.

Smith, Mary P. Wells. *The Boy Captive of Old Deerfield.* Dallas: Gideon House Books, 2016.

Smith, Roberta. "David von Schlegell, Abstract Artist, Is Dead at 72." *The New York Times* (October 6, 1992): http://www.nytimes.com/1992/10/06/arts/david-von-schlegell-abstract-artist-is-dead-at-72.html [.]

South Asia Collections, 17th-20th Centuries. Yale University: http://guides.library.yale.edu/c.php?g=296361&p=1974988 [.]

Steele, Timothy. *Missing Measures: Modern Poetry and the Revolt Against Meter.* Fayetteville and London: University of Arkansas Press, 1990.

Stein, Gertrude. "What Is English Literature." *Lectures in America.* Boston: Beacon Press, 1957. 11-58.

---. "Composition as Explanation." *Poetry Foundation*: http://www.poetryfoundation.org/resources/learning/essays/detail/69481 [.]

Stevens, Wallace. *The Collected Poems*. New York: Vintage Books, 1982.

Stout, Harry S. *The New England Soul: Preaching and Religious Culture in Colonial New England*. New York and Oxford: Oxford University Press, 1986.

Stratton, Billy J. *Buried in Shades of Night: Contested Voices, Indian Captivity, and The Legacy of King Philip's War*. Tucson: The University of Arizona Press, 2013.

---. "Captivity Narratives." *The Oxford History of Popular Print Culture*. Ed. Ronald J. Zboray and Mary Saracino Zboray. Oxford: Oxford University Press, 2019. 189-203.

Sturken, Marita. *Tangled Memories: The Vietnam War, the AIDS Epidemic, and the Politics of Remembering*. Berkeley and London: University of California Press, 1997.

Styles, Ezra. "Ezra Styles." *Encyclopedia.Com*: http://www.encyclopedia.com/people/philosophy-and-religion/protestant-christianity-biographies/ezra-stiles [.]

Sussman, Elisabeth, and Lynn Zelevansky. Eds. *Paul Thek: Diver, A Retrospective*. New York: Whitney Museum of American Art, 2010.

Thek, Paul. "The Personal Effects of the Pied Piper." New York: Whitney Museum of American Art, 2010: http://whitney.org/WatchAndListen/Tag?context=curators&play_id=332 [.]

"The Land Speaks: New Perspectives on the Falls Fight / A presentation by Archaeologists and Tribal representatives." (Thursday, November 16, 2017): http://www.montague.net/n/31/The-Land-Speaks-New-Perspectives-on-the-Falls-Fight [.]

The Transactions of the Charles Sanders Peirce Society: http://peircesociety.org/transactions [.]

Timreck, Ted, and Peter Frechette. *Great Falls: Discovery, Destruction and Preservation in a Massachusetts Town*. Oley, PA: Bullfrog Films, 2011.

Trumbull, James Russell. *History of Northampton, Massachusetts: From Its Settlement in 1654*. 2 vols. Northampton, MA: Gazette Printing, 1898 – 1902.

Tsatsanis, Peter. "On René Thom's Significance For Mathematics and Philosophy." *Scripta Philosophiae Naturalis* 2 (2012): 213-229.

Tucker, Arthur Holmes. *Hope Atherton and His Times*. Deerfield, MA: Pocumtuck Valley Memorial Association, 1926.

Vanderborg, Susan. *Paratextual Communities: American Avant-Garde Poetry Since 1950*. Carbondale and Edwardsville: Southern Illinois University Press, 2001.

Varzi, Achille. "Mereology." *The Stanford Encyclopedia of Philosophy*. Ed. Edward N. Zalta. Winter 2016: https://plato.stanford.edu/archives/win2016/entries/mereology/ [.]

Vaughn, Alden T., and Edward W. Clark. *Puritans among the Indians: Accounts of Captivity and Redemption 1676–1724*. Cambridge, MA: Belknap Press of Harvard University Press, 1981.

Vickery, Ann. *Leaving Lines of Gender: A Feminist Genealogy of Language Writing*. Hanover: Wesleyan University Press, 2000.

Vizenor, Gerald. Ed. *Survivance: Narratives of Native Presence*. Lincoln and London: University of Nebraska Press, 2008.

Washburn, Wilcomb E., and Alden T. Vaughn. *Garland Library of Narratives of North American Indian Captives*. 112 vols. Westport, CT: Garland, 1976–1983.

Watts, Charles, and Edward Byrne. Eds. *The Recovery of the Public World: Essays on Poetics in Honour of Robin Blaser*. Burnaby, BC: Talonbooks, 1999.

Webster, Noah. *American Dictionary of the English Language.* 1828 edition online: http://webstersdictionary1828.com/ [.]

---. *The Noah Webster Papers.* New York Public Library Manuscripts and Archives Division: http://archives.nypl.org/ [.]

Wells, Daniel White, and Reuben Field Wells. *A History of Hatfield, Massachusetts, in Three Parts.* Springfield, MA: F. C. H. Gibbons, 1910.

White, Hayden. *Tropics of Discourse: Essays in Cultural Criticism.* Baltimore: Johns Hopkins University Press, 1978.

---. *The Content of the Form: Narrative Discourse and Historical Representation.* Baltimore: The Johns Hopkins University Press, 1987.

Williams, Daniel E., Christina Riley Brown, Salita S. Bryant, et al. Eds. *Liberty's Captives: Narratives of Confinement in the Print Culture of the Early Republic.* Athens, GA: University of Georgia Press, 2006.

Williams, John, Rev. *The redeemed captive returning to Zion or, A faithful history of remarkable occurrences in the captivity and deliverance of Mr. John Williams, Minister of the Gospel in Deerfield.* Boston: Printed by B. Green, for Samuel Phillips, 1707.

---. *The redeemed captive returning to Zion or, A faithful history of remarkable occurrences in the captivity and deliverance of Mr. John Williams, Minister of the Gospel in Deerfield; who, in the desolation which befel that plantation, by an incursion of French and Indians, was by them carried away, with his family and his neighbourhood, into Canada. Drawn up by himself. Annexed to which, is a sermon, preached by him upon his return. Also, an appendix, by the Rev. Mr. Williams, of Springfield. Likewise, an appendix, by the Rev. Mr. Taylor, of Deerfield. With a conclusion to the whole, by the Rev. Mr. Prince, of Boston.* Boston: Samuel Hall, 1795: https://archive.org/stream/redeemedcaptive00willrich/redeemedcaptive00willrich_djvu.txt [.]

---. *The captivity and deliverance of Mr. John Williams, pastor of the church in Deerfield, and Mrs. Mary Rowlandson, of Lancaster: who were taken, together with their families and neighbors, by the French and Indians, and carried into Canada. Written by themselves.* Brookfield, MA: Printed by Hori Brown, from the press of E. Merriam & Co., 1811.

---. [Boston: Samuel Hall, 1795]. *The redeemed captive returning to Zion [...] With a conclusion to the whole, by the Rev. Mr. Prince, of Boston.* Springfield, MA: H.R. Hunting Co., 1908: https://archive.org/stream/redeemedcaptive00willrich/redeemedcaptive00willrich_djvu.txt [.]

---. "Williams, John." *Dictionary of Canadian Biography.* Vol. 2 (1701-1740): http://www.biographi.ca/en/bio/williams_john_1664_1729_2E.html [.]

Williams, William Carlos. "Cotton Mather's Wonders of the Invisible World." *In The American Grain.* New York: New Directions, 1933. 81-104.

---. *Paterson (Book I).* New York: New Directions, 1946.

---. *Paterson (Book Three).* New York: New Directions, 1949.

---. *The Selected Letters of William Carlos Williams.* Ed. John C. Thirlwall. New York: New Directions, 1957.

---. *Paterson (Book Five).* New York: New Directions, 1958.

---. *The Desert Music. The Collected Poems of William Carlos Williams.* Vol. 2: 1939-1962. Ed. Christopher MacGowan. New York: New Directions, 1988. 243-284.

---. *Paterson.* Ed. Christopher MacGowan. New York: New Directions, 1995.

---. "A New Measure." *Twentieth-Century American Poetics: Poets on the Art of Poetry*. Ed. Dana Gioia, David Mason, and Meg Schoerke. Boston: McGraw Hill, 2004. 49-50.

---. *The William Carlos Williams Collection*, 1902-1960. The Poetry Collection of the University Libraries. University at Buffalo, The State University of New York: http://library.buffalo.edu/pl/ [.]

Winthrop, John. *A journal of the transactions and occurrences in the settlement of Massachusetts and the other New-England colonies, from the year 1630 to 1644: written by John Winthrop, Esq; first governor of Massachusetts: and now first published from a correct copy of the original manuscript*. Books 1-2. Ed. Noah Webster. Hartford: Printed by Elisha Babcock, 1790.

---. *The history of New England from 1630 to 1649 by John Winthrop, from his original manuscripts; with notes to illustrate the civil and ecclesiastical concerns, the geography, settlement, and institutions of the country, and the lives and manners of the principal planters by James Savage*. Books 1-3. Ed. James Savage. Boston: Little, Brown, 1825-1826, 1853.

Yeats, W. B. *The Poems of W. B. Yeats*. New York: Macmillan, 1983.

---. *Last Poems: Manuscript Materials*. Ed. James Pethica. Cornell: Cornell University Press, 1997.

---. *New Poems: Manuscript Materials*. Ed. J. C. C. Mays and Stephen Parrish. Cornell: Cornell University Press, 2001.

---. "Cuchulain Comforted." *Collected Poems*. Adelaide: University of Adelaide Library, 2014: https://ebooks.adelaide.edu.au/y/yeats/william_butler/y4c/index.html [.]

Zeiger, Melissa F. *Beyond Consolation: death, sexuality, and the changing shapes of elegy*. Ithaca: Cornell University Press, 1997.

Zukofsky, Louis. "Program: 'Objectivists' 1931." *Poetry* 37.5 (1931): 268-272.

---. "Sincerity and Objectification: With Special Reference to the Work of Charles Reznikoff." *Poetry* 37.5 (1931): 272-285.

---. "Recencies in Poetry." *An "Objectivists" Anthology*. Ed. Louis Zukofsky. Le Beausset, Var, France: To, Publishers, 1932. 9-25.

---. *5 Statements for Poetry*. San Francisco: San Francisco State College, 1958.

---. "An Objective." *Prepositions: The Collected Critical Essays*. London: Rapp & Carroll, 1967; and New York: The Horizon Press, 1967. 20-26.

---. "An Objective." *Prepositions + The Collected Critical Essays*. Ed. Mark Scroggins. Hanover: Wesleyan University Press, 2000. 12-18.

A

Adams, Hazard, 61n99
Adams, Mary Manning Howe, 202–203n323
Adorno, Theodor, 85, 93n153
Althusser, Louis, 119
Altieri, Charles, 34–35, 35n68
Andrews, Bruce, 56–59n93
archive, 6, 9, 12, 15, 16, 19, 25, 26, 28, 29, 42, 55, 63, 68, 82, 86, 94, 97, 98, 101, 107, 112, 115, 120, 122, 126, 127, 155, 160, 162, 170, 174, 179, 180, 186, 189, 189–190n276, 201, 220, 235, 236–246, 245n441
Arendt, Hannah, 93, 157
The Argonauts (Nelson), 19
"Arisbe" (Howe), 25, 37, 42, 43–44, 45, 47, 49, 52
Arisbe (Howe), 12–13n31
Arosen, Marguerite Kanenstenhawi. *See* Williams, Eunice Mather
"Art in Art & Stone on Stone" (Howard), 17–30
Artaud, Antonin, 14
Articulation of Sound Forms in Time (1987) (Awede edition) (Howe), 5, 8, 9n20, 10–11, 12–13n31, 16, 54–189, 228, 233
Articulation of Sound Forms in Time (Wesleyan edition), 5, 76n131
artifact, 6, 9, 10, 12, 15, 16, 17, 21, 22, 23, 26, 27, 29, 42, 55, 62, 63, 68, 76, 86, 94, 97, 99, 101, 107, 115, 120, 122, 126, 127, 155, 160, 162, 170, 174, 175, 186, 201n318, 218n373, 220, 221, 236–246, 245n441
Atherton, Hope, 16, 55, 56–59n93, 71, 71–72n121, 72, 73, 79, 81, 82, 84, 85, 86, 87, 88, 89, 97, 98, 100–105, 109, 116, 118, 119, 120–121, 124, 126, 128–133, 131–132n231, 135, 137, 138–155, 149n246, 160–167, 169–170, 172, 173, 175–178, 181, 183–188, 233, 243

B

Back, Rachel Tzvia, 86, 88, 99, 127, 154, 164, 165, 166, 167, 169, 170
Baker, David, 56–59n93
Bazin, André, 207, 207n337
Of Being Numerous (1968) (Oppen), 109
Belding, Stephen, 132, 139, 140, 162, 163, 168, 169
Benjamin, Walter, 5, 14, 23, 92–93, 95, 156–159, 156n250
Bergland, Brita, 54, 59
Bernstein, Charles, 56–59n93, 76n131, 80n143, 202
betweenness, 6, 116, 118, 137, 209–210n348, 241, 246
Beyond Document: Essays on Nonfiction Film (1996) (Howe), 10, 13–

288

14

a bibliography of the king's book; or, eikon basilike (1989) (Paradigm Press edition) (Howe), 5, 8, 67n113, 96–97, 171, 216
The Birth-mark (1990) (Howe), 186
The Birth-mark (1993) (Howe), 18, 24, 26, 29, 30, 55, 73, 84, 86, 87, 89, 90, 91, 95, 156, 159, 166, 169, 171, 173, 181, 182–183, 204, 224, 231, 232, 237, 246
The Birth-mark (2015) (Howe), 95
Bishop, Elizabeth, 32–33n64, 33, 40, 52
Black Mountain School, 34
Blake, William, 79
Blaser, Robin, 34
The Book of the Dead (1938) (Rukeyser), 109
Bradstreet, Anne, 14, 30, 32–33n64, 40, 52
a bridge dead in the water (2007) (Stevens), 109
Bronk, William, 32–33n64, 33, 35n71, 40, 50, 52
Brown, Norman O., 233
Browne, Thomas, 33, 40, 52
Browning, Robert, 209
Brule, David, 131–132n231
Bunting, Basil, 110–111n191, 111, 111–112n196
Burch, Robert, 2n6, 13n34
Burt, Stephen, 51n87
Butterick, George F., 74–75n129, 80, 82, 101

C

Cabbage Gardens (1979) (Howe), 12–13n31, 232n421
Caldwell, Patricia, 90
Campbell, Bruce, 74–75n129, 83
captivity narratives, 71, 84, 85, 87, 96, 101, 103, 121, 123, 125, 128, 132, 135, 137, 140, 144, 145, 148, 150, 153, 154, 163, 164, 167, 173, 176, 179–181, 182, 183, 185. *See also* "The Captivity and Restoration of Mrs. Mary Rowlandson" (1985) (Howe); *Narrative of the Captivity and Restoration of Mrs. Mary Rowlandson* (Rowlandson)
"The Captivity and Restoration of Mrs. Mary Rowlandson" (1985) (Howe), 67n113, 78, 86, 171
Caruth, Cathy, 21
CDs, 30, 67n113, 69–70n117, 189, 203–204n325, 205n332, 218n373, 243, 245, 246n442
Champion, Martha, 111
Chanting at the Crystal Sea (1975) (Howe), 12–13n31, 232n421

289

"Childe Emily to the Dark Tower Came" (1983) (Howe), 86, 171
Circumnavigator (1970) (Howe), 30
Citizen (Rankine), 19, 109
Clark, T. J., 192–193
Clements, Arthur, 32n63
Clippinger, David, 74–75n129, 82, 85, 99
Close Listening: Poetry and the Performed Word (ed. Bernstein), 12–13n31
Collis, Stephen, 56–59n93, 67n113, 82, 84, 88, 99
Concordance (2019) (Howe), 30
Conte, Joseph M., 70n118
Cotton, John, 76n131, 125n222
Crane, Hart, 200, 221, 236, 238, 240, 241
Cronon, William, 90, 90n149
Crown, Kathleen, 74–75n129, 79, 82, 85, 87, 89, 90, 99

D
de Certeau, Michel, 65n109
de Portales, Juliette, 38
Debths (2017) (Howe), 9, 9n20, 122, 189, 189–190n276, 212–213n355
Defenestration of Prague (1983) (Howe), 12–13n31
Deleuze, Gilles, 56–59n93, 228, 233
Derrida, Jacques, 96–97, 165
Deux et (1998) (Howe), 12–13n31, 14, 15, 69–70n117
dialetheism, 68, 68n115, 245
Dickinson, Emily, 16, 27, 30, 32–33n64, 33, 35, 36, 37, 39, 40, 44, 45, 47, 48–49, 50, 51, 52, 53, 66, 67n113, 80, 86, 91, 130n228, 165, 169, 171, 173, 174, 179, 189, 195, 195–196n298, 197–198, 212, 220, 221, 228, 231, 236, 241, 246. *See also* Howe, Susan, "Arisbe"; Howe, Susan, *My Emily Dickinson* (1985)
"The Disappearance Approach" (Howe), 24, 193
A Discourse Concerning the Danger of Apostasy (1677) (Mather), 182
Diver: A Retrospective (exhibition) (Thek), 194–195
Donne, John, 31, 32–33n64, 33, 35, 36, 40–41, 52, 53
Drafts (DuPlessis), 109
Duncan, Robert, 32–33n64, 40, 52, 80, 80n143, 86, 169
DuPlessis, Rachel Blau, 56–59n93, 109, 111–112n196
Duran, Bob, 2n8

E
Eco, Umberto, 70

Edwards, Hannah (m. Hannah Edwards Wetmore), 16, 25, 26, 121, 208, 218, 236, 245
Edwards, Jonathan, 26, 125n222, 200, 241, 242
Edwards, Jonathan Jr., 107, 221, 240
Eliot, T. S., 32–33n64, 35, 39, 40–41, 42, 52, 73, 77, 77n132, 110–111n191, 225
Emmons, David, 3
"Encloser" (1990) (Howe), 9, 12–13n31, 15, 91–92, 96n159, 98
"The End of Art" (1974) (Howe), 24, 28, 122–123, 231
English Fairy Tales (1890) (Jacobs), 121
Eroding Witness (1985) (Mackey), 109
"Errand" (Howe), 26
"Escape of Jonathan Wells," 139, 140, 144, 165
"Ether Either" (1998) (Howe), 9, 12–13n31, 43–44, 198n306
The Europe of Trusts (1990) (Howe), 10, 20, 166, 177
The Europe of Trusts (2002) Howe, 10, 20, 65

F
fabric, meaning of, 3
factual telepathy, 6, 9, 10, 11, 12, 13–16, 13n34, 17, 19, 21, 66, 68, 70, 72, 97, 99, 105, 112, 115, 116, 119, 121, 124, 127, 129, 130, 133, 143, 157, 163, 169, 172, 175, 186, 211
faith, 23
Felman, Shoshana, 21
feminism, 56, 56–59n93, 80, 86, 169
Finlay, Ian Hamilton, 80n143, 83
"The First Chapter of Logic" (Peirce), 46–47
Firstness, Secondness, and Thirdness, 45 46, 49, 219n377, 220
Fisch, Max, 49
Foster, Edward, 24, 62n102, 95, 131–132n231
Frame Structures (1995) (Howe), 99, 164, 166, 232
Frame Structures (1996) (Howe), 12–13n31
Frame Structures: Early Poems, 1974–1979 (1996) (Howe), 6, 10, 232n421
"Frame Structures" (essay) (Howe), 24
Frolic Architecture (2010) (Howe and Grubbs), 9, 16, 25, 69, 69–70n117, 121, 200–201n317, 208, 217–218, 244–245n440, 245
Frolic Architecture (2011) (Howe and Grubbs), 16, 208n341, 218n373, 238
Frost, Elisabeth A., 74–75n129, 86, 88, 99, 127, 154, 165, 166, 167, 169, 170

G
Gaffield, Nancy, 74–75n129, 80, 82, 83, 85, 88–89, 99, 101, 127, 154, 165, 166–167, 170
Gerke, Robert, 3
Godard, Jean-Luc, 14
Goekjian, Greg, 37–38
Greenblatt, Stephen, 90, 90n149
Grosmann, Uta, 56–59n93, 80
Grubbs, David, Susan Howe collaboration with
  Frolic Architecture (2010). See *Frolic Architecture* (2010) (Howe and Grubbs)
  "Melville's Marginalia" (2005), 203–204n325
  overview, 25–26, 30
  Souls of the Labadie Tract (2007). See *Souls of the Labadie Tract* (2007) (Howe and Grubbs)
  THIEFTH. See *THIEFTH* (2005) (Howe and Grubbs); *THIEFTH* (2015) (Howe and Grubbs)
  TOM TIT TOT (exhibition) (2013). See *TOM TIT TOT* (exhibition) (2013) (Howe and Grubbs)
  WOODSLIPPERCOUNTERCLATTER. See *WOODSLIPPERCOUNTERCLATTER* (2013) (Howe and Grubbs); *WOODSLIPPERCOUNTERCLATTER* (2015) (Howe and Grubbs)
Guattari, Féix, 56–59n93, 233
gwawd, 23

H
Hamlet (Shakespeare), 14, 22, 222
Hare, Peter H., 192n282, 202–203
Hawthorne, Nathaniel, 30
Hayden, Robert, 109
H.D. (Hilda Doolittle), 76n131, 80n143, 86, 169
Hegel, Georg Wilhelm Friedrich, 93n153
Hegelian dialectics, 93, 93n153, 94, 157–158
Hejinian, Lyn, 80n143, 94
Heliopathy (Howe), 12–13n31
Heller-Roazen, Daniel, 193
Herbert, George, 32–33n64, 40, 51n87, 52, 200
"Heterologies: Community of Form in Practice and Imagination" (1999) (Howe), 12–13n31

Hindsell, Experience, 132, 140
Hinge Picture (1974) (Howe), 10, 12–13n31, 122, 232n421, 238
historical figuration, 65, 65n109, 70, 72, 95, 97, 98, 99, 104, 107, 109, 112, 118, 119, 124, 127, 129, 143, 153, 157, 158, 163, 169, 172, 175, 176, 186
A History of Deerfield, Massachusetts (1895–1896) (Sheldon), 16, 99–100n163, 102, 125, 127, 129, 133n233, 147, 147–148n245, 162n253, 165, 166, 168, 173, 175, 177
History of Hadley (1905) (Judd), 99–100n163, 126, 173
A History of Hatfield, Massachusetts: in Three Parts (1910) (Wells and Wells), 71n121, 99–100n163, 102, 126, 187
Hollister, Sarah, 130
Homer, 49, 77–78
Hope Atherton and His Times (Tucker), 5, 186
Hopkins, Gerard Manley, 54n89, 73
Howard, W. Scott, 12n28, 17–30, 26n55, 32n63, 35n71, 42n83, 65n109, 71n120, 73n127, 109n190, 116n205, 120n212, 120n213, 179n263, 185n272, 200–201n317, 200n314, 209–210n348, 211n352, 218n373
Howard, William, 132
Howe, Fanny (sister), 9, 20
Howe, Mark DeWolfe (father), 20
Howe, Mary Manning (mother), 20, 44
Howe, Susan
  "Arisbe," 25, 37, 42, 43–44, 45, 47, 49, 52
  Arisbe, 12–13n31
  Articulation of Sound Forms in Time (1987) (Awede edition), 5, 8, 9n20, 10–11, 12–13n31, 16, 54–189, 228, 233, 243
  Articulation of Sound Forms in Time (Wesleyan edition), 76n131
  Beyond Document: Essays on Nonfiction Film (1996), 10, 13–14
  a bibliography of the king's book; or, eikon basilike (1989) (Paradigm Press edition), 5, 8, 67n113, 96–97, 171, 216
  The Birth-mark (1990) (Howe), 186
  The Birth-mark (1993), 18, 24, 26, 29, 30, 55, 73, 84, 86, 87, 89, 90, 91, 95, 159, 169, 171, 173, 181, 182–183, 204, 224, 231, 232, 237, 246
  The Birth-mark (1993) (Howe), 156, 166
  The Birth-mark (2015), 95
  Cabbage Gardens (1979), 12–13n31, 232n421
  and captivity narratives, 67n113, 71, 78, 84, 86, 87–88, 96, 101, 103, 121, 123–124, 128

"The Captivity and Restoration of Mrs. Mary Rowlandson" (1985), 67n113, 78, 86, 171
career of, 11, 30, 233n424
Chanting at the Crystal Sea (1975), 12–13n31, 232n421
"Childe Emily to the Dark Tower Came" (1983), 86, 171
on Chris Marker, 14, 15, 22, 207
Circumnavigator (1970), 30
collaboration with David Grubbs. *See* Grubbs, David
collaboration with Leslie Miller, 198–199, 199n312, 206
Concordance (2019), 30
Debths (2017), 9, 9n20, 122, 189–190n276, 189–235, 212–213n355
Defenestration of Prague (1983), 12–13n31
Deux et (1998), 12–13n31, 14, 15, 69n117
"The Disappearance Approach," 24, 193
"Encloser" (1990), 9, 12–13n31, 15, 91–92, 96n159, 98
"The End of Art" (1974), 24, 28, 122–123, 231
"Errand," 26
"Ether Either" (1998), 9, 12–13n31, 43–44, 198n306
The Europe of Trusts (1990), 10, 20, 65, 177
The Europe of Trusts (2002), 10, 20, 65
Frame Structures (1995), 99, 164, 166, 232
Frame Structures (1996), 12–13n31
Frame Structures: Early Poems, 1974–1979 (1996), 6, 10, 232n421
"Frame Structures" (essay), 24
Frolic Architecture (2010) (with David Grubbs), 9, 16, 25, 69, 69–70n117, 121, 200–201n317, 208, 217–218, 244–245n440, 245
Frolic Architecture (2011) (with David Grubbs), 208n341, 218n373, 238
Heliopathy, 12–13n31
"Heterologies: Community of Form in Practice and Imagination" (1999), 12–13n31
Hinge Picture (1974), 10, 12–13n31, 122, 232n421, 238
Kidnapped (2002), 121
The Leisure of the Theory Class, 12–13n31
The Liberties (1980), 12–13n31
Marginalia de Melville (1997), 12–13n31, 67n113, 203–204n325
Melville's Marginalia (1993), 12–13n31, 16, 67n113, 203, 203–204n325, 204, 216, 231
"Melville's Marginalia" (2005) (with David Grubbs Grubbs), 69, 203–204n325
The Midnight (2003), 121, 201, 202, 231, 237

My Emily Dickinson (1985), 27, 38, 39, 42, 44–45, 47, 48, 49, 50, 52, 73, 86, 95, 171, 173, 189, 204, 209, 232, 237
My Emily Dickinson (1985) (Howe), 228
My Emily Dickinson (2007), 39
The Nonconformist's Memorial (1992), 12–13n31
The Nonconformist's Memorial (1993), 9, 10, 12–13n31, 15, 16, 67n113, 84, 86, 121, 203–204n325
One of Them (1969), 30
"Personal Narrative," 25, 69, 72, 113, 116, 154, 155, 158, 172, 175, 176, 178, 243
Pierce-Arrow (1999), 9, 12, 12–13n31, 31n61, 37–39, 40, 42, 45, 46, 47n85, 49, 50, 51, 52, 202, 205, 231, 237
Pythagorean Silence (1982), 12–13n31, 55–56n92, 65n108, 67n113, 177
The Quarry (2015). See *The Quarry* (2015) (Howe)
Scattering as Behavior toward Risk: The Europe of Trusts (1990), 12–13n31, 16, 67n113, 76n31, 232n422
Scattering as Behavior toward Risk: The Europe of Trusts (2002), 12–13n31, 16
Secret History of the Dividing Line (1978), 12–13n31, 55n92
Secret History of the Dividing Line (1978) (Howe), 86
Silence Wager Stories (1989), 12–13n31, 16
Singularities (1990), 9, 10, 12, 12–13n31, 16, 55n92, 56–59n93, 64n107, 67n113, 69n117, 72n122, 76n131, 82, 84, 86, 87, 89, 95–96, 101, 104n179, 121, 144, 146, 149, 152, 170, 172, 205n332, 232
"Sorting Facts; or, Nineteen Ways of Looking at Marker" (1996), 9, 10n22, 11n25, 12–13n31, 13–14, 22, 24, 69, 69–70n117, 116n206, 207n336, 211n352, 212
"Sorting Facts; or, Nineteen Ways of Looking at Marker" (2012), 14
"Sorting Facts; or, Nineteen Ways of Looking at Marker" (2013), 10n23
"Sorting Facts; or, Nineteen Ways of Looking at Marker" (2016), 14
Souls of the Labadie Tract (2007) (with David Grubbs), 2n7, 9, 16n39, 16n42, 26, 27, 55n91, 64n107, 99–100n163, 104n177, 116n204, 121, 155n249, 173, 176, 226, 229, 237, 238, 242, 243
The Sound of Poetry/The Poetry of Sound (2009), 104n177, 176, 177
Spontaneous Particulars: The Telepathy of Archives (2014), 6, 9, 16n40, 18, 107, 121n215, 189, 193, 197, 198–199, 200, 201, 212–213n355, 218n372, 219, 222, 223n388, 224, 225n395, 226–227, 236–246
Stray (2019), 30, 64n107

Talisman interview (1990), 24, 62n102, 64n107, 86–87, 95, 97–98, 101, 117, 173

THAT THIS (2010), 9, 69–70n117, 193n285, 208n342

"There Are Not Leaves Enough to Crown to Cover to Crown to Cover" (1982), 12–13n31, 20, 24, 64–65, 69

"There Are Not Leaves Enough to Crown to Cover to Crown to Cover" (1985), 178

"There Are Not Leaves Enough to Crown to Cover to Crown to Cover" (1990), 177, 178

"There Are Not Leaves Enough to Crown to Cover to Crown to Cover" (1992), 177, 178

"There Are Not Leaves Enough to Crown to Cover to Crown to Cover" (2002), 178

"There Are Not Leaves Enough to Crown to Cover to Crown to Cover" (2015), 178

THIEFTH (2005) (with David Grubbs), 67n113, 69n117, 203–204n325, 205n332, 238

THIEFTH (2006) (with David Grubbs), 189

THIEFTH (2015) (Howe and Grubbs), 203–204n325, 205n332

Thorow (2002), 16, 69–70n117, 76n131, 205, 205n332, 216, 232n422

"Thorow" (essay) (1987), 69, 69–70n117

TOM TIT TOT (book) (2014) (with R. H. Quaytman), 9, 25n54, 66n111, 69, 121, 189, 189–190n276, 194, 195, 195–196n298, 200–201n317, 205–206n333, 208–209, 230, 232, 233, 237

TOM TIT TOT (exhibition) (2013) (with David Grubbs), 19n49, 69–70n117, 189, 212, 213, 234

TOM TIT TOT (exhibition) (2015), 25–26

TOM TIT TOT (exhibition) (2018), 69–70n117

"Vagrancy in the Park" (2015), 24, 27, 28–29, 63n104, 123, 190, 193, 194, 198, 212–213, 228, 229, 229n411, 229n412, 231, 242

WOODSLIPPERCOUNTERCLATTER (2013) (with David Grubbs), 206n335

WOODSLIPPERCOUNTERCLATTER (2015) (with David Grubbs), 69–70n117, 189, 205–206n333, 238, 246n442

word squares of, 10, 56–59n93, 60n96, 74n129, 83, 140, 158, 159–160, 161–162n252, 162, 164, 165, 167, 175

Hunt, Erica, 109

Hutchinson, Anne, 16, 30, 84, 86, 87, 88, 89, 91, 118, 124, 133, 163, 165, 167, 169–170, 172, 173, 174, 179, 184, 224, 226

I

The Iliad (Homer), 77–78

J

Jacobs, Joseph, 121
James, Henry, 192, 211, 219–220, 245
James, William, 14, 28, 37n76
Jay, Ricky, 210, 211, 223
Jenkins, G. Matthew, 56–59n93
Johnson, Mark, 3, 5
Jones, John, 132, 140, 162, 163, 168, 169
Joyce, Elisabeth W., 82, 84–85, 88, 99, 170
Judd, Sylvester, 126, 135, 139, 143, 145, 146, 149, 152, 162, 173, 186. *See also History of Hadley* (1905) (Judd)

K

Kachergis, Anne, 75n130
kairic time, 92–93n152, 94–95, 98–99, 112, 124, 158
Kane, Brian, 207, 207–208n339, 217n369, 218n374
Keller, Lynn, 56–59n93, 76n131, 174
Kermode, Frank, 92–93n152
Kibbey, Anne, 90, 90n149
Kidnapped (2002) (Howe), 121
Kim, Myung Mi, 109
Klint, Hilma af, 30
Kristeva, Julia, 13, 84, 90, 90n149, 119, 120n212

L

L=A=N=G=U=A=G=E poetics, 3, 47, 55–56n92
La Jetée (1962) (film) (Marker), 14, 22
Lang, Amy Schrager, 90
Lanyer, Aemilia, 32–33n64, 40, 52
Laub, Dori, 21
Lazer, Hank, 74–75n129, 84, 99
The Leisure of the Theory Class (Howe), 12–13n31
"Letters to Lady Welby" (Peirce), 44, 45–46, 50–51, 219n377
Lewis, Joel, 56–59n93, 80
The Liberties (1980) (Howe), 12–13n31
The Little Edges (2015) (Moten), 110
Local History (1993) (Hunt), 109

M

Ma, Ming-Qian, 56–59n93
Macalister, R. A. Stewart, 193–194
Mackey, Nathaniel, 80n143, 109, 112
Magnalia (Mather), 226
Manning, Mary, 20. *See also* Howe, Mary Manning (mother)
Marginalia de Melville (1997) (Howe), 12–13n31, 67n113, 203–204n325
Marker, Chris, 13–15, 22, 30, 207
Marsh, Nicky, 56–59n93
Martin, Agnes, 80n143, 83
Martin, John Frederick, 187–188
Martz, Louis, 32n63
Mather, Cotton, 125n222, 226
Mather, Eunice (m. Eunice Mather Williams), 125n221, 125n222, 133, 133n233, 134, 136, 137
Mather, Increase, 76n131, 99–100n163, 105–106n181, 182
The Maximus Poems (1950-1970) (Olson), 109
Mays, James C. C., 195, 196
Mazzoni, Jacopo, 97n161
Mcallister, Andrew, 111–112n196
McCorkle, James, 74–75n129, 85, 87, 99
McGann, Jerome, 55–56n92, 191n280, 196–197, 198
McLane, Maureen N., 18, 190, 245
Melville, Herman, 24, 30, 67n113, 73, 78, 86, 87, 169
Melville's Marginalia (1993) (Howe), 12–13n31, 16, 67n113, 203, 203–204n325, 204, 216, 231
"Melville's Marginalia" (2005) (Howe and Grubbs), 69, 203–204n325
mereology, 13, 13n32
Merleau-Ponty, Maurice, 61
Metaphysical Club, 37n76
Metcalf, Paul, 56–59n93
Middleton, Peter, 74–75n129, 83, 84
The Midnight (2003) (Howe), 121, 201, 202, 231, 237
Miller, Leslie, 200–201, 200–201n317, 208, 209
Miller, Perry, 90n149, 182
Montgomery, Will, 74–75n129, 80, 84, 85, 88, 89, 91, 99, 119
Moore, Marianne, 32–33n64, 40, 52, 110–111n191
Moten, Fred, 110
My Emily Dickinson (1985) (Howe), 27, 38, 39, 42, 44–45, 47, 48, 49,

50, 52, 73, 86, 95, 171, 173, 189, 204, 209, 228, 232, 237
My Emily Dickinson (2007) (Howe), 39

N
Narrative of the Captivity and Restoration of Mrs. Mary Rowlandson (Rowlandson), 73–74
Naylor, Paul, 56–59n93
Nelson, Maggie, 19, 20
Nicholls, Peter, 74–75n129, 82, 85, 87, 89–90, 99, 127, 154, 164–167
Nichols, Miriam, 56–59n93
Niedecker, Lorine, 109, 111, 111–112n196
The Nonconformist's Memorial (1992), 12–13n31
The Nonconformist's Memorial (1993), 9, 10, 12–13n31, 15, 16, 67n113, 84, 86, 121, 203–204n325
North Central (1968) (Niedecker), 109

O
"An Objective" (1967) (Zukofsky), 110–111n191, 113, 113n199, 113n200, 114, 115
Objectivists, 3, 56–59n93, 80, 109, 110, 110–111n191, 112, 113
O'Hara, Frank, 223, 224n393
Olivier, Laurence, 22
Olson, Charles, 24, 34, 56–59n93, 80n143, 85, 86, 109, 169
One Big Self (1988) (Wright), 109
One of Them (1969) (Howe), 30
Oppen, George, 109, 110–111n191, 111, 111–112n196
ostranenie, 23
OULIPO, 3
Owen, Maureen, 56–59n93
"The Owl in the Sarcophagus" (Stevens), 16n43, 242

P
Palattella, John, 55n90, 83, 85, 99
Palmer, Michael, 32–33n64, 40, 52
Paterson (Williams), 78–79, 78–79n140, 103n176, 109, 163, 217, 217n370, 221, 222, 223, 223n392, 224–225, 225n397, 226, 227, 230, 231, 239–240
Peirce, Charles Sanders, 2n6, 13n34, 30, 37, 37n76, 38–39, 42, 43, 44, 45, 46–47, 48, 49, 50–51, 68, 189, 192n282, 202, 203–204n325, 210–211, 219, 221, 240. *See also Pierce-Arrow* (1999) (Howe)
Peirce, Harriet Melusina (Zina) Fay, 38

Penury (2009) (Kim), 109
Perloff, Marjorie, 55n92, 56–59n93, 74–75n129, 76n131, 80, 82, 83, 87, 99, 126, 164, 246
Pernu, Wayne, 3
Personal Effects of the Pied Piper (Thek), 194–195, 209
"Personal Narrative" (Howe), 25, 69, 72, 113, 116, 154, 155, 158, 172, 175, 176, 178, 243
Peskeompskutt massacre, 101, 105–106, 108, 108n188, 109, 119, 123, 124, 125–126n224, 126, 128, 132, 139, 146, 149, 150, 154, 159, 160, 161–162n252, 170, 174, 175, 176, 183, 184, 185, 186, 187, 188
Philip, M. NourbeSe, 109, 115, 116, 117, 124, 159
Pierce-Arrow (1999) (Howe), 9, 12, 12–13n31, 31n61, 37–39, 40, 42, 45, 46, 47n85, 49, 50, 51, 52, 202, 205, 231, 237
Pinsky, Robert, 51n87
poetics
    antinomian/nonconformist poetics, 84, 86, 87, 88, 89, 91, 118, 165, 191, 226
    cognitive poetics, 81n144, 82, 83, 170
    historical poetics, 80, 84, 102, 110
    L=A=N=G=U=A=G=E poetics, 3, 47, 55n92
    meaning of, 55, 61n99, 66
    metaphysical poetics, 31–53, 226
    Objectivist/Language poetics, 80, 109, 110–111n191, 113
    postlinear poetics, 83
    radical poetics, 84
    tropological constitutive poetics/constitutive tropological poetics, 120, 153
Poetry of Contemplation (Clements), 32n63
poiesis, 23
Pound, Ezra, 72n123, 77n132, 80n143, 85, 110–111n191
Powell, Michael, 2n8
Powell's Books, 1, 2, 2n8, 3–4, 5, 108, 186
praxis, meaning of, 23, 55, 61n99
Putnam, Hilary, 13n34, 70n119
Pythagorean Silence (1982) (Howe), 12–13n31, 55–56n92, 65n108, 67n113, 177

Q
quarry, meaning of, 29
The Quarry (2015) (Howe), 10, 14, 64, 69, 73, 87, 92–93n152, 94, 99, 102, 104, 116, 121, 126, 128, 144, 147, 153, 154, 171, 172, 173, 174,

176, 177, 178, 189, 213, 231, 232. *See also* "Arisbe" (Howe); "Art in Art & Stone on Stone" (Howard); "The Disappearance Approach" (Howe); "The End of Art" (1974) (Howe); "Frame Structures" (essay) (Howe); "Personal Narrative" (Howe); "Sorting Facts; or, Nineteen Ways of Looking at Marker" (1996) (Howe); "There Are Not Leaves Enough to Crown to Cover to Crown to Cover" (1982) (Howe); "Vagrancy in the Park" (2015) (Howe); "Where Should the Commander Be?" (Howe)

Quartermain, Peter, 56–59n93, 111–112n196

R

radical contingency, 11, 13, 63n105, 65, 70, 72, 80, 99, 104, 109, 112, 114, 116, 118, 119, 120, 124, 126, 127, 129, 133, 143, 146, 153, 157, 163, 172, 176, 186

Rakosi, Carl, 110–111n191, 111, 111–112n196

Ramke, Bin, 35

Rankine, Claudia, 19, 20, 109

Ratcliffe, Stephen, 56–59n93

The redeemed captive (1795) (Williams), 144

The Redeemed Captive (1811) (Williams), 134–138, 141, 146, 150

The redeemed captive, returning to Zion (1707) (Williams), 99–100n163, 125n222, 126, 128, 134, 144, 181

Reed, Brian, 60n96, 74–75n129, 82, 83

Reed, Thomas, 132, 140, 161–162n252, 162

Reinfeld, Linda, 56–59n93, 74–75n129, 84, 87, 99, 164

Reinhardt, Ad, 30, 80n143, 83

Renwick, Vanessa, 1

Reznikoff, Charles, 80n143, 85, 109, 110–111n191, 111, 111–112n196, 136

Rival, Bernard, 14

Rodney, Janet, 56–59n93, 80

Rorty, Richard, 63n105

Rowlandson, Mary White, 16, 73, 78, 84, 86, 87–89, 103, 118, 123, 124, 132, 133, 134, 135, 163, 165, 167, 168, 169, 170, 171, 172, 173, 174, 179, 181, 182, 183, 184. *See also* Howe, Susan, "The Captivity and Restoration of Mrs. Mary Rowlandson" (1985); *Narrative of the Captivity and Restoration of Mrs. Mary Rowlandson* (Rowlandson); *The Sovereignty & Goodness of God, together, with the Faithfulness of His Promises Displayed* (1682) (Rowlandson)

Rukeyser, Muriel, 109, 111–112n196

301

S

Sawyer-Laucanno, Christopher, 131–132n231
scape, meaning of, 54n89
scape esaid, 53, 54, 68, 75, 78, 108, 123, 132, 145, 155
Scattering as Behavior toward Risk: The Europe of Trusts (1990) (Howe), 12–13n31, 16, 67n113, 76n31, 232n422
Scattering as Behavior toward Risk: The Europe of Trusts (2002) (Howe), 12–13n31, 16
Schmitz, Neil, 56
Schultz, Susan M., 56–59n93, 74–75n129, 85, 87, 88, 89, 90–91, 99
Sebald, W. G., 20
Secret History of the Dividing Line (1978) (Howe), 12–13n31, 55n92, 86
The Secret Languages of Ireland (Macalister), 193, 194
Shakespeare, William, 27, 32–33n64, 35n71, 40, 52, 80
Sheldon, George, 16, 99–100n163, 123, 125, 125–126n224, 126, 127, 128, 129, 130, 130n228, 132, 133, 133n233, 134–135, 134n235, 136–149, 152, 161–162n252, 162, 163, 165, 166, 167–169, 173, 175, 177, 181, 185, 188. *See also A History of Deerfield, Massachusetts* (1895–1896) (Sheldon)
Shelley Memorials, 43
The Sight of Death (Clark), 192–193
Silence Wager Stories (1989) (Howe), 12–13n31, 16
Simpson, Megan, 56–59n93
"Sincerity and Objectification: With Special Reference to the Work of Charles Reznikoff" (1931) (Zukofsky), 110–111n191, 113, 113n198, 113n200
Singularities (1990) (Howe), 9, 10, 12, 12–13n31, 16, 55n92, 56–59n93, 64n107, 67n113, 69n117, 72n122, 76n131, 82, 84, 86, 87, 89, 95–96, 101, 104n179, 121, 144, 146, 149, 152, 170, 172, 205n332, 232
singularity, 15, 24, 83, 95–96, 96n157
Slotkin, Richard, 90, 90n149, 181–183
Sobin, Gustaf, 32–33n64, 40, 52
Sollers, Philippe, 14
"Sorting Facts; or, Nineteen Ways of Looking at Marker" (1996) (Howe), 9, 10n22, 11n25, 12–13n31, 13–14, 22, 24, 69, 69–70n117, 116n206, 207n336, 211n352, 212
"Sorting Facts; or, Nineteen Ways of Looking at Marker" (2012) (Howe), 14
"Sorting Facts; or, Nineteen Ways of Looking at Marker" (2013),

10n23

"Sorting Facts; or, Nineteen Ways of Looking at Marker" (2016) (Howe), 14

Souls of the Labadie Tract (2007) (Howe and Grubbs), 2n7, 9, 16n39, 16n42, 26, 27, 55n91, 64n107, 99–100n163, 104n177, 116n204, 121, 155n249, 173, 176, 226, 229, 237, 238, 242, 243

The Sound of Poetry/The Poetry of Sound (2009) (Howe), 104n177, 176, 177

The Soveraignty & Goodness of God, together, with the Faithfulness of His Promises Displayed (1682) (Rowlandson), 123–124, 132, 134, 181

Spicer, Jack, 32–33n64, 40, 50, 52, 97

Spontaneous Particulars: The Telepathy of Archives (2014) (Howe), 6, 9, 16n40, 18, 107, 121n215, 189, 193, 197, 198–199, 200, 201, 212–213n355, 218n372, 219, 222, 223n388, 224, 225n395, 226–227, 236–246

Stein, Gertrude, 30, 80n143, 86, 169, 211, 211n351, 223, 225, 236, 238

Stevens, James Thomas, 109

Stevens, Wallace, 16n43, 27, 29, 32–33n64, 40, 52, 63n104, 80n143, 110–111n191, 123, 189, 194, 199, 200, 212, 220, 225, 226–227, 228, 229, 229n412, 231, 234–235, 236, 241, 242, 243. *See also* Howe, Susan, "Vagrancy in the Park" (2015)

Stiles, Ezra, 125, 125n223, 143

Stray (2019) (Howe), 30, 64n107

Sturken, Marita, 23, 71n120

survivance stories, 106n183, 107, 151, 159, 240

synechism, 210–211, 210–211n350, 237

T

Talisman interview (1990), 24, 62n102, 64n107, 86–87, 95, 97–98, 101, 117, 173

Taylor, Edward, 32–33n64, 40, 52

Taylor, John, 135, 135–136n239, 138, 139, 152

Testimony (1934–1978) (Reznikoff), 109

THAT THIS (2010) (Howe), 9, 69–70n117, 193n285, 208n342

Thek, Paul, 194–195, 208, 209, 233

"There Are Not Leaves Enough to Crown to Cover to Crown to Cover" (1982) (Howe), 12–13n31, 20, 24, 64–65, 69

"There Are Not Leaves Enough to Crown to Cover to Crown to Cover" (1985) (Howe), 178

"There Are Not Leaves Enough to Crown to Cover to Crown to Cover"

(1990) (Howe), 177, 178
"There Are Not Leaves Enough to Crown to Cover to Crown to Cover" (1992) (Howe), 177, 178
"There Are Not Leaves Enough to Crown to Cover to Crown to Cover" (2002) (Howe), 178
"There Are Not Leaves Enough to Crown to Cover to Crown to Cover" (2015) (Howe), 178
THIEFTH (2005) (Howe and Grubbs), 67n113, 69n117, 189, 203–204n325, 205n332
THIEFTH (2006) (Howe and Grubbs), 238
THIEFTH (2015) (Howe and Grubbs), 203–204n325, 205n332
Thom, René, 24, 83, 95–96
Thoreau, Henry David, 205, 235, 235n429
Thorow (2002) (Howe), 16, 69–70n117, 76n131, 205, 205n332, 216, 232n422
"Thorow" (essay) (1987) (Howe), 69, 69–70n117
Thousand Plateaus (Deleuze and Guattari), 233
Tom Tit Tot: an essay on savage philosophy in folk-tale (Clodd), 68n114, 216
TOM TIT TOT (book) (2014) (Howe and Quaytman), 9, 25n54, 66n111, 69, 121, 189, 189–190n276, 194, 195, 195–196n298, 200–201n317, 205–206n333, 208–209, 230, 232, 233, 237
TOM TIT TOT (exhibition) (2013) (Howe), 213
TOM TIT TOT (exhibition) (2013) (Howe and Grubbs), 19n49, 69–70n117, 189, 212, 234
TOM TIT TOT (exhibition) (2015) (Howe), 25–26
TOM TIT TOT (exhibition) (2018) (Howe), 69–70n117
Traherne, Thomas, 32–33n64, 40, 52
Tucker, Arthur Holmes, 5, 71–72n121, 130, 131, 145, 147, 148, 149, 186, 188
Turner, William, 71–72n121, 100, 101, 129, 131–132n231, 132, 186
tychism, 2, 2n6, 41n81, 210, 224, 229n412, 237

V

"Vagrancy in the Park" (2015) (Howe), 24, 27, 28–29, 63n104, 123, 190, 193, 194, 198, 212–213, 228, 229, 229n411, 229n412, 231, 242
Vanderborg, Susan, 56–59n93
vates, 23
Vilgrain, Bénédicté, 14
von Schlegell, David, 14, 202n320

W

Waite, Benjamin, 132, 140, 145, 163
Waldrop, Rosmarie, 32–33n64, 40, 52, 74–75n129, 80n143, 85
Warnare, Danielle, 161–162n252, 162
Webster, Noah, 5, 29, 168, 220, 221, 238, 241
Welling, James, 61–62n100, 122
Wells, Daniel White, 99–100n163, 126
Wells, Jonathan, 128, 128n226, 130, 132, 133, 135, 137, 138, 139, 140, 141, 143–147, 150, 152–153, 154, 161–162n252, 163, 165, 167, 169, 174, 175, 183, 188. *See also* "Escape of Jonathan Wells"
Wells, Reuben Field, 99–100n163, 126
Wells, Susan, 2n8
Wetmore, Hannah Edwards, 16, 121, 218, 236, 245. *See also* Edwards, Hannah (m. Hannah Edwards Wetmore)
"Where Should the Commander Be?" (Howe), 24
White, Hayden, 65n109, 90n149
White, Rebekah, 238
Whitman, Walt, 40, 52
Whittelsey, Lucy Wetmore, 16, 121, 218, 221
Williams, Eunice Mather, 125n221, 125n222, 133n233, 134, 137
Williams, John, 99–100n163, 125, 125n221, 125n222, 126, 128, 133n233, 134, 135, 136, 137, 138, 139, 149, 181
Williams, Stephen, 56–59n93, 99–100n163, 125, 125n221, 126, 128, 129, 130, 131, 132, 133, 135, 135–136n239, 136, 137, 138, 139, 140, 141, 143, 144, 145, 146, 149, 152, 165, 170. *See also The Redeemed Captive* (1811) (Williams); *The redeemed captive, returning to Zion* (1707) (Williams)
Williams, William Carlos, 78–79, 78–79n140, 85, 109, 110–111n191, 189, 217, 221–222, 224, 225, 226, 227, 228, 229, 236, 239–240, 241. *See also Paterson* (Williams)
WOODSLIPPERCOUNTERCLATTER (2013) (Howe and Grubbs), 206n335
WOODSLIPPERCOUNTERCLATTER (2015) (Howe and Grubbs), 69–70n117, 189, 205–206n333, 238, 246n442
word squares, 10, 56–59n93, 60n96, 74n129, 83, 140, 158, 159–160, 161–162n252, 162, 164, 165, 167, 175
Words in the Mourning Time (1970) (Hayden), 109
Wright, Benjamin, 163
Wright, C. D., 109
Wright, Chauncey, 37n76
Wright, Ebenezer, 175

Y
Yeats, William Butler, 55–56n92, 80n143, 195–196, 209, 213, 215, 229, 230. *See also* Howe, Susan, *TOM TIT TOT*

Z
Zohn, Harry, 93, 157
ZONG! (2008) (Philip), 109, 115, 115n202, 116n203, 117, 118, 159
Zukofsky, Louis, 110–111n191, 111, 111–112n196, 113–115, 113n200, 117, 215

The Author

W. SCOTT HOWARD received his Ph.D. (1998) in English and Critical Theory from the University of Washington, Seattle, where he was a member of the *Subtext Collective*. At the University of Denver, he teaches in the Department of English & Literary Arts; and in the Emergent Digital Practices Program, the Critical Theory Program, the University Honors Program, and the DU-Iliff Ph.D. Program. His teaching, research, and publications engage the fields of modern and postmodern American poetry; Renaissance and early modern literature & culture; poetics and historiography; literary & cultural theory; and digital humanities. Scott worked at Powell's Books (1990-1993) where he managed the *Critical Theory* section and the *prism* interdisciplinary discussion series, and co-managed (with Vanessa Renwick) the *Small Press & Journals* section and the *dew.claw* reading series. His literary arts interviews appeared in *PLAZM* magazine (1993-1997), one of which was noted in the documentary film, *Helvetica* (2007). Scott is the founding editor of *Appositions: Studies in Renaissance / Early Modern Literature & Culture*; and of *Reconfigurations: A Journal for Poetics & Poetry / Literature & Culture*. His digital multigraphs for *Reconstruction* include *Water: Resources and Discourses* (2006) co-edited with Justin Scott Coe; and *Archives on Fire: Artifacts & Works / Communities & Fields* (2016). *The Divorce Tracts of John Milton: Texts & Contexts*, co-edited with Sara van den Berg, is available from Duquesne University Press (2010). His edited volume, *An Collins and the Historical Imagination,* is available from Ashgate (2014). Scott's collections of poetry include the e-book, *ROPES* (with images by Ginger Knowlton) from Delete Press (2014), and *SPINNAKERS* from The Lune (2016). *Poetics and Praxis 'After' Objectivism,* co-edited with Broc Rossell, is available from the University of Iowa Press (2018). Scott's work has received support from the Modern Language Association; the Pew Charitable Trusts; the National Endowment for the Humanities; the Beinecke Library, Yale University; and the Andrew W. Mellon Foundation. Scott lives in Englewood, CO where he gardens, writes, and commutes year-round by bicycle, following *what crow dost.* At the University of Denver, he is professor of English & Literary Arts; and editor of *Denver Quarterly*.

Praise for *Archive and Artifact*

"In his book-length study of Susan Howe's poetry and prose, W. Scott Howard investigates the wealth of criticism that has been devoted to Howe's work by skillfully considering what has been addressed well and why it has been so pertinent, but more importantly, what particular aspects of her work have been overlooked by previous criticism. An example of this approach is in his discussion of Howe's *Articulation of Sound Forms in Time*. After an extensive review of what critics have argued, Howard states that 'no one has yet even considered the possibility that Howe's engagement with the poem's historical sources engenders a critical reading of those very documents'. Howard's canny and insightful approach has made it possible for him to see what the rest of us missed—that Howe might be critical of Atherton's historiographic treatment and might be embarking, therefore, on a mission of restorative justice in her poem. For this poem and for many others in Howe's oeuvre, Howard uses the breadth of his knowledge of history and a wide range of texts and carefully detailed archival materials to provide us with new approaches to these works, approaches that are considered and well-reasoned and will be essential for scholarship moving forward."
—Elisabeth W. Joyce

"W. Scott Howard captures the entire arc of Susan Howe's considerable and crucial body of work in this many-faceted, deeply researched study. Tracing the role of the meticulously ecstatic in Howe's dissolution and reconstruction of historic and literary particulars into new artifacts, he deftly negotiates the difficult line between reading Howe's work in relation to tradition and reading it autonomously, in relation only to its own terms. Just as all of Howe's work brings us into the quick of the moment in which history continues to be constructed, Howard's incisive tracking brings us into the quick of Howe's own contribution to that construction."
— Cole Swensen

"*Archive and Artifact* is passionate criticism, driven by careful attention to the work of Susan Howe and reinforced by archival scholarship. W. Scott Howard is scrupulously alert to the many modes in which Howe's project of poetic documentary unfolds. At the centre of the book is an extended examination of Howe's crucial 1987 text, *Articulation of Sound Forms in Time.* Elsewhere—and unusually—Howard reflects on the experience of teaching Howe's poetry. He also discusses her recent multimedia works, her trajectory as a wayward scholar-poet, and her practice of factual telepathy. In a long and illuminating interview, Howe's *Spontaneous Particulars* becomes the platform for wide-ranging reflections on her life and writing. Howard's *Archive and Artifact* is a book of 'betweenness' that adeptly treads the lines between criticism and poetry, stillness and vagrancy, discipline and chance, objects and metaphysics. In the words of the book's subject, revoicing Williams: 'Beauty is chance and there is a rigor in the quest'."

—Will Montgomery

ARCHIVE AND ARTIFACT:
SUSAN HOWE'S FACTUAL TELEPATHY

W. SCOTT HOWARD

The essays collected in this volume are cross-genre hybrids of creative and critical enchantment with the multifaceted works of Susan Howe from 1969 to 2019. Through print and electronic, video and vinyl, manuscript and typescript, gallery installation and special collection media and methods, W. Scott Howard illuminates Howe's "invisible colliding phenomena" of folding floreate flare. Howard's prose modulates from lyrical invocations to theoretical discourses, becoming increasingly embedded in generative, unpredictable intersections among Howe's archives, artifacts, and factual telepathy. The book also includes an extensive interview with Susan Howe concerning chance and discipline in her poetics and praxis from *My Emily Dickinson* to *Debths*. Howard's writing moves within and against fields of study (mainly history, literature, and philosophy plus a few others here and there); across and through time periods (from the early modern to now), following a nonconformist's helical quest 'after' the poet's signal escapes.